THE MIDDLE AGES SERIES

Ruth Mazo Karras, Series Editor
Edward Peters, Founding Editor

A complete list of books in the series
is available from the publisher.

The Beguines of Medieval Paris

The Beguines
of Medieval Paris

Gender, Patronage,
and Spiritual Authority.

Tanya Stabler Miller

PENN

UNIVERSITY OF PENNSYLVANIA PRESS

PHILADELPHIA

Published by
University of Pennsylvania Press
Philadelphia, Pennsylvania 19104-4112
www.upenn.edu/pennpress

Printed in the United States of America on acid-free paper
10 9 8 7 6 5 4 3 2 1

Library of Congress Cataloging-in-Publication Data
Miller, Tanya Stabler.
The Beguines of medieval Paris : gender, patronage, and
spiritual authority / Tanya Stabler Miller. — 1st ed.
    p. cm. — (The Middle Ages series)
Includes bibliographical references and index.
ISBN 978-0-8122-4607-0 (hardcover : alk. paper)
 1. Beguines—France—Paris—History—To 1500. 2. Women
in Christianity—France—Paris—History—To 1500.
3. Monastic and religious life of women—France—Paris—
History—To 1500. I. Title. II. Series: Middle Ages series.
BX4272.Z5F877 2014
282'.44361082—dc23
                                        2013044479

For Drew

CONTENTS

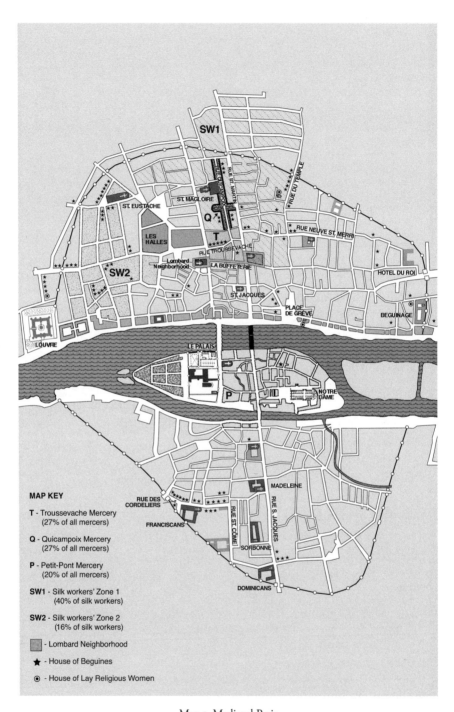

Map 1. Medieval Paris

Introduction

In everything a Beguine says
Listen only to good
Whatever happens in her life
It is religious.
Her word is prophecy;
If she laughs, it is amiability;
If she weeps, it is devotion;
If she sleeps, she is ravished;
If she dreams, it is a vision;
If she lies, think nothing of it.
If the Beguine marries
That is her conversion:
Since her vows, her profession
Are not for life.
Now she weeps and then she prays
And then she will take a husband:
Now she is Martha, now she is Mary
Now she is chaste, now she marries
But do not speak ill of her:
The king will not tolerate it.

—Rutebeuf, "Li diz des beguines"

Not long after returning from his first crusade in 1254, Louis IX (r. 1226–1270) founded a house on the eastern end of Paris for "honest women who are called beguines."[1] Prior to gaining this royal recognition and patronage, beguines— lay religious women who took personal, informal vows of chastity and pursued a life of contemplative prayer and active service in the world—were a significant and widely recognized phenomenon in the bustling streets and marketplaces of medieval Paris. Never canonically recognized as religious in the strict sense of the word, beguines did not follow an approved rule, did not live in convents, and did not give up their personal property.[2] They were free to abandon their religious vocation at any time, since it was not enforced by any binding monastic vow. Nevertheless, they were generally recognized as "religious women." Dressed in humble garb evocative of habits and publicly pursuing a "more perfect" Christian life, they provoked admiration in some, hostility in others, and bewilderment in many. As the Parisian satirist Rutebeuf complained, the woman who adopted the beguine life could pursue charitable action in the world (a spiritual path represented by Martha in the Gospel of Luke) or engage in contemplation (the path represented by her sister Mary); she could espouse celibacy one year and marry the next if it suited her.[3] On the other hand, admirers such as Robert of Sorbon (d. 1274) noted that beguines exhibited far more devotion to God than even the cloistered, since they voluntarily pursued a religious life without vows, while living in the midst of the world's temptations. The Franciscan theologian Gilbert of Tournai, a contemporary of Robert as well as a regent master in theology at Paris, wrote of the beguines, "There are among us women whom we have no idea what to call, religious or lay, because they live neither in the world nor removed from it."[4]

Yet, it was the flexibility and dynamism of the beguine life that encouraged thousands of women all over medieval Europe to take it up in the first place. Inspired by the new apostolic piety of the thirteenth century, with its emphasis on poverty, preaching, and imitation of Christ, beguines found ways to pursue their spiritual ambitions, despite injunctions against women's participation in these central features of the *vita apostolica*. Gathering in households or joining formal beguine institutions (known as beguinages), they worked and prayed, engaged with theological questions, bought and sold property, maintained ties with their families, and utilized their personal resources to aid their fellow beguines. Moreover, with its pursuit of both the active and the contemplative modes of religiosity in the world, the beguine life resonated with medieval Parisians at all levels. King Louis IX himself experienced the challenge of living a religious life in the world despite the mockery and ridicule with which observable expressions of piety were often met. His commitment to supporting beguines was inspired not only by his personal admiration for the *vita apostolica* but also by a desire to support new religious opportunities for the women of his realm. Clerical observers, particularly in the schools of medieval Paris where Gilbert of Tournai himself was trained, took up ideas about beguines in discussions of a range of issues, from the professional to the pastoral. Robert of Sorbon, for example, claimed that beguines were illuminated by the fire of charity and worked more to save the souls of their fellow Christians than did trained theologians. Robert's colleague, William of Saint-Amour (d. 1272), however, targeted beguines as "silly women" and frauds in his attacks on the mendicant orders during the secular-mendicant conflict of the 1250s. Beguines pursued their spiritual ambitions under the watch of ecclesiastical and secular observers who struggled to define, protect, and circumscribe the women's status. At the same time, beguines carved out a place for themselves in medieval society—whether quietly living a life devoted to chastity, prayer, and service in their own homes; actively and publicly seeking to convert others to live a more "perfect" Christian life; or taking up residency in a beguine community. As lay women widely recognized as "religious," they called into question binary categories of religious or lay and active or contemplative; nevertheless, historians continue to approach their history from one perspective or the other. Indeed, as a recent essay on the field of beguine scholarship has noted, the inclination to define such women "in terms of the singularity of what they were not, rather than the spectrum of what they were," has obscured the range of options open to women who wished to live a religious life in the world.[5]

This book examines communities of beguines, their support networks, and their direct participation in—as well as their discursive importance to— the economic, intellectual, and religious life of thirteenth- and fourteenth-century Paris. While scholarship on beguines and their communities has grown in the past half century, Paris has been largely ignored in the historical literature.[6] An examination of Paris's beguine communities offers a unique window onto the social, occupational, and religious networks of lay religious women while shedding new light on medieval Paris, a city of considerable importance intellectually, politically, and economically. In the thirteenth century, Paris was the largest city in Western Europe. It was the French royal capital and the seat of one of medieval Europe's most important universities, and was developing a thriving industry in luxury textiles. A vibrant and cosmopolitan medieval city, Paris attracted scholars and preachers; merchants, artisans, and day laborers; nobles and courtiers. It also drew large numbers of immigrants, both male and female, from the surrounding areas, a factor crucial to the development of a beguine community.[7] Intellectuals moved back and forth between Paris and other major urban centers with substantial populations of beguines, linking

Paris's communities with those of the southern Low Countries, the very heart of the beguine movement. There is also evidence that beguines from other regions came to Paris to take up new opportunities. One of the first mistresses of the Paris beguinage, for example, was from Douai, a town in French Flanders. Preachers casually mentioned beguines who came to Paris from other towns to purchase pastoral texts, and manuscript evidence suggests that Parisian clerics were part of a lively exchange in vernacular devotional literature written about or for beguines. This context shaped both the nature and the success of the beguine communities in Paris.

Paris is also significant to the history of the beguines because it was the city where the central drama of beguine history—the trial and execution of Marguerite Porete—played out. In 1310, Marguerite Porete was burned at the stake at the Place de Grève in Paris for writing and circulating a book that, according to the judgment of twenty-one theologians from the University of Paris, contained doctrinal errors.[8] In 1311, at least six of the twenty-one Parisian theologians called upon to judge Marguerite's book participated in a church council in Vienne where ecclesiastical officials made several specific connections between Marguerite's ideas and deeds and the beguine status. These connections were expressed in two decrees. The first decree, *Cum de quibusdam*, targeted the beguine status specifically, claiming that beguines "having been led into insanity, dispute and preach about the highest Trinity and the divine essence and introduce opinions contrary to the Catholic faith concerning the articles of the faith and the sacraments of the church." Because of these alleged activities, the decree declared that the beguine status "ought to be perpetually prohibited and completely abolished."[9] The second decree, *Ad nostrum*, listed eight "errors" allegedly espoused by beguines and their male counterparts, beghards, who according to the decree constituted an "abominable sect." Like *Cum de quibusdam*, this decree condemned the beguine status but specifically targeted women and men in German lands.[10]

Despite historical interest in several strands of this story—Marguerite Porete's trial, royal concerns about heresy in the French realm, and the ways these events and concerns converged at the Council of Vienne—the ties between the university, the king, and the beguines of Paris have almost completely escaped notice.[11] Yet they are essential to understanding the history of beguines in and beyond Paris. While the waves of persecution and inquisitorial activity unleashed by the Vienne decrees negatively affected beguine communities all over northern Europe, the Parisian beguinage weathered the crisis, in spite of local concerns about beguines engaging in the very activities referenced in *Cum de quibusdam*.[12]

Modern Historians and Medieval Beguines

Because beguines were the subjects of numerous medieval hagiographies as well as the targets of church decrees accusing them of ideas deemed heretical, these women have long fascinated modern historians of religion, heresy, and gender. But the same clerically authored writings—hagiographies lauding their sanctity and church decrees warning of their heresy—have in many ways shaped historical approaches to the study of beguine communities.

These two bodies of sources have also determined the regions upon which scholars traditionally focus. The most influential publications on the beguine movement concern communities in the southern Low Countries, the region credited with the birth of the beguine movement, or beguines in German lands, the region specifically named in the second of the two decrees pronounced against the beguines at Vienne.

Many of the earliest publications on beguines were local histories seeking to uncover the birthplace of the beguine life or the location of the oldest beguinage.[13] In 1935 Herbert Grundmann published his seminal study *Religious Movements in the Middle Ages*, which identified beguines as participants in the broader religious movements of the twelfth and thirteenth centuries. Drawing attention to the beguines' place in a wider European phenomenon, as well as their role in the rise of vernacular literature, Grundmann established the beguines' importance in the history of gender, heresy, and religion.[14] His central argument that "all religious movements of the Middle Ages achieved realization in religious orders or in heretical sects," however, placed beguines—who never achieved recognition as a religious order—on the wrong side of orthodoxy.[15] Two important and influential studies focused on German cities appeared in the 1970s, Robert Lerner's *Heresy of the Free Spirit in the Later Middle Ages* and Richard Kieckhefer's *Repression of Heresy in Medieval Germany*. They illustrated the consequences of the beguines' lack of canonically approved status by detailing inquisitorial activity targeting these women in specific German towns, especially the middle-Rhineland cities of Strasbourg, Mainz, and Basel.[16] Although focused on the broader issues of heresy and inquisition, both studies have profoundly shaped Anglophone scholarship on beguines in general, to the extent that many scholars understand the history of beguines to be characterized by relentless persecution and widespread hostility.[17]

The best-known studies that focus on the history of beguines concern the beguine communities of the Low Countries and tend to emphasize the foundation, patronage, and social composition of beguinages (large, walled complexes governed by house rules and closely supervised by ecclesiastical and secular officials). Ernest McDonnell's influential study, while ostensibly focused on the Belgian scene, covered the history of beguine foundations within and beyond the Low Countries, offering short chapters on beguine communities in France and the Empire.[18] A wide-ranging and encyclopedic work, McDonnell's study emphasized residency in a beguinage and economic self-sufficiency as staves against heresy accusations. Comparing the Low Countries with the Rhineland, McDonnell claimed that the beguinage marked the key difference between these two regions.[19] More recently, in Walter Simons's magisterial work *Cities of Ladies*, one finds a valuable corrective to numerous misconceptions about beguine history, some of which were perpetuated in McDonnell's study.[20] Equally important to the field is Simons's emphasis on the centrality of religion to the beguine life. Whereas earlier studies had portrayed beguine communities as second-best options for women unable to gain entry into an approved religious order or as shelters for the unmarriageable, Simons has shown that the beguine life had its own particular appeal as a locally recognized expression of the new apostolic ideal.

Studies on beguine communities in the Low Countries, in contrast to the dominant narratives in Anglophone scholarship concerning German beguines, have stressed survival and continuity, attributing the endurance of the beguine status in this region to the local tendency for lay religious women to reside in officially recognized houses, especially large court beguinages.[21] Beguinages were similar enough to traditional convents to satisfy some ecclesiastical authorities in that they effectively minimized occasions for the women to leave the enclosure. In their focus on the beguinage, these studies, albeit not intentionally, have encouraged the general perception that residency in a beguinage served as a marker distinguishing between "good" and "bad" beguines.[22] McDonnell most vividly expressed this focus on the beguinage as a protector against heretical leanings. In his discussion of the beguine Marguerite Porete, he asserts, "She must have been an unattached beguine, with no fixed residence, regarding mendicancy as a means of livelihood, pursuing a life of moral laxity, and refusing to submit to authority. For the fourteenth century, she was a sectarian, far removed from the *beginae clausae* who dominated the extraregular scene in Belgium."[23] Embedded in this statement is the view that beguinages, with their ecclesiastical and noble founders and supporters, rules and walls, were environments in which beguine spirituality might be restrained and contained; that somehow the walls might prevent residents from "producing, debating and teaching theology."[24]

On the question of the factors leading to the development and ultimate condemnation of the beguine movement, feminist scholarship has drawn attention to the beguines' relationship with their male clerical advisers. Employing male-authored hagiographies of individual beguines, several studies have presented the relationship between beguines and their spiritual advisers as a partnership, with varying degrees of advantage to the beguine. According to this view, the beguine acquired informal personal authority by virtue of her spiritual gifts, while the male cleric's formal powers were enhanced by virtue of his relationship with the beguine.[25] Recent scholarship has suggested the ways in which the relationship between beguines and their confessors was always suspect or dangerous to the female penitent.[26] While these works have brought much to our understanding of individual religious laywomen and their relationships with male authorities, many scholars of beguine communities characterize the religious expression described in hagiographies and mystical writings as "atypical," arguing that the Christocentrism and mysticism associated with beguines in literary sources do not appear to have been part of the devotional practices of "ordinary" beguines.[27] Yet this opposition raises questions about what is meant by "ordinary." The religious practices and spiritual expression of beguines were extraordinarily diverse, drawing on a range of ideas and influences. Beguines sought to teach and learn from one another—as the letters of Hadewijch show.[28] They disagreed with one another, too. Marguerite Porete noted that other beguines considered her to be in error. Clearly, beguines have been pushed into categories that obscure the rich diversity of their spiritual lives as well as the complexity of medieval attitudes toward their communities.

The Beguines of Medieval Paris

With some studies focused on the foundation and social composition of beguine communities and others concerned with a handful of beguine "mystics," the scholarship on beguines in some ways reflects the frustration voiced by Gilbert of Tournai in that beguines are often treated either as laywomen seeking economic support or as religious women seeking spiritual fulfillment.[29] Yet the beguine life melded social engagement with religious expression. Both were essential to the character and perception of this status. Moving away from the notion that a beguine community was a second-best option to marriage or the cloister, this book argues that such gatherings offered a unique space in which to pursue an apostolic life of chastity, poverty, and active engagement with one's fellow Christians. Fiscal and property records place individual beguines within extensive networks composed of urban clerics, royal officials, and civic authorities, bringing to view the ways in which Paris's beguines pursued religious interests *and* economic opportunities.

Illuminating the spectrum of lay religious activity in medieval Paris, this book, while focused primarily on the royal beguinage, examines the range of options open to lay women who wished to live a religious life in medieval Paris. Moving between the officially recognized and royally supported community of the city beguinage and the clusters of beguines living in small, informal houses located throughout the city, this book explores the ways in which the beguine status offered women of different socioeconomic backgrounds and lifestyles opportunities to pursue lives of active engagement in their communities combined with religious contemplation. The beguinage received regular support from the French monarchy, which maintained the buildings, provided stipends to its residents, and protected beguines from criticism and suspicion. Nevertheless, not all laywomen who aspired to live a religious life joined the beguinage, whether out of choice or prohibitive circumstances. Still recognized as beguines in their neighborhoods, these women established significant commercial networks, employed their fellow beguines, and maintained close ties with merchants and workers in the silk-producing sectors of Paris. Life in the beguinage perhaps had less appeal to these women, some of whom may have felt that their commercial activities or familial connections were hindered by its rules and walls. On the other hand, the beguinage of Paris accommodated and nurtured a broad spectrum of social activities and spiritual expression. Secluded from the bustle of the city, yet open to royal, clerical, and bourgeois visitors, the beguinage permitted the circulation of property, the expansion and deepening of social networks, and the cultivation of close spiritual friendships.

The flexibility of the beguine life accounted in part for its appeal among Parisian women. The enthusiasm of the French kings and civic elites for Saint Louis's foundation helped support the beguinage, a relatively secure environment in which to pursue work opportunities and cultivate spiritual connections. Important too were opportunities for religious instruction. Clerics studying and preaching at the University of Paris frequently delivered sermons at the beguinage chapel, sermons that provide invaluable evidence of interaction between laywomen and theologians. Exploring these interactions offers another perspective on medieval intellectuals, demonstrating that university clerics were intimately connected with beguines and looked to these women for inspiration in their pedagogical and pastoral endeavors. Parisian theologians, through sermons, moral treatises, and theological tracts, had tremendous influence on medieval thought and belief outside Paris. By analyzing their interactions with the beguine communities of Paris, this book contributes to scholarship on beguines and other lay religious communities beyond Paris as well as broader issues concerning gender, knowledge, and authority.

The fragments of the beguines' history, scattered in archives all over Paris, survive mostly by accident. The Paris beguinage was turned over to the Filles de l'Ave Maria—a group of Observant Franciscan nuns—in 1485. Espousing poverty (indeed, the nuns lived from alms alone), the new occupants of the house maintained few documents relating to the property holdings of the beguinage, and no foundation documents survive. Moreover, Parisian notaries did not record private documents in registers, and no notarial archives exist prior to the fifteenth century. Thus, many of the wills and property records concerning Parisian beguines that have been preserved, primarily by confraternities and religious houses with which individual women had ties, were uncovered thanks to guesswork and, especially, the painstaking efforts of scholars of medieval Paris.[30] Fortunately, Parisian archives are rich in royal account books, tax rolls, and sermon manuscripts, all of which bear witness to the social and religious significance of Paris's beguine communities.

The chapters that follow proceed chronologically and thematically. Laying out the spiritual and ideological climate in which Louis IX founded the beguinage in Paris sometime in the early 1260s, Chapter 1 examines perceptions of lay religiosity in thirteenth-century Paris as it reconstructs the king's efforts to establish a "court beguinage" modeled on the distinctive beguine houses of the southern Low Countries. Inspired by new spiritual currents flowing through thirteenth-century Europe and guided by a deep sense of responsibility to rule morally, justly, and charitably, Louis's patronage of beguines fit a larger pattern of support for men and women committed to living a life in accordance with new conceptions of the apostolic ideal. Louis's personal spiritual ambitions resonated with aspects of the beguine life, particularly the challenge of living a religious life in the world despite the derision with which visible

expressions of piety were often met. Importing this court beguinage model
from the Low Countries (indeed, Paris is the only city outside this region to
have a court beguinage), Louis played a central role in supporting its residents
and smoothing the way for the women to receive reliable and appropriate
pastoral care. In addition to laying out the origins of the Paris beguinage, this
chapter also introduces some of the currents of opposition to unregulated
forms of lay religiosity in medieval Paris. Louis, like the beguines, endured
criticism by those opposed to laypeople assuming religious dress and publicly
exhibiting religious devotion, behavior that seemed to violate distinctions between clerical and lay status, distinctions that were vociferously defended in
thirteenth-century Paris. Thus, the chapter introduces one of the central issues
of the book, specifically the ways in which the existence of a formally recognized, royally supported institution for lay religious women shaped understandings of the term *beguine*, a term that came to be loaded with powerfully
charged meanings.

Chapter 2 moves to the beguinage itself, a house with deep and enduring
connections to a broad cross-section of medieval Parisians. Attracting women
of diverse backgrounds—noble, patrician, and artisan women gained admittance to the beguinage well into the fifteenth century—the Paris beguinage
enjoyed the support of medieval Parisians—both clerical and lay—who valued
the beguines' intercessory and social services. No less important were family
ties. Many beguines, particularly the mistresses of the beguinage, hailed from
elite bourgeois families, who had a vested interest in supporting a royal foundation. In its organization and administration, the beguinage was flexible and
well suited to the Parisian context, accommodating women of diverse socioeconomic backgrounds pursuing a wide spectrum of religious practices. As
in beguine communities all over northern Europe, an important component
of this flexibility was control over property. Observing an inheritance system
that allowed unmarried women to maintain independent control over inherited property, Paris provided the material means necessary for the adoption
of the beguine life. Importantly, unlike convents and other houses for lay
religious women, the Paris beguinage did not require its residents to hand
over their property to the community, permitting women to join or leave
the community without significant loss of personal investment. Such flexibility was essential to the cultivation of strong relationships within and outside
the beguinage.

Following this discussion of piety, property, and patronage, the book
turns to unenclosed beguine communities, specifically loosely organized

households of beguines unaffiliated with the Paris beguinage. Compiling data from tax rolls, guild records, and property sales, Chapter 3 examines the beguines' occupations, social networks, and contributions to Paris's growing silk industry, an industry that historians have largely overlooked until recently.[31] Modern scholars have frequently focused on the beguines' socioeconomic status and residence in an effort to explain why church officials accused beguines of heresy and attempted to suppress the beguine status in the early fourteenth century. Such studies imply that beguines received praise and escaped blame merely by avoiding mendicancy, remaining self-sufficient, and most important, residing within a beguinage. This chapter shows that access to property, credit, and work opportunities enabled many of these "unenclosed" beguines not only to survive but even to prosper despite the realities of life as single women in medieval Paris. While Paris offered women opportunities to pursue a life of prayer and work as beguines, it was an environment in which such women were vulnerable. The beguinage offered safety, but not all beguines lived in the enclosure. Fiscal records, especially a set of tax rolls compiled during the reign of Philip the Fair, show that a significant number of Parisian beguines set up alternative households, established workshops, and employed or worked for other beguines. These beguine households or home workshops provided another option for beguines outside the beguinage, made possible in part by Paris's silk industry, which was just getting off the ground in the thirteenth century.

Chapter 4 returns to the religious and intellectual climate of the later thirteenth century, focusing in particular on the relationship between university clerics and the beguines of Paris. While recent work has illuminated the complex dynamic between religious women and their clerical guardians or mentors, this chapter enters largely uncharted territory: the intimate ties between university clerics, in particular those affiliated with the Sorbonne, and the beguines of Paris.[32] Sermon collections and preaching material housed at the medieval library of the Sorbonne reveal that some Sorbonne clerics, starting with the college's founder, Robert of Sorbon, perceived beguines as essential to their pastoral work. University clerics also seemed to see the beguine as engaged in the same kinds of spiritual work and activities in which the clergy were occupied. Far from shunning the pastoral care of women, many university scholars perceived contact with beguines as useful to their pastoral mission. Of broader significance here is that this chapter shows that it was not at all unusual for Parisian beguines to have sustained contact with university theologians, a fact that provides important context for the activities of Marguerite Porete, who acquired the approbation of three learned clerics—one of whom was the emi-nent Paris-based theologian Godfrey of Fontaines—for her book, *The Mirror of Simple Souls.*[33]

Chapter 5 examines the vibrant spiritual and intellectual culture of the Paris beguinage. The beguines' access to a wide range of preachers, scholars, and texts that the women were exposed to a variety of teachings. Their receptivity to and engagement with such teachings made beguines an ap-pealing audience for preachers seeking to hone their skills behind the pulpit. Indeed, the beguinage was a space in which preachers might take inspira-tion from the beguines' activities, aspirations, and tastes, testing new ways of speaking about such themes as penance, contemplation, and love. Founded and supported by the French kings, frequented by Parisian theologians, and inhabited by the daughters and widows of the Parisian bourgeoisie, the Paris beguinage was the site at which courtly, monastic, and urban influences in-termingled. It was also a space in which clerics and beguines interacted and shared ideas. Sermons preached to the beguines by the mistress of the begui-nage, sermons that both cite clerical authorities *and* were themselves included in sermon manuals intended for clerical authorities, provide some insight into the dialogue and collaboration that characterized the religious culture of the Paris beguinage.

As Chapters 4 and 5 establish the beguines' active religious roles, both in thought and reality, Chapter 6 addresses the negative consequences of these roles, suggesting that the very same features of the beguine life praised by Robert and some of his contemporaries were also points of contention among intellectuals in medieval Paris. As several accounts of the beguine life indi-cate, beguines were thought to assume active religious roles beyond what was permissible for laypeople, taking seriously what some viewed as the central mission of the beguine life: to exhort fellow Christians to live more moral, Christian lives. This active interpretation of the beguine life was not one to which all medieval clerics subscribed. Sermons preached to the beguines of Paris reveal clerical apprehension over the women's lack of enclosure and sus-picions about beguines becoming too proud of their reputations for having special access to God. Moreover, as Parisian theologians defended the clergy's exclusive control over preaching, they also debated the right of women to give religious instruction.[34] Over time, the notion of a lay apostolate, exem-plified by feminine exhortation, became increasingly suspect, even if car-ried out privately.[35] Chapter 6, then, by examining the ways in which clerics discussed the beguine status, sketches an important part of the backdrop to the condemnation and execution of the brilliant beguine mystic Marguerite Porete, as well as the Council of Vienne, where ecclesiastical officials applied Marguerite's ideas to all beguines.

Chapter 7 returns to royal patronage of the beguinage, particularly in the wake of the Council of Vienne. Even as the kings of France, particularly Philip IV (r. 1285–1314), sought to utilize a reputation for sanctity to enhance their political authority—thus cracking down on perceived religious dissidents such as Marguerite Porete with ferocity—they were careful to protect the reputation of Paris's beguinage. For the kings of France, Paris's beguinage was a royal foundation that symbolized the power, prestige, and piety of the royal family. Even as the king's beguines were implicated in the Vienne decrees, the French rulers took charge of rehabilitating the reputation of the beguinage, calling attention to the community's sainted founder and tying their own support of the beguines to their place in this saintly line.

To tell the story of Paris's beguines necessitates taking these multiple perspectives, which I hope will shed light on the urban context out of which the beguines' approach to *religio* emerged and on which the women depended for support. In doing so, this book aims to contribute to a growing body of scholarship on lay religious women that emphasizes interaction and collaboration over marginality and persecution.[36] Paris's beguine communities interacted with the city's "masters, princes, and merchants" in ways that had lasting significance.[37] Paris's silk industry took off just as beguines were flocking to the trade in the late thirteenth century. University clerics found inspiration in the beguine life, which served as a model for their own religious lives in the city. Bourgeois and royal patrons viewed the beguines as powerful intercessors for their souls, demonstrating the importance of the beguines' spiritual practices. Finally, the ties among beguines suggest the ways in which the beguine life was shaped by the spiritual goals and social situations of Parisian single women. A new, visible, and provocative example of conversion, beguines were a significant part of urban life in medieval Paris and represent a useful focus through which to understand the social, intellectual, and economic history of an important medieval city.[38]

CHAPTER I

The *Prud'homme* and the Beguines

Louis IX and the Foundation of the Beguinage of Paris

By the mid-thirteenth century Paris was home to an increasingly visible population of religious women who lived in a manner that earned them the label *beguinae.* In the early 1250s, the secular cleric William of Saint-Amour (d. 1272) complained of "young women who are called beguines," lamenting that they were becoming "widespread throughout the kingdom."[1] In the late 1250s and early 1260s, William's contemporary Robert of Sorbon (d. 1274) found the beguine life worthy of extensive commentary and praise in his sermons and treatises addressed to students in Paris. Although details about informal beguine communities are lacking, such women had become a widely recognized phenomenon in Paris before Louis IX (r. 1226–1270) purchased lands in the parish of Saint-Paul for the purpose of building a house for "honest women who are called beguines."[2] It is likely that prior to Louis's foundation, religious laywomen in Paris—as in other northern European cities—gathered in informal communities or attached themselves to one of the city's churches or religious houses (see map 1).[3] In any case, it is clear that Louis's beguinage found immediate success attracting large numbers of lay religious women. In his *Bonum universale de apibus*, which was completed before May 1263, the Dominican Thomas of Cantimpré (d. 1272) marveled at the "great multitude" of beguines Louis had "gathered together" (*collegerit*) in the royal beguinage.[4] The king's Dominican confessor and biographer, Geoffrey of Beaulieu (d. 1275), claimed that Louis's foundation housed "around four hundred" beguines.[5] While there is no way to verify Geoffrey's estimate, it was probably close to accurate.[6] The size of the enclosure, as well as the substantial funds Louis invested in the foundation, indicate that the beguinage of Paris, like the court beguinages in the Low Countries on which it was modeled, housed hundreds of women.[7]

By all accounts, Louis was deeply invested in the success of his foundation, which represented the spiritual and practical sensibilities of a king influenced by new forms of spirituality and driven by an acute sense of responsibility to rule justly.[8] Known for his admiration for the mendicant, or "begging," orders, which extended beyond the established Dominican and Franciscan orders to lesser-known groups such as the Friars of the Sack and the Crutched Friars, Louis's patronage of beguines fits a larger pattern of support for groups of men and women committed to living a life in accordance with new conceptions of the *vita apostolica*.[9] Most accounts of Louis's religious and charitable foundations, however, limit mention of the beguinage as just one of many "works of mercy" undertaken by the pious king.[10]

While there is little doubt that Louis perceived beguines as a group of women in need of royal support and protection, his personal admiration for the beguine life as well as his practical reasons for supporting a certain type of beguine community merit greater scrutiny. An examination of the socio-religious context in which Louis established the beguinage not only provides important insight into the significance the beguine life held for Louis on a personal level, it illuminates the circumstances under which beguines in Paris first gained official recognition. This recognition was crucial for the beguine community as it developed and endured in medieval Paris. Indeed, the king's central role in the foundation and support of the beguinage set the course for the treatment of the beguine community throughout the history of its existence in medieval Paris.

The Conversion of Louis IX

In the summer of 1254, Louis returned to France from his failed first crusade. As nearly all accounts of his life attest, his personal disappointment over the crusade and sense that the loss was in some ways attributable to his own sins precipitated a major life turn in Louis.[11] His hagiographers report that the king, in an effort to expiate his sins, submitted himself to flagellation and extreme fasting. In evident disregard for his own health, he fed lepers with his own hands and personally ministered to the poor and the sick. The hagiographical reports accord well with documentary evidence, which bears witness to the king's generous support of the poor and the sick.[12] Louis also threw himself into the task of spiritually and administratively reforming the kingdom from which he had been absent for six years. On the administrative front, he set to work reforming royal government, personally settling disputes and investigating local problems and complaints.[13] He also turned his attention to promoting spiritual reform in his realm. To this end, he gave generously to religious and charitable houses throughout the kingdom and founded several new houses, such as the Quinze-Vingts (a hospital for the blind) and the beguinage of Paris.[14]

Among the many acts celebrated in Louis's *vitae*, the foundation of a house for beguines is usually treated as but one example of the king's pious concern for the sick, the poor, and the vulnerable.[15] Geoffrey of Beaulieu, Louis's confessor and the author of the earliest hagiographical account of the king's life, reported that Louis founded the beguinage in Paris for "honest women called beguines."[16] Geoffrey's account emphasizes the charitable impulse driving this foundation, reporting that Louis provided daily sustenance—or pensions—especially for beguines hailing from impoverished noble families.[17] Similarly, Jean of Joinville, who penned his vita sometime between 1270 and 1309, reports that Louis founded and endowed the beguinage in order to house women who "wished to devote themselves to a life of chastity."[18]

Louis undoubtedly held women who chose to live a religious life in the world in particularly high regard. His own sister Isabelle (d. 1270), who embodied the ideals of thirteenth-century lay sanctity, devoted herself to a life of chastity at an early age.[19] Significantly, Isabelle never became a nun, remaining at court for sixteen years after rejecting a politically significant marriage alliance and eventually retiring to Longchamp, the Franciscan convent near Paris she founded in 1260. As several scholars have noted, Isabelle's religiosity paralleled, and probably helped shape, that of her sainted brother.[20] Both siblings pursued lives of devotion that did not always mesh with the wishes and expectations of others. Sometime before Louis made his crusader vow in December 1244, Isabelle famously resisted what must have been considerable pressure from her family—and even the pope—to marry the son and heir of Emperor Frederick II.[21] Isabelle's steadfast rejection of marriage impressed courtly observers and her virginity was a prominent theme in her biography.[22]

In his *Bonum universale de apibus*, Thomas of Cantimpré draws explicit connections between Isabelle of France's chastity and rejection of a worldly life and her brother's support for beguines. In a chapter dedicated to the virtue of chastity, Thomas praises Isabelle for rejecting marriage, even to the son of the Holy Roman Emperor, and "giving herself so much to contemplation and virtue that she seemed to have no care for any transitory things."[23] Having extolled Isabelle's virginity, Thomas immediately turns to Louis's foundation of the beguinage in Paris. According to Thomas, the French king founded the beguinage out of great admiration for "the modesty of virginal dignity," so that the beguines could "employ themselves in the submission and salvation of humility."[24] While Thomas's praise for Isabelle is delivered within the context of a broader discussion of chastity, it is also a commentary on Isabelle's rejection of social expectations and embrace of a beguine-like lifestyle. As Sean Field puts it, Isabelle was an example "not only of resolute devotion to virginity in the face of parental opposition but also of a devout laywoman's ability to remain in the world."[25]

Thus, the various accounts of Louis's foundation for beguines tend to emphasize the king's charitable motivations as well as the worthiness of the beguinage's residents, who, Louis's hagiographers insisted, lived honestly and chastely and came from noble backgrounds. Yet the term *beguina* originally seems to have been used pejoratively to describe someone of ostentatious, and thus probably insincere, piety.[26] By dress and demeanor, beguines made a claim to live a religious life and their behavior, consequently, invited a great deal of scrutiny. In Paris, lay religious women were highly visible, attracting both positive and negative commentary for their refusal to conform to the expectations of urban life, such as marriage, cultivation of reputation, and acquisition of wealth. While Louis's hagiographers stressed the beguines' chastity and respectability, some contemporary observers strongly objected to their adoption of humble dress, expressed skepticism regarding their pious self-representation, and accused them of mendicancy, hypocrisy, and sexual impropriety.

The writings of the secular cleric William of Saint-Amour (d. 1272), a vociferous critic of the beguines, give voice to some of the suspicions regarding the beguine life in Paris at the time of Louis's foundation. William's principal objection to the beguines seems to have been their association with the mendicant friars, against whom he composed his famous eschatological treatise *De periculis novissimorum temporum* (*On the Perils of the Last Times*) in 1256 at the height of the bitter and protracted dispute between the secular and mendicant orders at the University of Paris.[27] But it was not just the beguines' association with the friars that drew William's ire. The beguines' assumption of religious dress and public displays of devotion violated what William viewed as important distinctions between clerical and lay status, a pernicious trend that even the king himself followed.[28] By making a claim to lead a religious life, the beguines exposed themselves to intense scrutiny and inevitable charges of hypocrisy.[29] In William's attacks on the beguines, then, can be detected some of the broader suspicions some Parisians harbored against them.

Employing biblical exegesis and drawing on apocalyptic themes, William's treatise aimed to warn the secular clergy in particular about the dangers posed by the mendicant friars, whom he associated with the "pseudo-Apostles," or the forerunners of the Antichrist.[30] Citing Paul's Second Letter to Timothy ("Know also this, that in the final days, dangerous times will threaten . . . for of this sort are those who penetrate homes and lead captive silly women laden with sins"),[31] William warned that the friars unlawfully penetrated the house of the soul by usurping the pastoral tasks of preaching and confession from the secular clergy who rightfully exercised them.[32] As for the *mulierculas* (or silly little women) of verse 6, William was quick to associate them with certain women of his own time, who, laden with sins, preferred the friars to their own parish priests.[33] Embedded in the apocalyptic message of the treatise were the secular clergy's concerns about mendicant appropriation of the pastoral responsibilities of the secular clergy, a concern that intensified with the appearance of lay religious women who sought spiritual experiences apart from and beyond those of the ordinary parish laity.[34] By accusing the friars of unlawfully entering houses and seducing "silly women laden with sin," moreover, William gave voice to suspicions that the beguines, who were unenclosed and unprofessed, were inappropriately intimate with the friars.

When compelled to defend his attacks on the friars, William avoided direct mention of the orders themselves, claiming that his work was not directed against any approved order.[35] The beguines, never recognized as an official order by the papacy, therefore represented an easy target. These beguines, William complained, seemed to be multiplying throughout the kingdom and posed a burden to society since, although young and able-bodied, they shamefully begged for alms.[36] Here, William's critique turns from the beguines' gullibility and attachment to false preachers to their mendicancy. According to a list of accusations against the secular cleric, William had criticized the beguines' claims to live a religious life as false and prideful, criticizing the beguines for donning humble clothes and cutting their hair in order to be thought holier than others. This assumption of "religious" clothing, he argued, deceitfully advertised a religious vocation when in fact, he insisted, they were ordinary laywomen. Such women, he charged, were guilty of the sin of hypocrisy.[37]

William's characterization of the beguines acknowledges the appeal the *vita apostolica* had for these women while, at the same time, exploiting the doubts and suspicion some observers had about the ability of such women to pursue such a life honestly and chastely. According to William, while Christ and his apostles had female followers, to whom they ministered, the pseudo-apostles had beguines. Weak and vulnerable to seduction, beguines were easily led away from their proper teachers (i.e., the parish clergy, who were, according to William's ecclesiology, the rightful successors of the apostles) by the false teachings of the mendicant pseudo-apostles. Unlike the women of the Gospels who were fed by the Word of God, the beguines of William's time preferred to be fed by the alms that rightfully belonged to the deserving poor. Not even their claims to chastity were to be trusted. Although the beguines might initially be drawn to the friars by means of the confessional, it did not take long for the relationship to become sexual.[38] Of course, this accusation of sexual immorality, here directed at beguines, aimed to damage the friars' reputations by capitalizing on suspicions about unattached women.[39] Indeed, friars, according to William, were "lovers of beguines" and could not be trusted to minister to the youthful and beautiful beguines without falling into sin.[40]

William's accusations against beguines were echoed in thirteenth-century vernacular literature. Drawing on commonly held suspicions about the ability of women to live a religious life in the world, as well as male confessors' intimate contact with their female penitents, the poet Rutebeuf (d. 1285), a supporter of William of Saint-Amour, pilloried the beguines in several poems written just after William's exile in 1256.[41] In *Les Ordres de Paris*, the Parisian *jongleur* mocks the beguines' claims to live a religious life, asserting that the "Order of Beguines" is easy. The women can leave to marry, since they take no vows. Moreover, to enter the "order," all one has to do is bow one's head and wear a wide garment.[42] Thus, for Rutebeuf, religious commitment was not a true commitment without the permanent pledge of self and property.[43] The beguines' clothing and sexual immorality are also targeted in his poem *La chanson des ordres*, in which Rutebeuf quips, "We have many beguines who have wide garments; whatever they do beneath them, I cannot tell you."[44]

As in the writings of William of Saint-Amour and Rutebeuf, Jean de Meun's continuation of the *Roman de la Rose*, composed around 1270, attacks beguines as hypocritical intimates of the friars. The poem features Constrained Abstinence (*Atenance Contrainte*), the companion of the friar False Seeming (*Faux Semblant*), dressed "like a beguine."[45] It is noteworthy that this beguine costume consisted of a cameline robe—a woolen garment of

high quality—and a silk *couvrechief,* not exactly humble attire. Constrained
Abstinence also held a psalter and wore a paternoster around her neck. The
latter was a generous gift from her mendicant partner False Seeming, echoing
William of Saint-Amour's references to the friars' gifts to their female penitents. In one memorable scene, Jean highlights the sexual intimacy between
the friar and the pseudo-beguine as Constrained Abstinence makes her confession "with such great devotion that it seemed to me that their two heads
were together under a single cap."[46] These criticisms of beguines in vernacular
literature indicate that the image of the beguine as a hypocrite whose close ties
with the friars were more sexual than spiritual must have had some currency
within certain circles in medieval Paris. It is little wonder, then, that Louis's
hagiographers emphasized the honesty and chastity of the women for whom
he built the beguinage.

Prud'homme or beguin?

Louis IX, who returned to France at the height of the secular-mendicant conflict, must have been aware of William's vitriolic attacks against mendicants
and beguines. Indeed, for Louis such criticism struck home, as he too found
himself a primary target of William's invective.[47] The secular clergy had long
regarded the French king as the protector of the university and its privileges.
Under Louis, however, the situation had tipped in the friars' favor. Before
embarking on crusade in 1248, Louis was already an enthusiastic patron of
mendicant convents.[48] He chose Dominicans as confessors, and friars were
placed in prominent positions at court.[49] Friars also served as *enquêteurs* responsible for ensuring the king's justice in the realm.[50] Upon his return from
crusade in 1254, however, Louis's affinity for the friars seemed to have moved
beyond a preference for mendicant confessors and administrators.[51] Louis's
dress and behavior, which for many observers seemed at odds with the dignity
of his office, suggested that the friars' influence at court had grown to the extent that the king himself wanted to live as a mendicant. As Joinville reports,
after Louis returned from crusade he "led so devout a life that he never again
wore ermine or miniver, or scarlet, or gilt stirrups or spurs. His clothing was
of undyed or dark-blue wool."[52] Joinville also describes Louis's simple meals,
claiming that Louis never asked for special dishes but rather ate whatever was
placed in front of him and watered down his wine.[53] Louis was also known to

follow a monastic routine of prayers and vigils, rising to say matins, attending several masses a day, and chanting the canonical hours.

In the eyes of his critics, the change in Louis was due to the influence of the friars at court. After the secular clergy expelled the friars in 1253 over their refusal to participate in a university-wide strike, Pope Alexander IV, an ardent supporter of the mendicant orders, ordered the seculars to readmit them.[54] Under papal pressure, the secular clerics found themselves unable to call upon their traditional supporter, whose sympathies seemed increasingly aligned with the mendicants.[55] Even as the king attempted to arbitrate the dispute on several occasions, the seculars generally perceived him as unfairly favoring the friars.[56] William of Saint-Amour was especially convinced that Louis's personal deportment and governmental policies were dictated by the mendicants. In several poorly concealed references to the French king, William criticized "Christian princes and people who had entrusted the governance of their souls to the said seducers [i.e., the pseudo-apostles]." Conveying his dismay at the king's foolish choice of counselors, William referred to the royal court as a place where the false preachers may incite "sympathetic leaders" against their enemies.[57]

Louis was surely aware of the criticism his intimacy with the friars provoked among members of the antimendicant party at the university. It was apparently a sentiment shared by some of his subjects, who were most likely as convinced as William that Louis's behavior and governmental policies were dictated by the friars. William of Saint-Pathus relates in his *Vie de Saint-Louis* that a certain woman, upon seeing Louis dressed in his humble garb, cried, "Shame, shame that you should be King of France! It would be better that another be king than you, for you are only king to the Friars Minor, the Friars Preachers, and to the priests and clerics."[58] William reports that Louis accepted the woman's criticisms with patience, responding that she was right and that he was, in fact, unworthy of being king.[59]

Setting aside for the moment William's account of Louis's reaction to criticism of his personal piety, an anecdote clearly presented as evidence of Louis's humility, such criticism of lay piety demonstrates that there existed considerable tension over the issue of what it meant to live a religious life in the world. Communities of lay religious men or women, such as the beguines (or individuals like Louis), raised questions about the possibility of living a religious life outside a monastic order. The more traditionally minded clerics, monks, and laypeople mocked or feared these new expressions of piety, insisting that only those who entered an approved monastic order and bound themselves to its rules with formal, perpetual vows might be considered "religious" in the strict sense of the word.[60] Others were more willing to recognize as "religious" anyone who lived a life of devotion to God, even if they did so outside a monastic setting.[61] James of Vitry, one of the best-known clerical supporters of lay religious women, effectively summarized the latter perspective in his *Historia occidentalis*: "We do not consider religious only those who renounce the world and go over to a religious life, but we can also call religious all the faithful of Christ who serve the Lord under the one highest and supreme Abbot."[62] Some even suggested that exposure to the temptations of the world as well as the endurance of mockery and humiliation were essential markers of a truly religious life. Louis's friend Robert of Sorbon, embraced and advocated the discomfort and social marginalization that came with living a devout life in the world as opposed to the cloister, claiming that those willing to endure criticism were better able to find the Kingdom of Heaven than even the professed religious.[63] In his sermons and moral treatises on this issue, the secular cleric and university master frequently invoked contemporary views—both positive and negative—regarding beguines.

A moralist and pastoral theologian, Robert of Sorbon seems to have had a profound influence on King Louis. Although few studies have explored the extent of Robert's influence, historians have generally recognized the secular cleric as a significant presence in the king's court.[64] Indeed, Joinville's *Life of Saint Louis* conveys a close friendship between Louis and the secular cleric, as well as a friendly rivalry between Robert and the seneschal for the king's attention. Robert carried the title of clerk of the king in 1256 and was involved in several property transactions with and on behalf of Louis throughout the late 1250s and early 1260s.[65] Louis, moreover, played an important role in the foundation of the Sorbonne, the college Robert established sometime around 1257.[66] The Obituary of the Sorbonne states that Robert was one of Louis's confessors, a claim that has not met with universal acceptance.[67] Whether or not Robert served in this capacity, he seems to have had some influence on Louis's thought. This influence is conveyed indirectly through Jean of Joinville, whose vita relates a debate between himself and Robert that touched upon fundamental tensions in lay expressions of religious devotion, tensions that Louis was compelled to negotiate as king and devout layman.

The debate took place at the king's request. Joinville reports that "when the king was in a gay mood" he addressed him, saying, "Seneschal, give me the reasons why a *preudome* is better than a *beguin*."[68] The contrast between these two terms, and the lifestyles they evoked, was an important one for all three men and has significant implications for understanding Louis's piety as well as his support for women adopting the beguine life. *Prud'homme*, a word used in courtly literature to refer to the ideal knight and later applied to men recognized as experts in their professions, designated someone of esteem and good reputation.[69] The term *beguin* could have much more negative connotations, denoting someone of ostentatious, sanctimonious piety.[70] Yet this was obviously not an interpretation to which Louis himself subscribed, given his desire to hear a debate on the superiority of one over the other. While Robert defended the beguin, Joinville took up the cause for the prud'homme. Without recording the details of either side's argument, Joinville tells us that the king, after hearing both men, responded "Master Robert, I would dearly love to have the name of being a *preudome*, so long as I deserved it, and you would be welcome to the rest. For a *preudome* is so grand and good a thing that even to pronounce the word fills the mouth pleasantly."[71]

Although we do not know the details of the debate that took place before the king, Robert's sermons and treatises provide some insight, at least into the secular cleric's side, which may have had more influence on the king than Joinville lets on.[72] In Robert's view, the beguin, and his female counterpart the beguine, lived religious lives in the world in spite of the ridicule they attracted for their humble appearance and pious behavior.[73] The prud'homme, on the other hand, was excessively concerned with preserving his good reputation. The beguin's publicly observable piety, deemed excessive or sanctimonious, attracted disdain, yet the beguin refused to tone down his practices, ever striving to bring about the conversion of others. To the beguin, the Kingdom of Heaven—for himself and for his fellow Christians—was far more important than earning and preserving the admiration of others. Louis's devotional practices, judged excessive and beneath his station by his critics, fitted Robert's portrayal of the beguin, suggesting that Louis's claim that he would "dearly love to have the name of being a *preudome*" should not be taken as the last word on the topic.[74] Louis may have wished to earn the esteem of others; after all, he was king. And he understood that his desire to live a more perfect Christian life was in some ways difficult to reconcile with the expectations related to his position.[75] Indeed, this conflict is perfectly encapsulated in the debate between Robert and Jean of Joinville.

The king's conversion to a stricter religious life after returning from crusade, although celebrated in the mendicant-authored hagiographies, engendered a great deal of discomfort among his contemporaries, and even among members of his own family.[76] While aspects of Louis's sanctity were suitable—indeed expected—of a thirteenth-century lay saint, they did not always fit comfortably with the standards of thirteenth-century kingship. As William Jordan has argued, Louis's behavior was reconciled with ideals of kingship with difficulty, and probably only in retrospect.[77] Even the vitae, as we have seen, provide glimpses of this discomfort over the king's dress and devotional practices. In perhaps a direct reference to the king's position between prud'homme and beguin, Robert declares in one sermon—which, it is worth noting, was preached at the beguinage of Paris—that he himself would prefer to be a beguin than to be king, so long as he was able to be.[78]

Like Robert's beguin, Louis accepted criticism with notable patience. Well aware that his dress and behavior were targets of derision, the king generally resisted any temptation to conceal or tone down his practices. Nevertheless, the criticism must have bothered him.[79] Indeed, there is evidence that even Louis had his limits. While he probably knew of William of Saint-Amour's thinly veiled criticisms circulating in De periculis, he took no immediate action.[80] This situation changed abruptly in June 1256 after William publicly preached a sermon in Paris highly critical of the king. The sermon targeted Louis's religious practices, specifically his nightly vigils, humble clothing, and excessive solicitude for the poor, claiming that such practices were not appropriate for kings, who ought to focus their attention on upholding justice in the realm and preserving the dignity of their position.[81] Perhaps stung by William's criticism of his failure to uphold justice in the realm, Louis finally acted, ordering William's exile from the kingdom.[82] Not long afterward, Louis submitted William's treatise De periculis to the pope, who condemned the work in October 1256 and approved William's banishment. The letter from the pope confirming these orders states that the decision was in accord with the wishes of the king, leaving little doubt that Louis was directly responsible for William's punishment.[83]

Whatever we are to make of Louis's response to William's sermons, it is clear that the king struggled to reconcile his religious commitment with commonly held expectations of kingship. This was a struggle that his friend Robert of Sorbon attempted to resolve in debates held in the king's presence. The conflict between reputation and religious devotion was also a subject Robert frequently addressed in sermons and treatises directed at university scholars, pressing his students to model their behavior on that of the beguin, in spite of the derision that such behavior would inevitably attract.[84] The fact that Robert also articulated these ideas at the beguinage of Paris demonstrates that he perceived a clear connection between advocating the beguine life in general and supporting the Paris beguinage. It is likely that Louis, upon whom Robert had a demonstrable influence, did as well. While hagiographical accounts of Louis's support for the beguine life emphasize his charitable motivations, Louis's connection with the beguine life was much more personal than the vitae suggest. Indeed, it was a tangible manifestation of his support for lay religious expression.

The context in which Louis founded the beguinage, a city where new modes of religious expression were tested and debated, suggests that his own pursuit of a religious life in the world, which was by no means universally admired during his lifetime, was informed as much by the example of the beguines as by the mendicant orders. His ardent support for the beguine life was so well known, in fact, that Rutebeuf in his poem "Li diz des beguines," which lampoons the beguines' pseudo-religious practices, wryly notes that one should avoid speaking ill of the beguines, for the king would not tolerate it.[85]

"Good and Holy Works": Louis's Foundation for Beguines

Beguine communities arose as like-minded women sought to adopt a communal life and, as James of Vitry phrased it, "incite one another to do good by mutual exhortations."[86] Formal communities needed secular and religious patrons willing to support these aspirations both ideologically and materially. As a ruler concerned with advancing religious reform in the realm as well as bettering the earthly lives of its people, Louis recognized the advantages of sponsoring a certain *type* of beguine community. In practical terms, a beguinage—organized by regulations, surrounded by walls, and protected by royal patrons—was a response to a demonstrable need. The beguinage provided a substantial and visible population of lay religious women with the opportunity to pursue a life of contemplative prayer and charitable action in relative security. A court beguinage also had the advantage of bringing together a large number of women who could perform a wide range of valuable services, such as hospital work and the teaching of children.[87] Thus, from the beginning, Louis endeavored to set up a house that would nourish and protect the spiritual needs and aspirations of lay religious women without undue interference from secular or ecclesiastical authorities. A potent symbol of the king's support of the religious aspirations of lay religious women, the beguinage brought together the king's twin concerns of personal piety and Christian kingship.

Louis's religious and charitable foundations began in earnest upon his

return from the Holy Land in the summer of 1254.[88] Around 1260, Louis
founded the Quinze-Vingts and established six new mendicant houses in Paris
alone between 1255 and 1259, including houses for the short-lived Friars of the
Sack and the Crutched Friars.[89] He endowed hospitals and convents throughout the realm and gave a large subsidy to the Filles-Dieu, a house for reformed
prostitutes. Royal support for beguine communities is evident in the first years
after Louis's return from crusade. Accounts for 1256 record several donations
made to support or establish small beguine convents throughout the realm,
including communities in Senlis,[90] Tours, Orleans, Rouen, Caen, and Verneuil.[91] In May 1256, Louis donated ten *livres* to the beguines in his kingdom, as well as ten livres for the mistress of the beguinage of Cambrai;[92] and
in September 1256, he designated forty livres "pro beguinis."[93] Most beguine
communities in northern Europe were small convents of varying organization
and pastoral affiliations accommodating about ten to fifteen women who were
directed by a *magistra* or mistress.[94] These convents were usually located near
a church—often a parish church—where the women attended Mass with the
ordinary laity.[95]

Louis's plans for a beguine house in Paris, however, were on a much
grander scale. Inspiration may have come from Flanders, a region with a significant population of beguines and important political connections with
France. Evidence that Louis was inspired by the Flemish model comes from a
statement sent to the bishop of Tournai in 1328 attesting to the morality and
orthodoxy of the beguines of Saint Elizabeth in Ghent. The statement, composed by clerical supporters of the Ghent beguines, claims that Saint Louis
had once visited the beguinage and had observed their way of life.[96] According to the report, Louis was so impressed with the beguines of Ghent that he
secured several privileges for the women and decided to found a beguinage
in Paris on the model of Saint Elizabeth's, which was a *curtis*, or "court," beguinage.[97] Less common than the beguine convent, court beguinages were
enclosed complexes that usually included a chapel for religious services, individual houses for beguines with the means to purchase their own dwellings,
and a communal house or convent for beguines living in common. Many
court beguinages, like that of Ghent, included a hospital and school.[98]

While the report of Saint Louis's admiration for the beguines of Ghent
clearly aimed to present the beguinage's residents in the best possible light,
there is no reason to doubt that Louis had visited Saint Elizabeth's. Soon after
his return to France in 1254, he made his way to Flanders to mediate a dynastic dispute between the sons of Countess Margaret.[99] An act concerning

the sale of some property to the abbey of Bonne-Fontaine confirms that he was in Ghent in November 1255.[100] Moreover, there is evidence to suggest that he recruited beguines from French Flanders as the first residents of the Paris beguinage. One of the first mistresses of the beguinage, Agnes of Orchies (d. 1284), was from Flanders, possibly Douai, and may have been invited to direct the Paris beguinage by Louis himself.[101] By placing the beguinage under Agnes's direction, Louis benefited from the expertise of someone with experience in the organization and administration of a court beguinage. Throughout the history of the Paris beguinage, the mistress wielded broad powers over the community. She kept track of finances, presided over decisions about who might join the community, advised the beguinage's religious and secular directors on the regulations governing the residents, and provided the women with religious instruction.[102]

Given the active role Louis played in the foundation and administration of the various religious and charitable houses he set up in Paris and throughout the realm, it is no surprise that he would seek to establish the Paris community in emulation of a demonstrably successful model from one of the main centers of the beguine movement in northern Europe. Hagiographical sources portray Louis as personally involved in the construction, organization, and material support of his charitable and religious foundations. William of Saint-Pathus's vita describes the king visiting construction sites and determining the layout of the houses and buildings.[103] As Sean Field has shown, Louis personally recruited women, including the first abbess, for the Franciscan convent at Longchamp.[104] Extant sources concerning the beguinage indicate that Louis was equally involved in this project. The preface to the rules of the Paris beguinage, which date from 1327, cites the active role he played in founding the beguinage and recruiting residents. According to the rule, he "acquired an enclosure of houses in Paris . . . and placed there good and honest beguines," suggesting that the saintly king had a direct hand in choosing the women who came to reside in his beguinage.[105]

Although the details relating to Louis's foundation of the Paris beguinage are extremely fragmentary, they provide a picture of a king deeply invested in supporting and protecting a beguine community in Paris. The earliest mention of the foundation is found in a document dated November 1264, which records the abbot of Tiron's acknowledgment of receipt of one hundred *livres tournai* from the Crown for a tract of land just inside the city walls on the Right Bank in Paris, in the parish of Saint-Paul.[106] While no formal documentation of the beguinage's foundation has survived (unfortunately, typical of such houses) it is certain that Louis began the process of founding the Paris beguinage at an earlier date.[107] Paris was home to a noticeable population of beguines by the mid-thirteenth century, as the complaints of William of Saint Amour attest. Gervais Ruffus, a Parisian merchant who composed his testament in April 1260, gave sixty livres to the "Beguines of Paris," indicating the existence of a recognizable beguine community in the city.[108] Thomas of Cantimpré's *Bonum universale de apibus*, written before 1263, refers to the beguinage of Paris as a completed project. Rutebeuf's *Ordres de Paris*, composed in the early 1260s, likewise refers to the numerous beguines residing at the Paris beguinage.[109] Several documents affirm that the beguinage possessed urban properties along the rue des Fauconniers by the early 1260s, clear evidence that the community had already become well established in the area.[110]

Most of the available evidence concerning the founding of the Paris beguinage is hagiographical. What is known about the organization of the beguinage, its privileges, and pastoral relationships, comes primarily from fourteenth-century sources. Nevertheless, the historical record holds a few clues that serve to illuminate Louis's efforts to secure rights and privileges for the beguinage. Although the lands on which the beguinage was built—extending from the rue des Poulies in the north down to the rue des Barres (later rue des Béguines) on the southern end—were located in the censive of the Benedictine abbey of Tiron and the parish of Saint-Paul, the city walls cut the area off from seigneurial and parochial authority, thus facilitating the beguinage's relative independence from both and effectively bringing the area under royal power (map 2).[111] The location was significant for the history of the Paris beguinage for several reasons. Depending upon the balance of powers in a particular town, beguines had to negotiate with a constellation of authorities for the privilege of setting up their communities.[112] Powerful patrons helped smooth this process. As laywomen, beguines were subject to parochial and seigneurial authority, obliged to pay taxes and tithes, and subject to secular courts. Thus, beguines relied on their patrons to grant and secure privileges, such as exemptions from certain financial obligations, as well as the right to receive pastoral care from their own confessors or from a specially designated chaplain in the service of the beguinage. On the other hand, patrons had to ensure that parochial and seigneurial authorities were not unduly disadvantaged by the presence of a beguine community in their jurisdictions. Louis took care to uphold the rights of the seigneurial lords and to compensate adequately the parish priests of Saint-Paul, thereby avoiding unnecessary conflict between the beguines and local authorities while nourishing the spiritual

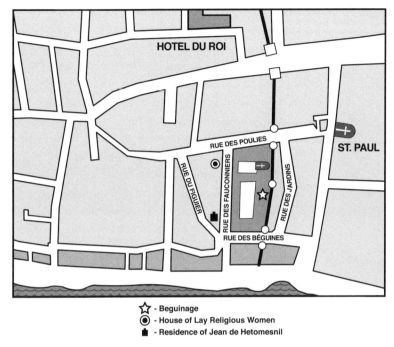

Map 2. Beguinage

ambitions of the beguines and, at the same time, protecting the reputation and financial solvency of the beguinage.

Royal accounts show that the Crown paid the seigneurial dues the beguinage owed to the abbey of Tiron and compensated the parish priests for the losses they incurred as a result of the construction of a beguinage in their parish. The king's negotiations with these authorities were important for the beguinage's survival. Although the king was in a strong position to provide the beguines with substantial privileges, such as exemptions from certain taxes (the residents of the beguinage never show up in the tax rolls, for example), the beguines were subject to a nexus of authorities, and the king recognized the need to uphold the rights of the other interested parties as far as possible.[113]

As religious women who organized themselves into communities with varying degrees of formality, many beguines took the initiative in arranging for their own spiritual care. The beguine households just outside the Franciscan convent in Paris, for example, may have been set up by women who wished to receive pastoral care from the friars (see map 1). Other informal

beguine communities probably made similar ad hoc arrangements with individual clerics regarding care of souls. Nevertheless, as laywomen, beguines
were subject to parochial authorities, who frequently objected to parishioners
seeking pastoral care from other clerics, particularly friars.[114] Formal beguine
communities, such as convents and beguinages, were often administered by
an array of local clerics in conjunction with secular officials, who negotiated
issues of pastoral care and general governance. In many of the larger beguine
communities of the Low Countries, the mendicant orders—especially the
Dominicans—took on supervisory roles as spiritual guardians and financial
administrators. While these arrangements demonstrated the intense interest
local clerics and secular patrons took in the spiritual and financial health of beguine communities, in some cases the pastoral care of beguines could be every
bit as contentious an issue as the pastoral care of nuns. As religious women,
beguines required more than the minimal religious services. The beguines
of Paris heard Mass daily and, like other beguine communities, observed a
monastic routine of prayers and vigils.[115] Patrons of the beguinage, including
Louis, requested anniversary masses, prayers, and vigils from the residents.[116]
Sermons preached at the Paris beguinage indicate that the beguines were particularly eager to hear sermons and received regular religious instruction from
university scholars.[117] The mistress also played a significant role in the spiritual
instruction of beguines and may have participated in negotiating the provision of pastoral care for the community. The mistress's competencies can be
discerned in excerpts from sermons she preached to the beguines under her
care.[118] Her close relationships with the preachers who came to the beguinage
chapel also suggest that she exercised some influence in arranging religious
instruction at the beguinage.

Louis was deeply concerned with arranging pastoral care at his foundations
and cultivating the religious devotions of its residents. The better-preserved archival sources for the Quinze-Vingts show that he devoted considerable attention to ensuring that regular religious services were held at the hospital for "the
poor blind of Paris."[119] He arranged to have a chapel built within the enclosure
of the hospital and chose the first chaplain, to whom he entrusted the task of
performing the divine services.[120] Employing his considerable influence, Louis
persuaded the pope to grant the hospital parochial status, further attesting to
the king's active role in the spiritual direction of the residents.[121]

The fragmentary evidence suggests that Louis also provided the beguinage
with its own chapel and arranged for the women to receive pastoral care from
their own specially appointed chaplains. It is likely that Louis, and perhaps the

women themselves, preferred that the beguinage's residents attend Mass and receive pastoral care within the enclosure rather than mingle with the laity in the parish church, which, it will be remembered, was located outside the city walls.[122] Moreover, it would have been difficult for the parish church to accommodate such a large number of women.

There is some suggestion, in fact, that the parish priests were unwilling or unable to provide pastoral care to the beguine community. Unlike the court beguinages of the Low Countries, the Paris beguinage did not have independent parochial status, perhaps out of deference to the parish authorities of Saint-Paul.[123] Yet, in spite of the beguinage's subjection to their authority, the priests of Saint-Paul had minimal involvement in the women's pastoral care and little say in the governance of the enclosure. Sermon evidence from the 1270s reveals that the beguinage hosted at least twenty-five different preachers over the course of a single year. The extent of the parish priests' involvement at the beguinage can be surmised further from a document recording an agreement between the parish priest and the Crown in March of 1290. By this date, the parish priest agreed to say one mass per year at the beguinage, "among other things," indicating that his pastoral obligations were quite small.[124]

Thus, while the beguinage remained part of the parish of Saint-Paul, with its priests only partially involved in the pastoral care of its residents, the beguinage was served by several specially designated chaplains.[125] Significantly, royal accounts demonstrate that the French kings compensated the parish priests by paying them around fifteen *livres parisis* per year "for the chapel of the beguinage."[126] The payments may have been compensation for their services as well as the losses the parish priests incurred as a result of the beguines' chapel being erected within the boundaries of the parish, since the chapel would result in a loss of parishioners. Certainly, given the number of university preachers—secular and mendicant—that the beguinage hosted, the parish priests were probably justified in any complaints they had against the beguinage.

Significantly, there is no evidence to suggest that the mendicant orders were in any way involved in the spiritual or administrative oversight of the Paris beguinage until the reign of Philip IV.[127] This may seem surprising, given Louis's close ties with the friars, not to mention the beguines' own connections with both orders. In many of the beguinages of the Low Countries, the prior of the Dominican order presided over the community as an administrator and spiritual director.[128] In Bruges, the prior of the Dominican order aided the mistress of the beguinage in naming the chaplain. The Dominican prior nominated the mistress of the beguinage of Ghent as well as the chaplains who served the community.[129] Nevertheless, the involvement of the mendicants in the supervision of beguine communities should not be overstated. In Lille, for example, parish priests appointed the chaplains serving the beguinage and similar arrangements existed in other northern European cities.[130] Although there is no evidence to suggest that this was the arrangement observed in Paris, it was a possibility. Overall, the evidence suggests that Louis worked to affect a series of compromises in order to fulfill the spiritual needs of the beguines and address the practical concerns or objections of the parish priests, all the while protecting the reputation of the beguinage as a house of honest and holy women. While we have much more direct evidence concerning his efforts to provide for the beguinage materially, the pastoral and seigneurial arrangements in place early on in the foundation's history point to Louis as a major force in the long-term success of the foundation.

The king's efforts to ensure material support for his foundation are evinced in both the hagiographical and the documentary records. Geoffrey of Beaulieu's vita emphasizes the King's charitable motivations, specifically providing for the daughters of impoverished nobles.[131] These "poor" beguines, who may not have been impoverished at all but rather counted as "deserving poor," seem to have been of special concern for Louis. They were probably the beneficiaries of royal pensions, an arrangement alluded to in the various accounts of Louis's charitable deeds and elaborated upon in William of Saint-Pathus's vita. William, who composed his work in 1302 at the request of Louis's widow, Margaret of Provence, reports that Louis provided individual beguines with pensions, which the women were to receive on a regular basis in the same manner that Louis provided financial support to poor scholars of the Sorbonne.[132] Specifically, a certain number of women were to receive weekly subsidies, and perhaps housing, from the royal treasury.[133] By insisting upon the need to support the "poor beguines" in the beguinage, Louis committed his successors to providing for a specific, apparently needy, sector of the beguinage's population.

As was the case with his other foundations, Louis continued to support the beguinage throughout his reign, leaving the institution generous bequests at his death. In his testament, he expressed concern for maintaining both the buildings and the residents of his foundation. Specifically, he bequeathed one hundred livres "for the purpose of improving and enlarging the beguinage in Paris," indicating, perhaps, that the beguine population was outgrowing the original buildings.[134] In addition to leaving aside funds for the maintenance and enhancement of the beguinage, he left twenty livres for its poorer members.[135] His testament also provided for "poor beguines"—perhaps the small beguine convents throughout the realm—designating one hundred livres to be distributed among these women.[136] It is not without significance that, toward the end of his testament, Louis returns to the beguines once more, singling the women out for special consideration and binding his successors to continue to support a foundation that was of great personal importance. Specifically, the testament requests that his successors uphold certain provisions that he had established for the beguines of the realm.[137] These provisions are alongside similar arrangements made for clerics and converted Jews, suggesting that these three groups held special importance.[138] Indeed, the Crown later set up a special account to fund pensions for beguines, poor scholars, and converted Jews, a triad of special significance to the "work of the realm," that also affirmed the French kings' commitment to emulating the deeds of their saintly predecessor.[139]

As a layman who chose to live a religious life in the world, in many ways Louis embodied the ideals of thirteenth-century lay sanctity, yet his pious image fitted awkwardly with his position as ruler. Even granting the constructed nature of hagiographical accounts of his piety, it is evident that Louis cultivated a reputation as a devout layman given to dramatic expressions of humility and charity, in spite of opposition and ridicule, during his life. Beguines, who were both mocked and praised for their public displays of devotion, represented an important and visible example of lay religiosity played out in the world rather than removed from it. This mockery and humiliation, while passed over by Louis's hagiographers, who preferred to emphasize the worthiness of these recipients of royal support, was an important characteristic of the beguine life, and it was part of what made it worthy of Louis's admiration and support. Alongside these personal or spiritual reasons for supporting the beguine life, we must balance the king's practical reasons. Beguinages served as refuges for lay religious women committed to performing "good and holy works," such as caring for the sick and ministering to the poor. Although accounts of the beguinage's foundation naturally do not mention the social utility of such houses, Louis was most certainly aware of the advantages beguinages brought to the city and its inhabitants.

By establishing a certain type of beguine house, moreover, Louis shaped the beguine life in Paris in significant ways. Although large numbers of beguines continued to live outside the beguinage in their own homes, often with other like-minded women, attitudes toward the beguine status—for good or for ill—were informed by the existence of the royally sponsored beguinage.

The beguinage, with its rules and walls, in some ways approximated a convent, to the extent that some observers, especially clerics, expressed disapproval toward women who lived a religious life outside it. On the other hand, to the women living within the enclosure, rules, walls, and carefully controlled admission criteria may have provided much more freedom to pursue a life of chastity and work in an environment where they were relatively safe from physical harm and public suspicion of their reputations.

CHAPTER 2

The World of the Beguinage

When Louis IX commissioned the building of a court beguinage on the eastern end of the city, Paris was already home to a recognizable community of lay religious women. Although little is known about the first few years of the beguinage's existence, Louis's foundation clearly resonated with the social needs and religious sensibilities of a broad cross-section of medieval Parisians. Attracting noble, patrician, and artisan women well into the late fifteenth century, the Paris beguinage succeeded not only due to strong royal support but also because medieval Parisians—both clerical and lay—found it worthwhile to support the foundation and its residents. The beguinage, in its organization and administration, was flexible and well suited to the Parisian context, accommodating women of diverse socioeconomic backgrounds pursuing a wide spectrum of religious practices. As Rutebeuf groused, the beguines could be both "Martha" and "Mary." They could work in the city to support themselves, pursue an active apostolate among their fellow Parisians, and withdraw to the beguinage to enjoy seclusion and contemplation. They could leave at any time to live as lay religious women outside the beguine community. Some women left to marry.

An important component of this flexibility was control over property. Paris, like many northern European cities, observed an inheritance system that gave women significant control over property, a factor that contributed to the popularity and success of the beguine life.[1] Both formal and informal religious communities relied on the resources of their members, who invested their wealth and supported themselves and their fellow beguines with their own property.[2] The rules governing the Paris beguinage and its assets were adapted to and dependent on the particular customary laws and practices regulating Parisian women's property rights and shaping bourgeois family strategies.

Unlike convents and other houses for lay religious women, the Paris beguinage did not require its residents to hand over their property to the community, allowing women to join or leave the community without significant loss of personal investment. This compatibility gave propertied beguines the ability to forge strong relationships with other women, as well as members of the Parisian bourgeoisie, while maintaining flexible ties to their families, who were certainly not disinterested parties with regard to their female relatives' decisions to become beguines. Able to inherit, invest, and donate property within a secure environment, beguines were important transmitters of wealth. Goods and annuities circulated in and out of the beguinage, supporting lay religious women and their friends and families, as well as other religious and charitable institutions in and around Paris, giving beguines the opportunity to act as leaders and benefactors within this socioeconomically diverse community.[3]

Exploring issues of property and socioeconomic status, factors that tied beguines to the bustling world beyond the beguinage walls, serves to address several interrelated points frequently raised by historians of beguine communities. Early studies of the beguine movement argued that beguine communities formed in response to economic and demographic pressures of urban life, with primarily unmarried, destitute women joining the community out of economic need.[4] Beguine houses seemed to be one solution to what historians viewed as the problem of "too many women," a phenomenon historian Karl Bücher in 1882 termed the *Frauenfrage*, or "the woman question." Influenced by Bücher's thesis, some scholars argued that beguine houses served as charitable foundations for indigent and unmarried women, effectively denying the religious motivations of individual beguines.[5] Later studies, most influentially Grundmann's, countered this interpretation, arguing that beguinages mainly attracted women from the wealthier sectors of society who wished to live an apostolic life of poverty.[6] These conflicting historical perspectives on the background and motivations of beguines, in many ways, reflect the divergent views of the beguines' contemporaries. James of Vitry, for example, focused on wealthy beguines who, turning their backs on their families' wealth and status, lived lives of voluntary poverty.[7] The beguines' detractors, such as William of Saint-Amour, by contrast, portrayed beguines as destitute burdens on society.[8] Linking socioeconomic status and general support for the beguine life, scholars have often cited changes in beguine recruitment as a reason behind or a consequence of changing attitudes towards beguines over the course of the Middle Ages.[9] Yet the participation of women from different backgrounds both created and contributed to the beguinage's unique function as a place in which women could come together to live, work, and care for one another in a supportive and spiritually nurturing environment. Wealthier women might join a beguinage in pursuit of apostolic ideals. They also might find the beguine life a more flexible, and thus more appealing, alternative to the cloister, where they would be cut off from their family, friends, and associates. At the same time, beguinages offered women of middling and lower socioeconomic status a safe haven in which to worship and work.[10] Whatever a woman's personal wealth and status, it is clear that her reputation and social networks were key factors in securing a place in the community.[11] These networks continued to link women to the world outside the beguinage even as beguines forged enduring ties to their lay religious sisters within the enclosure.

Life in the Beguinage

A social and cultural microcosm of the city, the Paris beguinage accommodated and nurtured a broad spectrum of spiritual expression. Abutting the walls of Philip Augustus on its eastern end, the beguinage was both within the city boundaries yet effectively secluded from Paris's bustling, mercantile Right Bank (figure 1). To the north, the beguinage was bordered by buildings running along the rue des Poulies. Rows of buildings (possibly individual residences) along the rue des Fauconniers separated the beguinage from its neighbors on the beguinage's western periphery (see map 2).[12] Traffic in and out of the enclosure was channeled through the main gate, located on the rue de Barres, later called the rue des Béguines, to the south. Within the enclosure there existed a variety of residential and communal spaces. Depending upon their individual means or personal preferences, beguines could live either in private homes, sometimes with one or two companions, or in the communal dormitory, which must have housed dozens of women. The beguinage also had its own chapel, as well as a hospital for elderly or ill beguines. By the fourteenth century, the beguinage had a school where young girls from the city, and perhaps beguine residents, were taught the fundamentals of reading and writing.[13]

The walls surrounding the beguinage literally separated its female inhabitants from the city in order to protect the women from threats to their bodies and reputations. In reality, however, the beguinage was remarkably porous. Acting as a magnet, the beguinage and its chapel drew royal patrons, bourgeois supporters, and clerical visitors. Its residents were likewise drawn out of the enclosure to nurture spiritual friendships with clerical advisors, carry out property

Figure 1. Remnants of the wall of Philip Augustus. CJ Dub, Restes de l'enceinte de Philippe-Auguste, mitoyen du Collège Charlemagne, Wikimedia Commons.

negotiations with family members and business associates, and fulfill spiritual and social obligations. Within the relative seclusion of the beguinage chapel or private room, beguines were able to engage in solitary contemplation, but the porosity of the beguinage meant that they were free to nurture horizontal and vertical networks that included family, friends, and work associates.

Contact with the world outside the beguinage was frequent and relatively uncontroversial. Although the earliest surviving statutes for the community date from 1327, and thus reflect a community struggling to cope with the anti-beguine decrees of the Council of Vienne, some of the earliest sources concerning the Paris beguinage indicate that residents were reasonably free to travel outside the enclosure. One of the miracles ascribed to Saint Louis in William of Saint-Pathus's *Miracles of Saint Louis* describes two beguines who had been cured after traveling to the dead king's tomb.[14] Casual mention of the beguines' forays outside the enclosure is also found in records of sermons preached at the beguinage chapel. In a sermon encouraging beguines to embrace contemplation and solitude, one Franciscan preacher tells his audience that, wherever they go, whether to church, or sermons, or public places, they must do everything for the honor of God.[15] Another preacher laments that, because the beguines were not enclosed, they were vulnerable to outside "invasion."[16]

A canon of Saint-Eloi complained of beguines who wandered about the towns, insisting that such women be "enclosed" both in habit (or dress) and "other things," presumably their living spaces.[17] Several *exempla* relayed by Parisian preachers mention beguines who travel from one town to another and engage in conversation with university masters.[18] While fragmentary, the evidence suggests a community with ties to the world outside the beguinage.

The surviving statutes regulating life at the beguinage, although composed in the wake of the Council of Vienne, portray a community of women with relative freedom to enter and leave the enclosure, suggesting perhaps that the original statutes had been more lax in this respect. These statutes emphasized supervision over the beguines' comings and goings and increased vigilance regarding the types of visitors that residents were permitted to receive. The very first rule in the revised statutes concerns the circumstances under which beguines might travel out into the city, decreeing that any beguine who wished to leave the beguinage was required to obtain the permission of the mistress. If permission to travel outside the enclosure was granted, the mistress would designate a companion to accompany the beguine to and from her destination.[19] It seems to have been acceptable, however, for beguines to leave the enclosure for the day or even overnight. One rule decrees that beguines should return to the enclosure before dark, unless they had reasonable cause not to return.[20] Another rule prohibits sleeping or dining outside the beguinage without the permission of the mistress, indicating that beguines were able to leave for extended periods of time, so long as they had the mistress's approval.[21] Given the beguines' involvement in hospital work and other social services, it was reasonable to allow beguines to stay overnight outside the enclosure in order to attend the sick or dying.[22] The rules further suggest that the house was relatively open to male visitors, provided that the mistress gave her permission and residents met with their male visitors in public areas, such as the refectory or chapel.[23] While traffic in and out of the beguinage was closely monitored, its residents were by no means cut off from the world outside the walls. Testaments and property records show that its inhabitants managed to cultivate a wide network of female and male associates.[24]

Overseeing the community was the mistress, who was charged with managing the institution's finances, monitoring the everyday comings and goings of residents and visitors, enforcing the rules of the community, and deciding how violations should be punished.[25] According to the beguinage's earliest extant statutes, the mistress, with the counsel of three or four senior beguines, determined who could be admitted to the community and decided which visitors, male or female, beguines might entertain within the enclosure.[26] To ensure that residents of the beguinage conducted themselves appropriately while outside the beguinage, the mistress appointed trustworthy companions to accompany beguines on approved outings.[27] Finally, the mistress was delegated the task of keeping track of the beguinage's day-to-day expenditures and for rendering the community's accounts to the Dominican prior.[28] Nurturing essential ties to the city that sustained the beguinage, the mistress secured annuities for its support. Several cases show the mistress approving the sale of the beguinage's properties, including the individual houses within the enclosure and serving as executor for beguines' testaments. It also fell to the mistress to apply the proceeds from the sale of beguinage property for the common profit of the beguine community.[29]

In addition to these disciplinary and administrative roles, the mistress assumed responsibility for the beguines' spiritual direction. Poised between a community of women with varying spiritual objectives and a diverse population of clerics, she cultivated ties with university scholars, parish priests, and local churchmen. Like beguine communities all over northern Europe, the Paris beguinage came to have special ties to the Dominican order, which was charged with the responsibility of supervising the beguine community sometime during the reign of Philip IV.[30] The mistress of the beguinage, as representative of the community, was accorded the honor of burial in the Dominican chapel since the time of Agnes of Orchies (d. 1284), suggesting a long-standing affiliation between the Dominicans and the beguinage of Paris.[31] Sermon collections from the 1270s further attest to connections with local clerics. University masters and students—both regular and secular—frequently preached in the beguinage chapel.[32] Without doubt, the advantages of living in close proximity to some of the most learned theologians of medieval Europe were not lost on the mistress, who welcomed preachers of the highest caliber to preach sermons in the chapel of the beguinage. Sermon material compiled by the Sorbonne cleric Raoul of Châteauroux sheds light on the collaborative nature of her interactions with university scholars. It is through these sources that we have evidence of the mistress's sermons to the beguine community, which Raoul copied into his sermon collections. The inclusion of the mistress's sermons in what was intended as a preaching guide for clerics attests to Raoul's high esteem for the mistress and her religious instruction, as well as the personal nature of his relationship with the leader of the beguine community.[33]

Indeed, life in the beguinage did not isolate lay religious women; rather, it facilitated the creation of a vast network of patrons, supporters, and spiritual advisors. Individual beguines also forged close spiritual friendships with clerics. Jeanne du Faut, who lived in the beguinage for a time, left substantial bequests to a chantry priest named Roland Helloin, with whom she maintained a close spiritual friendship.[34] Alison Roullonne named the Franciscan theologian Étienne de Bléneau as one of the executors of her testament. Étienne had served as confessor and executor to the Countess of Étampes, Jeanne d'Eu.[35] It is likely that Alison too looked to Étienne for spiritual guidance. Other relationships are illuminated through property transactions. In 1372, the beguine Jeanne Daufay received a life rent from a priest named Pierre Chagrin, an enthusiastic supporter of lay religious women.[36] The beguine Perrette la Mairesse received an annuity from Henri le Bourguignon, the procurer general of the Dominican order in 1324.[37] In his testament, Jean de Hétomesnil (d. after 1380), the canon of Sainte-Chapelle and counselor to King Charles V who lived just across the street from the beguinage, made special mention of several beguines who lived in the enclosure. These references indicate that Jean was particularly close to one beguine, Bourges de Mortières, whom he employed in his household.[38] Other beguines maintained close ties with merchant elites, intimates of the court, and Parlementary officials.[39]

The beguinage fostered communal life while, at the same time, allowing for independence and solitude. Like monks and nuns, the beguines of Paris attended sermons and chapter meetings in common.[40] Although not required to by the statutes, beguines dined together in the refectory.[41] Most of the residents of the beguinage lived together in the convent or hospital, and even beguines with private homes within the enclosure lived with companions.[42] Indeed, it may have been common for beguines to have other women, servants or young girls, living with them in their homes.[43] In some cases, such companions were required. The statutes decreed that no woman under the age of thirty was permitted to live alone.[44] For these younger beguines, the mistress, in consultation with three or four senior beguines, would choose a suitable (presumably older) companion.[45] Thus, even as it was possible for some beguines to live and work in solitude in their own homes or rooms within the enclosure, the beguinage encouraged a sense of community and mandated mutual responsibility.

Socioeconomic Composition

This spirit of community was particularly important in a house composed of women of different ages, religious objectives, and social conditions. More important, perhaps, was the beguinage's accommodation of this diversity, which not only gave the beguine life great appeal for Parisian women of all classes and conditions but also helped attract support for the community as a whole. Poorer women found work opportunities in Paris's wool industry, which was centered in the neighborhoods around the beguinage.[46] The presence of poor women, moreover, helped preserve the beguinage's image as a group of women worthy of Christian charity. Wealthier women, for their part, were able to maintain control over their personal property, a boon in a city where women inherited, managed, and bequeathed property with relative freedom. Since it is unlikely that the beguinage was able to support all of its residents, wealthier residents were obliged to contribute to the support of their poorer sisters. The diversity of the beguinage undoubtedly led to some tension among residents, but it was what helped sustain the community and its image.[47]

For the Paris beguinage, little is known about the backgrounds of most of the residents of the community. If indeed the beguinage housed hundreds of women, very few are named in the extant records. Geoffrey of Beaulieu's vita claims that Louis IX established the beguinage as a house for "worthy" poor women, that is, the daughters of noble families who lacked the means to marry them off according to their status.[48] These sources echo reports concerning the beginnings and growth of the beguine movement in northern France and the southern Low Countries. James of Vitry and Thomas of Cantimpré describe the first communities of lay religious women there as composed of the daughters of nobles and urban elites. Narratives describing the foundation of the Grand Beguinage of Ghent—the model on which the Paris beguinage was based—cite the poverty of noble and respectable families who were unable to contract suitable marriages for their daughters as a key impetus behind the foundation.[49] From the founding of the beguinage by Louis IX, French kings arranged to provide pensions for some of the residents. It is possible that these stipends were reserved for the "impoverished nobles" for whom Louis ostensibly founded the beguinage; however, no extant source outlines how these recipients of royal alms were selected. Louis's successors likewise bestowed gifts on the "poor" beguines of Paris and throughout the French kingdom.[50]

Sermon evidence from medieval Paris presents the beguinage as a possible option for noble and patrician women. In a sermon delivered at the beguinage in 1273, the Dominican friar Giles of Orleans describes how he attempted to convince a certain noble lady to become a beguine. According to Giles, the noblewoman scoffed at the notion, complaining of the beguines' bad reputations. It is noteworthy, however, that the noblewoman did not reject the beguine life because she thought it was beneath her status.[51] Indeed, the entire exchange, as relayed in Giles's sermon, highlights familial and socioeconomic considerations as important factors in recruitment to the beguinage. Complaining that she was unable to marry off her daughters to suitable husbands, the noblewoman tells the preacher that she will place them in convents rather than a beguinage, but only because religious devotion was not expected in a convent.[52] Several sermons preached at the beguinage chapel refer to women of exalted backgrounds in the audience. In one sermon, the secular master Gerard of Reims relayed an amusing story about a noble beguine who, after hearing a sermon on the virtue of patience, decided to test her own ability to bear the disrespect of her inferiors by asking her servant to say something insolent to her. Her servant dared not comply. Later on, when the beguine was with her family and friends, the servant decided to honor her mistress's earlier request. The beguine, of course, became furious about this public affront.[53] Another sermon, preached sometime in the late thirteenth century, complains of the expensive books owned by beguines, indicating that many of the beguinage's residents were thought to be women of significant means.[54]

Even as sermons and official narratives tended to emphasize the beguinage's more exalted residents, the community was composed of women from a range of socioeconomic backgrounds. Indeed, the structure of the beguinage, with its common and private residences, indicates that socioeconomic diversity was expected. Certainly, no effort was made to efface class distinctions within the enclosure. Although the residents of the beguinage wore special habits to signify their membership in the community, women of higher status were apparently permitted to advertise their gentle birth with habits appropriate to their station.[55] Beguines with sufficient means could purchase, rent, or build their own houses within the enclosure. Beguines of more modest means, however, lived in common in the beguinage convent or hospital.[56] An unspecified number of beguines, possibly those who were recipients of royal stipends, were permitted to live in private residences rent-free.[57] The statutes of the beguinage show, moreover, that special provisions were made to aid the community's poorer members. For example, beguines who could not afford to make repairs to their homes were to receive aid from the community.[58]

Parisian testators recognized this diversity in the beguinage's population, singling out groups of beguines they considered deserving of charitable support. For example, in 1313, Jeanne la Fouacière left one hundred sous to the "poor women living behind the beguinage."[59] Margaret Loisel likewise bequeathed twenty sous to the "hospital of the poor beguines."[60] In his testament, the canon and royal counselor Jean de Hétomesnil also recognized different groups of beguines within the beguinage.[61] Indeed, among the few testaments that survive for medieval Paris, most bequests intended for the beguinage targeted the "poor" beguines as a group or the beguinage hospital.[62] This emphasis on the poor members of the community accords with medieval patterns of charitable giving, which tended to focus on segments of the population perceived as "honest poor," especially women from reputable families who were vulnerable to falling into destitution.[63]

Although it is difficult to determine the socioeconomic backgrounds of most of the residents of the beguinage, patrons, governors, and mistresses undoubtedly paid special attention to a prospective recruit's character before admitting her to the community. The mistress was probably appointed by or with the approval of the king, but perhaps (at least after the reign of Philip IV) on the advice of the Dominican prior.[64] The mistress's council, too, was probably composed of well-connected and reputable women. We know from the statutes that, by the early fourteenth century, it was the mistress and the members of her council who took charge of determining who might be admitted into the community.[65] The smattering of names mentioned in royal account books compiled during the reign of Philip IV and his successors confirm that many residents of the royal beguinage were drawn from the ranks of the upper bourgeoisie, and at least one noblewoman lived in the beguinage in the late fourteenth century.[66]

Indeed, a woman's connections and reputation, more than any other factor, earned her admittance into the royal beguinage. In some cases, the relationship between a beguine and the court is quite clear. Louis IX's brother, Alphonse of Poitiers (d. 1271), knew the porteress of the beguinage by name. In 1267, Alphonse entrusted the beguine with the task of delivering a gift of fifty sous to the beguine community.[67] Louis's widow, Margaret of Provence, received a substantial payment for a house on the Left Bank on behalf of a beguine named Alice, suggesting a close relationship with the French queen.[68] The noblewoman Jeanne de La Tour, who entered the Paris beguinage sometime before 1432, had served as a lady-in-waiting to Isabelle of Valois, the Duchess of Bourbon.[69] No doubt Jeanne's connection with the court facilitated her entry into the beguinage of Paris.

This relationship with the royal court, as we might expect, was especially important for the mistress of the beguinage. The mistress's responsibilities, as we have seen, presumed a high level of education as well as broad contacts. Although the first mistress and perhaps several of the beguinage's first residents were recruited from northern France and the Low Countries, the region in which the beguinage organization was most entrenched, by the early fourteenth century mistresses were drawn from royally connected Parisian families, particularly the daughters of city administrators and intimates of the royal court.[70] Perrenelle Chanevacière, mistress of the community in 1306, was related to several well-connected Parisian merchants and aldermen.[71] Other mistresses of the beguinage were from important Parisian families whose male members served noble and royal households as well as the city government. Martine Canu, mistress until 1430, was the sister of a royal official.[72] Jeanne Brichard, mistress in 1311, was from a prominent bourgeois family with multiple ties to the royal court. Both Jeanne's father and brother served as royal moneyers, and Jeanne's aunt, Isabelle Tremblay, was a major supplier of luxury wool cloth to the French royal household.[73] Jeanne Arrode, mistress in 1352, was from a prominent aldermanic family.[74]

Significantly, women from some of Paris's most powerful bourgeois families identified as beguines, both within and outside the beguinage enclosure. In a tax register drawn up in 1292, Genevieve and Agnes Senliz were listed next to their brother Girard on the rue du Four, a street with a strong beguine presence (see map 4).[75] The son-in-law of the prominent alderman Jean Hescelin, Girard eventually divided the family business with his sisters and moved away from the family home on the rue du Four.[76] By 1300, the sisters had moved as well, this time to a neighborhood populated with some of Paris's most powerful families, including the Hescelins, suggesting that the sisters moved to a residence where they might live as lay religious women with the social and economic support of their peers.[77] Similarly, the beguine sisters Jeanette and Perette Chanevacière lived with their brother Jean on the rue de la Croix du Tiroir until 1300, when the sisters moved to another location on a nearby street.[78] Although we do not know if these women eventually joined the beguinage, there is little doubt that their family connections would have facilitated their admission into the community. Indeed, the Perrette la Chanevacière listed in the tax rolls was probably the same Perrenelle la Chanevacière who served as mistress of the beguinage in 1306.

No source illuminates the specific processes and criteria for entering Paris's beguinage; however, it is clear that its residents had connections that probably helped them gain admission to the community. As in beguine communities across northern Europe, some women gained admission to the Paris beguinage through the sponsorship of an employer or well-connected patron. The prominent beguine mercer Jeanne du Faut attempted to use her connection with the beguinage to gain a spot within the enclosure for her silk spinner Guillamette.[79] A beguine called Bourges de Mortières was employed as the *chambrière* for Jean de Hétomesnil. It is not known whether Jean used his influence at court to obtain a spot at the beguinage for his chambrière or if his relationship with Bourges was due to her proximity; the beguinage was located just across from Jean's residence on the rue du Figuier. In any case, Bourges served as an intimate of Jean's household, storing the canon's personal effects in her own home within the beguinage after Charles V bought Jean's house in 1364 and delivering the clothing and linens in which Jean wished to be dressed and shrouded upon his death in 1380.[80] Jean released another beguine resident of the beguinage, the silk worker Jeanne la Mareshalle, from all obligations and debts she owed him.[81]

Support for the beguinage was particularly strong among royal counselors, officers, and members of Parlement, who seemed to value in particular the beguines' intercessory activities. In 1432, Parlementary official Pierre Michel, for example, gave a fifty-sou annuity to the beguinage with the request that masses be sung in the chapel of the beguinage for the salvation of his soul.[82] Similarly, Denis de Mauroy, an attorney and procurator of the king, gave twenty sous to the beguinage, requesting vigils and masses for himself and his wife, Richarde, who had special affection for the community.[83] Jean de Creté, master of the Chambre des Comptes, gave cloth to the "six bonnes femmes des Béguines."[84] Another master of the Chambre des Comptes, Pierre du Châtel, gave two francs to the beguinage (as well as to two other houses of lay religious women) in 1394.[85] In 1418 Robert Mauger, president of Parlement, gave twenty sous to the beguinage for masses and vigils.[86] Alice Cournon, a noblewoman with close ties to Parisian Parlementary officials, gave the beguinage twenty sous, requesting masses and prayers be said at the beguinage for her soul.[87] Alice also gave eight sous to the chaplains and clerics of the beguinage and ten sous to the beguinage's hospital.[88] As this small sample of surviving testaments show, intercessory prayers and masses tied the beguines to important Parisian officials, underscoring the beguines' spiritual role in the city.[89]

Labor, Property, and Charity at the Beguinage

Although reliant on royal support and donations for the upkeep of its chapel and common buildings, the beguinage of Paris was relatively self-sufficient. A handful of sources hint that the beguinage possessed urban properties, much like other urban hospitals and institutions.[90] Individual residents, too, invested in the beguinage by using their personal resources to build houses within the enclosure. The community also claimed a portion of the profits earned when beguines sold or rented the properties they possessed within the beguinage.[91] Around 1341, the beguinage began requiring a small fee—a minimum of twelve deniers for young girls and more for women older than twelve years of age—who received special permission to live within the enclosure.[92] Of course, a few deniers were hardly sufficient to support a beguine for any length of time. As in the beguinages of northern France and the southern Low Countries, the residents of the Paris beguinage were expected to support themselves and one another through their own labor or private incomes. Some residents of the beguinage entered the community with substantial assets or received royal pensions. Others, however, were obliged to work.

Work opportunities, in fact, were a key impetus behind the creation of the beguinages.[93] Within the beguinage itself, beguines could serve as hospital workers or schoolteachers, or in any number of official positions within the enclosure.[94] Some probably worked as domestic servants or assistants.[95] Domestic work was, of course, also abundant outside the enclosure. The beguine Bourge des Mortières worked for Jean de Hétomesnil as a chambrière.[96] A beguine like Dame Agnes, referred to by the Goodman of Paris in his treatise on household management, could have started or ended her career at the beguinage of Paris.[97] The beguine Jeanne la Mareschalle, who entered the beguinage sometime before 1397, worked for or with the wealthy mercer Jean Charles, probably as a silk weaver.[98] Jeanne de La Tour served as a lady-in-waiting to Isabelle of Valois even after Jeanne had taken up residence in the beguinage of Paris.[99]

While acknowledging the religious function of the court beguinages of the Low Countries, Walter Simons has argued that these houses functioned as "a reservoir for relatively cheap labor."[100] Although the extant evidence for the work activities of the beguinage's residents makes it difficult to make a strong case for the beguinage's importance for the local textile industries, several valuable clues suggest that the Paris beguinage, like those of the Low Countries, provided an abundance of cheap labor. While never reaching the same level of importance of Bruges's and Lille's industries in wool cloth, Paris had important industries in wool, silk, and linens, which relied in part on low paid workers.[101] Scholars have deduced that Paris's estimated 450 wool weavers would have required at least seventeen hundred wool spinners to supply them with spun wool.[102] Clearly, opportunities for unskilled work in the wool industry existed in Paris, a factor that must have affected the success of the beguinage.[103] Located in the very center of the wool-producing sector of Paris, the royal beguinage was perfectly situated for women seeking work opportunities in textiles (see map 1). There is some evidence of beguine residents engaged in wool carding and weaving, tasks in which women predominated and for which they were poorly paid. A miracle story recounted by the Franciscan friar William of Saint-Pathus reports that a woman named Alice Malachine, a wool carder, "frequented" Paris's beguinage, where she evidently worked.[104] A fascinating entry in a royal account book alludes to the production of wool cloth at the beguinage of Paris. In 1320, the French queen Jeanne of Burgundy gave six ells of *marbre*, a multicolored woolen cloth, to one of the women in her entourage. The account states that Jeanne bought the marbre from the Paris beguinage for 108 sous parisis.[105]

As in the southern Low Countries, there existed in Paris a close connection between manual labor—particularly in textiles—and life as a lay religious woman.[106] Tax rolls reveal that dozens of beguines living outside the Paris beguinage supported themselves in the much more profitable tasks related to the silk industry.[107] Other lay religious communities in Paris expected their members to support themselves through personal income and labor. The Haudriettes, for example, produced handwork items, such as pillowcases and quilts, as well as wool cloth, which they sold for the common profit of the community.[108] The streets surrounding the beguinage of Paris, moreover, were home to several smaller houses of lay religious women, including the foundation of Agnes and André Marcel on the rue de Paradis and the foundation of Jean Roussel at the porte Barbette, suggesting the confluence of economic, social, and religious forces behind such foundations.[109]

The success of the beguinage depended not only on the availability of work opportunities but also the ability of individual beguines to invest and utilize property. Provisions concerning the control of property, in fact, were essential to making beguine life attractive to propertied women and their families. Unlike other religious and charitable institutions in Paris, the beguinage did not make claims to the properties of its residents. Indeed, the beguinage was one of the only religious communities in Paris not to require its residents to hand over their properties upon admittance into the community. Two other houses for lay religious women, the Haudriettes and the Bonnes Femmes of Sainte-Avoye, which both accommodated considerably smaller numbers of women than the royal beguinage, required entrants to commit themselves and all of their property to the community.[110] In other words, all movable and immovable properties, including annuities, became the possession of the community as a whole upon the reception of a new member.[111] The beguine status, on the other hand, allowed women considerable latitude in disposing of their property. Such a feature undoubtedly made the beguine life appealing to Parisian women who, as was the case with their sisters in northern European cities, had the ability to acquire and maintain property with relative independence.[112]

An examination of the beguinage's rules concerning property illuminates the ways in which family interests, royal patronage, and the active religious character of the beguine life came together to promote the success of the beguinage. Thoroughly embedded in the realities of an urban context in which women inherited freely, single women managed property, and families maintained important economic and emotional connections with their daughters, the rules protected the interests of the Parisian bourgeoisie, whose daughters and donations contributed to the success of the community. Yet the statutes also maintained that the beguinage's buildings and properties ultimately belonged to the king, who had final say over how these properties should be managed. Asserting these rights was important for preserving the resources and corporate identity of the institution. Because the beguines did not render their property to the community, wealth could move in and out of the beguinage in unexpected ways. The beguinage's rules reflected these concerns, even as they provided the beguines with an environment in which they could best carry out the active, charitable impulses of the beguine life.

The advantages of the beguinage's property regime were many. Residents of the Paris beguinage were able to invest in annuities, which they sometimes passed on to their coreligionists. Patrons of individual beguines, moreover, could keep their spiritual investments in play, so to speak, since they could stipulate that whatever annuities they gave to individual residents had to be passed on to another person or community upon the beguine's death. Beguines themselves could utilize their personal resources to aid individuals or make donations to the religious or charitable institution of their choice. Life in the beguinage, then, did not entail a break from the economic and social world outside the enclosure. Within the networks of each individual beguine could be found any number of hospitals, institutions, clerics, patrons, and clients.

One particularly intriguing example centers on a woman named Perrenelle de Vemars, who had been married to Guillaume Rose, a member of Parlement, and who entered the beguinage soon after her husband's death in 1376.[113] In 1375, Guillaume and Perrenelle had drawn up a contract vowing to donate five hundred francs to the Chartreuse de Vauvert upon their deaths.[114]

This substantial sum was intended for the founding of a chapel, where masses were to be said for the souls of the couple. After Guillaume's death, Perrenelle maintained control of the promised bequest, holding her property in usufruct.

Whatever Perrenelle's religious motives for joining the beguinage, the community was the perfect refuge for a woman of means who had committed a substantial portion of her wealth to another religious institution. The entry requirements for other houses for lay religious women—the Haudriettes or the Bonnes Femmes of Saint-Avoye—would have involved some complicated negotiations for a woman like Perrenelle. Another propertied woman connected with the monks of Chartreuse, Perrenelle d'Yerres, joined the beguinage sometime before she composed her testament in 1349. In her testament, which makes no mention of a husband, father, or male relative, Perrenelle gave a considerable amount of landed property just outside Paris to the monks of Chartreuse, a gift to which the beguinage of Paris would have had no claim.[115] The beguine Marie de Gonesse also maintained control over her personal resources while living at the Paris beguinage. Upon her death in 1321, Marie commissioned the construction of a monumental tomb at the Cistercian abbey of Barbeau, on which she is portrayed in her beguine habit with her girdle book (figure 2). Significantly, her tomb identifies Marie as a resident of the Paris beguinage, suggesting the extent of the beguine's social network.

Because the community did not make claims on the property of its residents, propertied beguines were able to acquire, invest, and dispose of their assets freely, facilitating the circulation of wealth in and out of the beguinage. Propertied beguines used their wealth to acquire annuities for their own support or pass them on to their fellow beguines. In 1370, for example, a resident of the beguinage, Marie de Charru, sold two annuities to a fellow beguine named Alison Roullone for twenty-five *livres tournois*.[116] By 1389, Alison had died, and her executors, the Franciscan master Étienne de Bléneau and a secular master Jean Fignot, along with the mistress of the beguinage, sold one of the annuities on Alison's behalf to another beguine, Jeanne la Mareschalle, for eighteen gold francs.[117] By 1397, Jeanne had bequeathed this rent—along with a few others—to the hospital and confraternity of Saint-Sépulcre, requesting masses for her soul.[118] This transfer of property from one beguine to another suggests some of the ways that the circulation of property helped sustain members of the community. It also serves to illustrate the ways in which wealth moved in and out of the beguinage. Because beguines maintained control over their personal property, they could choose to utilize it in support of other beguines, or they could pass it on to an individual or community

Figure 2. Drawing of the tomb of Marie of Gonesse, beguine of Paris (d. 1321). The tomb was located at the now destroyed Cistercian abbey of Barbeau. The sketch comes from the collection of tomb drawings by François-Roger de Gaignières (1644–1715). Collection Gaignières, fol. 20. By permission, Bibliothèque nationale de France.

outside the enclosure. Some beguines did both. In 1403, the beguine Agnes de Fresnes granted a fellow beguine, Jeanne de Mortières, usufruct over an annuity that Agnes ultimately bequeathed to the Hôtel Dieu.[119]

In some respects, beguines were ideal carriers of property for Parisians who wished to maximize their returns on their spiritual or social investments. The beguine Jeanne la Mareschalle, who had bequeathed about fifty-two sous' worth of annuities to Saint-Sépulcre in her testament, herself received an annuity valued at four livres parisis from her employer or work associate Jean Charles, a wealthy mercer. In his testament, Jean stipulated that the annuity was to pass to Saint-Sépulcre upon Jeanne's death.[120] Jean Charles, then, was able to gift the beguine with a generous annuity while, at the same time, ensuring that his bequest eventually ended up in the possession of the confraternity and hospital of Saint-Sépulcre.

Although beguines maintained control over their personal property, as residents of the beguinage they were expected to utilize these resources in the support of their poorer sisters within the enclosure. Beguines, like other groups of single women, typically banded together in mutual support of one another, worked and lived in common, and remembered one another in their testaments.[121] Affluent beguine merchants employed poorer beguines as spinners, weavers, or domestic servants, sometimes rewarding them with generous gifts.[122] Such concern for the poorer members of the community fitted well with the beguine ethos, which stressed charity and active service. Like all women and laymen, beguines were not permitted to preach and teach publicly; therefore the active element of the beguine life was ideally limited to charitable works, such as caring for the poor and sick and teaching children. The rules of the Paris beguinage formalized the active charity of the beguine life by requiring propertied beguines to contribute to the support of poorer residents.[123] The rules also mention houses that were freely given to poorer beguines, as well as the obligation of the community to pay for repairs to houses when their owners were too poor to pay for their upkeep.[124]

An illuminating example of the socioreligious bonds that developed between beguines is found in the testament of the beguine silk merchant Jeanne du Faut. In addition to bequeathing gifts to numerous religious houses, the poor, and her private chaplain, gifts that amounted to more than five hundred livres in cash, Jeanne bequeathed substantial properties to her beguine employees.[125] Despite the existence of several male relatives, who, according to the customary laws governing Parisian inheritance practices, could have made a legitimate claim to Jeanne's properties, Jeanne bequeathed most of her properties to her companion and business partner Beatrice la Grande. In her testament, Jeanne specifies that the properties she bequeathed to Beatrice were acquired through her own industry and labor.[126] In this way, Jeanne labeled her annuities, houses, and workshop as property that she was freely able to give away.[127] Still, Jeanne's insistence that Beatrice should inherit all of her movable and immovable properties without exception suggests that Jeanne wanted to make Beatrice her primary heir, although Beatrice was not related to her by blood, a move indicating that her socioreligious affiliations were stronger than her attachments to her kin. Indeed, in her testament, Jeanne expresses concern that her male relatives might dispute the will, offering each family member a gift of eight livres, on the condition that they not dispute the testament.[128]

The testament of Martine Canu, the mistress of the Paris beguinage until her death sometime after 1408, attests to the close ties among beguines within the beguinage.[129] Martine favored her beguine companions over her male relatives, specifically her brother, Robert. In her testament, Martine granted life usage of one of several houses she owned within the beguinage to another beguine, Marion Guerart, along with a cloak of rabbit fur, a hood, and a kerchief.[130] To another beguine, Guillamette la Petite, Martine gave several articles of clothing, thirty-two sous parisis, and a book of hours, instructing Guillamette to pass the book to another beguine upon her death.[131] To her brother, Martine gave only usufruct of one of the three houses she owned within the enclosure. Because only beguines were permitted to live within the enclosure, Robert effectively inherited from his sister only the right to collect rents on the house. Robert's gift, moreover, probably came with a price: according to the statutes governing beguinage properties, one-third of Robert's profits from renting the house had to go to the beguinage.[132] Martine requested that upon Robert's death the house go to another beguine, Marguerite de Stain, whom she designated as her primary heir.[133] In addition to all of the movables and immovables not named in the will, Martine gave two additional houses to Marguerite. One of the houses was Martine's residence, a large two-story house called "Le Coven." The other house was on the rue des Escouffles, not far from the beguinage.[134] Martine bequeathed these properties with the request that Marguerite arrange to have masses sung for her and her brother Robert's souls.[135] Although Martine may have left it to customary law to give her brother what he was due, the testament indicates that she intended to leave the bulk of her estate to her beguine companion Marguerite. Further signaling her attachment to her lay religious sister over her flesh-and-blood brother, she named Marguerite, not Robert, as an executor of her will.[136] Such close connections among women, fostered by the beguine life, were also found in informal gatherings of lay religious women outside the beguinage.[137]

Family, Property, and the Rules of the Beguinage

While property and work opportunities may have allowed wealthy women to adopt the beguine life, familial support was also an important factor. Parisian elites supported the beguinage as both a royal foundation and a religious and charitable institution. Parisian testators remembered the beguinage in their testaments, and, as we have seen, a significant number of beguine residents were members of some of the city's most powerful families. The beguine life, however, also proved compatible with elite property strategies and social aspirations. In fact, some Parisian families may have permitted their female relatives to enter the beguinage because its rules allowed women to adopt or abandon the beguine life without losing property or, presumably, reputation.

The communal but independent, active but contemplative nature of the beguine life is reflected in the beguinage's living arrangements within the enclosure, as well as its rules concerning property. As described above, the beguinage included private houses, communal residences, and common buildings for meals and prayer. The beguinage, then, accommodated the active, communal impulses of the beguine life while allowing women of means to live in solitude if they desired. It also, however, had to accommodate the needs of the bourgeois families from which many beguines were drawn. These families maintained close ties with their female relatives, whether these women joined a monastery or a beguinage.[138] Elite families regarded their female relatives as a reflection of their own morality, spirituality, and social aspirations. Women were important in the forging of alliances with other elites through marriage or with certain religious houses through monastic profession. Elite Parisian families, like noble families, desired to place their sons and daughters in convents for the prayers, prestige, and social capital these placements provided.[139] These houses did not, however, offer women and their families the same flexibility the beguinage offered. A nun's vows were irrevocable. Elite women who entered a convent were no longer marriageable, and entrance gifts cost their families a portion of the patrimony. Although bourgeois families probably saw more advantage—both spiritually and socially—in placing their daughters in an officially recognized convent than in the beguinage, the latter offered families some flexibility and enough prestige to make the community a viable option for their daughters and widows. The beguinage, after all, was a royal foundation. In addition, the flexibility of this status allowed families to maintain connections with their beguine relatives, connections that could be both economic and affectionate. Since beguines ideally did not have children, any inherited properties they received over the course of their lives were supposed to return to their natal families. Further, because the beguine could leave the beguinage to marry—indeed, the statutes specifically mention marriage as a possibility—elite beguines were still available to their families for advantageous marriages.[140]

Beguines, both in and outside the royal beguinage, maintained social and economic ties with their families.[141] Several beguines remembered godchildren, nieces, and nephews in their wills, indicating that their ties with their natal kin remained strong long after they adopted the beguine life. In her testament, Jeanne Brichard, mistress of the beguinage until 1312, bequeathed an annuity worth four livres to her niece, also named Jeanne.[142] Both Jeanne du Faut and Martine Canu gave generously to their godchildren in their wills.[143] Perrenelle de Vemars gave a four-livre annuity to her niece, Perrenelle Auberde, who was a nun at the Franciscan convent at Longchamp just outside Paris.[144] Perrenelle and her niece also combined portions of their considerable resources for vigils and masses to be said for their souls at Longchamp, again demonstrating the close relationship between the two women.[145] Some women took on the beguine life with their female relatives.[146] In the Paris beguinage, Bourges de Mortières lived with her niece, Jeanne, who was also a beguine.[147] Similar patterns held in the dozens of beguine households outside the beguinage. The Chanevacière sisters lived as beguines in their family home for several years before setting up their own home workshop on the rue Guillaume Bourdon in 1300. The Senliz sisters likewise adopted the beguine life together, even as they lived among extended family outside the beguinage.[148]

While allowing beguines considerable freedom to manage and bequeath their property, the beguinage's rules asserted the French kings' control over the buildings within the enclosure. A beguine could buy, sell, renovate, rent out, or bequeath her house in the beguinage, but only under certain conditions. The houses within the enclosure technically did not belong to their occupants; rather, they belonged to the king and his successors.[149] According to the rule, beguines who purchased or received houses within the enclosure could not transfer their houses to anyone without the approval of the Dominican governor, the mistress, and the small group of senior beguines who composed the mistress's council. The rule further decreed that any sale or rent transacted without the permission of these authorities was automatically void.[150] Any beguine who failed to obtain permission to sell or rent her house forfeited her rights over the house, which was seized by the community.[151] It is likely that the intent of these rules was to prevent beguines from selling, renting, or bequeathing houses within the enclosure to nonbeguines, including family members. This concern was well founded. Although the rules state that only women who were willing to observe the ordinances of the community and to live lives of good works could reside within the enclosure, beguines sometimes tried to transfer their houses to outsiders.[152]

This practice seems to have been a major concern of the king and the administrators of the beguinage. A dispute over a house within the enclosure dating from 1432 illustrates the ways in which property interests could clash within the beguinage.[153] The house had belonged to a noble beguine named Jeanne de La Tour. Jeanne apparently lived in the house for twelve years until her death in 1385, after which her executors sold the house.[154] By 1432, the house had come into the possession of a certain Guy le Cesue and his wife. It was at this time that the beguinage disputed Guy's claim to ownership of the house, bringing the case before the Châtelet. Guy claimed that his wife (who is not named in the document) inherited the house from her father, Jean le Maire, who had himself inherited it from his mother, Alice de Malaisie. According to Guy, Alice bought the house from Jeanne de La Tour's executors, the Duke of Bourbon and Pierre Saint-Rémy, shortly after Jeanne's death in 1385.[155] Guy's argument, which accords with property practices in medieval Paris, rested on the claim that, because his wife's grandmother, Alice, had purchased the house from Jeanne, the house rightfully belonged to her and her heirs.[156] Indeed, the claimants asserted that the mistress herself had sold the house to Jeanne de La Tour "not only for [Jeanne] to keep during her life, but for her heirs."[157]

Claiming that the beguinage had been founded "in honor of God," the beguines' advocates argued that "the beguines and those who have the said houses are not at all owners of these [houses]." Instead, "the property belongs to the king, who has retained and reserved these [houses] by keeping the said foundation for himself and his successors." The beguines living in these houses possessed only "right of habitation" over these residences, which could only be rented, sold, or bequeathed to women who honestly live in the beguinage, wear the beguine habit, obey the ordinances of the beguinage, and perform good works.[158] Ultimately, the Châtelet ruled in favor of the beguinage, and Guy lost his claim over the house, which, according to the customary law governing most urban properties, should have belonged to him through his wife.

The conflict between customary law and the beguinage's rules are also evident in an earlier case, concerning the house of the beguine Jeanne du Faut. In 1330, Jeanne du Faut composed her testament, leaving her house in the beguinage to her silk spinner, Guillamette la Grande. The testament dictated that after Guillamette's death, the house was supposed to go to Jeanne's companion and business partner Beatrice la Grande.[159] By March 1334, Jeanne had died, and her executors attempted to carry out the provisions of her testament. The documents recording this attempt reveal that Beatrice, Jeanne's primary heir and executor, had also died, leaving the remaining executors to sell Jeanne's house in the beguinage.[160] It is not clear why Jeanne's executors took it upon themselves to sell the house. According to Jeanne's testament, the house was supposed to devolve ultimately to Beatrice and her heirs.[161] It is possible that Beatrice died intestate and that she had no known heirs to whom the executors could deliver the property. Another possibility is that Beatrice did not wish to live in the beguinage and hoped to sell or rent the house to another party. Or perhaps the executors were selling the house on behalf of Beatrice's heirs. In any case, the beguinage objected to the sale and brought the matter before Parlement in March 1334. The beguinage argued that the executors did not have the right to alienate the property of the beguinage; only living beguines could manage the houses within the enclosure. In accordance with the rules of the beguinage, the case was decided against Jeanne's executors.[162]

These cases suggest some of the ways in which interests, especially concerning property, might clash within the beguinage. While independent control over property enabled women to become beguines, the beguinage itself had to limit this freedom in order to protect the identity and reputation of the community. If the beguinage's rules permitted beguines to alienate their houses however they pleased, or allowed the houses to fall under the inheritance regime of customary law, the institution would not have survived as a house for beguines. Moreover, since the Paris beguinage allowed for the possibility of leaving the community to marry, it was necessary to impose rules to ensure that the houses within the enclosure would not become family residences or fall into a married couple's conjugal fund. In order to preserve the community, the houses in the enclosure had to be subject to a property regime that differed significantly from customary law. Thus, the rules attempted to impose some permanence on what was a very flexible arrangement.

The rules and structure of the beguinage offered beguines a secure environment in which they might work, pray, and provide social services to their neighbors. Propertied beguines could manage and invest their property and even act as community leaders and financial benefactors to other beguines. Significant too is the ways in which the beguinage facilitated the creation of networks that might include fellow beguines, patrons, clients, and family members. Permitting traffic in and out of the enclosure, the beguinage allowed its residents frequent contact with the outside world. The rules of the community allowed individual ownership of movable and immovable properties, thereby enabling beguines to use their wealth to support themselves and their fellow beguines and to contribute to the local economy, whether by investing in annuities, establishing workshops, or loaning money.[163] Thus, the beguinage provided women with the opportunity to use their wealth for charitable or economic purposes and to support a religious life that best suited their individual situations or desires. Beguine communities all over Europe were shaped by contexts, including property laws and family strategies. Within these contexts, lay religious women and their supporters found ways to carve out a space for women to pursue their spiritual ambitions in a safe, supportive environment. In Paris, the royal beguinage was not the only option for lay religious women. As we have seen, the Haudriettes and the Bonnes Femmes of Saint-Avoye represented alternative contexts for laywomen seeking spiritual community and service. Some women simply chose to live as beguines in their own homes, supporting themselves by their own labor. It is to these households—poignant examples of the diversity of lay religiosity in medieval Paris—that we now turn.

CHAPTER 3

Beguines, Silk, and the City

Sometime before 1292, Jeanne du Faut left her home in the Paris beguinage to take up residence on the rue Troussevache, a street dominated by wealthy mercers and located at the center of Paris's silk-producing sector. Although her reasons for leaving the beguinage are not known, she left in good standing.[1] Moreover, Jeanne continued to live as a lay religious woman, supporting herself through her own labor and income from various properties she owned throughout the city.[2] Leaving behind the security and prestige of the royal foundation for lay religious women, she seems to have found companionship and spiritual fulfillment—along with economic success—outside the beguinage. A successful mercer by the early 1290s, she cultivated relationships with silk workers, many of whom also lived as lay religious women. One of these women was Jeanne's neighbor Marie Osanne. Both beguines lived and worked with female spinners, weavers, and factors, and they engaged in business transactions with nobles, Italian merchants, and Parisian elites. On a nearby street in the parish of Saint-Merry, the well-to-do beguine mercers Isabelle of Cambrai and Marguerite of Troyes lived among a larger cluster of beguine silk workers, many of whom they employed as spinners and weavers in their workshops. This combination of economic success and lay religiosity was not unusual in medieval Paris. Dozens of similarly constituted households are referred to throughout the sources of the time period.

These home workshops—centered on beguine entrepreneurs and composed of beguine silk workers—underscore the diversity of lay religious communities in medieval Paris. As recent scholarship has noted, the beguine life was one pursued in a wide variety of contexts, both formal and informal.[3] In medieval Paris, the existence of the royal beguinage undoubtedly complicated understandings of what it meant to identify as a beguine, but it was not the only recognized framework in which lay women might pursue their spiritual aspirations, even if some Parisian preachers insisted otherwise.[4] Some medieval authorities, for example, sought to affix the label firmly to residents of a beguinage, calling into question the authenticity of women who claimed to live as beguines outside the institution's walls.[5] For others, however, the label referred to any woman who lived a religious life in the world, whether in her own home or in a more formal setting.[6] Fiscal and property records are peppered with references to women identified by the descriptor "la beguine," women who lived alone, with family members, or with other lay religious women. Some of these women took up residence in the beguinage for a time—as Jeanne du Faut had. Some may have entered any one of Paris's formally-recognized institutions for lay religious women, such as the Hospital founded by Stephen Haudry, whose members had close ties with the beguines of the royal beguinage. Understandings of what it meant to live as a beguine were multiple, and medieval Paris was home to dozens of small households whose residents were known as "beguines."

These households were usually set up in close proximity to one another, as religious and temporal concerns drew lay religious women to particular streets and neighborhoods. A look at these independent households of beguines—composed of like-minded women who pooled their resources and trained one another in textile work—offers some glimpses of the female initiative that led to the creation of lay religious communities while underscoring the importance of local factors and support networks. Certainly, a close examination of these households provides a more nuanced picture of the development of beguine communities than is possible to glean from sources concerning the foundation of the beguinage, which, of course, tend to portray the institution as a project conceived and executed on the initiative of Saint Louis alone. Although not without significant limitations, fiscal and property records demonstrate that even as Louis was "collecting" women to populate his beguinage, Parisian women who aspired to live religious lives were grouping together in households and supporting themselves by their own labor.

For many clerical and secular observers, the legitimacy of the beguine life depended on the degree to which these women avoided mendicancy and wandering the towns. Although in some cities beguine houses forbade women to work, preferring that they support themselves from private incomes, manual labor was an important component in the ethos—as well as the success—of the lay religious life in Paris.[7] Work opportunities enabled beguines unaffiliated with the beguinage or any other formal institution to support themselves and their lay religious sisters while maintaining good reputations. The Parisian theologian William of Saint-Amour accused beguines of laziness, claiming that, although young and able-bodied, they did not work, preferring instead to beg for alms. According to William, by their mendicancy the beguines scandalously defrauded the truly deserving poor.[8] Similarly, in a report sent to Pope Gregory X in preparation for the Second Council of Lyons (1274), the Dominican Minister General Humbert of Romans complained that many beguines wandered and begged, and in so doing brought scandal upon both themselves and society.[9] On the other hand, Robert Grosseteste reportedly praised the beguines as "the most perfect and holiest of religions," since they supported themselves by their own labor and therefore did not pose a burden to society.[10] In the wake of the Council of Vienne, the beguines' defenders in Ghent emphasized the women's industriousness, asserting that they posed no burden to anyone because they supported themselves by their own labor.[11]

Labor was, in Paris at least, a significant component of the beguine life. Manual labor not only helped protect reputations, it facilitated the creation of informal beguine communities and served as a framework in which beguines might carry out their active apostolate. Familial connections and wealth were important, but so were connections with other lay religious women. In Paris, as elsewhere, like-minded women from a range of socioeconomic backgrounds grouped together in households, with wealthier members supporting their poorer sisters. As we have seen, such an arrangement was institutionalized in the beguinage and enforced by the community's rules. But it was also present in the informal communities of lay religious women that sprang up all over medieval Paris. Coming together for the purposes of prayer, work, and mutual support, Parisian beguines could support themselves and their households through earnings from a profitable, well-respected craft—specifically silk work—that was culturally feminine and open to any woman who wished to take up the métier. Here, local circumstances were important. Providing women with access to "high-status labor" apart from the traditional family context, silk work afforded a degree of social capital, which Parisian beguines utilized in their efforts to navigate life in the world as lay religious women.[12] Thus, whether these women lived outside the beguinage by choice or because they lacked the wealth and connections to gain admittance to the royally sponsored community, they had access to work opportunities and a stable network of religious women and their supporters.

The silk industry, which was just getting off the ground in late thirteenth-century Paris, played a major role in the formation of independent beguine communities. As a communal, well-remunerated craft dominated by women, the silk industry facilitated connections among women, served as a powerful magnet drawing immigrant women to Paris, and fostered the development of strong work identities. In short, silk work provided opportunities for lay religious women to support themselves and other lay religious women living outside the royal beguinage. While certainly not all Parisian beguines worked with silk, extant sources point to a striking association between silk work and the beguine life. Silk provided unmarried women with opportunities to give and receive training in a well-respected, profitable craft, binding women together in female-centered households. In addition to forging strong ties among lay religious women of diverse socioeconomic backgrounds, silk work broadened the beguines' social networks. Raw silk made its way into the city via Italian merchants. Silk technologies arrived in Paris via foreign workers.[13] Marketing silk entailed making connections with silk artisans, merchants, and noble clients. Working silk necessitated ties with urban elites, as well as Italian and Jewish entrepreneurs. Through their participation in the silk industry, beguines were part of the very fabric of Parisian life.

Reconstructing Beguine Communities: The *Livres de la Taille*

Rarely do medieval sources reveal the status, occupations, and networks of ordinary medieval people, especially women. Fortunately, the tax registers from the reign of Philip IV (r. 1285–1314), offer a window through which these informal beguine communities can be glimpsed. Early in his reign, Philip ordered a tax of one hundred thousand *livres tournois* to be levied in Paris over a period of eight years.[14] Only rolls for the last five years of this levy (1296, 1297, 1298, 1299, and 1300) have survived.[15] Two additional registers, however, exist. A register dating from 1292 does not include notations of payment and was probably a preliminary list of possible taxpayers drawn up to determine eligibility for the hundred-thousand-pound levy that would begin in 1293.[16] In 1313, the king imposed another tax to collect sums from the tax-paying populace for the knighting of his eldest son.[17] All seven of these extant rolls record the name, residence, amount of tax assessed, and often the occupation of Parisians obligated to contribute to the levies, making it possible to identify beguines living outside the beguinage, as well as to determine their familial and parochial associations and sometimes even their professions.

While the tax rolls provide precious details on the occupational activities and relationships of Parisian beguines, they present some challenges. First, the tax rolls do not list all of the city's inhabitants.[18] Nobles, clergy, residents of exempted ecclesiastical jurisdictions, and the unemployed were exempt from taxation and therefore are not mentioned in these sources. Many Parisians, moreover, were too poor to pay the minimum tax of twelve deniers, equivalent to a day and a half's wages for a day laborer in the construction business.[19] Sharon Farmer estimates that about half of Paris's population in the late thirteenth century lived near or below the poverty line. Thus the majority of Parisian households do not appear on these lists.[20] Further rendering large numbers of Parisians invisible, the assessors typically listed only the person they regarded as the household's primary taxpayer. Consequently, married women, apprentices, and servants, although occupied in a profession, are typically not listed in the tax assessments.

Second, although the assessors were residents of the parish and quarter to which they were appointed and thus presumably described taxpayers according to how they were known in the neighborhood, they did not record the names, occupations, or household composition of Parisian taxpayers with much consistency.[21] The assessors identified people by métier, place of birth, nickname, or, in the case of widows, their deceased husband's name. Since homonyms were common, second names and nicknames are crucial for distinguishing individuals across the tax assessments.[22] Of particular importance here is the fact that lacunae in the sources, as well as inconsistencies in the recording of various descriptors, mean that not all lay religious women were identified as such in these sources. It is likely that Paris was home to a number of women who lived as beguines—and were recognized in their communities as such—but were not labeled with the descriptor "la beguine" in the tax registers. To take one example, none of the extant tax registers includes the identifier "la beguine" in listings for Jeanne du Faut, a wealthy beguine mercer. In this case, we are fortunate to have other sources identifying Jeanne as a beguine.[23]

Occasionally, however, the assessors neglected to include any identifying descriptors other than the fact that the woman being assessed was recognized as a beguine. For example, in 1292 the assessors described a woman listed below a certain Pierre au Leu only as "the beguine in his [Pierre's] hostel."[24] Fortunately, it is possible to track individuals across the various assessments, allowing one to pick up any additional details the assessors might happen to include in subsequent rolls.[25] In 1292, for example, the assessors described the beguine Marie Osanne as "Marie, the daughter of Dame Osanne," thus identifying Marie according to her relationship to her wealthy and prominent mother.[26] In 1298, however, the assessors identified Marie by her religious identity and occupation ("Marie la beguine, mercer"); the following year, Marie appears in the register as "Marie Osanne, mercer."[27]

While the records conceal as much as they reveal, they yield intriguing details about household composition as well as women's relationships with one another. For most Parisian households, the assessors only listed the person regarded as the head (typically a male representative).[28] In several cases, however, the tax assessors listed other people in the household whom they considered either liable for the tax or important partners of the household's head. These were typically households composed of a surviving parent—usually a widow—and her children or households made up of siblings or unrelated persons.[29] For households composed of beguines, the assessors frequently mentioned the existence of companions, partners, or employees, suggesting that the household composition was worth mentioning. For example, when listing the beguine Alice of Saint-Joce, who earned her living as a maker of silk alms purses, the assessors made note of "her companion," a woman identified as Philipotte.[30] Mention of Alice's companion, however, is inconsistent: she is listed in 1296 and 1297 but omitted in 1298. The omission does not mean that Philipotte had left the household; she reappears in the 1313 roll.[31] Although the relatively short time span covered by the tax rolls—twenty-one years—makes it impossible to argue that the assessors were describing beguine convents (and indeed, no official record of these households exists apart from the tax assessments), the practice of mentioning companions and employees indicates that these beguines households were recognized as stable, perhaps even as corporate, entities. More important, the tax assessors, by making special note of the women's "status" as beguines, recognized these female taxpayers as religious women.

Treating beguine households as units sometimes led to the omission of useful details, however. In 1292, the assessors taxed a beguine named Perrenelle and "her companions" as a single unit, without providing the names, or even the number, of these companions.[32] In 1296, assessors taxed Isabelle of Cambrai, a mercer and beguine, as the head of her household along with an unspecified number of "beguines who are with her."[33] In 1299, the beguine Ade of Senlis was taxed beside an unknown number of "beguine companions."[34] The 1292 tax roll vaguely describes one beguine household as "the beguines at the house of Laurens of Saint-Marcel," making it impossible to determine the identities, or even the number, of the women who lived there.[35]

Beguines and Silk Work

In spite of these omissions, the tax rolls provide enough detail to identify 106 individual beguines, as well as four clusters of unnamed beguines, who contributed to the levy between 1292 and 1313. Significantly, silk played a major role in binding together and sustaining many of these independent, informal beguine households. Although the tax assessors left out the occupations for the majority of female taxpayers, it is possible to discern some striking patterns. Tracking entries for individual beguines across the seven extant tax assessments yields specific details on the occupations for forty-two individual beguines. Of these forty-two, thirty-seven (88 percent) performed tasks related to the production and marketing of silk cloth and luxury items made from silk. The tax assessors describe these beguines either generically as silk workers (*ouvrières de soie*) or specifically as silk spinners (*filleresses de soie*), makers of silk headdresses, silk altar cloths, silk alms purses, or embroiderers of silk mercery items such as belts, ribbons, and gloves.[36]

A few words about the tax rolls' descriptions of beguine silk workers are in order here. As I mentioned, the assessors were not consistent in how they described taxpayers, suggesting that they were observing different tasks related to the silk industry being performed within these beguine households. In many cases, a taxpayer's métier is described in slightly different terms from one year to the next. For example, the tax roll for 1298 lists the beguine Alice of Saint-Joce as an *ouvrière de soie* (silk worker).[37] The following year, Alice is identified as a maker of silk alms purses.[38] Thus, one roll describes Alice generically as a silk worker while the later roll describes the specific product she makes: silk alms purses.[39] Similarly, the beguine Marie des Cordeles, described as an *ouvrière de soie* in 1299, is listed as a *fabricante de couvre-chef* (maker of silk head coverings) the following year.[40] In a few cases, a worker's occupation is clearly different, though related, from one year to the next. In 1298, the beguine Isabelle du Rouer is described as a silk spinner. In 1299, the tax rolls report that Isabelle earned a living selling silk (*vendeur de soie*). In 1300, however, the assessors again listed Isabelle's occupation as "silk spinner."[41] While the occupations attributed to Isabelle are related, manufacturing and marketing are clearly two different professions. It is possible that Isabelle worked as a silk spinner one year and a silk seller the next, but her relatively high assessments indicate that she sold silk.[42] Her tax assessments (sixty-two sous in 1300), in fact, place Isabelle in the upper range of Parisian taxpayers, suggesting that she worked as a mercer rather than as a silk spinner.[43] The assessors' inconsistency may in some ways be attributed to the kind of work they witnessed in Isabelle's workshop. As Isabelle was frequently taxed with and alongside beguine companions, it is possible that she managed a group of silk spinners, turning a profit from selling finished silk thread or cloth.

While the tax registers do not identify the occupations of sixty-four of the 106 unenclosed beguines in these sources, they do indicate that many—if not most—of the beguines for whom no occupation is known were engaged in the manufacturing or sale of silk goods. Specifically, three of the sixty-four beguines for whom no occupation is specified were taxed as members of a household in which silk goods were produced. In all probability these women were silk workers, and they possibly contributed to the silk workshop. For five more beguines, evidence in the tax rolls strongly suggests that they were silk workers. For example, the tax rolls provide enough information about the beguine Agnes de La Tache to conclude that she worked with silk, most likely as a mercer. Agnes lived in the parish of Saint-Joce on the rue Quicampoix, a street located in the center of Paris's silk-producing sector (map 3).[44] Moreover, her high tax assessments—she paid an average of eighty sous each year—are consistent with taxes paid by other mercers in her neighborhood.[45] Finally, it is not without significance that thirteen beguines were taxed next door to a silk worker and twenty-five beguines lived in neighborhoods in which silk workers predominated.[46] The majority of the women on the rue des Cordeliers, for example, whether labeled in the tax registers as beguines or not, were identified as silk workers. Among the forty different women listed in the tax rolls between 1292 and 1313, the occupations for eighteen are known. Of these eighteen women, fifteen (83 percent) practiced some sort of métier related to the silk industry. It is probable, then, that "Belon la beguine" and "Marguerite la beguine," both residents of the rue des Cordeliers, also worked with silk.[47] Of course, it would be unwise to assume that every beguine who lived in a neighborhood dominated by silk spinners and weavers also worked in the métier. Nevertheless, the fact that all but five of the forty-two beguines for whom a profession is known were silk workers or silk merchants is suggestive of much more than just a coincidental connection between beguines and silk.[48]

Contemporary sources, in fact, offer further evidence of this association. The testament of the prominent beguine mercer Jeanne du Faut shows that

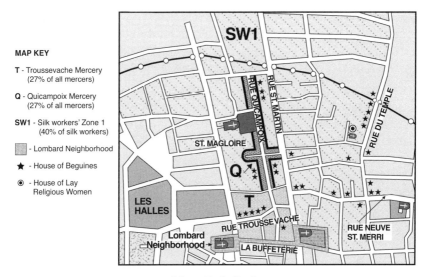

MAP KEY

T - Troussevache Mercery
(27% of all mercers)

Q - Quicampoix Mercery
(27% of all mercers)

SW1 - Silk workers' Zone 1
(40% of silk workers)

▨ - Lombard Neighborhood

★ - House of Beguines

◉ - House of Lay
Religious Women

Map 3. Right Bank

Jeanne employed other beguines as silk spinners. Her relationships with her beguine employees are particularly evident in the terms of her will, which named another beguine as the primary heir to Jeanne's workshop and substantial urban properties.[49] A list of members of the embroiderers' guild, a métier closely connected with the silk industry, includes a beguine named Jeanne.[50] Beguines also turn up in the handful of published and unpublished account books that include descriptions of silk garments and accessories purchased by and for members of the royal household.[51] Significantly, the connection between beguines and silk work is assumed in an inventory for King Charles V (r. 1364–1380), which includes descriptions of religious chasubles edged with "orfroiz de beguines."[52]

Beguines, Silk, and the City

What accounts for this overlap between religious identity and work identity?[53] Did life as a beguine somehow make women more likely to engage in silk work? Did the silk industry facilitate the adoption of life as a lay religious woman outside the beguinage? The nature of the silk industry, as well as particulars of the beguine life, suggest some of the reasons why unenclosed beguines engaged in this type of work. As lay women living outside the beguinage, they were particularly vulnerable to accusations of mendicancy and heresy, not to mention physical danger. Moreover, as single women, beguines did not have access to the same resources and work opportunities available to some Parisian wives and widows.[54] Silk work, however, had earning potential, conferred social capital, and facilitated connections among women—all factors that helped sustain communities of lay religious women like the beguines. Most important, it was an industry that, at least in the late thirteenth and early fourteenth centuries, was especially welcoming to unmarried women, even as most other areas of the Parisian economy were not.

Historians of women and work in medieval Paris have argued that although women faced certain restrictions and limitations that men did not, almost no profession was closed to them.[55] Yet these studies have not acknowledged the fact that most of the professions to which women had access were only open through the family.[56] In order to ensure the continuity of family businesses, most guilds permitted wives and widows to stand in for their husbands in cases of illness and to carry on the family business after their husbands' deaths.[57] Single women, or widows unable to draw on the wealth of the conjugal household or continue their deceased husbands' professions, found many crafts closed to them. The wool weavers' guild, for example, admitted no women save for the widows of masters.[58] The tax rolls show that most female wool workers were concentrated in the lowest-paid crafts in this industry, such as wool spinning, a task that required minimal tools and little technical knowledge.[59] Regulations for other guilds were hostile to unmarried women. The statutes for the strap makers' guild, for instance, state that wives could not learn the craft unless they themselves were the daughters of strap makers. Daughters, moreover, were not permitted to enter the guild independently and could practice the craft only if they married within the guild.[60] These regulations express a general distrust of single women, a distrust that was, of course, not restricted to guild regulations and undoubtedly limited the choices and opportunities available to women such as beguines.[61]

Despite prevailing attitudes toward single women, unmarried women seem to have found attractive work opportunities in Paris's silk industry. A well-remunerated, highly skilled, communal craft, silk work was culturally regarded as "women's work."[62] Indeed, silk work was relatively easy for unmarried, unattached, and even immigrant women to break into, a fact borne out by the tax assessments, which attest to women's domination of the silk industry in the late thirteenth century. The assessments list an average of six hundred silk workers for each year, 92 percent of whom were women.[63] Guild regulations and membership lists further point to the association between women and silk. The *Livre des Métiers*, a collection of statutes for 101 workers' associations initially compiled between 1268 and 1270 and revised and expanded throughout the period we are considering here, contains guild regulations for six craft associations primarily limited to women: two silk spinners' guilds, one employing large spindles and the other employing small spindles; the *ouvrières de tissuz de soie* (weavers of silk narrow ware items such as belts and ribbons); the *queuvrechiers de soie* (weavers of silk head coverings); the *liniers* (sellers of linen fibers); and the *fesseresses de chapeaux d'orfrois* (makers of embroidered hats).[64] Significantly, all of these crafts, with the exception of the liniers, are related to Paris's silk industry.[65] The regulations for these crafts employ predominantly female terms, such as *maistresse, filleresse, ouvrière,* and *apprentice,* suggesting that membership in these silk guilds was assumed to be almost exclusively female. The tax assessments show that two other métiers reliant on the silk industry—the *crépinières* (makers of silk headdresses or hairnets) and *fabricantes aumônières* (makers of silk alms purses)—although officially open to both sexes, were in practice dominated by women.[66] A royal ordinance dating from the late thirteenth century concerning the makers of "Saracen alms purses" (*faiseuses d'aumônières sarrazinoises*) includes the names of 124 workers, all of whom were women.[67] Women seem to have been prominent in the embroiderers' guild as well: legislation dating from the late thirteenth century lists ninety-four embroiderers in Paris, seventy-nine of whom were women.[68]

Even more important for our understanding of how silk work sustained Parisian beguines and their communities is the fact that silk work provided women with unique opportunities to work in an industry that was profitable yet able to be pursued independently of the conjugal household. Because women did not need to be married or widowed in order to break into the silk industry, their marital status was irrelevant; they could enjoy guild protection in their own right, rather than as the widows or daughters of masters. The silk guilds, moreover, allowed unmarried women to give and receive formal training, sanctioning the transmission of silk technologies between female masters and apprentices apart from the kin-based household. Parisian silk women trained apprentices and participated in guilds and confraternities—not as wives or widows of masters but as mistresses themselves. On the apprenticeship side, silk workers did not necessarily receive training from their parents but instead could apprentice under another women who was mistress of the trade.[69] Guild statutes permitted silk spinners using large spindles to employ three apprentices; spinners using small spindles could retain two.[70] The regulations for two other métiers dominated by women, the weavers of silk tissu and weavers of silk head coverings, also included statutes concerning the training of apprentices.[71] These apprenticeships were formalized by contracts and could last for up to ten years.[72] Such long periods of training, which suggests perhaps the high level of skill required to become a mistress of these crafts, meant that silk women maintained long-term affiliation with their craft. In other words, silk work was not a craft one practiced in the short term or only during certain phases in the life cycle.[73] Women could work in the silk industry their entire lives as apprentices and mistresses.

The acquisition and transmission of specialized knowledge, as well as long-term affiliation with their craft, would have enhanced the beguines' sense of identification with their labor and importance in their field. Confraternities reinforced this sense of work identity. The crépinières, a craft association the tax rolls indicate was dominated by women, and the weavers of silk tissu both had confraternities, for which each member contributed a monetary sum as a requisite of membership in the guild.[74] Within these silk guilds, women also took on supervisory roles. Some of the silk guilds offered opportunities for women to act in official capacities as officials or jurés. Although supervised by male jurés, the spinners using small spindles relied on preudfemmes—presumably senior mistresses of the guild—to judge whether or not an apprentice had mastered the craft well enough to take on an apprentice herself.[75] The weavers of silk tissu were organized by guilds headed by three male and three female jurés, who were charged with overseeing apprenticeship contracts, inspecting work quality, and enforcing ordinances. Members of the guild were obliged to pay these officials for their trouble, indicating that this was a task recognized as involving significant responsibility.[76] Unique among the Parisian guilds, the weavers of silk head coverings (queuvrechiers de soie) were governed by female jurés alone. Charged with the responsibility of enforcing the rules of the métier, especially with ensuring that their fellow weavers did not buy silk from or pawn silk to Jews, Lombards, or any other unauthorized person, the jurés were respected members of the guild, possessing broad contacts as well as intimate knowledge of the workings of the silk industry.[77]

Although it is not possible to determine if any of the beguine silk workers listed in the tax assessments served as jurés, or even if they were guild members in the first place, it is reasonable to assume that they possessed a strong work identity.[78] Even in cities where silk workers were not organized into guilds, such as London, silk women nevertheless possessed a strong work identity, acting collectively to advance and protect their interests.[79] Silk work, unlike most types of "women's work," required the acquisition of special skills, investment in special tools, and the forging of close ties among workers at all stages in the production process.[80] It is likely that even silk workers who operated outside the guild structure worked in the craft long-term, trained other women, and established non-kin-based forms of mutual support. For beguines, this sense of affiliation with a trade, and with other members of the trade, might have received some reinforcement from their religious identity.

We should not, then, think of the beguines who engaged in silk work as unskilled laborers for whom no other options were available. Silk work was skilled work. Women were able to participate in this industry not because it was low status but rather because silk technologies were valued, no matter who possessed them. Guild regulations for both silk spinners' guilds declare that these crafts were open to any woman with knowledge of the craft, including women who had immigrated to Paris from elsewhere.[81] Indeed, there is reason to believe that the French kings played a role developing the industry in Paris.[82] As a highly valued craft, silk work opened up opportunities for unmarried women to live and work apart from the traditional conjugal household, a key factor in the success of the beguine movement.

Beguine Households

Profitable, respectable, and based in the home workshop, silk work allowed beguines to create female-centered home workshops that made products for the urban market.[83] It also provided opportunities for women to take on entrepreneurial roles in the silk industry as mercers. Mercers came to dominate the silk industry by the late thirteenth century, organizing silk workers and marketing finished silk cloth and accessories at Les Halles or other venues.[84] One of the four most influential and politically powerful corporations in medieval Paris, the mercers nevertheless permitted women to attain the status of mistress of the craft.[85] Many mercers rose to prominence supplying high-value luxury cloth to aristocratic households. Mercers with more modest clients also dealt with silk, albeit less prestigious items such as narrow ware and mercery goods.

The tax rolls reveal that several beguines worked as mercers, managing silk home workshops composed of lay religious women. While much about these households is obscured by the nature of the sources, it is clear that silk served to bind these women together in supportive and stable communities that mirrored the support systems mandated in the rules of the royal beguinage. Bonds among workers would have been particularly valued in Paris's nascent silk industry. Silk spinners, weavers, and craftswomen worked in their homes using materials purchased from the mercers. Mercers supplied silk spinners with raw silk, the silk weavers with silk thread, and silk craftspeople with the cloth, thread, and precious metals and stones out of which these workers made silk headdresses, belts, purses, and other mercery items. Mercers paid their silk workers by the piece, not for their time, and marketed the finished products out of their own workshops, or at Les Halles and the fairs in Saint-Denis and Champagne.[86] This system required extensive cooperation and trust among the workers engaged in the various stages in the production of finished silk cloth or goods. In order to assure the quality of the silk and silk-made goods they marketed, the mercers' guild sought to maintain tight control over silk workers. The mercers' guild regulations contain numerous restrictions on the materials the mercers could use in the goods they marketed.[87] The guild imposed stiff penalties for lying about the materials from which products were made.[88] For the sake of their reputations and profits, then, Parisian mercers often lived and worked in close proximity to the silk workers they supervised.[89]

The workshops of the beguine mercers Isabelle of Cambrai and Marguerite of Troyes, located on the rue de Quicampoix, were at the center of a cluster of beguine silk workers appearing in the tax assessments between 1296 and 1300. In 1296, Isabelle paid eighteen sous for herself and an unidentified number of beguines, who apparently lived and worked with her.[90] With the help of these companions, she ran a modestly successful workshop that produced small silk goods, such as kerchiefs.[91] The rolls indicate that she continued to run a home workshop with other beguines at least until 1300. One of these beguine workers was Marguerite de Troyes, whom the assessors identified as Isabelle's "companion" in 1297.[92] Perhaps Isabelle's chief business partner, Marguerite paid her own tax of sixteen sous, which was more than what Isabelle owed that year.[93] In 1298, the rolls record a payment made by another beguine—Ade of Senlis—between the entries for Isabelle and Marguerite, suggesting that she lived and worked either next to or in the same household as Marguerite and Isabelle.[94] By 1299, Isabelle was once again described by the assessors as the head of a household, but this time with an unknown number of beguine "companions."[95] Marguerite and Ade, although taxed separately, were listed next to Isabelle, indicating that all three beguines continued to live and work either with or next door to one another.[96] By 1300, Isabelle and Marguerite were managing separate silk shops on the same street. Isabelle remained in the original workshop on the rue Quicampoix next to Ade. Marguerite, however, had set up her own shop on the other side of the street with a new companion, named Bienvenue.[97] Although it is impossible to know how these households were organized or even how many women came and went during the four years these households turn up in the records, it is clear that Isabelle and Marguerite, both beguines and mercers, tended to employ other beguines in their workshops.

Similarly, the beguine mercers Jeanne du Faut and Marie Osanne maintained successful workshops side by side on the rue Troussevache, a street at the heart of the city's silk-producing sector. Naming patterns show that both Jeanne and Marie employed several women, some of whom were beguines, either as silk workers or as apprentices. In 1292, the tax assessors listed Marie Osanne alongside two other women identified only by their first names, Perette and Agnes, indicating that these women were connected to Marie. While the tax rolls do not provide further information about Perette, we learn from the 1296 assessment that Agnes was a beguine.[98] In 1292, Jeanne du Faut was also taxed alongside a woman identified only by her first name, Isabelot. Jeanne probably employed Isabelot as a silk worker, or perhaps as an apprentice. Isabelot disappears from the rolls after 1292, depriving us of further details.[99] Fortunately, Jeanne's testament offers a clearer window into her workshop, in which she employed other women as silk spinners and factors.[100]

This pattern of beguine entrepreneurs and workers living and working together in households of two or more is in evidence throughout the tax rolls. In 1292, Isabelle du Rouer, a beguine who ran a silk workshop on the rue du Temple for more than twenty years, lived next to—or perhaps with—another beguine (also called Isabelle).[101] The two Isabelles lived in close proximity to several other beguine silk workers, who appear and disappear in subsequent tax rolls. Paris's streets were peppered with such households. Taxed together as a unit, the beguines Ameline and Basile worked together making embroidered hats. Their workshop was located near those of mercers, other embroiderers, and weavers of fine silk cloth.[102] The tax assessment for 1292 lists several unnamed beguines living "in the house of Laurens de Saint-Marcel" in the parish of Saint-Nicolas-des-Chans.[103] Indeed, most of the beguines identified in the tax rolls lived with, or next to, other women, suggesting a tendency among beguine silk workers to cluster together in households and on the same streets. Of the 106 unenclosed beguines discussed in this chapter, the tax rolls describe thirty-six as living in households composed of several women and thirty-one as being taxed next to another beguine.[104] The remaining households, while represented by single individuals in the tax rolls, also may have been composed of several women.

The most striking overlap between religious identity and work identity is found in the cluster of beguine silk workers living on the rue des Cordeliers in front of the Franciscan convent on the Left Bank.[105] This street was, in fact, home to at least sixteen individual households of beguines in the late thirteenth century. Throughout the 1290s, the beguine Martine de Maule lived with an embroiderer named Jeanne. Consistently taxed as a unit, Martine and Jeanne paid a relatively high assessment (averaging about forty-eight sous), indicating that their workshop was reasonably successful.[106] Jeanne and Marie probably embroidered silk goods, since their workshop was surrounded by silk-working beguines. Of the sixteen individual beguine households on the rue des Cordeliers, seven were identified as being composed of silk workers, while five other beguines were taxed either with or alongside a beguine silk worker, suggesting that they too worked with silk. While some of these households disappear and reappear in different tax years, eleven of the sixteen households appear in more than one tax register, suggesting a stability that is sometimes obscured by the nature of this source. This clustering of beguine silk workers on the rue des Cordeliers is particularly noteworthy, since this part of the city did not have easy access to any of the major mercery zones of medieval Paris.[107] Likely drawn to the street by the presence of the mendicant orders, or perhaps university clerics in general, these beguines set up households on the Left Bank, taking their knowledge of silk production with them.[108] There, beguine silk workers may have obtained raw materials from Jewish entrepreneurs—who seem to have organized silk production on the Left Bank—further attesting to the broad contacts silk women made as a result of their work.[109]

A significant number of beguines also settled on two streets framing the parish church of Saint Eustache, an area that seems to have been a magnet for lay religious women.[110] The tax registers make note of several beguine households on the rue Raoul Roissole, with at least six different beguines appearing in the same area from 1292 to 1300.[111] Several beguine households were also recorded at the intersection of the rue Raoul Roissole and the rue du Four.[112] These beguines may have lived next door to or in the same household with other beguines throughout the 1290s. The tax rolls do not specify. Either way, it is clear that throughout the 1290s the streets immediately surrounding the parish church of Saint Eustache was home to several clusters of beguines. In all likelihood, the women were drawn to the area by both work opportunities

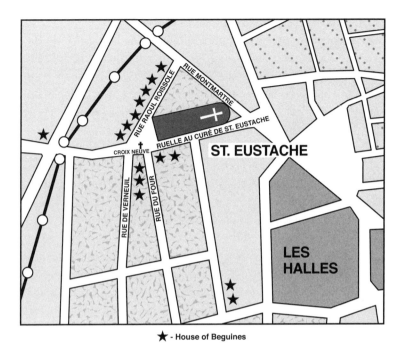

★ - House of Beguines

Map 4. Saint Eustache

and spiritual companionship. Significantly, beguines congregated especially near the intersection at which the parish church had its entrance, called the Croix Neuve, suggesting that pastoral care was also a draw.[113] Clerics associated with the church of Saint Eustache were deeply involved in the pastoral care of lay religious women. Specifically, the curé of Saint Eustache, Bernard de Pailly, had, by 1308, become the governor of a community of lay religious women called the Haudriettes, a community modeled in large part on the beguinage.[114] Bernard's brother William, also a supporter of the Haudriettes, was known as "le Béguin," undoubtedly a reference to William's own lifestyle.[115] Proximity to clerical supporters of lay religious women, as well as work opportunities as silk spinners and weavers, perhaps explains the long-term presence of the beguine households around the church of Saint Eustache. Even in the assessment for 1313, which listed only the wealthiest Parisian taxpayers and thus included references to only a few beguines, the assessors recorded the presence of "Les Beguines" on the rue du Four.[116]

Did these small households listed in the rolls represent a type of beguine convent? There is little in the historical record to conclude one way or the

other. None of the beguines is referred to as *magistra* or in any way identified as a leader of a formal community. Although the sources do not allow us
to track beguine households beyond 1313, it is possible that some may have
transformed into formal institutions over the course of the fourteenth century, perhaps under pressure from the Vienne decrees. For example, beguine
households on the rue de Richebourg, located just outside the walls on the
western side of the city, might have been transformed or co-opted into a formal house for lay religious women by the fifteenth century.[117] Whatever their
eventual fate, these clusters of women, which tended to form around wealthier
beguines, shed some light on informal beguine communities in medieval Paris
(map 4). In many cases, it appears that wealthier beguines oversaw households
in which other women might take up the beguine life for a time while supporting themselves by their own labor. These households functioned as both
convent and workshop, offering lay religious women a place to live and work
with other like-minded women. Moreover, they suggest that informal beguine
households, like the beguinage of Paris, were composed of women from varying socioeconomic backgrounds and perhaps offered more affluent beguines
the opportunity to serve as patronesses of their less well-off beguine sisters.
Studies of beguines in the southern Low Countries and of the Humiliati in
Italy have noted similar relationships among lay religious women in those
regions.[118] Although it would certainly be naïve to romanticize these relationships as motivated solely by charitable impulses—indeed there is much to suggest that these relationships were shaped by business interests—it is evident
that beguine silk workers at all levels benefited economically and spiritually
from their connections with one another. We cannot know if the driving initiative behind the households was a mercer's need for silk workers or a wealthy
beguine's desire to support and sustain a religious community. Nevertheless,
the overlap between work identity and religious identity suggest that both factors were mutually reinforcing.

Jeanne du Faut's testament provides the most detail about the nature
of a beguine mercer's relationship with her workers, particularly the level of
personal affection such relationships could potentially foster. Her will, which
Jeanne made in 1330, portrays a beguine at the center of a wide network
of women. The nature of these relationships is not always clear; although
it is evident that Jeanne favored these female associates over her own kin.
After leaving large sums of money to various women—for example, twenty-
four livres to a certain Dyonisette of Gentilly—Jeanne gave forty sous to

each of her godsons and eight livres to her male relatives. The testament also mentions generous bequests to several silk workers. Jeanne granted one silk spinner, Guillamette la Grande, usufruct over a house Jeanne owned in the beguinage.[119] Jeanne's bequest suggests that Guillamette identified as a beguine and was inclined to live as a lay religious woman within a more formal setting, since, in order to take up residence in one of the beguinage's houses, Guillamette would have had to have adopted the habit and obeyed the rules of the beguinage.[120]

Jeanne bequeathed the lion's share of her property to her factor, Beatrice la Grande, despite the existence of several male relatives, who, according to the customary laws governing Parisian inheritance practices, could have made a legitimate claim to Jeanne's movable and immovable properties.[121] The testament refers to Beatrice as Jeanne's "puella," a possible reference to Beatrice's identity as a beguine.[122] Beatrice is also identified as Jeanne's "factor," indicating that Beatrice worked as Jeanne's broker or receiver.[123] Beatrice may have been a fellow mercer, a colleague and close associate who put herself in the employ of Jeanne. In any case, Beatrice's knowledge of the workings of Jeanne's workshop was certainly extensive, since Jeanne planned to hand over the workshop to her. The properties bequeathed to Beatrice were substantial. After the death of Guillamette la Grande, Jeanne wished for Beatrice to inherit her house in the beguinage in perpetuity, evidence, possibly, that Beatrice identified as a beguine.[124] Jeanne also gave Beatrice her house on the rue Troussevache, where Jeanne resided from at least 1292 until 1313. Finally, Jeanne named Beatrice as her primary heir and executor, instructing that the remainder of her estate, that is, all of the annuities, houses, and personal effects Jeanne did not mention in her will or donate *inter vivos*, go to Beatrice.[125]

Jeanne's designation of Beatrice as the primary heir of her estate illustrates the personal nature of occupational relationships between silk workers identifying as beguines. The testament states that Jeanne wished to leave her substantial properties to Beatrice in compensation for her "pleasing services" as an "agent and supplier," undoubtedly of silk.[126] Jeanne's executors referred to this affection when they executed Jeanne's testament in October 1334. The documents recording the executors' efforts to fulfill the terms of Jeanne's testament reveal that, by this date, Beatrice la Grande had died.[127] As Jeanne's executors attested to Jeanne's wish that a sixty-sou annuity be delivered to the church and confraternity of Saint Jacques, they indicated that the masses the confraternity's members were to say as a condition of Jeanne's gift were to benefit the souls of both Jeanne and her factor Beatrice. Moreover, this document describes Beatrice as Jeanne's "beloved," revealing that Jeanne's relationship with her associate was affectionate as well as professional.[128]

Beguines, Wealth, and Commercial Ties

Silk, by necessity, widened beguines' social networks. Jeanne du Faut and Marie Osanne both managed to attain entrepreneurial success as unmarried women. Their workshops represented some of the more profitable in Paris while providing work opportunities and companionship for like-minded religious laywomen. Possessing specialized knowledge of silk technologies, both enmeshed themselves in networks of other prominent mercers, foreign workers, merchants, and entrepreneurs, some of whom may have come to Paris at the invitation of the French kings. Silk work widened their networks, connecting them with Jews, Italian merchants, and visiting nobility. Jeanne's testament suggests a wide social network. In her will, Jeanne forgives the debts of several women—possibly fellow silk workers or mercers—including a substantial debt of ten livres owed by a woman named Isabelle la Tyceline.[129] In 1283, Jeanne du Faut and her fellow mercer Agnes Cauda purchased an annuity from a knight and his wife.[130] The annuity was on a house located on the rue Neuve-Saint-Merri, a street at the center of Paris's silk-producing district (see map 3). In 1308, Jeanne paid a converted Jew and his wife thirty livres for another annuity on the same street.[131] Jeanne's testament reveals that she likewise collected income from investments she had made in properties located on the Left Bank.[132]

Jeanne conducted numerous transactions with other mercers, gave generously to confraternities in which mercers predominated, and named a fellow mercer as executor of her will in 1330.[133] Jeanne was also affiliated with the confraternity of Saint-Sépulcre, founded in the early fourteenth century with the aid of royal patronage.[134] Most of the members and governors of this confraternity came from the city's merchant and bourgeois elite.[135] The confraternity's records attest to special devotion to Saint-Sépulcre among prominent Parisian mercers and expatriate Italian merchants (especially Lucchese), who founded chapels in the church and donated costly silk cloths and liturgical garments.[136] Several beguine mercers gave annuities to the confraternity, suggesting some of the ways in which silk work drew lay religious women into networks of merchants and entrepreneurs.[137]

As the seat of the French monarchy and the part-time residence of count-less barons, dukes, bishops, and familiars of the royal family, Paris hosted a huge number of nobles and their entourages. These distinguished residents and visitors knew that Paris was the place to shop for fine cloths for their robes, furnishings, carriages, horses, and luxury items such as belts and purses.[138] Paris's merchants worked to provide these royal residents with such items for these nobles' own personal use as well as to give as gifts. The account books of the Countess Mahaut of Artois (d. 1329), who visited Paris at least once, and often twice, a year, attest to the nobility's fondness for acquiring and distributing such gifts. The countess rewarded the dozens of men and women in her household with belts, purses, and other items purchased from Parisian drapers and mercers.[139] Mahaut and other nobles kept Paris's mercers and drapers busy, and it is likely that beguines like Marie Osanne, Jeanne du Faut, and Agnes la Tache supplied noble and royal households with silk cloth and commodities. Jean de Laon, a mercer who supplied the Countess Mahaut with belts, purses, and hats for her entourage, was a neighbor of Marie Osanne and Jeanne du Faut on the rue Troussevache.[140] Marie and Jeanne had equally important clients. In 1295, a certain Damoiselle Marie de Val, a member of the household of the Countess of Flanders, made several purchases of silk cloth from the beguine mercer Marie Osanne.[141] The royal household purchased a silk chasuble and altar cloth, valued at just over twenty-two livres, from a Pari-sian beguine named Jeanne des Granches for the occasion of the ill-fated mar-riage of Blanche of Bourbon and Pedro of Castile (1353).[142] The same Jeanne des Granches sold silk undergarments to the royal household in 1350, which purchased the items for the counts of Anjou and Étampes.[143]

Far from being the poor and itinerant outcasts portrayed in some essays and monographs on beguines, Parisian beguines were deeply embedded in the fabric of Parisian life. A visible presence in the city, beguines stood out by virtue of their public espousals of a religious life as well their contributions to the city's industry in luxury textiles. Silk work enabled lay religious women to traverse religious, social, and cultural boundaries; to move in and out of different regions; to live lives of charitable action combined with religious contemplation; to survive and even prosper from their specialized skills; and to establish important connections as a result of their work. Directing home workshops that made products for an international market, some beguines experienced economic success while utilizing the fruits of that success to the benefit of their lay religious sisters. Their work might bring them into contact with Italian merchants, converted Jews, and noble clients and could end up

adorning ecclesiastical vestments as well as noblewomen's attire. Their workshops, moreover, should change our views on women, work, and the household production unit, which scholars traditionally associate with the family.
Rather than envision a household in which women contributed as wives, widows, or daughters of masters, we might imagine a community organized and
sustained by women who trained, worked, and prayed together.

CHAPTER 4

Masters and Pastors

Sorbonne Scholars, Beguines, and Religious Instruction

At his death in 1306 the secular theologian Pierre of Limoges bequeathed his personal library—about 120 manuscripts—to the college of the Sorbonne. Pierre had been a student at the Sorbonne, a college for secular clerics studying theology, and an admirer of its founder, Robert of Sorbon. Pierre's donation represented a significant contribution to the library, which was quickly becoming the best in medieval Paris.[1] Among the numerous preaching aids Pierre bequeathed to the college was a pastoral miscellany composed of sermons and exempla attributed to James of Vitry, a treatise on preaching, and several sermon extracts.[2] Toward the end of the miscellany is a fragment containing material for preachers, including several *exempla* and sermon excerpts under the heading "De benignis" ("On Beguines").[3] One section neatly summarizes the attitude of its author: "No one is a good preacher or confessor unless he supports the beguinage."[4]

This connection between pastoral ministry and support of the beguine life is evident in many of the manuscripts once housed in the medieval library of the Sorbonne. One such manuscript, also donated by Pierre of Limoges, contains copies of sermons preached at the chapel of the Paris beguinage.[5] The manuscript indicates that its compiler had been a regular presence at the beguinage chapel and considered sermons preached to beguines to be especially valuable to his pastoral project. In a related manuscript, which contains *distinctiones,* sermon extracts, exempla, and collations, are found excerpts from sermons preached to beguine audiences, including several preached by the mistress of the community herself.[6] Manuscripts donated to the Sorbonne by theologians affiliated with the college, such as Godfrey of Fontaines (d. c. 1309) and Jean of Essômes (d. 1310), also feature sermons preached at the Paris beguinage or sermons and exempla about beguines.

Beguines, then, featured prominently in texts composed and copied for the instruction of preachers, bringing together the pastoral mission of the early Sorbonne and the admiration for the beguine life that characterized many of Robert of Sorbon's writings.[7] That Sorbonne clerics compiled and donated manuscripts for the use of preachers is well known among scholars of the University of Paris.[8] Indeed, the mission of the college as conceived by its founder, Robert of Sorbon, centered upon pastoral ministry, especially preaching. Richard and Mary Rouse have discussed the major contributions Sorbonne scholars made to the library, as well as its members' enthusiasm for creating, copying, and collecting preaching aids.[9] What has received less attention is that clerics affiliated with the early Sorbonne perceived beguines as important to that mission.[10]

This chapter explores the multiple reasons why university clerics, especially those affiliated with the Sorbonne, were drawn to beguines, both in the abstract as models of piety and as flesh-and-blood women eager to receive— and impart—religious instruction. Sermons and preaching material suggest that Sorbonne clerics perceived beguines as meaningful to their role as pastors, and that this meaning operated on several levels. For Robert of Sorbon, the beguine life resonated with that of the secular cleric personally and professionally. In the context of debates over preaching authority and secular-mendicant conflict, Robert employed ideas about the beguine life to explore and promote an alternative conception of the religious life for the secular clergy. More broadly, he promoted the beguine as a model for the university cleric and explicitly tied this model to the administration of effective pastoral care. As lay religious women gathered together in the beguinage just across the Seine, however, he recognized beguines as objects of care who could also serve as active disseminators of the fruits of their interactions with preachers. Inspired in part by the sermons and writings of Robert of Sorbon, secular clerics affiliated with the college were attracted to the community of women at the Paris beguinage, exhibiting an intense interest in their religious instruction as well as an appreciation for the utility of sermons preached to beguine audiences.

That medieval clerics were drawn to religious women comes as no surprise to scholars of medieval women, gender, and religion. Recent scholarship has illuminated the ways in which representations of holy women served to defend and promote sacramental authority.[11] Studies of holy women and their male confessors have explored the intense, personal relationships some men established with women in their care.[12] Less attention, however, has been paid to the importance the *cura mulierum* held for men on the general level.[13] Papal and mendicant legislation regarding the cura has left the impression that clerics generally wished to avoid providing pastoral care to communities of women, including beguines.[14] Grundmann's influential *Religious Movements in the Middle Ages* describes the beguines' struggles to attach themselves to the mendicant orders, in spite of official resistance on the part of the friars as well as opposition from parish priests, who claimed that the beguines, as lay-women, were under parish authority.[15] Indeed, discussions of the pastoral care of beguines usually center upon instances of parish conflict, as parish priests opposed beguines' efforts to detach themselves from the parish.[16] As we have seen, the kings of France took an active role ensuring the provision of pastoral care at the Paris beguinage, while apparently allowing the women some latitude in selecting confessors or personal spiritual advisors. Nevertheless, the well-known attacks of the secular cleric William of Saint-Amour, as well as the oft-cited complaints of bishops and parish clergy, have left the impression that the secular clergy was invariably hostile to beguine communities.

Such a focus, while important for illuminating the difficult context in which beguines arranged their religious lives and fulfilled their spiritual needs, obscures instances of cooperation, collaboration, and mutual benefit in relations between beguines and clerics. Recent work on the pastoral care of nuns has shown that male clerics often approached the cura as an opportunity to "store up treasure in heaven through . . . service to women on earth."[17] Rather than a burden they were eager to escape, pastoral interactions with female religious communities could be understood as a means of salvation. By ministering to these brides of Christ, clerics could vicariously enjoy the fruits of this spiritual intimacy.[18] Sermons preached, copied, and preserved in Paris suggest that religious women could also be important to clerics on the professional and pastoral levels. In other words, beguines could play an important role in the education of the university cleric. Yet the relationship between the Sorbonne—a college whose history and importance is certainly well known among medieval intellectual historians—and the beguine community of Paris has gone almost entirely unnoticed.[19] Although the university was without question a man's world and women did not feature prominently in theological disputation, in the realm of pastoral ministry, women, especially beguines, served an important, albeit not undisputed, role.[20] As a manifestation of new, urban, religious enthusiasm, beguines were thought to be ostentatiously pious, religiously active, and unmoved by the ridicule with which their zeal for souls was often met.[21] While this image of the beguine was met with scorn and skepticism by some, to secular clerics like Robert of Sorbon beguines could be worthy exemplars for preachers, who were expected to work assiduously for the conversion of souls, lead exemplary lives as representatives of God, and maintain an image of "holy simplicity" as human ministers to the laity.[22] For Robert and many of his students, tending to the religious instruction of beguines was not only personally meritorious, it was pastorally useful. As sermons and preaching materials produced by Sorbonne clerics show, beguines were thought to both inspire and support the pedagogical and pastoral endeavors of the secular clergy, even as these clerics disagreed over the precise nature of the beguines' role in these endeavors.

Preaching and Pedagogy in Medieval Paris

Before turning to this relationship between the beguinage and the Sorbonne, it is necessary to lay out the context in which preaching and pastoral care, the tasks that brought the Sorbonne masters into close contact with beguines, had become an extremely important, and contentious, issue in thirteenth-century Paris. The late twelfth and early thirteenth centuries witnessed a new emphasis among ecclesiastical leaders and intellectuals on the role of preaching as a primary means of providing religious instruction to the laity. This attention to the role of sermons in church ministry was motivated by an explosion of lay religious enthusiasm in the late twelfth century, as dualist Cathars questioned the sacramental authority of the clergy and as lay religious groups such as the Waldensians and Humiliati, independently of the institutional church, embraced the *vita apostolica*, which they interpreted as a commitment to poverty and preaching.[23] Unauthorized lay preaching was of great concern to church leaders, who not only feared lay competition in pastoral ministry but also considered lay preaching a source of theological error and a major cause of lay criticism of the clerical hierarchy. Ecclesiastical leaders found themselves in the position of needing to reach out to the laity but lacking the personnel to do so.[24]

The response to both lay criticism of clerical leadership and demand for religious instruction came from several quarters. Moralists—theologians and intellectuals—in Paris looked to the schools as a resource for providing much-needed instruction in doctrine as well as the art of preaching.[25] In the late twelfth century, Paris was fast becoming the intellectual center of medieval Europe, as students flocked to its schools seeking training in biblical exegesis and theological discourse.[26] Railing against the "evil silence" of the secular clergy, the Parisian master Peter the Chanter (d. 1197) was among the first to articulate the idea that preaching was the fundamental task of the clergy and was best carried out by theologically trained preachers. Preaching, Peter argued, was only to be undertaken after, not before, "the reading of Holy Scripture and the investigation of doubtful matters by disputation."[27] Thus, he clearly regarded the schools as the place to train a more educated and effective secular clergy. At the same time, he encouraged and defended lay participation in religious ministry. Recognizing that the clergy could not effect change without lay support, he made the case for greater lay participation in advancing the faith. According to Peter, the laity had a role, indeed a responsibility, to spread and defend the faith, especially through private exhortation and admonition.[28] In fact, the "simple" and the "unlettered," he suggested, could do far more good than the mute, ineffectual secular clergy.[29]

Yet, in the course of offering this praise of lay ministry to shame those who possessed the preaching "office" yet failed to exercise it, Peter strove to define, and therefore limit, lay participation.[30] He and members of his circle, which included the future Pope Innocent III, distinguished between preaching and private exhortation: the former being the privilege and duty of the ordained clergy, and the latter permitted to the laity.[31] Commentators who spoke favorably of a lay apostolate did not necessarily intend for this apostolate to be open to all, nor did they deny that the role of public preaching properly belonged to the ordained.[32] This distinction represents a significant, but by no means decisive, effort to define preaching as a professional office for which one must receive a specific kind of training.[33] It was a distinction that, as Michel Lauwers has argued, simultaneously included the laity in religious instruction while excluding laypeople from public preaching.[34] By defining lay religious speech as *exhortatio*, medieval thinkers limited and circumscribed it, adamantly reaffirming the clerical monopoly on preaching.[35] Exhortatio was also, simultaneously, associated with women.[36] As "quintessential laypersons," women easily fitted on the exhortatio side of the imagined line between lay exhortation and professional preaching.[37]

Whatever his intentions in promoting exhortation as an acceptable, even necessary, form of lay ministry, Peter the Chanter's efforts to expand the church's preaching mission and to create a trained, professional clergy to carry out this mission were canonically reinforced by the Fourth Lateran Council of 1215. It was certainly no coincidence that the council had been called by a pope who had been a member of Peter's circle in Paris.[38] The council's canon 10, among other things, decrees that bishops must appoint "suitable men . . . powerful in word and deed" who will administer to the laity in the bishop's place, "since these by themselves are unable to do it." This campaign to professionalize preaching and authorize "suitable men" was carried out to great extent with the subsequent formation of the mendicant orders. Avowing lives of poverty and itinerant preaching, the Franciscan and Dominican orders represented an effective response to the church's critics. Their popularity was such that the first two decades of the thirteenth century saw a dramatic expansion of both orders.[39] The Dominican order quickly established a pyramidal system of schools, setting up a *studium generale* in Paris at the Convent of Saint Jacques, where select friars were sent to study theology. The Franciscans soon followed suit, receiving royal assistance to set up the Convent des Cordeliers on the Left Bank in 1230.[40]

Although secular clerics like Peter the Chanter and his followers stressed the connection between theological education and pastoral ministry, it was the mendicant orders that exemplified the drive to utilize the schools for the purpose of preaching.[41] The Dominicans and Franciscans were founded as preaching orders, conceiving their mission as going out to the urban centers to preach and hear confession, tasks over which the secular clergy claimed exclusive responsibility. In addition to challenging the secular clergy's pastoral authority, the mendicants attacked the secular clergy's image by criticizing them for their worldliness and reliance on benefices, which contrasted sharply with the mendicants' poverty.[42] Moreover, the friars competed successfully with secular masters for positions within the church and at the French court, especially as royal confessors and almoners.[43] Their theological program worked to undercut the secular clergy, and Franciscan and Dominican friars soon gained a reputation for superior theological learning and attracted secular students to their schools.[44] By challenging the intellectual and pastoral leadership of the secular clergy and undermining their relationship with the laity, the mendicants revived the criticisms unauthorized preachers had leveled against the secular clergy in the twelfth century. Secular clerics, for their part, were not slow to compare the mendicants with the unauthorized, itinerant preachers with whom the church had been battling.[45]

The arrival of the mendicants, then, led to an explosive debate over preaching rights as secular clerics challenged mendicant claims to apostolic activity.[46] The secular master, William of Saint-Amour, who emerged as the spokesman for the secular clergy during the height of the secular-mendicant conflict in the 1250s asserted that the friars were not called—that is, *non missi* (following Romans 10:15, "And how will they preach unless they are sent?")— to preach and hear confession. These responsibilities, he asserted, were reserved for the ordained priests, who were the descendants of Jesus' apostles, and thus were the only legitimate followers of the vita apostolica.[47] The mendicants, on the other hand, claimed that the secular clergy's ignorance and moral failings made them unworthy of the preaching office. Consequently, as pastoral theologians in Paris were thinking of preaching as an art requiring a specific kind of training and technique (which they could get in the Parisian schools), preaching authority was also tied up with issues of personal morality and official ecclesiastical status or authorization. Beguines—both real and in the abstract—could be useful to clerical efforts to assert and defend all of these positions.

The Sorbonne and the "Ordo Caritatis"

It was within the context of the secular-mendicant conflict of the 1250s that Robert of Sorbon founded a college for secular clerics studying theology. An admirer of the mendicant orders but a firm believer in the necessity of the secular clergy, Robert sought to develop a program at the Sorbonne based on the principles of collegiality, morality, and intellectual rigor.[48] Such a college was truly novel—and sorely needed—in thirteenth-century Paris. Students belonging to the regular orders were able to pursue their studies with the material and intellectual support their orders provided. Secular students pursuing masterships in theology, a course of study that could take over ten years, faced the persistent problems of securing shelter in an increasingly overcrowded city, gaining access to resources, such as books, and meeting other personal needs. A college for secular clerics, Robert hoped, would allow secular scholars to pursue their studies without interruption while benefiting from the collegial support, internal cohesion, and intellectual collaboration made possible by the communal life.[49]

It should be pointed out, however, that Robert's plan for his college was not driven solely by a desire to help the secular clergy compete with the mendicant orders.[50] Rather, like Peter the Chanter, Robert saw the university as a remedy to social ills and sought to utilize the schools to train effective preachers to the laity. Robert considered university theologians essential to the preservation of orthodoxy. Scholastic disputation was the means by which the theologian discerned correct doctrine, which he then imparted to priests and other ministers to the laity. The theologian's responsibilities, then, went far beyond study and disputation, which were simply the prerequisites for effective preaching and teaching, tasks best carried out by moral pastors committed to the care of their flock.[51]

Indeed, Robert was particularly attuned to the fact that the challenges of the preaching office extended beyond the acquisition of theological knowledge. He spent the better part of his career composing sermons and moral treatises on the issue of clerical morality, which he connected explicitly to the provision of effective pastoral care.[52] According to Robert, theological study and disputation should serve the community of believers, not the individual renown of the scholar.[53] The Sorbonne's statutes brought these elements together, emphasizing personal morality, intellectual ability, and a commitment to pastoral ministry.[54] Specifically, the statutes required students of the Sorbonne to demonstrate a commitment to both preaching and teaching. The lengthiest of the college's statutes has a distinctly pastoral emphasis, decreeing that "those who reside in the house at the expense of the house . . . shall within a short space of time prepare and dispose themselves to make progress in public sermons throughout the parishes and in disputations and lectures in the schools; otherwise, of the benefits of the house they shall be totally deprived."[55]

At the Sorbonne, Robert sought to train clerics who would pursue the active life of pastoral ministry, going out to the parishes and instructing the laity in the spirit of *caritas*. This spirit of caritas, as Robert's sermons, treatises, and college statutes show, started with the community of scholars. It was also what connected the Sorbonne with the beguine life, at least as Robert conceived it. As a college of secular scholars—living communally but not as monks— the Sorbonne, in a sense, was like a beguinage. Both groups were engaged in similar attempts to construct new possibilities for living as religious men and women in the world. Their discipline depended not on a papally recognized rule or monastic oversight but rather upon individual efforts to exhort one another to live exemplary lives.[56] Both constituted a visible presence in Paris, and their actions attracted much scrutiny.

While several studies have noted Robert's consciousness of the connections between theological training, personal morality, and the office of preaching, his use of ideas about beguines to advance a model of humility and caritas for university clerics has been completely overlooked in the scholarly

literature. Like mendicant friars who identified with the humility and devotion of Mary Magdalene, Robert adopted beguines as models of holiness with
the aim of turning secular clerics to a more truly religious life, which would
not only benefit their immortal souls but help them to fulfill their pastoral
obligations.[57] Robert's many anecdotes and exempla about beguines reflect an
admiration for what he considered the fundamental mission of the beguine
life: to draw others to a more perfect Christian life through moral exhortation
and example.[58] According to Robert, *beguine* and its male form *beguin* were
terms derisively applied to men and women who confessed frequently, heard
the word of God eagerly, and corrected their fellow Christians unfailingly.
Nevertheless, as Robert asserted, no community was more reviled than the
beguinage. Thirteenth-century Paris was abuzz with opinions on beguines,
many of them negative.[59] Mocking the beguines as fools and frauds, some contemporary observers found their ostentatious piety discomforting or insincere.
Robert, however, embraced the negative connotations of the term in order to
encourage university clerics to practice humility and show love for one another (in other words caritas, an important theme in Robert's writings, as we
will see). According to Robert, beguines endured skepticism and accusations
of hypocrisy with patience, refusing to tone down their practices, even in the
face of ridicule. In the context of secular-mendicant conflict and concerns over
preaching authority, Robert undoubtedly felt that the secular clergy would do
well to emulate such devotion.

   Robert outlined this connection between the beguine life, humility, and
moral exhortation in a sermon preached to a university audience around 1260
in which he described the beguines as an "ordo caritatis," or "order of love,"
over which Jesus is abbot.[60] An apparent play on the term "ordo," which can
refer to a recognized group, including a religious community, or refer to a
state in which things are put in their proper order, Robert uses the phrase to
describe the centrality of caritas to the beguine life. Explicitly comparing the
beguines to a monastic "order," Robert asserts that those who wish to be a
monk of this order must possess patience and kindness.[61] Unlike traditional
monastic orders, however, this ordo caritatis was open to anyone, male or
female, religious or secular, who rightly ordered his love, specifically in the
Augustinian sense of love of God and neighbor for the sake of God.[62]

   In the same sermon Robert quoted Paul's famous statement on love in
Corinthians 13:4 ("Love [caritas] is patient, love is kind"), proposing a particularly flattering etymology for the term "beguine" in order to support his
assertion that the beguine represented the highest of all virtues. Claiming that

the term "begina" (beguine) came from the Latin word "benigna" (meaning "kind"), Robert declared: "Love is kindness, that is, Love is Beguine." According to Robert, those who wish to enter the "order of beguines" or "order of love" are those who possess patience, kindness, and a zeal for souls.[63] In an obvious criticism of university clerics out for their own gain, Robert declares that anyone who sees his neighbor fall into fire (that is sin) and fails to help him is not "noble" (*debonair*). Thus, Robert declares, "if you see your colleague [*socium*] or anyone fall into the infernal fire . . . and you do not bring the water of holy admonition or prayer . . . you are cruel."[64] On the other hand, Robert asserts, it is *begina* to draw that neighbor to the good through moral exhortation. Robert further claimed that the beguine was thoroughly ablaze (*bene ignita*—another invented etymology for the term "beguine") with love/caritas. The beguine's burning love for God had the effect of attracting all to her and her pious life, even her enemies.[65] Apparently, even those hostile to the beguine can be converted by her good words and examples. The beguine life, here understood as a life of caritas, was a life focused on love of God and neighbor: a life suitable to Sorbonne students in particular and the university in general.

The utility of the beguine as an exemplar for the secular clergy is particularly evident in a sermon Robert preached at the Paris beguinage in the early 1270s on the feast of the discovery of Saint Stephen's relics (August 3). Significantly, this venue provided Robert with an opportunity to promote his reform agenda with flesh-and-blood exemplars of caritas, as well as the very men he wished to persuade, in attendance. Manuscript evidence for this sermon testifies to its importance to Robert as well as its interest to scholars affiliated with the Sorbonne. Robert possessed a personal copy of the sermon, which includes some marginal notes in his own hand in which he develops specific points made in the sermon.[66] At least two students of the Sorbonne also owned copies. The reported version of the sermon preached at the beguinage exists in a manuscript belonging to Godfrey of Fontaines and was probably initially copied by Godfrey himself, suggesting that he attended the sermon.[67] The other known copy exists in a manuscript owned by the Sorbonne cleric Jean of Essômes.[68]

The sermon was based on a passage from the Gospel of Matthew (Matt. 13:44: "The kingdom of heaven is like a treasure hidden in a field. Which a man having found, hid it, and for joy thereof goes, and sells all that he has, and buys that field"). In the version preached at the beguinage, Robert explained to his audience that the beguinage itself represented the field, playing on a double meaning of the term "beguinage" as both a residence for beguines—that is, the very location of Robert's preaching—and a "beguine" way of life.[69] While conceding that the beguinage, being exposed to the dangers of the world, was not a place where the wealthy and the powerful, who preferred towers and walled cities, would hide something of such value, Robert asserted that God left his treasure (that is, the Kingdom of Heaven) available to all. This beguinage (or open field) was planted with the seed of the Word of God and cultivated by contrition and confession.[70] Indeed, Robert argues that the beguines' public visibility is necessary for the salvation of others; beguines are not cloistered away, "so that they may help others spiritually" through their good example.[71]

Pursuing this theme of openness and accessibility, Robert portrays beguines as exercising a kind of lay ministry: "And that treasure especially seems to be hidden in the beguinage, because those men and women [i.e., beguins and beguines] have burning desire for God, and they are more fervent in converting sinners than others, and they labor more for the salvation and conversion of sinners than others do."[72] Explicitly crediting the beguine life—which he understands as communal and characterized by mutual exhortation—with bringing others to God, Robert claims that the beguines have more of the grace of God than others because they encourage and incite one another to lead more perfect lives.[73] His praise of the beguines' fervor for the conversion of souls undoubtedly flattered the beguines in his audience, but his use of both the masculine and the feminine forms of the term "beguine," as well as the presence of secular clerics at the sermon, suggests that his message was meant to resonate with the male members of his audience.

Nowhere are Robert's intentions more obvious than in his criticism of "great masters" who are unable to find the treasure hidden in the field of the beguinage. Disdaining the beguine life, the great masters say "*Fi de beguinage*! I want to be a *prud'homme* [or respected man] but never a *béguin*."[74] Citing Matthew 11:25 ("I confess to you, because you have hidden these things from the wise and revealed them to the little ones"), Robert issues a direct critique of university masters who are unable to find the treasure in the beguinage because they fail to recognize anything not found in study or reason.[75] Yet, he continues, the "little ones" know that what seems contrary to reason is in fact possible: the fire of caritas may mix with the waters of tribulation; the beguin may be esteemed, while the prud'homme is despised.[76] Intriguing in its critique of the intellectual culture of the University of Paris, in which masters insisted on the ability of human reason to illuminate truth, Robert's sermon draws on paradoxes (fire and water; honor and scorn) to urge university masters to put aside their pride and focus on their souls. In a personal aside reminiscent of the Sorbonne cleric's debate with Jean of Joinville in the presence of Louis IX, Robert tells his audience that he counted himself among these "little ones," declaring that, for his part, he would rather strive to be a beguin than to be king.[77]

Given before a mixed audience of beguines and clerics—and subsequently copied into manuscripts belonging to Sorbonne clerics—Robert's sermon suggests several interpretations. It is obviously a criticism of clerical pride (a concern evident in many of Robert's sermons and treatises) via praise for the "simple" beguine. But it is also a commentary on the related issue of pastoral care. Bearing in mind the dual sense of the term "beguinage" (a life committed to action in the world *and* a community of lay religious women), Robert's chastisement of the masters who fail to recognize the treasure in the beguinage is a criticism of both the clerics' personal morality and their failure to carry out their pastoral duties. In other words, disdain for the beguinage can be taken to mean a rejection of a life of piety and active exhortation of others, as well as a rejection of the flesh-and-blood beguines in the enclosure. The fact that Robert gave this sermon on the feast of the discovery of Saint Stephen's relics—a saint Robert explicitly associated with the pastoral care of religious women—also points to this association between personal morality, pastoral care, and support of the beguine life.[78]

This association receives further emphasis in Robert's own personal, polished version of the sermon, which was copied into one of his manuscripts (perhaps by a professional scribe) and included notations in his own hand. In Robert's version, the theme of the hidden treasure serves as an admonition to preachers who fail to reach the laity. Quoting the passage from Matthew "The kingdom of heaven is like a treasure hidden in a field," Robert pointedly observes that the passage does not say that the treasure is hidden in a tower, castle, cloister, or garden. Thus, those who hide themselves, failing to tend to the needs of neighbors through counsel, aid, or example are the same ones against whom Gregory the Great said: "Who by life and knowledge choose for themselves a life of the aforesaid solitude, they are responsible for as many souls as those to whom they might have been useful."[79] Robert's distinctly pastoral admonition is followed by the Gospel story of the servant who had squandered his talent (Matt. 25:24–30), thus further driving home the argument about the pastoral obligations of trained clerics. As the citation of Gregory the Great suggests, Robert's praise of the beguines' openness to the criticisms of the world, as well as their caritas, had pastoral implications, pointing to the larger issues with which Robert was preoccupied. In a direct challenge to negligent pastors, Robert claimed that the beguines were "cultivated by the plow of confession and penance, and sown by the word of God," and thereby "drew more to sermons and confession than many great clerics."[80] Most important, the beguine zealously worked to draw her fellow Christians to confess and hear sermons without regard for how her interventions would be received by others. The worldly cleric, however, preferred to preserve his reputation at the cost of his immortal soul.

In an extensive discussion of the Song of Songs, that classic biblical source in monastic discussions of divine love, Robert further pushes his pastoral message via a commentary on the beguines'—and by association the secular clergy's—active religious life. Citing passages from the Song of Songs 3:1–4, which was, since Origen of Alexandria, traditionally interpreted as the soul's search for God, Robert makes a case for the active, engaged life of preaching over contemplation. His interpretation of chapter 3, verse 1 ("In my bed at night I sought him whom my soul loves, I sought him and I found him not"), for example, stands as an explicit criticism of the contemplative life. Drawing on the twelfth-century *Glossa ordinaria,* which, as Suzanne LaVere has shown, advocated the active life of preaching over the contemplative life, Robert interprets the bride in her bed at night as the soul withdrawn from the cares of the world.[81] In this state, however, the soul cannot find her beloved. Even as the soul rises from her bed and goes out to the city, she finds her beloved neither in the streets, which Robert interprets as the religious orders, nor in the squares, which represent the secular life. These "religious and secular men . . . want to be called *prud'hommes* . . . and are unwilling to be reviled on account of Christ," and consequently "found him not."[82] Moving to verse 3 ("The watchmen who keep the city found me: Have you seen him whom my soul loves?"), Robert explains that the preachers, as the watchmen, are those of whom the Soul asks about her Beloved. The Holy Soul, described as one who supports the preachers and "bears fruit in her example of good works," represents the beguines who, according to Robert, do this better than others.[83] Yet the Holy Soul must still "pass by them a little" (verse 4). After fulfilling the counsels of religion or the precepts of the secular life and after frequenting sermons and consulting with preachers, the Soul must "pass by a little" by accepting mockery and reproaches for the sake of Christ. Only then will she find her Beloved.[84] Clearly, Robert's beguine is an exemplar of the active religious life but also of humility and caritas, a life that embraced the mockery and derision that came with the task of exhorting one's fellow Christians to live a more moral life.

Yet Robert's praise of the simple, humble beguine certainly does not imply a disdain for learning and intellectual debate, nor does it suggest that he considered the beguines' private exhortations a substitute for the public preaching of the ordained clergy. Robert's decision to found a college for secular clerics studying theology is proof enough that he considered university-trained clerics essential to the growth and unity of Christendom. Robert promoted the beguine as a symbol of humility and caritas in order to reform the secular clergy while helping them to bridge the divide between themselves and the laity, a divide that the Gregorian Reform and the decrees of Lateran IV had done so much to emphasize. Emphasis on the sacramental powers of the clergy resulted in the elevation and separation of the clergy from the laity; yet this separation threatened to undermine the clergy's ability to persuade and teach the laity. As preachers seeking to reach out to lay audiences, clerics had to be more eloquent, accessible, and even approachable. Robert's representation of the beguine as someone who tirelessly sought to convert others through word and deed, enduring ridicule and scorn for her efforts, was a useful model for the pastoral theologian.

Preaching Aids and the Sorbonne

As we have seen, students of the Sorbonne were required to study theology, attend disputations, and preach in the parishes, activities Robert, like Peter the Chanter before him, deemed essential to the training of a university master. Manuscripts donated to the Sorbonne library show that Robert's students enthusiastically applied themselves to the task of preaching in the parishes and diligently collected and composed preaching aids to assist them in this task. The need for such tools was driven by two, somewhat contradictory, features of preaching: first, the need to connect with and persuade lay audiences and, second, the need to establish pastoral authority. As Claire Waters has argued, the medieval preacher needed both to "distinguish himself from and to resemble his flock."[85] He needed training in both "Latinity" and "vernacularity" in order to communicate the Word to the simple laity. This was especially important for university clergy, whose learning and culture worked to create distance between themselves and the laity they wished to reach and teach.[86] For these reasons, manuals advised preachers to employ exempla, amusing stories, and personal accounts in order to communicate effectively.[87] The concern with bridging the gap between preacher and laity was evident in Robert's sermons and moral treatises. Robert's frequent references to the humble, simple beguine were in many ways an attempt to persuade clerics to span the divide between learned and lay culture.

At the same time, however, preaching was a task over which the trained clergy claimed an exclusive right. Preaching, as ecclesiastical and university authorities insisted, required training and an evident mastery of the Word. Over the course of the thirteenth century, university preachers, immersed in biblical exegesis, came to adopt a new approach to preaching that reflected this training. The school sermon, or *sermo modernus* as it was called, built upon a specific theme drawn from a line in scripture, then elaborated upon in (usually three) divisions. These divisions came to be based on biblical *distinctiones*, citations of biblical, patristic, or classical *auctoritates*, and exempla, which functioned to support the preacher's conclusions and to showcase the preacher's university training.[88] The use of these sorts of devices defined the school sermon and depended upon access to preaching aids, such as alphabetized, searchable collections of *distinctiones*, *florilegia*, and biblical concordances.[89] This mastery of the Word was important in sermons preached to university audiences, particularly when the preacher's acceptance as *magister* depended in part on successful preaching before his own masters and peers.[90] It was also, however, important for establishing the preacher's authority before his lay audience.

Given the importance of both rhetorical strategies and technical mastery of the Word, Sorbonne clerics energetically composed, copied, and acquired manuals, sermon collections, and other types of preaching tools. Robert himself composed several treatises that, while focused on the sacraments—especially penance, confession, and marriage—were ultimately designed for the edification and guidance of clerics with pastoral responsibilities.[91] His sermons, moreover, were widely copied by his students, making their way into collections that served to guide other clerics in the composition of sermons.[92] Fourteenth-century library inventories for the Sorbonne list dozens of sermon collections, preaching manuals, collections of distinctiones, and other tools for the use of preachers, attesting to the students' zeal for collecting such works, as well as their recognition of the need to pass these tools on to their colleagues at the college.[93]

Many of the early members and supporters of the Sorbonne recognized the need to supply it with books, including preaching manuals and sermon collections. Indeed, support for the college often took the form of donations of large numbers of books. One of its first supporters, the secular cleric Gerard of Abbeville (d. 1272), famously donated approximately three hundred manuscripts to the Sorbonne.[94] Robert himself donated about seventy manuscripts to the college, among which were scriptural commentaries, sermon collections, and moral treatises.[95] Pierre of Limoges bequeathed around 120 manuscripts to the Sorbonne, including *reportationes* of sermons preached by Robert of Sorbon and other preachers of note, including Guiard of Laon, the bishop of Cambrai known for his preaching as well as his support of beguines.[96] Jean of Essômes's donation to the college was more modest, but characteristic of Sorbonne students during the early years of the college's history. At his death in 1310, Jean left seven manuscripts to the Sorbonne, including sermons and other pastoral texts.[97] Thomas of Ireland, who was a student at the Sorbonne, compiled the *Manipulus Florum*, a searchable compendium of excerpts from scriptural, patristic, monastic, and classical authorities designed for the use of preachers composing sermons.[98] He bequeathed a copy of the work to the Sorbonne at his death in 1306. Thanks to the support of secular clerics and graduates of the Sorbonne, within the first four decades of its existence it possessed the best library in Paris.[99] Clearly, the first generation of Sorbonne scholars took the college's pastoral mission to heart, applying themselves to the task of compiling and acquiring preaching aids—particularly sermon collections—with notable enthusiasm.

Beguines and Preaching Aids: Women, Exemplars, and Exempla

The obligation to preach—emphasized in the statutes of the Sorbonne as well as the sermons and moral treatises of its founder—and the need for tools to better carry out this obligation came together (indeed, the two are consciously fused) in the dozens of sermons recorded at the Paris beguinage by Sorbonne clerics. The sermon materials compiled by the secular cleric Raoul of Châteauroux (d. 1286) provide compelling evidence of the ways in which the pastoral mission of Sorbonne clerics came to be connected with the beguinage of Paris.[100] During the 1272–1273 liturgical year, Raoul recorded at least 216 sermons preached by seventy-three different preachers in twenty-seven different places of worship in and around Paris.[101] From late October 1272 to November 1273, Raoul recorded at least fifty-four sermons (or about

25 percent) preached at the beguinage chapel, far more than any other place of worship in and around Paris. A related manuscript composed of alphabetically arranged *distinctiones*, many of which are developed using excerpts from undated sermons preached in Paris, includes an additional three sermons preached at the beguinage.[102] Significantly, Raoul also copied extracts from sermons preached by the mistress of the beguinage into this particular manuscript, which, as indicated by its organization and contents, was intended as a collection of authorities for the use of preachers. Raoul's inclusion of sermons preached by the mistress of the beguinage indicates that he counted her as one of these authorities.[103]

As several scholars have observed, Raoul's sermon collection not only stands as a remarkable compilation of reported sermons preached in the "modern" style, it is also unique in that it is one of the only collections in which the location, preacher, and occasion of each sermon are regularly, if not consistently, identified.[104] The sermons are also presented, with a few exceptions, chronologically, providing a week-by-week record of sermons preached in medieval Paris. Nicole Bériou has argued that Raoul, who clearly approached his task with deliberation and care, chose to hear sermons at specific chapels because he was interested in recording sermons preached to the "simple laity."[105] As a student studying theology in Paris, he was expected to attend university sermons. He was also expected to preach before his peers. Yet, true to the pastoral emphasis of his college, he chose to frequent parish churches rather than the usual venues for university sermons, such as the mendicant convents.

Taking into account details about the manuscript—its contents, relationship with other sermon *reportationes*, and eventual home in the Sorbonne library—it is evident that Raoul compiled the manuscript to serve as a preaching aid and that he probably intended to make it available to other clerics training to give sermons of their own.[106] Raoul clearly favored certain preachers and venues over others because he felt that they were better suited to his task. Mendicant sermons, for example, dominate both manuscripts, suggesting two possible interpretations, which are in fact complementary. The first is that Raoul purposely sought to record mendicant sermons, and the second is that the friars dominated preaching in thirteenth-century Paris.[107] Indeed, Dominicans seem to have monopolized preaching at several of the parish churches (or at least the ones Raoul chose to frequent), especially Saint Gervais and La Madeleine. The Franciscans are the only preachers whose sermons are recorded at the Champeaux, the field just outside the cemetery of

Les Innocents.[108] Occasionally, Raoul's choices seem to have been dictated by convenience; he probably recorded sermons at the church of La Madeleine because it was on the way from the Sorbonne to the parish churches he usually frequented on the Right Bank.[109] Other times, friendship or loyalty dictated his schedule.[110] In short, Raoul had his reasons for attending the sermons of certain preachers at certain venues. This sense of purpose in the manuscript's contents renders the extraordinary number of sermons recorded at the beguinage chapel all the more significant.

The itinerary our copyist followed over the course of the 1272–1273 liturgical year affirms that the beguinage chapel held a special attraction. Raoul did not attend sermons preached at the beguinage because he expected to hear mendicant preaching, however. Based on this collection, it is clear that no single group dominated preaching at the beguinage; secular clerics, Franciscans, and Dominicans are all represented in the collection, suggesting that university scholars from all of Paris's schools were involved in the religious instruction of beguines.[111] It is impossible to know how often university clerics preached at the beguinage, but Raoul's collection shows that the beguinage chapel was a popular venue for university scholars. Raoul seems to have taken advantage of this opportunity to hear sermons preached by a variety of preachers (both secular and mendicant), making his way from the Sorbonne to the beguinage almost on a weekly basis. An examination of the days he actively recorded sermons indicates that he was often free to attend and record sermons on Sundays: of the fifty weeks he actively recorded sermons, he missed only one Sunday sermon.[112] On most of these Sundays, he made his way to the beguinage, recording sermons preached in the beguinage chapel on thirty of the forty-nine Sundays he was active. He was, however, notably absent from the beguinage on major feasts such as Christmas, Easter, and Pentecost, when we might assume that the beguinage's own chaplain—or perhaps the parish priest of Saint-Paul—would have exercised his right to preach at the chapel. Raoul clearly was only interested in recording sermons preached by university clerics. Over the summer months, when he had time off from his studies, as well as from the official university sermons he was required to attend, he almost exclusively recorded sermons preached at the beguinage.[113]

Given these details, we can conclude that Raoul copied sermons at the beguinage because he considered them particularly useful to his pastoral project. The fondness Robert of Sorbon had for the beguine status, as well his attempts to equate the beguine life with the lifestyle of the secular cleric, likely

influenced Raoul—and his colleagues—to some degree. Several students of
the early Sorbonne, as we have seen, owned copies of Robert's sermons and
treatises praising the beguine life. The Sorbonne cleric Pierre of Limoges, an
ardent admirer of Robert and his preaching, appended a quire of preaching
material in praise of beguines into one of his personal manuscripts.[114] The
quire has been identified as the work of another Sorbonne cleric, Stephen of
Abbeville (d. c. 1288), providing yet more compelling evidence of a close association between beguines and the early Sorbonnists.[115] On the reverse side
of the final page of this fragment is a short list, in French verse, of characteristics attributed to beguines, entitled "Les XXXII propriétés des beguinages."[116]
Further attesting to the esteem Sorbonne clerics had for beguines, the quire
features numerous favorable discussions of the beguine life, including an exemplum in which a former usurer confronts a legate who had spoken against
beguines. The legate argued that he had never heard of the beguine status,
which was unknown in Rome, and that he did not wish for people to adopt
this way of life. While the legate's audience listened in silence, a man who had
once made his living through usury spoke up to defend the beguines, arguing
that the words and example of these women persuaded him to hear sermons,
attend Mass, and return all that he had acquired through usurious activity.[117]
Another exemplum describes a conversation between a Parisian master and
a beguine. When the master discovers the beguine weeping in a church out
of love for Christ, her spouse, he marvels that the beguine, who understands
nothing of theological mysteries, is so moved by love of God when he himself
feels nothing. Seeking the advice of the beguine, the master asks her to explain
to him how he might experience a similarly emotional response.[118] In a reply
somewhat reminiscent of Robert's criticism of clerics who refuse to believe
anything that is not found through study or reason, the beguine avers that it is
the cleric's constant study of scripture that prevents him from knowing God.[119]

The beguines' prominence in Raoul's manuscripts, as well as those of
many of his colleagues, invites a deeper examination of this connection between the Sorbonne and the beguinage of Paris. Clearly, as models or exemplars, beguines were useful to preach with. The usefulness of beguines as
exemplars could be enhanced, however, by contact with actual beguines, as
Raoul's sermon collection demonstrates and the exempla cited above suggest. As real women in need of religious instruction, beguines were important
to the pastoral aims of university preachers. Robert's sermon comparing the
prud'homme and the beguin is but one example of the ways in which the

actual presence of women could be used to convey or reinforce lessons intended for male clerics.[120]

Beguines as Mediators Between Preacher and Audience

Clearly, the sermons in Raoul's collections are not just examples of preaching
directed at the "simple laity." In the case of the dozens of sermons preached to
beguines, we might see the sermon as a site of mutual exhortation and influence. As religious women, beguines were thought to be eager consumers of
religious instruction, and thus a particularly receptive audience for preachers.
As an example, one need look no further than James of Vitry's account of the
prototypical beguine, Mary of Oignies. James portrays Mary as an ardent supporter of priests and their ministry, frequently referring to her love of priests
and desire to hear sermons.[121] He records that even as she lay dying, "she would
prick up her ears" when she heard someone preaching in the church.[122] While
we know Mary only through the writings of her male confessor, she appears
as a major impetus behind James's pastoral work. She encourages his preaching, and he credits her with helping him to become a better preacher.[123] Mary
was not a passive listener, however. James describes how she would discuss
sermons with those around her.[124] As John Coakley has argued, Mary's revelations and spiritual interventions complemented the pastoral work of male
theologians.[125] Eager to hear sermons and bring errant souls back to God,
Mary is a priest's perfect partner. As a woman, moreover, she ostensibly poses
no threat to the priest's authority; rather her feminine powers of persuasion
and access to divine grace aid and abet the priest's work.

Beguines, then, were not only useful to preachers as abstract models; they
could also be useful as actual mediators between preacher and audience. The
beguines' role was most forcefully asserted by Robert of Sorbon, who frequently referred to the beguines' success in drawing others to sermons and
confession, calling to mind the traditionally feminine mode of religious instruction through private exhortation. As Sharon Farmer has shown, pastoral
theologians such as Thomas of Chobham credited women with extraordinary
powers of oral persuasion, which they encouraged women to use to persuade
their husbands to live moral, Christian lives.[126] Although oral persuasion was
traditionally regarded with mistrust, twelfth-century moralists saw positive
potential in womanly influence. This favorable view of feminine speech connects with the new emphasis on preaching discussed above, which sanctioned

rhetoric as "a means of persuading a lay audience to conform to Christian morality."[127] In fact, preaching handbooks from the thirteenth century indicate
that medieval thinkers were aware that, in order to persuade their audiences,
preachers needed to be well versed in the art of persuasive speech, an art often
associated with women and seduction.[128]

To return to Robert for a moment, this positive view of female speech—so
long as limited to private exhortation—is related in a sermon he preached to a
university audience on the theme of the good pastor. In this sermon, the master contrasted the simple priest with university masters of theology, asserting
that the unlearned priest accomplished more in the parish than masters of theology. Although the university masters knew more about the law of God, and
therefore were better trained to preach to the laity, the simple priest accomplished more because of his genuine desire to convert souls.[129] Significantly,
rather than support his argument using the example of the simple priest with
which he began his sermon, Robert shifts the discussion to beguines, saying,
"Sometimes good women do more good in the parish than even priests, or Regent Masters in Theology in Paris, by their good works and examples and good
words."[130] He then launches into an exemplum about a beguine who travels
from Cambrai to Paris to obtain a copy of a *Summa of Vices and Virtues*. The
beguine actively circulates the *Summa* by lending it to local priests, thereby
facilitating the copying of a useful pastoral aid throughout the region.[131]

Robert's exemplum has several implications regarding the role of feminine virtue and professional preaching tools in pastoral efforts to instruct the
laity. As we have seen, Robert associated the beguine with her tireless efforts
to draw others to sermons and confession, a virtue he urged university clerics
to emulate. His exemplum, however, portrays the beguine as playing a more
active role in pastoral ministry by persuading local priests to utilize preaching manuals produced by university theologians. Clearly, Robert recognized
beguines as more than symbols or abstract models for the secular clergy. Their
actions and words mattered. As religious women with ample opportunity to
commune with the ordinary laity, beguines might aid the preacher's work by
sharing the fruits of what they heard in sermons. They could also travel between cities, acquiring preaching aids to share with their local priests. Even
as Robert employed the beguines as exemplars, he frequently shifted to the
words and deeds possible of real beguines. His representations of the beguines'
words and deeds are strictly positive. But he was, when it comes down to it,
describing a community of living women. This was a bold move indeed, since
the behavior of real women put his entire model at risk.

For Robert, the beguine was a model for secular clerics, as well as a useful focus through which he negotiated the competing codes of behavior associated with his—and his students'—clerical identity. Alongside this abstract utility, however, was the real beguine who might serve to persuade wayward, or simply indifferent, Parisians to attend sermons, go to confession, and do penance. The multiple connections between pastoral ministry and support for the beguine life, succinctly expressed in the Sorbonne manuscript mentioned at the start of this chapter, is nowhere more apparent than in Raoul of Châteauroux's sermon reportationes. Raoul's frequent presence at the beguinage attests to this connection between the Sorbonne, a college originally conceived as a supportive community for pastoral theologians, and the lay religious women who might inspire and aid their work. The collection shows, however, that the beguines of Paris were important not only to the secular clerics of the Sorbonne. Mendicants and regular canons also frequently preached to Parisian beguines, clear evidence that members of the regular clergy were also interested in the instruction of lay religious women. One benefit of the beguine life was the availability of a range of spiritual teachers—secular, mendicant, or even monastic—and a variety of contexts in which to learn and discuss. In the beguinage chapel, out in the streets of Paris, or within their common quarters or private rooms, beguines could engage with and impart religious teachings.

CHAPTER 5

Religious Education and Spiritual Collaboration at the Beguinage of Paris

Robert of Sorbon's exemplum about the beguine who travels to Paris from Cambrai to acquire a copy of the *Summa of Vices and Virtues* lauds the informal means by which beguines engaged in religious instruction, taking for granted that a beguine might travel from one region to another circulating texts and preaching aids. This association between beguines and religious instruction is echoed—although in a much less positive context—in a report addressed to Pope Gregory IX in preparation for the Second Council of Lyons (1274) written by the Franciscan friar and theologian Gilbert of Tournai. In his report, Gilbert sourly complained of beguines who possessed vernacular scriptures and read these faulty copies in common.[1]

Several recent studies have shown that beguines were indeed intensely interested in obtaining, composing, and circulating religious texts, particularly in the vernacular. Within the past decade or so, research on the best-known beguine writers—Mechthild of Magdeburg, Hadewijch of Brabant, and Marguerite Porete—has drawn attention to the didactic aim each woman had in composing and disseminating her teachings. Sara Poor, for instance, has argued that Mechthild of Magdeburg's use of the vernacular and employment of courtly motifs must be understood as a deliberate strategy to advance her book's universal message.[2] Similarly, recent publications on Marguerite Porete's *Mirror of Simple Souls* has challenged the standard view of the book as esoteric and elitist, arguing that Marguerite clearly intended her book to be read aloud to mixed audiences of both religious and laypeople.[3] It is well known, moreover, that Marguerite deliberately and energetically circulated copies of her book, showing it to clerics, monks, and theologians and reading it to lay audiences, actions for which she eventually paid with her life.[4]

The role of lay religious women as producers and consumers of religious and devotional texts in the vernacular has long been recognized. Indeed, the same factors that contributed to the growth of lay religious communities such as the beguines—including a laicization of medieval piety, increased literacy among the laity, and the embrace of more active expressions of religious devotion—contributed to the proliferation of religious texts in the vernacular.[5] Women in particular embraced the vernacular as a vehicle for expressing religious devotion, fusing the language and ethos of courtly love literature with the more traditional monastic themes of bridal mysticism, creating "a hybrid of court and cloister, of bridal mysticism and *fine amour.*"[6] Such innovations in language and style allowed writers to blend, challenge, and reinterpret courtly and mystical literary traditions, producing new theological insights and reaching a broader lay public.[7] Male writers, too, embraced the vernacular in part as a way to direct or encourage female spirituality. Indeed, collaboration and dialogue characterize much of vernacular theology, which reflects "encounters between clergy and laity, men and women, teachers and disciples, patrons and writers."[8]

Although sometimes understood as personal, solitary effort, the pursuit of a more perfect Christian life—even one oriented toward mystical experience—necessitated dialogue, models, and texts to read and share. This mission of teaching, learning, and exhortation was furthered within the Paris beguinage, which fostered collaboration between and among lay religious women and their clerical advisors and supporters.[9] This chapter explores these themes of collaboration and dialogue as it sketches the spiritual topography of the beguine life. The beguine status accommodated women who wished to pursue lives of religious contemplation and/or action in the world. It suited women eager to receive religious instruction, women who were not cloistered and who conceived their mission as directed toward the exhortation of one another as well as the general laity. As Robert of Sorbon observed, the beguines' holiness was enacted publicly and stood as a positive example to others. Adding to this association between beguines and religious exhortation and inspiration, Parisian preachers assumed beguines to be conversant in both courtly and pastoral theological discourses and inclined to impart spiritual teachings in communal prayers, writings, and personal conversations.

A forum in which various modes of religious expression intermingled, the beguinage was a space in which clerics might take inspiration from the beguines' activities, aspirations, and tastes, testing new ways of speaking about such themes as penance, contemplation, and love. Indeed, the spiritual teachings and practices of Paris's beguines both shaped and were shaped by new vernacular modes of expression as well as the more traditional monastic and scholastic discourses of their clerical mentors, making the beguinage a space in which courtly and pastoral, popular and learned discourses converged and intersected. Commenting on the beguines' level of learning, explaining theological questions, and—in some cases—encouraging the women to impart what they learned to other Christians, some preachers saw beguines as important allies and exemplars in the pursuit of pastoral goals. For these reasons, many clerics, even as they drew personal and pastoral inspiration from their contact with holy women, sought to direct and control beguine religious expression, channeling it along traditional sacramental and penitential lines.[10] Yet beguines were far from passive recipients of clerical teachings, as their advisors knew only too well. Exposed to a variety of teachings and religious models, particularly through socially oriented activities, communal reading and singing, sermons, and contemplation, beguines constituted a community receptive to a wide spectrum of religious teachings and expressions. Particularly compelling evidence of this relationship of collaboration and resistance are sermons preached to the beguines by the mistress of the beguinage, which Sorbonne clerics recorded and incorporated into sermon collections intended for the use of Parisian university students and preachers. These sermons provide an example of beguine teachings aimed at a beguine audience while functioning as a citable authority for preachers to include in their own sermons. The sermons convey a universal message while at the same time suggesting resistance to aspects of the sacramental and penitential model associated with beguines. Thus, even as clerics sought to instruct beguines, they consciously and deliberately drew on beguine teachings, which did not always fall in line with the teachings of their clerical advisors.

The Religious Education of Beguines

Despite ongoing medieval debates about the right of women to give religious instruction, conveying religious teachings to others was an acknowledged feature of the beguine life from the very beginning. As we have seen, early discussions of the beguine status, including the first papal acknowledgment of beguines, describe such women as living in common in order to mutually exhort one another to live more perfect Christian lives.[11] The "beguine *vitae*" abound with examples of lay religious women receiving instruction from beguine teachers. Ida of Gorsleeuw (c. 1200–1262/70) lived with a group of beguines for seven years, during which time she learned Latin.[12] Beatrice of Nazareth (1200–1268) was sent to a beguine community for a year, specifically for the purpose of being educated.[13] Ida of Nivelles (1199–1231) was educated by local beguines before entering the Cistercian convent of Kerkom in 1216.[14] Beguines living outside the Paris beguinage tended to cluster around other women—perhaps senior beguines—from whom they received instruction in silk work. It is certainly possible that this training would have been in conjunction with religious instruction.[15] And as we have seen, Robert of Sorbon singled out exhortation as a defining attribute of beguines.

At the Paris beguinage, there were several communal forums in which beguines received and imparted religious instruction.[16] The rules of the beguinage required the beguines to attend chapter, at which residents read in common and received religious instruction from the mistress.[17] The sermon collection of the Sorbonne cleric Raoul de Châteauroux shows that Paris's beguines regularly met and worshipped communally, attending Mass on a daily basis.[18] Although not specifically mandated in the statutes for the community, Paris's beguines performed the Divine Office daily.[19] As in the beguinages of the Low Countries, women in the Paris community performed readings from the psalms or other texts appropriate to particular feast days and a choir of beguines, educated and trained in music at the beguinage's school, sang the chant texts—antiphons and responsories—proper to the office.[20] Testamentary gifts to the beguinage choir specifically request the performance of such offices, indicating their significance to the broader community of Parisians.

Chosen by the mistress or schoolmistress, members of the choir performed the divine service as well as vigils for patrons or deceased beguines, activities for which they were compensated.[21] For example, in 1380, the canon of Sainte-Chapelle, Jean de Hétomesnil, gave one hundred gold francs to the beguines Bourges and Jeanne de Mortières, women with whom he had a close relationship, directing them to use part of the money to arrange for anniversary masses to be sung at the beguinage chapel for the salvation of his soul.[22] Jean left a separate bequest specifically for the beguine choir.[23] Several fifteenth-century testaments include requests for vigils and prayers from the beguines. In 1411, Denis de Mauroy, an attorney and procurator of the king, gave twenty sous to the beguinage with the request that the beguines perform vigils and a *messe à note* (a high mass in plainsong) for himself and his wife, Richarde, who had special affection for the community.[24] In 1418 Robert Mauger, president of Parlement, gave twenty sous to the beguinage for masses and vigils.[25] Alice Cournon specifically asked the beguines to perform nine readings of psalms and nine scriptural readings, a final commendation, and a requiem mass.[26] It is likely, too, that the beguines celebrated anniversary masses for their saintly founder, King Louis IX, and his successors.[27]

Contemporary observers confirm these details about the beguines' daily spiritual routines. In the wake of the publication of the Vienne Decrees in 1317, the Parisian chronicler Jean of Saint-Victor described the negative effects of the condemnations on the women living in the Paris beguinage. In his report, Jean alluded to the religious practices he associated with the community, stating: "The beguines were deprived of their beguinage, and their order was condemned; they neither sang nor read there."[28] That the chronicler singled out singing and reading—two communal activities through which beguines learned Latin and basic religious teachings—indicates their centrality to beguine religious practices and points to striking similarities between beguines and nuns.[29]

Given the diverse socioeconomic composition of the beguinage, it is impossible to generalize about the level of literacy and education residents of the beguinage possessed. Without doubt, the mistress and at least some residents possessed a degree of literacy in Latin and were able to read and write in the vernacular. Sermons preached at the Paris beguinage acknowledge the beguines' literacy and refer to their meditative prayer, singing, and reading. Several preachers casually mentioned the beguines' basic knowledge of Latin.[30] In a sermon he preached at the beguinage in 1273, the Dominican William of Auxerre described the beguines as "often in prayer" and acknowledged their ability to read the psalms. Referring to members of the audience who did not know the psalms because they were neither learned men (*clerici*) nor learned women (*clericae*), William advises those among his audience who were not able to read instead to recite the Paternoster and Ave Maria. Those beguines who knew their Psalters were directed to read from them.[31] The use of the term "clerica," of course, is a clear acknowledgement of the level of learning some beguines in the audience were thought to possess.

Some beguines may have received a rudimentary education in Latin at the beguinage school, which seems to have been known for musical instruction and perhaps functioned as a song school in which reading and writing basic Latin were also part of the curriculum.[32] A typical feature of beguinages in the southern Low Countries, beguine schools focused on teaching good manners and basic letters, as well as instruction in music and theology.[33] Paris's beguinage most likely played a similar role in the education of the daughters of the urban elite. It is evident from sermons that beguines had some knowledge of theology, knowledge that they could have acquired at the beguinage school.[34]

Intersecting with the beguines' emphasis on contemplation and action in the world, education was not only personally beneficial to the individual beguine, it was a social service beguines provided to their cities. Hence the schools helped fulfill the stated mission of the Paris beguinage. According to the rules of the house, women entering the community were to "obey and keep the ordinances and to persevere in good and holy works."[35] Similarly, documents recording a property dispute the beguinage brought before the king in 1432 refer to this aspect of the institutional identity of the community. In the records of the dispute, the beguinage's representatives argued that the community "was founded in honor of God and in order to receive women of devotion who do and perform good and holy works."[36] These good works included religious services, such as prayers and vigils for the dead, and social services, especially hospital work and teaching.[37] In their testaments, Parisians mentioned the hospital in the beguinage, indicating that the active element of the beguine life, specifically caring for the sick and the poor, was important to patrons.[38]

While education and learning were features of the beguine life, there is no evidence that the Paris beguinage produced or collected manuscripts, and no book belonging to an individual Parisian beguine has yet been identified. Testaments composed by Parisian beguines, however, provide evidence of the significance of books in the beguines' devotional practices. The testament of Martine Canu, mistress of the beguinage in 1408, lists a book of hours among her personal effects, which she bequeathed to another beguine of the community.[39] The beguine Jeanne du Faut likewise left a missal, as well as several chapel ornaments, to a priest named Roland de Helloin.[40] Sermons, too, refer to book ownership among beguines. In an anonymous sermon preached in Paris sometime in the late thirteenth century, the preacher compared plain, holy books with the books carried by beguines and wealthy ladies, saying that, while these lovely tomes were beautiful on the outside, within they were corrupt.[41] Leaving aside the obvious negative analogy the preacher drew between beguines and their outwardly lovely but inwardly corrupt books, its assumptions regarding book ownership among lay religious women imply the existence of a book culture among Parisian beguines.

Indeed, book ownership among Parisian beguines was probably more common than extant evidence indicates. Since beguinages did not recognize communal ownership of property, these institutions did not have libraries. Beguine-owned books, in the words of Walter Simons, were "fragile items of personal property and highly movable objects, easily transferred along ties of family or friendship."[42] The beguines of Paris freely disposed of their personal property, including books, to whomever they wished, whether to other beguines or to women outside the community. Martine Canu gave her book of hours to another beguine, Guillamette la Petite, who was then obliged to pass the book on to another woman, named Robinette.[43] It is not certain that Robinette herself identified as a beguine. In any case, Robinette was free to pass the book on to someone outside the community if she wished.

While no books remain to shed light on the reading tastes and practices of Parisian beguines, tombstones attest to the existence of a book culture at the beguinage. The tomb of Agnes of Orchies, mistress of the Paris beguinage until her death in 1284, portrays her dressed in her habit and surrounded by smaller etchings of beguines pictured in prayer or carrying books, perhaps Psalters (figure 3). The tomb of Jeanne Brichard, mistress until her death in 1312, represents the beguine wearing a girdle book (figure 4), as does the tomb of another Parisian beguine, Marie of Gonesse (see figure 2).[44] These artistic renderings of beguines with girdle books—purse-like book holders used to keep books close at hand while protecting them from the elements—is telling. As a recent survey of girdle books argues, these items "were used symbolically to denote knowledge, wealth, intellectual curiosity, and learning."[45] They enabled their owners to carry books easily and safely, assuming both mobility and a close attachment to books, features that, given what is known of the beguine life, suggest further evidence of a universal mission to disseminate religious knowledge outside the beguinage.

The Order of Perfect Lovers

As literate lay religious women, beguines constituted the ideal audience for texts, poems, and songs that brought together learned and popular religious traditions. Literary scholars have recently drawn attention to the dozens of poems written for—and perhaps by—beguines, noting their distinctive style and shared themes, particularly their employment of language and imagery drawn from secular romance. Examining a body of thirteenth-century

Figure 3. Drawing of the tomb of Agnes of Orchies,
mistress of the beguinage of Paris (d. 1284). Engraving by
Jean-Baptiste Scotin and included in Jean Aymar Piganiol de La Force's
Description de Paris, vol. 5 (Paris, 1742), 143. The tomb was located
in the Dominican convent of Saint-Jacques in Paris (now destroyed).
By permission, Bibliothèque nationale de France.

Figure 4. Drawing of the tomb of Jeanne Brichard,
mistress of the beguinage of Paris (d. 1312). The tomb was located
at the now destroyed Dominican convent of Saint-Jacques in Paris.
The sketch is part the collection of tomb drawings made
by François-Roger de Gaignières (1644–1715). Collection Gaignières,
fol. 21. By permission, Bibliothèque nationale de France.

anthologies from northern France, Geneviève Hasenohr has argued that the
beguines' communal religious practices, specifically reading and singing,
encouraged the memorization, recitation, and dissemination of vernacular
poems, love songs, spiritual treatises, and prayers both within and beyond
their immediate circles.[46] Tony Hunt and Barbara Newman have drawn attention to the contributions of beguines to vernacular literature, noting a
plethora of poems, songs, and didactic texts that seek to define the beguine
life or assume a beguine audience.[47] Drawing on secular songs and trouvère
lyrics, these poems and songs characterize the beguine life according to the
possession of specific virtues, especially those that express the beguine's status
as *fin amant*. Specifically, beguines are those who love loyally, passionately, and
completely. Defined by their love, which exceeds that of all others, beguines
alternately experience the ecstatic presence of God and suffer periods of distance and alienation.

Pastoral miscellanies once housed at the medieval library of the Sorbonne
include vernacular poems and verses aimed at beguine audiences with similar
features and themes. One manuscript donated to the library in 1306 includes
several snatches of verse in Latin and French describing the signs by which a
beguine might be recognized. Under the rubric "de benignis," for example, is
a list of qualities that center on the beguines' outward comportment. Echoing
James of Vitry's *Life of Mary of Oignies*, the text asserts that the beguine's inner
purity of heart will be manifest in her modest appearance, somber expression, and mature gait.[48] Toward the end of the manuscript is a poem entitled
"Les XXXII propriétés de beguinage," which likewise defines the beguine life
by moving back and forth between the beguines' observable behavior (their
bowed heads, praying mouths, weeping eyes) and their internal disposition
(desiring hearts "burning love," and "spiritual courtliness").[49] Utilizing courtly
modes of expression, the poem describes beguine spirituality in paradoxical
terms: the beguines "go while staying, speak while silent, weep while laugh-
ing"; they "die by living, live by dying, fast by feasting, feast by fasting." Drawing on themes and imagery recognizable to beguines and presenting them in
an easily memorized format, the "XXXII propriétés" attempts to define—and
therefore shape—beguine spirituality by stressing outward comportment and
ascetic practices.

A late thirteenth-century devotional text entitled *La Règle des fins amans*
(The Rule of Perfect Lovers) offers another interesting example of efforts to define and shape beguine spirituality through the deployment of courtly themes
and ideals. Despite its name, the *Règle* is not so much a rule as a vernacular

treatise describing what the author perceived to be qualities and religious practices of beguines, whom the text refers to collectively as the "Order of Perfect Lovers."[50] What is more significant, the text seeks to capture the distinctive culture of the beguinage and its community of lay religious women. Although featuring Picardian words and expressions, the linguistic criteria place the *Règle* within the region of the Ile-de-France. Indeed, the manuscript's editor posits that the *Règle* could have been written for the beguines of Paris.[51] Its contents, too, suggest a Paris connection: the *Règle* borrows from the popular allegorical poem the *Roman de la Rose*, which was becoming widely known within educated Parisian circles by the late thirteenth century.[52] It is worth mentioning that one of the earliest versions of the *Rose* was among the chained books in the Sorbonne library, evidence that the *Rose* was much read and prized by clerics studying at the Sorbonne.[53] The *Règle*, moreover, references definitions of the beguine life that turn up in sermons preached at the Paris beguinage, as well as treatises—particularly those of Robert of Sorbon—that circulated among Parisian clerics. Like Robert, the author of the *Règle* refers to the beguines as an order of love (*ordo caritatis*) over which Jesus is abbot and to which the Virgin Mary herself belongs. The treatise also features the familiar assertion that the term "begina" is drawn from the Latin word for kindness (*benigna*) or refers to the beguines' burning caritas (*beguine comme bons feus*), the vernacular equivalent of the Latin *bene ignita*, which Robert himself had offered as a flattering etymology for "begina" in his sermons.[54] Whatever the provenance of the *Règle* and whoever its intended audience, it is entirely possible that the beguines of Paris knew this text, or something quite similar to it.

Conveying the distinctive culture of the beguinage, the *Règle* intermingles discourses of both human and spiritual love, catering to an audience of women whose interests and activities span the worlds of city, court, and beguine community.[55] Moreover, the *Règle* acknowledges the active and contemplative aspects of the beguine life and even valorizes the beguines' unenclosed status. Presenting love as central to the beguine ethos, the *Règle* draws on the language and imagery of *fin' amors* to describe the love that God has for humanity and the beguines, the Order of Perfect Lovers, in turn have for God. It is this passionate love of God that defines the beguine. The *Règle* asserts that among the four pillars of the beguine life—purity, poverty, humility, and love—love is the pillar that "carries everything . . . guards everything, and does everything."[56] Giving the beguines' lack of canonical status and regular oversight a courtly twist, the *Règle* claims that God himself is the guardian of the beguines because he is *jalous*, an emotion essential to "perfect love," according to that tradition.[57] In other words, God's jealousy is such that he cannot allow an earthly guardian to oversee his Order of Perfect Lovers. Certainly, the *Règle*'s description of the beguines as an order can be read as a defense of the beguines' status as a religious association lacking official papal sanction. The *Règle* argues that the beguines are not a monastic order of *this* world; rather, they are an order sanctioned directly by God, who recognizes the beguines' greater devotion, which is fueled by love, not enforced by vows and walls.

As in "Les XXXII propriétés de beguinage," the *Règle* is preoccupied with describing qualities and activities that define the beguine, presenting the beguines with a type of code that draws on the ideals of courtly behavior outlined in secular literature while giving them an otherworldly objective. Beginning with the "Twelve Signs" by which one can identify a *fin amant*, the *Règle* asserts that a beguine "love[s] loyally," "think[s] often and attentively of her lover," "keep[s] the commandments of her lover," "go[es] often and willingly to her lover," and "receive[s] devotedly the jewels her lover sends, which are poverty, suffering, maladies, and tribulations."[58] The beguine is known as one who "grieves over the suffering of her lover" and offers gifts to her Lover in return, which include "anguished tears and heavy sighs," an allusion to the affective piety associated with women in general and beguines in particular.[59]

Urging the beguines to visualize his suffering body, the *Règle* vividly connects Jesus' suffering to his worthiness as Lover and invites the beguine listener or reader to imagine herself taking Jesus' heart and giving him her own in return:

> He showed us love of his heart when he wished to have his side
> opened right next to his heart, as if he wants to say, "I cannot speak,
> but I have opened my side to you. Fair sweet son, fair sweet daughter,
> put your hand in my side, take my heart, because it is yours. . . ."
> With all of his strength [Jesus] loved us, he even appeared on the
> cross. There, he spent all of his strength for us; there he was broken
> for all of humanity. . . . And he says through Solomon, "Fair son, give
> me your heart!" He does not say "lend it to me!" . . . The fair King of
> Paradise exchanges with us his heart, and for this we should love him
> with all of our might.[60]

In this sense, the *Règle* functions as an "intimate script" for beguines to follow, guiding them to perform and experience the emotions appropriate to their relationship with Christ.[61] Like the meditative texts composed for nuns and female recluses, the *Règle* seeks to cultivate compassion for the suffering Christ, encouraging the reader or listener to imagine events in the life of Christ and to participate mentally in these events using her imagination.[62] In the *Règle* these practices and emotions are relayed through an intermingling of nuptial and courtly motifs, with the latter being particularly well suited to beguines who, as religious laywomen, might be considered lovers rather than brides. One might even argue that the beguines' expressions of fidelity to their divine Lover had to be "hotter, louder, brighter, riskier," conveying a passion more intense than that expected of Christ's official, canonically recognized brides.[63] Asserting the special intensity of the beguines' passion, the *Règle* exclaims: "What marvel! If they love more virtuously and more fervently and they know to love better than any other, because they are the order of lovers, just as Mary Magdalen, who loved Jesus Christ so ardently! And [the beguines] have and will have 12 delights that God does not give except to his lovers."[64] Thus, in true courtly fashion, God returns and rewards the beguines' intense love.

Deploying the courtly theme of *amor de lonh* (love from afar), the *Règle* encourages the beguines to engage in prayer and meditational practices in order to help comfort them during their divine Lover's absence. The *Règle*'s didactic function is clear in its detailed description of the four stages of prayer, which function as steps in the beguine's spiritual progress and aim to culminate in a mystical encounter with the Lover. In the first stage of prayer, the beguine begins her spiritual progress by praying at the appropriate times and occasions, specifically matins, the canonical hours, and whenever she is required for penitential purposes.[65] In the second stage of prayer, the beguine prays for specific communities, such as the church, sinners, and the dead, highlighting the beguines' role as intermediaries for sinners and souls in purgatory.[66] In the third stage, the beguine prays for "special friends," a directive that acknowledges the beguines' exclusive circle of *fins amans*.[67] Finally, in the fourth stage, the beguine is directed to engage in an extended meditation on Christ's humanity and divinity and the mystery of the Trinity, a practice that will result in the soul being transfixed and the body losing its corporeal senses.[68] Like Saint Paul, Saint John the Evangelist, and the quintessential contemplative, the Queen of Sheba, the beguine will experience mystical rapture, a state referenced in the short *roman* at the end of the *Règle*.[69] In an obvious nod to the *Roman de la Rose*, the *Règle* concludes with Conscïence searching for her absent lover, Christ, whom "the Cloistered" (monks and nuns) have imprisoned in their garden.[70] Significantly, it is Jalousie who informs Conscïence of her divine Lover's whereabouts in the garden of the Cloistered, declaring that, once Conscïence and her allies find Christ there, they will forcefully bring him out.[71] With this acknowledgment of beguine jealousy toward the cloistered—which is a sign of their true love—Hope, Fine Amour, Charity, and Wisdom help bring Christ to Conscïence.[72]

As we have seen, Robert of Sorbon perceived the beguine as someone, male or female, religious or lay, who, burning with the fire of caritas, actively exhorted his or her fellow Christians to attend Mass, confess their sins, and do penance. The *Règle*, by contrast, was less interested in the beguines' caritas, preferring to imagine the beguine as someone languishing in *amour*. Nevertheless, as in Robert's writings, the *Règle* presents the beguines as exemplars for others. Their "good fire" both lights the way for errant Christians to reform their lives and stokes the fires of those within their circles, making them more fervent in their desire for God.[73] The *Règle*, then, seeks to direct beguine spirituality along sacramental and contemplative channels, while at the same time acknowledging the beguines' position out in the world and appealing to popular literary tastes. We might even imagine that the *Règle*'s glowing, romantic description of the beguines as *Ordres des Fins Amans* had more appeal to beguines steeped in courtly literature than Robert's sober discussion of the beguines as an ordo caritatis.

Like devotional literature and spiritual treatises, sermons preached at the Paris beguinage sought to shape the spirituality of their hearers by advancing models of piety that resonated with beguine audiences while serving pastoral ends. Such models were informed by the hagiographical writings of James of Vitry, Thomas of Cantimpré, and other clerics involved in promoting the new religious movements of the late twelfth and early thirteenth centuries.[74] James of Vitry's *Life of Mary of Oignies*, completed in 1215, in many ways set the course for clerical representations of the lay religious women who came to be known as beguines.[75] Although scholars have helpfully analyzed sources to describe a distinctive female spirituality that was centered on the sacraments—especially penance, confession, and communion—and distinguished by paramystical experiences and a close identification with Christ's humanity, recent scholarship has focused more upon the objectives of the hagiographers, arguing that these texts must be read with an eye for the ways in which the sex of the authors and subjects, as well as the hagiographical genre, shaped the content.[76]

As tensions in the vitae suggest, the actions and aspirations of lay religious women were nuanced or explained to conform to gender expectations. Indeed, as Michel Lauwers has argued, the beguine vitae convey a certain ambiguity regarding the roles of action and contemplation in the women's lives.[77] The ways in which lay religious women diverged from traditional forms and contexts of female religiosity—the absence of a monastic rule and lack of strict enclosure—could not be ignored by the hagiographers, who took great pains to defend the purity and sincere religious commitment of their female subjects. The active element of the beguine life, manifested in manual labor, hospital work, and care for the poor, although admired by some, also necessitated justification and reinterpretation on the part of the hagiographer.[78] For example, according to the first part of the *Life of Mary of Oignies*, Mary's piety centered on charitable activities in the world, such as caring for lepers, spinning wool, and giving alms, activities that subsequent hagiographers depicted as typical of the praiseworthy beguines in their own locales.[79] Later in the vita, however, Mary no longer engages in manual labor; rather, she focuses her attentions on Christ alone, devoting herself solely to a life of contemplation.[80] As a contemplative, Mary was blessed with visions and revelations, clear evidence of the greater spiritual rewards of contemplation over action. This shift from the active life to the contemplative life—or abandoning "Martha" for "Mary"—takes place in the vitae of other beguines.[81]

Tensions between the active and contemplative aspects of beguine spirituality were attenuated in some ways by clerical emphasis on penitential practices. Even as lay religious women sought to imitate Christ in his poverty, care for others, and preaching, social norms limited women's range of activity, and canon law prohibited female preaching. The only sanctioned, admired form of *imitatio Christi* for women was to suffer.[82] Indeed, in several vitae, the actions their female subjects perform in the world "take the form, almost solely, of ascetic and contemplative work for sinners on earth and in purgatory."[83] The hagiographies describe the beguines' intense concern for the souls of others, for whom they weep, fast, and suffer severe, often self-inflicted, pain.[84] Through their extraordinary penitential feats, which went far beyond what their own sins merited, these women were able to free souls from purgatory. Thus, penitential practices serve to maintain the beguines' link to the larger community without challenging clerical prerogatives or gender norms.[85]

Sermons preached at the Paris beguinage touch on penance, contemplation, and visionary experience, suggesting that clerical expectations and representations of beguine spirituality were influenced, at least in part, by these hagiographical models and that preachers hoped to provide a kind of script for performing the type of sanctity associated with the ideal beguine. Perhaps reflecting the effect of hagiographical tropes on clerical attitudes toward

beguines or testifying to the extent to which beguines internalized these ideals, penance figured prominently in sermons preached at the Paris beguinage.
In her examination of sermons preached there, Nicole Bériou noted that half
of the sermons addressed to beguines feature the word *penitere, penitentia,* or
penitens.[86] Calling to mind the painful images of suffering, not only of Christ,
but also of souls in purgatory, the secular cleric William of Montreuil urged
the beguines to "pray and weep" for those suffering in purgatory.[87] The Dominican Giles of Orleans specifically associated the beguines with confession
and penance, focusing especially on the benefits of the latter, which included
delivery from purgatorial suffering, the strength to resist the devil, and a positive example to others. For these reasons, Giles claimed, penance was especially recommended to beguines, suggesting that the Dominican perceived the
beguines as having a special intercessory role both in this world and the next.[88]

   While there was no consensus among Parisian preachers as to the form and
frequency with which beguines ought to do penance, it was indeed a prominent theme in sermons preached at the beguinage. An unnamed preacher from
the monastery of Mont Saint-Eloi recommended to the beguines contrition
and tears, fasting and prayer, followed by confession.[89] Likewise, an unnamed
Franciscan recommended contrition, penance, fasting, good works, singing,
and confession to prepare the way for Christ.[90] In a sermon preached at the
beguinage chapel in 1272, the secular cleric and Sorbonne student Humbert of
Sorbon advised the beguines to perform the work of penance, saying "Lord,
I give myself completely to you and I rise up at night in order to praise you,
I put on a hair shirt, I fast, I give alms, and I do other things in secret." Acknowledging that it was possible for the beguines to take on too much, Humbert concedes, "If it is a thing that burdens you, the priest will willingly release
you, provided however that you did not vow that."[91] The secular cleric Ranulph of Houblonnière alluded to the beguines' obligation to perform penance
during a brief discussion on the women's habit, saying, "The dress you wear
signifies the life you ought to lead." Specifically, he informed the beguines that
"the veil by which your head is covered signifies humility and obedience." The
white color of the veil, according to Ranulph, "signifies charity and purity;"
the dress's russet color "signifies mortification of the flesh."[92] Once again, exterior signs, in this case clothing, are called upon to prove the beguines' interior purity and holiness. In this case, clothing also signifies the penitential
practices—mortification of the flesh—expected of beguines. Linking penance
with visionary experience, another prominent theme in the beguine vitae,
some preachers described penance as a stage in contemplative practice. An

unnamed Franciscan who preached at the beguinage in 1273 described penance as the essence of the active life, which is a stage through which one moves toward the contemplative life focused on prayer. It is through this prayer, the Franciscan preacher claims, that the beguines will obtain remission of sins, deliverance from temptation, and the revelation of divine secrets.[93] Similarly, the Dominican friar Giles of Liège positioned penance and mortification of the flesh as a stage preceding contemplation and culminating in holy meditation and the fire of perfect love.[94]

Love was also a prominent theme in sermons preached to beguines. As we have seen, Robert of Sorbon declared that "Love is Beguine" and praised the beguines' socially oriented caritas.[95] Sermons and exempla concerning beguines took a different approach, associating the women with love but using this virtue as a means of defining the beguines as a traditional religious order, specifically an order of love in the sense of a community of women preoccupied with prayer and the contemplation of the divine Lover. Troubled by the beguines' lack of enclosure, some Parisian preachers suggested that beguines needed to exhibit total commitment to their divine Lover in order to prove themselves worthy of his love. In what was no doubt a reference to traditional nuns, Giles of Liège claimed that "good spouses" of Christ were "completely enclosed."[96] When Christ wished to speak privately to his unenclosed lovers (beguines), he required their complete attention, a demand of which beguines needed reminding, given all of the distractions in their daily lives. In this spirit, Giles advised the beguines to bear in mind that, wherever they might go, whether to church or to hear sermons, or out in public, they ought to do everything in honor of their divine Lover and look for the next private moment to commune with him, for it is in solitude that Christ reveals his secrets.[97] Thus, the beguines ought to apply themselves to "prayer and contemplation in a solitary place with God." Emphasizing the benefits of solitude, Giles demanded, "Do you think that when you spend the day in the town, that lover [that is God] will descend to you? Certainly not, but [he may] when you kneel before an altar, or an image of the cross or the Virgin Mary, or if you are not able to go to Church, next to your bed, kneeling or prostrate upon the floor."[98]

Similarly, in a sermon preached at the beguinage chapel in 1273, a Franciscan preacher instructed the beguines to pray to God as they would to a king, saying (and here the copyist provides the vernacular), "Lord, I want only you, your Love, and your company."[99] Another Franciscan friar identified in Raoul of Châteauroux's sermon collection as "Gosoinus" told the beguines that they ought to have a desire for God on par with that of the prophets, and that, through this desire, God would inflame their souls in the knowledge of his Love, melt it in devotion, and raise it up in contemplation.[100] The secular cleric Arnoul le Bescochier preached that the beguines would win God's Love through their great faith and obedience and that their souls would progress stage by stage from virtues of mercy and piety to the heights of contemplation, where they will be embraced by this love like Elijah in his chariot of fire.[101] In February 1273, Jean Tempier, a Dominican, preached to the beguines on Love, which he described as the greatest and most powerful of all virtues. Echoing beguine writings on Love's power, Jean asserted that it was Love that brought God from heaven to earth and bound Jesus to the cross.[102] A sermon by the secular cleric Humbert of Sorbon cites contemplation as the highest goal of the beguines, which they achieve by overcoming temptations and tribulations and focusing their thoughts on Love of God.[103] Citing the Song of Songs 2:16 ("My Beloved to me and I to him"), Humbert describes the heights of contemplation, which is experienced as a brief encounter with the Beloved. Clearly, rather than express their love through action in the world (caritas), the beguines are encouraged to languish in a love that brings them to the heights of contemplation.

The Masters and the Magistra

Even as Parisian clerics sought to direct beguine spirituality along penitential channels, they also recognized the personal and professional benefit they might draw from collaborative relationships with beguines. The collection of distinctiones compiled by Raoul de Châteauroux offers important insight into this dynamic. Composed of selections from sermons preached in and around Paris and quotes from patristic and scholastic sources, Raoul's collection included six excerpts from sermons preached by the mistress of the Paris beguinage.[104] That Raoul included the mistress's sermons in this particular type of preaching manual is significant. With the development of the sermo modernus—a sermon centered on a particular theme—preachers now needed to pull together biblical, patristic, and scholastic authorities to support and develop their chosen themes.[105] To meet this need, preachers developed aids such as collections of distinctiones: searchable, alphabetized collections of words or themes under which quotes or passages from citable authorities were collected. Raoul's collection, although not widely copied, became part of the library's chained, noncirculating collection, indicating that it was among the most frequently used books of the Sorbonne's library. Raoul's inclusion of the mistress's sermons alongside the writings of Parisian masters, preachers, and church fathers stands as compelling evidence of the esteem in which she—and her teachings—were held. The association between beguines and teaching were not lost on Parisian clerics. The association was so powerful, in fact, that Raoul identified the mistress of the Paris beguinage with the title *magistra*, a term with scholarly implications that would have been well understood in medieval Paris.[106] Moreover, the excerpts themselves have a dual significance: first, as artifacts of beguine teachings and, second, as citable authorities intended for incorporation into university sermons.

It probably comes as no surprise that the first reference to the *magistra beginarum* appears under the theme of *Amor*. As we have seen, beguines were thought to be experts on the subject as well as receptive listeners to teachings that drew on courtly love themes. In this light, Raoul's citation of the magistra makes sense. Indeed, much of the material collected under *Amor* had some connection with beguines and vernacular spirituality. For example, Raoul's authorities on Love leads with an early version of an Old French rhyme known as the *Amour* verses, a popular, easily memorized, and widely diffused poem on the Passion.[107] With its repetitive rhymes and courtly motifs, the *Amour* verses circulated both in oral and written form, like much of the poetry associated with beguines.

The mistress's contribution, which appears to be a fragment from a poem or song, is presented in Latin followed by a French translation. Drawing on secular expressions of romantic love, especially the power of love over God himself, the excerpt begins with the declaration that there are "four ways that the Love of God is acquired."

> God is acquired by loving,
> In loving he is held captive
> And he guards those who love him,
> And he is sufficient for those who love him.[108]

Thematically, the mistress's ode to love is typical of beguine poetry with its borrowing of courtly themes to describe Love's power: Love is a force by which God is held captive. Stylistically, too, the beguine's contribution seems to be intended to be memorized, suggesting that Raoul included the excerpt for the benefit of Parisian preachers seeking to connect with beguine audiences.

This collection of authorities assembled under a theme closely associated with beguine spirituality highlights the beguinage's role as a site of collaboration, a place in which preachers might take inspiration from the beguines and experiment with new ways of addressing spiritual themes.[109]

Raoul also included the mistress's sermons among authorities compiled under the themes of Christian faith (*Exemplum de fide Christianitatis*) and tribulation (*Tribulatio*). In both cases, the excerpts do not seem to have an obvious connection with a beguine audience. The sermon extract found under the rubric *Exemplum de fide Christianitatis* contains an exemplum about a Tartar who, having inquired into many other religions, came to Rome seeking baptism. After being met with skepticism about his intentions, the Tartar eventually convinced the pope himself of his sincerity by telling him that it was the Christians' superior caritas—their love for one another—that moved him to desire baptism.[110] Similarly, under *Tribulatio*, one finds a sermon extract attributed to the mistress that relates an allegory about a powerful lord who, wishing to sell his wine, closes down all of the local taverns in order to ensure the sale of his own product.[111] This great lord, the mistress reveals, is Christ, who wishes to sell the wine of misery, sickness, poverty, and the loss of worldly friends, and thus shuts down the taverns of wealth, health, honor, respect, and companionship. Pursuing this rather conventional theme, the beguine mistress highlights suffering as a sign of God's great love, one that will be rewarded with the wine of paradise. Both exempla, likely included in Raoul's distinctiones for their value as interesting anecdotes with which preachers might pepper their sermons, reflect the mistress's role in engaging and imparting pastoral teachings. Addressing universal Christian themes, the mistress's teachings resonate beyond the beguine audience before which it was originally preached.

Reading these sermons as records of the mistress's work—or what she might have said to her community—it should come as no surprise to find a learned beguine addressing matters such as confession, contrition, penance, charity, and meditation, subjects with which women—especially beguines—were associated. The mistress's sermons, however, suggest some resistance to hagiographical models of lay piety, specifically aspects of the penitential system, which was one of the main pillars of female sanctity in general.[112] In a sermon on confession, the mistress engages and amends Peter the Chanter's influential statement on penance: "Confession is the greatest part of satisfaction," asserting instead: "Confession is the *least* part of satisfaction."[113] According to the mistress, contrition is the greatest—that is, the most onerous—part of satisfaction. The mistress's shift in emphasis from confession to contrition, from external act to internal emotion, is significant in light of current theological positions on the topic as well as clerical representations of beguine spirituality, both of which placed greater emphasis on confession and penance. By the early thirteenth century, theologians tended to emphasize auricular confession as the "greatest part" of the penitential system, which consisted of three elements (contrition, confession, and satisfaction), arguing that without confession to a priest, there could be no satisfaction (the penance imposed by the priest) and thus no absolution.[114] It was these external stages of the penitential system—confession and satisfaction—that received the most emphasis in hagiographical accounts, too, which presented their female subjects as "professional penitents" engaged in extravagant feats of asceticism undertaken on behalf of themselves and others.[115] In a sermon warning against the dangers of pride and hypocrisy in confession, the mistress emphasized instead the primacy of interior contrition, suggesting resistance to clerical emphasis on confession.[116] With regard to confession itself, the mistress cites a certain Jean de Bethune—perhaps a clerical advisor—who taught that confession must be motivated by grief, given of one's own free will, and accomplished with alacrity, completeness, and purity, thus highlighting the importance of the individual penitent's internal disposition over confession and penance.[117]

In a sermon preached on the occasion of the dedication of a church, perhaps the chapel of the beguinage, the mistress similarly engages with ideas and practices with which beguines were assumed to be familiar.[118] Following a well-established tradition in sermons preached on the occasion of church dedications, the mistress takes as her theme the idea of the human soul as a temple of God.[119] Describing the bishop's ritual sprinkling of holy water, the mistress compares the rite with the punishment of three types of sins, namely, ignorance, the sins of the flesh, and the sins of malice, the last being, according to the mistress, the worst of all.[120] Utilizing the visual imagery in the church as a mnemonic device, the mistress directs the beguines to contemplate the lamps (which represent the light in the soul) and the crosses in the church and to imagine the crosses within their own souls, in which the memory of the Passion should be inscribed. Rather than focus on the images in the church to meditate on the life of Christ or cultivate compassion for the suffering Christ, the mistress instructed the beguines in the audience to hold the image in their minds in order to better follow the major themes presented in the sermon.[121] The church itself, the mistress asserts, is only a building; it is the holiness of the people within its walls that make it a true church blessed by

God. Likewise, outer penance, such as fasting, is only a sign of inner devotion. True inner penance is in the memory of Christ's Passion, "which the holy soul ought to have always in its heart."[122]

We might detect in the mistress's sermon some resistance against the view that the beguine life was defined by outward behavior, a prominent theme in clerical discussions of these women. Several details in the mistress's sermon, in fact, suggest a desire to downplay the importance of fasting and asceticism, emphasizing instead interior faith and love. In a discussion of the dangers from which the soul must be guarded, the mistress specifies sins of slander, vile thoughts, and desire for praise. After simply mentioning the sin of slander, she elaborates on the second and third types of sin. She warns her listeners to repel and reject vile thoughts but not to become too distressed by their occurrence; so long as the beguines do not delight in or consent to them, they are only thoughts.[123] To support her assertions, again the mistress cites the teaching of a male cleric, this time a certain Abbot Nicholas, who warned against becoming discouraged when plagued by "imaginings and phantasms."[124]

Most striking is the mistress's discussion of the third danger to the soul, which she identifies as the desire for divine praise for the smallest of good works, a desire, she asserts, that reduces the relationship with God to nothing more than a transaction.[125] All good works, the mistress counsels, should be done with good intention and on account of God alone. Here, the mistress's sermon seems to urge the beguines toward disinterested love of God, a message similar to that of Marguerite Porete's *Mirror of Simple Souls*. Intriguingly, the mistress's church-dedication sermon ends with a reference to the Augustinian triad of will, reason, and memory that most certainly relates to the mistress's criticism of beguines who perform good works for the sake of earning divine praise. In a brief allusion to these three faculties of the soul, the mistress asserts that when the Will wills (that is, conforms itself to God), Reason accords itself and memory is pure, making the soul a church dedicated and married to God.[126]

Whether Raoul came to possess copies of the mistress's sermons by recording her words himself or by working from a written copy, the inclusion of the mistress's teachings in a preaching manual for university clerics stands as compelling evidence of male and female collaboration in the accomplishment of pastoral goals.[127] The mistress's teachings were no doubt valued for their utility in helping preachers connect with the general laity, once again underscoring the ways in which some university clerics sought to learn from beguines as they prepared to carry out their pastoral duties. The symbiotic nature of this relationship is evident too in the fact that, in her sermons, the mistress cites the male clerics from whom she has learned. The mistress states that she learned the exemplum about the Tartar who came to Rome seeking baptism in a sermon she heard by "a great preacher," and several other excerpts specifically cite a clerical source.[128] In this manner, the mistress is enacting the advice of preachers like Robert of Sorbon, who recognized the role of beguines in imparting what they learned from their clerical mentors to the broader community. Of course, the inclusion of such citations also serves to authorize the beguine's teachings, not an insignificant point given the context. Moreover, in line with canonical injunctions against female preaching, the sections Raoul included do not record the mistress expounding on scripture. To shift perspective a bit, the mistress's sermons, although clear evidence of male and female collaboration, hint at beguine resistance to clerical representations of female spirituality, suggesting that beguines did not passively accept and adopt the predominant models of beguine piety.

The sermons themselves, therefore, represent instances of dialogue among university scholars and between these scholars and lay religious women. University clerics approached beguine audiences with certain assumptions about their religious practices, interests, and abilities, hoping to encourage and benefit spiritually from contact with such women. Moreover, the sermons demonstrate that beguines were not passive recipients of religious instruction. They asked questions, reacted to the preacher's words, absorbed and challenged the teaching to which they were exposed. To illustrate this point, I turn once again to Robert of Sorbon. In a sermon preached to a university audience, he relayed a story about a certain preacher's attempt to explain the virtue of charity to a beguine audience. According to Robert, the preacher explained that "a man whose charity goes straight cannot but act in a way above reproach." To this, the mistress of the beguines asked, "Where in Holy Scripture, master, have you seen that charity is lame? If it limps and no longer follows a straight course, it is no longer charity."[129] Clearly, in Robert's view, preachers had an attentive, knowledgeable, and outspoken audience in the beguines. While Robert clearly hoped that such dialogue made for better preachers, others may have been less enthusiastic about beguines who presumed to question and instruct. Alongside Robert's beguine who doggedly encouraged her fellow Christians to lead more perfect lives was the arrogant laywoman who boldly instructed priests and foolishly misled the laity.

CHAPTER 6

"There Are Among Us Women Called Beguines"

Robert of Sorbon deployed the image of the beguine in support of his pastoral agenda, presenting beguines as worthy models for university clerics by emphasizing their zeal for souls, active lay ministry, and humility. According to Robert, it was the beguine's actions (namely, exhortation of her fellow Christians) and humility (specifically acceptance of the skepticism and ridicule with which her actions were met) that defined her. Yet, while setting up the beguine as a model for university clerics, Robert referred to the actions possible of real, flesh-and-blood women with whom he, his colleagues, and students at the University of Paris had contact. Such emphasis on deeds and demeanor subjected lay religious women—in all their visibility and vulnerability—to intense scrutiny and skepticism. Offering the beguine as a cleric's model, counterpart, or superior (whether consciously or unconsciously) could have negative consequences for the women with whom Parisian clerics interacted as some began to suspect that lay religious women internalized discourses lauding female spiritual authority.

Among the men preaching to audiences of beguines were some who expressed doubt that all of the women who took the name "beguine" and who wore the beguine habit lived up to the positive attributes associated with the name. A few preachers even contended that some women took up the name so that they might pass themselves off as holy women, when in reality they lived wicked, dissolute lives. Moreover, as women who could claim religious authority based on the idea that they had special access to God, beguines were frequently accused of spiritual pride. Adding to this growing cloud of suspicion over lay religious women, the notion of a lay apostolate became

increasingly suspect over the course of the thirteenth century, even if this apostolate was carried out privately.[1] Enduring fears of heretical groups and their
alleged tolerance (or even encouragement) of female preachers—as well the
ongoing conflict between secular and mendicant clerics at the University of
Paris— made preaching authority one of the most hotly debated issues in medieval Paris.[2] As several scholars have noted, Parisian theologians defended the
clergy's exclusive control over preaching by debating the right of women to
give religious instruction.[3] Thus, while Robert of Sorbon extolled the beguine
for her zeal for souls, some of his contemporaries were suspicious of women's
involvement in religious instruction, preferring to relegate beguines to a more
passive role as the quintessential recipients of pastoral care. By the late thirteenth century, some of the very same features of the beguine life praised by
Robert and certain of his contemporaries were also points of major contention
among intellectuals in medieval Paris.

It was within this context that the beguine Marguerite Porete (d. 1310),
who had actively disseminated her spiritual writings to bishops, theologians,
other beguines, and members of the laity, was sentenced to burn at the stake
as a "relapsed heretic" for writing and circulating a book that, according to the
judgment of twenty-one theologians from the University of Paris, contained
doctrinal errors.[4] While Marguerite was active in northern France, her inquisitorial process— directed by a Dominican who served as both confessor to the
French king and papal inquisitor of France—took place in Paris and included
consultations by university theologians and canon lawyers. Marguerite's trial
must have been the talk of Paris, and her actions widely (if not accurately)
discussed. Her actions and ideas, moreover, came to be associated with the
beguine status in general when church leaders, including six of the twenty-
one Parisian theologians called upon to judge her book, met at the Council
of Vienne (1311–1312) the year after her execution. Examining how Marguerite
Porete's career intertwined with clerical representations of Parisian beguines illuminates questions about what it meant to be labeled a beguine and the wider
consequences of the term.

What Did It Mean to Be Called a Beguine?

In many ways, by identifying as a beguine a woman seemed to make a claim to
lead a religious, even saintly, life. Such claims, not surprisingly, were regarded
with mistrust. Moreover, some clerics expressed discomfort with the fact that

it was not quite clear who counted as a beguine and who did not. The existence of beguinages in northern European cities in some ways complicated clerical understandings of what it meant for a woman to identify—or to be labeled—as a beguine. With the establishment of the beguinage, a woman who wished to live as a beguine could now join an official, recognized community and submit herself to its rules, thus visibly taking on an identity laden with a complicated and somewhat contradictory set of expectations. Moreover, it was an identity that one might adopt or abandon with relative ease. In their interactions with women who self-identified as beguines, many clerics insisted that the beguine status was contingent upon entry into the beguinage, attempting to impose some permanence upon a status that was unofficial and voluntary. Aware of the informal nature of the beguines' vows and their freedom to abandon these vows with minimal consequences, many preachers expressed skepticism that women would remain committed to such a life for more than one or two years.[5] Others discussed the beguine status in terms similar to discussions of recognized religious orders, warning the residents of the Paris beguinage that leaving the institution constituted an abandonment of their vows, and that in order to be considered "religious," one had to remain bound to the community.[6]

Nevertheless, the informality of the status thwarted clerical efforts to distinguish between "true" and "false" beguines to any degree of satisfaction. For these reasons, the beguine identity invited close scrutiny and high expectations of outward behavior. Even close scrutiny failed to satisfy some observers, however. If behavior and dress served as markers of the beguine, such markers were easily imitated by those who wished to benefit from the good reputations of local beguine communities. Moreover, the reputation of a beguine community depended on the behavior of individual women, who may or may not have been sincerely committed to a life of chastity and good works. As living, visible, unenclosed holy women, beguines had to maintain their claims to sanctity "on an on-going basis."[7] Yet this too could lead to negative assessments of the beguine status, as some beguines were criticized for excessive attachment to the sacraments, ostentatious piety, and spiritual pride. Even as the Parisian poet Rutbeuf acidly claimed that whatever the beguine did, one was expected to perceive her as holy ("In everything the Beguine says, listen only to good"), it was clear that, in some circles, the actions and demeanor of the religious laywoman were consistently read as hypocritical.

Two curious incidents involving beguines and the French court illustrate the striking range of interpretations of beguines in the late thirteenth century.

The first involved a beguine from Nivelles, perhaps Elizabeth of Spalbeek, a woman apparently famed for her prophetic abilities. Rumor of Elizabeth's powers reached the French court by the mid-1270s, where a scandal surrounding Philip III's second wife, Marie of Brabant, was in process of unfolding. According to the chronicle account of the events, when Philip's eldest son Louis suddenly died in 1276, Philip's chamberlain Pierre de la Broce instigated a rumor that Marie had poisoned the dauphin.[8] Reportedly motivated by a desire to curb the influence of Philip's new wife, whom the king had married in 1274, Pierre and his accomplices suggested that Marie murdered the dauphin in order to ensure that her own children would succeed to the French throne.[9] Called upon to weigh in on the accusations against the queen, Elizabeth, after some resistance to the questioning, confirmed her innocence.[10] Curiously, while the Latin and French versions of the incident are nearly identical, they diverge markedly in their assessment of Elizabeth's character. The Latin version, presumably intended for a clerical audience, portrays Elizabeth as a hypocrite and fraud who "lied to God."[11] The French translation, however, characterizes the beguine as a prophetess and "holy woman."[12]

The second incident involved Philip IV. In 1304, a certain "pseudo-mulier" from Metz "under the beguine habit" drew the attention of the French court with her claims to have revelations, which, the chronicler reports, she used to deceive the king, his wife, and members of the court.[13] Ultimately exposed as a fraud, the beguine was arrested and tortured at the instigation of Philip's brother, Charles of Valois. Clearly, the French kings were quick to associate beguines with prophecy, calling upon individual women to advise them on matters of personal and political import. Significantly, chronicle reports on these incidents express extreme skepticism, suggesting that beguines were increasingly viewed as women who falsely and opportunistically claimed to possess the revelatory powers with which they were associated.

Sermons preached to and about beguines in thirteenth-century Paris reveal that some clerics believed that an opportunistic woman could conceal her impious ways beneath her beguine habit and behind the beguinage's walls. In a sermon he preached at the Paris beguinage in 1272, the secular canon Ranulph of Houblonnière expressed his suspicion that the beguine life, which he tellingly associated with the adoption of the beguine habit, could serve as a cover for irreligious behavior. After declaring that the beguinage ought to be a garden of God, Ranulph claimed that among the beautiful roses and violets, there were thistles, ill-smelling violets, and thorny roses.[14] These undesirables in God's garden represented the bad beguines, who, he warned, could discredit the entire community: the beguine whose habit advertises a humble demeanor, but who lashes out when chastised; the beguine who appears chaste and pure but burns with lust; and the seemingly wise beguine who refuses to be instructed.[15] Significantly, Ranulph's sermon presented three "types" of bad beguines posing as their good counterparts. Indeed, the roles these bad beguines assumed corresponded to the models of holiness presented in beguine hagiographies and exempla. In these texts, James of Vitry and his fellow hagiographers depicted their female subjects as humble, chaste, and wise. The bad beguines were expert imitators of these characteristics; underneath their pious exterior (again, represented by their habits) they were proud, lustful, and foolish. By claiming that the beguinage offered the thistles a cover for their evil ways, Ranulph's sermon expressed deep skepticism of the beguine life.

Ranulph's contemporary, the Dominican preacher Giles of Orleans, also expressed the suspicion that there were bad women in the beguinage, warning that the beguines—because already suspect—should hold themselves to a higher standard than other religious women, namely, nuns. Giles's sermon at the beguinage in 1272 warned "corrupt beguines" against leading people into error and especially against bringing scandal to the entire beguinage.[16] Giles opens his sermon with a story about a certain noblewoman who had expressed astonishment when she heard him praise the beguine life, citing the beguines' terrible reputation. The Dominican tells his audience that he defended the beguine life by explaining to the noblewoman that she should not wish to cut down a tree on account of a few bad pieces of fruit. He further pointed out to her that among Christ's apostles there was Judas, and even monasteries were not free from vice.[17] Even as Giles defended the beguinage's reputation, he clearly intended his sermon as a warning to beguines about how easily public perception might turn against them.

Rejecting Giles's defense of the beguinage, the noblewoman insisted that beguinages were to be held to a higher standard than monasteries. In a fascinating critique of the monastic life, she asserted that no one was surprised when a monk or nun behaved badly, since monks and nuns entered the religious life to preserve family status. To illustrate her point, she explained that she herself had several daughters but was unable to make marriages for them according to their station. Rather than marry them off to cobblers, she opted to place them in a convent.[18] This decision, she admitted, was made not out of piety or according to her daughters' religious aspirations, but out of a desire to protect family status. For these reasons, when a nun behaved badly, no one was surprised, since women did not become nuns out of religious zeal.[19] On the other hand, the noblewoman continued, a woman enters a beguinage of her own free will. In a chilling conclusion to her comparison of beguines and nuns, the noblewoman—as reported by Giles—argued that beguines who behaved badly, and thus brought scandal to the entire community of holy and honest women, ought to be stoned.[20]

Clearly, a lot depended on the deportment and reputation of even one beguine. Giles's anecdote, however, calls for closer scrutiny. According to Giles's sermon, social considerations were paramount in the decision to assume the nun's habit. No such considerations were attached to the beguine status. The adoption of the beguine life—whether signaled by a public declaration of conversion (in the sense of a life turn), entry into a beguine community, and/or adoption of special clothing—announced the convert's claim to live a religious life. [21] But evidentiary problems remained. The lay religious woman's lack of a canonically recognized (and therefore canonically protected and monitored) corporate identity meant that she had to take care to live up to the claims that her name announced to others. According to Giles's sermon, a woman who allowed herself to be known as a beguine made a personal promise to live a truly religious life—a life set apart from ordinary Christians—and she did so of her own free will. Thus, medieval observers were particularly scandalized if a beguine failed to live up to this promise. Indeed, her failure cast doubt upon the sincerity of *all* beguines. Unlike nuns, whose reputations could be protected by walls and rules, as well as the reputations of their orders, the beguines' reputations rested upon the name "beguine" itself and the women who laid claim to it.

The secular cleric (and later Victorine canon) Arnoul of Bescochier (d. 1286) also believed that women identifying as beguines should take care to live up to the name. In a sermon preached sometime in the late 1270s, Arnoul argued that the beguine was "benigna" (or kind) on account of her being anointed by the Holy Spirit with the oil of compassion.[22] Those so anointed, Arnoul asserted, were those who took the misfortunes of others upon themselves by virtue of compassion while sharing the good with others by virtue of caritas.[23] Arnoul declares that these virtues ought to be in every holy soul but especially in a woman who is called a beguine. Since the thing (that is, the beguine) is the same as the name (benigna), Arnoul understood the beguine as one who exhibited an outwardly directed piety, manifested in a desire to comfort others while sharing the fruits of her own privileged relationship with God.[24] Women who claimed the name "beguine" without exhibiting love and compassion for others, however, were beguines in name only; and there were consequences for the beguine who failed to live up to her name. Specifically, Arnoul warns that "whatever [the beguine] does is weakened, unless she is as kind as she is able," suggesting that the beguine who does not live up to her name calls into question other aspects of her (public) behavior.[25] Beguines, therefore, had to walk a fine line. Unenclosed, visible, and thus subject to public scrutiny, a beguine who behaved badly brought all women who held the name into disrepute.

Even the Sorbonne cleric Raoul de Châteauroux, a keen supporter of beguines, included some musings on public perceptions of beguines in his collection of distinctiones. In this case, Raoul included an observation by a certain Abbot Nicholas, most probably the same Abbot Nicholas the mistress of the beguinage cited in two sermons she delivered to the beguines.[26] Succinctly presenting the pitfalls the beguine must navigate with regard to her public reputation, Abbot Nicholas declared, "If I were a beguine, I would not want to be of great name, nor less, because less causes scandal, more is occasion for vainglory."[27] The abbot's point, which Raoul significantly categorized under the heading *hypocrisis,* is that the beguine has much to lose either way. Admiration will lead to pride, but defamation will bring irreparable harm to her reputation, as well as that of others known by that name. The decision to live as a beguine, then, was a voluntary assumption of a religious identity loaded with expectations. Beguines had to be ever vigilant in living up to the claim to holiness their name and dress signified.

Love and Knowledge

As we have seen, the beguines' supporters acknowledged and even valued such skepticism of the beguine life. Keenly aware of their responsibilities toward and authority over Christian society, some Parisian preachers embraced these negative images of beguines in order to demonstrate their own desire to humble themselves. Robert of Sorbon's sermons expressed the notion that the contempt with which some observers regarded the beguines was a positive, indeed essential, aspect of the beguine life. Moreover, it was an aspect Robert advocated for university clerics, who, he believed, were too concerned with studying, debating, and advancing their careers. Yet his efforts to present beguines as models for university clerics presented some challenges to clerical masculinity. The university was an environment in which clerical manliness was molded through competition with other men.[28] Over the course of the thirteenth century, as theologians struggled to preserve their positions within the university and demonstrate their theological expertise, the model of the humble beguine became increasingly incompatible with these goals.

In fact, rather than recognize the similarities noted by clerics such as Robert, many saw only difference. Here, too, the gender implications were complex. As John Coakley has shown, some clerics believed that the holy women in their care were favored with a more intimate relationship with God than the clerics themselves could experience. Such clerics were both fascinated by and envious of their female penitents, since these women brought to mind the clerics' own perceived limitations.[29] Coakley suggests that this relationship between female mystics and male clerics was initially based on the notion that the women's mystical experiences and the clerics' religious authority served complementary goals, namely, to fight heresy and strengthen the resolve of wavering Christians.[30]

Several Parisian sermons and exempla reflect this gendered division of religious roles. The pastoral miscellany Pierre of Limoges donated to the Sorbonne library at his death in 1306 contains a particularly detailed exemplum describing an encounter between a Parisian master and a weeping beguine. The master asks the beguine to explain to him the cause of her weeping. She tells him that the cause of her tears, which outweighs the sorrow she feels for her own and others' sins and the plight of the poor, is the absence of her spouse, that is, Christ.[31] Persisting in his questioning, the master asks the beguine to explain to him what she knows about the one for whom she weeps. In response, she admits that she knows only that Jesus suffered, died, and was resurrected for all of humankind. At this, the master wonders how it is that, though he knows more about God than the beguine, he is not affected in the same manner as the beguine, namely, with this gift of tears.[32] Comparing love (*affectus*) with knowledge (*intellectus*), the master, citing the Book of Job, laments that he has "fed the barren," meaning knowledge, but has "done no good to the widow," meaning love.[33] He proceeds to ask the beguine to teach *him* how to experience the affective love by which the beguine is so consumed. Employing the tools of the medieval preacher, she instructs the master by relaying to him an exemplum. This exemplum compares the master's pursuit of knowledge and deeper meaning in Holy Scripture to a tigress gazing at her reflection in a mirror. Hunters plot to steal the tigress's young but naturally fear their ferocious mother. To avoid encountering the tigress, they place a mirror in her path in order to distract her. Believing her own reflection to be her offspring, the tigress gazes upon the mirror, thus lingering in the path and allowing the hunters to escape with her young.[34] The beguine explains the meaning of her exemplum: "Because you see many mirrors in Holy Scripture, upon which you gaze, your love [*affectum*] is impeded."[35] It is the beguine's lack of text-based knowledge, then, that allows her to surpass the cleric in experiential knowledge of God.

This exemplum expresses a consciousness of the different types of knowledge in which the beguine and the cleric excel. The beguine's knowledge, she admits and the master knows, is simpler in terms of its content, but more direct and experiential than scholarly, text-based knowledge. The master knows that he knows more about theology, but he does not feel rewarded, nor does he feel that he has been looking in the right places. Thus, he seeks to learn from the beguine.[36] By presenting the beguine mystic as the theologian's superior in matters of devotion, the exemplum, like other texts in this pastoral miscellany, aimed to encourage male clerics to focus more on prayer and contemplation rather than solely on study and disputations. Yet this exemplum also suggests a rivalry between the learned master and the beguine. As women, beguines were supposed to remain under the control of their confessors; however, as holy women, through their spiritual gifts, they were able to connect with God (and perhaps the wider laity) on a level that the learned cleric did not conceive as possible for himself. Significantly, the association of beguines with mystical experiences, a common theme in the beguine vitae, became part of a discourse comparing beguines with learned theologians.

Comparisons between the beguine and the Parisian master appeared in several thirteenth-century sermons and exempla. In a sermon he preached to the nuns at Saint-Antoine in 1272, Giles of Orleans related a story about a well-spoken beguine. Giles declared that this beguine's explanation of the value of listening to the word of God could not have been better if it had been articulated by "the best cleric in Paris."[37] Several exempla depicted beguines and Parisian clerics in conversation. In one such exemplum, a Parisian theologian asks a beguine to explain her way of life. The beguine answers: "We know to love God, to confess, to know God, the seven sacraments, to love our neighbors and to distinguish between the vices and virtues, to have humility without pride, love without hate, patience in tribulation, clear knowledge of God and the Holy Church, and are ready to suffer everything for God: all this is the beguinage."[38] After the theologian heard the beguine's description of her way of life, he remarked, "Thus you know more about divinity than all the masters of Paris."[39]

It is not without significance, moreover, that leaders of beguine communities were often called *magistra*, a term with clear scholarly implications that would have been well known in medieval Paris. As Walter Simons has noted, the term "magister" was used to describe clerics who had completed their studies at a studium generale and, by the early fourteenth century, graduates who had earned their teaching licenses.[40] Indeed, any cleric with a reputation for teaching and preaching might be known by this title. To draw on one other parallel between university scholars and beguines, it is worth noting that the chapel of the Paris beguinage was dedicated to Saint Catherine of Alexandria, patron saint of scholars and co-patron of the University of Paris. Catherine of Alexandria was also, significantly, associated with preaching.[41]

As we have seen, preaching was a fraught issue for the medieval church, both internally and with regard to its relationship with the laity. Disagreement about the mendicants' role in teaching the laity, as well as enduring concerns about the unauthorized preaching of Cathars and Waldensians, compelled theologians, particularly at the University of Paris, to debate the question of what sectors of medieval society had the right to preach. Further, saintly examples of female preachers, known to the laity through the Bible and collections of saints' lives, especially James of Voragine's popular *Legenda Aurea* (compiled 1255–1266), posed difficulties.[42] Over time, theologians felt increasingly compelled to reconcile their position on women preachers with their own justification for preaching: in other words, was the preacher authorized by grace or by training? Theologians argued that only properly trained clerics could claim the right to preach; a female apostolate carried out by saints such as Mary Magdalen and Catherine of Alexandria was permissible only during the early days of the church, when there were few to carry out the task.[43] As Carolyn Meussig has shown, sermons preached on the feasts of Mary Magdalen and Catherine of Alexandria pointedly mention the preaching gifts of these two women, characterizing their abilities as exceptional.[44]

Parisian preachers could hardly deny that beguines frequently assumed an active lay apostolate. Negative commentaries about beguines, such as those articulated by the Parisian poet Rutebeuf, indicate that beguines were known for assuming this function from the very first mention of their communities in the historical record. In *Les Ordres de Paris*, Rutebeuf referenced the beguines' proselytizing efforts as neighbors of the Carmelites:

The Carmelites are near the beguines.
They have a hundred and eighty of them for their neighbors[.]
They only have to go out the door
So that by divine authority,

By example and by doctrine
They can teach each other
Not to fall into error.[45]

It is not without significance that it was precisely at this time, not long after theologians such as Thomas Aquinas, Henry of Ghent, and Humbert of Romans debated the right of women to give religious instruction (of course, all concluding that women were explicitly barred from preaching), that Raoul de Châteauroux included sermons preached by the mistress of the Paris beguinage in his collection of distinctiones.[46] In one sense, the position of the mistress as both preacher and representative beguine imbued her preaching with authority. The inclusion of her sermons in a text intended for the use of preachers in the composition of future sermons places the mistress's preaching on a level reserved for male clerics. If preaching is citational—meaning that it must draw on authoritative texts while, at the same time, exist as a potentially citable authority for future preachers—the inclusion of the mistress among patristic, scholastic, and pastoral authorities is particularly noteworthy.[47] Significantly, Raoul's inclusion of the mistress's sermons is not accompanied by any note of apology for including the words of a woman. There is no reference to the mistress's preaching being inspired by God or legitimized by divine inspiration. Of course, we may assume that the sermons were originally preached to the beguines themselves—in other words, in private—but Raoul does not go to the trouble to assure the reader of this fact. It is not at all clear how he came to possess these sermons to begin with.

The image of the beguine who possessed a spiritual authority from which male clerics were barred, or carried out a lay ministry independently of the ordained clergy, was one over which clerics recognized they might lose control, particularly if real women began to enact the model. Several Parisian preachers, in fact, accused the beguines of pride and arrogance. In 1272, the secular cleric Gérard of Reims targeted beguines in a sermon focused on the theme of judgment. In his first elaboration of the theme "the judgment of rashness," Gérard employed Matthew 7:1 ("Do not judge, so that you may not be judged"), warning beguines (and nuns) that in judging others, they themselves will be judged by God.[48] Paraphrasing a letter from Jerome to a mother and daughter living in Gaul, Gérard referred to beguines, saying, "It is unsuitable to isolate oneself while the tongue wanders through the world."[49] Here, Gérard alludes to the beguines' ostensibly isolated life while criticizing those who judge the whole world but wish to be condemned by no one.[50]

The Franciscan minister general Bonaventure warned the beguines against having too much pride in their knowledge. His concern that the beguines thought too highly of their intellectual and spiritual gifts is clearly expressed in a comparison of two sermons preached on the same day in 1273. Bonaventure preached first to the Cistercian nuns at Saint-Antoine and then to the beguines in the Paris beguinage, choosing wisdom as his theme in both sermons. As Nicole Bériou has observed, Bonaventure's discussion of wisdom varied significantly in the two sermons. In the sermon to the Cistercian nuns, Bonaventure encouraged his audience to retreat from the world, quoting Ecclesiastes 27:12 ("In wisdom remain"). In this sermon, he claimed that wisdom was best attained through the contemplative, isolated existence. In the sermon at the beguinage, however, he based his message on the Wisdom of Solomon 7:13 ("I have learned without guile and imparted without grudging"). He did not emphasize contemplation in the sermon to the beguines. Instead, he warned them against arrogance and teaching things about which they lack sufficient knowledge, saying, "Just as he sins who knows and does not wish to learn first, so also does he who does not know and wishes to be master."[51] Like Ranulph of Houblonnière, who complained about seemingly wise beguines who refuse to be instructed, Bonaventure represented beguines as too proud of their knowledge. The difference in Bonaventure's approaches to the two groups of women suggests a growing suspicion that beguines were active, not only in charitable works, but also in discussing matters of faith.

The clearest and most famous expression of clerical concern about the Parisian beguines' noncontemplative activities was Gilbert of Tournai's report to Pope Gregory IX in preparation for the Second Council of Lyons (1274). In this report Gilbert voices his extreme disapproval of certain activities in which he believes beguines are involved, claiming:

> There are among us women called beguines, and some of them
> thrive on subtleties and delight in novelties. They have in translation
> mysteries of the Scriptures, rendered into ordinary French, which
> are hardly understood even by experts in Holy Scripture. They
> read them in common, irreverently, audaciously, in study groups,
> workshops, and in the public squares. I have seen, and read and
> held a Bible in French, whose exemplar is displayed publicly by the

booksellers of Paris so that heresies and errors, dubious and absurd interpretations might be copied.[52]

Gilbert's commentary conveys clerical anxieties about beguine encroachment upon the intellectual territory of the educated male elite. The commentary demonstrates that some clerics believed that beguines audaciously engaged in activities unsuitable for the laity, especially women.

The "Beguine Clergesse" in Paris

Parisian sermons not only reflect clerical confusion about how to classify and categorize beguines, they demonstrate that Parisian scholars found in the beguine status a useful focus through which to debate some of the pressing issues and concerns of their day. Parisian clerics worked out the basis of their own preaching authority by vociferously denying women the right to preach. All the while, preachers (paradoxically) alluded approvingly to certain female preachers and copied sermons preached by beguines into pastoral manuals. Beguine involvement in actively promulgating the Word, whether as praiseworthy disseminators of collections of vices and virtues or as sinister propagators of erroneous copies of scripture, seemed to blur the already dim line between *exhortatio* and *praedicatio*. Finally, while questioning the legitimacy of their intellectual approaches to divine knowledge, Parisian clerics referred to the knowledge beguines acquired by virtue of their mystical encounters with God.

By the early fourteenth century, many of these issues remained unresolved. Moreover, they were evident in the person and work of the "beguine clergesse" Marguerite Porete. Sometime during the mid-1290s, Marguerite wrote her *Mirror of Simple Souls* in the French vernacular, describing the annihilation of the soul, specifically its descent into a state of no-thingness, of union with God without distinction. Structured as a courtly dialogue between Love, Reason, and the Soul, Marguerite's book was clearly intended in part as a guide for other would-be "simple" souls. Although often perceived as a lone figure, Marguerite likely had connections with a community of clerics, beguines, and laypeople, upon whom she drew for support and among whom she circulated copies of her book.[53] Within Marguerite's *Mirror* are critiques of both reliance on Reason and reliance on works, broadly reflecting two communities—scholars and laywomen—with which she evidently had close relations.[54]

For Marguerite, Reason was what ruled "Holy Church the Lesser," since Reason was incapable of understanding Love's teachings. Throughout the first eighty-seven chapters of *The Mirror of Simple Souls*, Love attempts to explain to Reason how the Soul can become annihilated in God's love. Reason, however, is constantly perplexed, often complaining that Love's teachings are full of confusing paradoxes. The Soul responds to Reason's complaint, declaring, "What strange conclusions you reach! You take the straw and leave the grain, because your understanding is too base."[55] Marguerite's book further asserts that the Annihilated Soul seeks guidance in God, "whose teaching is not written down either in books or examples or in the teachings of men."[56] Marguerite even criticizes the learned elite, saying that by living by the counsel of Reason, these clerics are "stupid and asinine," and because of their stupidity, she must "be silent and . . . circumspect in [her] words."[57]

Here, perhaps, Marguerite was referring to her own frustrating experience trying to convince churchmen that the *Mirror* was theologically sound. The proceedings against her indicate that, sometime around 1300, Marguerite's book came to the attention of the bishop of Cambrai, Guido of Collemezzo.[58] While it is not known why or how the book came to his attention, it is possible that Marguerite herself sent him a copy in the hopes of gaining his approval.[59] Certainly, the extant records of her trial suggest a woman confident in the truths expressed in her book and determined to have her ideas heard and understood. Instead of endorsing the book, however, the bishop declared it heretical and ordered it to be publicly burned in Valenciennes, the town where Marguerite probably lived at that time.[60] According to the records of her trial, he informed her that she would be handed over to secular authorities should she attempt to disseminate her ideas, whether in oral or written form.[61] Apparently undeterred by his warning, she added several chapters to the original version, probably in an effort to clarify her ideas for those whose understanding, like that of the bishop of Cambrai, was "too base."[62]

It was most certainly at this time that Marguerite sought authoritative support for her book by sending or showing copies of the revised *Mirror* to churchmen whose approval—she hoped—would carry some weight with ecclesiastical authorities.[63] Ultimately, she managed to obtain statements of approval from three clerics—a Franciscan called John of Querayn; Dom Franc, chanter of the Cistercian abbey of Villers; and Godfrey of Fontaines, a secular master of theology. As Sean Field has shown, Marguerite's connection with Godfrey of Fontaines is worth exploring in some detail, since it sheds considerable light on Marguerite's relationship to ecclesiastical authority and her "seemingly paradoxical" actions, specifically the energy and determination with which she circulated her work contrasted with her resolute silence at her trial in Paris.[64] This connection is also significant when we consider Godfrey's affiliation with the Sorbonne and Paris's beguine community. While a student in Paris, Godfrey was in attendance at the beguinage chapel when Robert of Sorbon delivered his sermon praising the beguine life as superior to that of the prud'homme.[65] Evidently, Godfrey valued the sermon enough to record and preserve it in one of his personal manuscripts.[66] Although we cannot know the extent to which he shared Robert's admiration for the beguine life, he was, perhaps, particularly inclined to consider the views of this determined beguine, the book's previous condemnation by the bishop of Cambrai notwithstanding.

Having acquired statements from a Franciscan, a Cistercian, and one of the best-known secular theologians in the region, Marguerite appended these approbations to a new epilogue and proceeded to circulate her book anew, eventually sending a copy to John, bishop of Châlons-sur-Marne. There is very little in the historical record that helps explain why she thought it wise to share her book with Bishop John. Whatever her reasons, it is clear that she held out hope that she would eventually win ecclesiastical approval for her work. Perhaps she believed that the approbations of respected churchmen, including a renowned theologian, in some ways outweighed the condemnation of the bishop of Cambrai. In any case, she seems to have had a great deal of confidence that the bishop of Châlons-sur-Marne would read and understand her book.

In this assumption, Marguerite could not have been more wrong. Finding that the bishop of Cambrai had previously condemned the book, John brought Marguerite to the attention of the inquisitor of Lorraine, who summoned the new bishop of Cambrai, Philip of Marigny. Bishop Philip, brother to Philip IV's influential chamberlain Enguerran and himself closely affiliated with the royal court, soon handed Marguerite over to the inquisitor of Paris.[67]

It is worth pausing here to speculate why. On the surface, Marguerite's case seems to have been straightforward enough for the new bishop of Cambrai to have handled himself. After all, Marguerite had confessed to disobeying the previous bishop's order to cease circulating her book. The previous bishop had warned her, in writing, that persisting to circulate her ideas would lead to her being declared a heretic and handed over to secular authorities. Yet, as Sean Field has argued, there is much to suggest that Philip of Marigny sent the case to Paris either out of a desire to pass the problem on to someone better qualified to decide the question of Marguerite's orthodoxy (especially if the bishop had been aware of the three churchmen's approbations) or because of his political connections to Philip IV.[68] At the time of Marguerite's transfer to the Parisian inquisitor, William of Paris, the latter was embroiled in the controversial trial of the Templars. A royal confessor and inquisitor, William was charged with both "the spiritual safety of the realm and the personal salvation of the monarch."[69] It was in this capacity and within this context that he prosecuted Marguerite's case.

Marguerite, for her part, refused to take the oath that would allow William of Paris to proceed with the case. Her refusal to cooperate might be explained as a strategy designed to drag out the proceedings in hopes that some other form of support might emerge.[70] Proceeding with the utmost care, William eventually gathered together twenty-one theologians, to whom he showed fifteen excerpts from Marguerite's book.[71] That so many theologians—almost the entire faculty of the University of Paris—turned up to judge the book suggests that they considered the matter one of significance and within their purview, not the bishop of Cambrai's or even the inquisitor's.[72] It seems likely, moreover, that the approbation of Godfrey of Fontaines would have given both the inquisitor and the university faculty pause.

According to the trial records, the assembled theologians unanimously declared that the *Mirror* "should be exterminated as heretical and erroneous."[73] Having established the heretical content of the *Mirror*, and thus canceling out the positive statements of Godfrey of Fontaines and others, William consulted four regent masters of canon law in an effort to determine Marguerite's fate. It was at this consultation, on 9 May 1310, that William informed the canonists that the accused not only defied ecclesiastical orders but also preached her ideas by sharing her work with "many other simple people—*beghards* and others—as a good book."[74] In light of these facts, the canonists decreed that "this *beguina* . . . be judged relapsed and deservedly relinquished to the secular court."[75]

Thus, according to the judgment of Paris's preeminent experts in theology and canon law, Marguerite and her book were heretical. Not long after, on 31 May, William gathered clerics, royal officials, and ordinary laypeople at the Place de Grève. Before this crowd, he publicly pronounced Marguerite "not only as one fallen into heresy, but as a relapsed heretic," and relinquished her to the secular authorities for justice.[76] The very next day she was publicly burned in the Place de Grève on the order of the provost of Paris.[77]

According to the record of William's public statements against Marguerite, the inquisitor did not refer to her as a "beguine," possibly in an effort to avoid jeopardizing the reputation of the king's beguines. Yet contemporary chroniclers easily made the association, for in many ways this "clergesse" was emblematic of the learned, active beguine both criticized and praised in the sermons of Parisian preachers. John Baconthorpe, an English theologian who came to study in Paris not long after Marguerite's execution, described her as a "certain beguine who published a little book against the clergy."[78] The vernacular *Grandes chroniques de France* described Marguerite as a "beguine clergesse" who had circulated errors regarding the articles of the faith and sacrament of the altar.[79] Even if William of Paris deliberately left out any reference to Marguerite's identity as a beguine in his public condemnation of her ideas and behaviour, observers were quick to use the label.

As home to a well-known and generally well-regarded community of beguines with close ties to the University of Paris, the French royal family, and the urban elite, Paris could have been an ideal place for Marguerite to make a case for herself and her book. Yet the beguine's dogged efforts to disseminate her teachings, her defiance of clerical authority, and her criticism of reason and works must have raised concerns among Parisian clerics who already perceived in the local beguine community arrogance, hypocrisy, and a threat to learned male authority. Indeed, it did not take long for clerics to attribute Marguerite's ideas and behavior to all beguines. In 1311, at least six of the twenty-one Parisian theologians who passed judgement upon Marguerite's book participated in the Council of Vienne, where ecclesiastical officials made several specific connections between Marguerite's ideas and deeds and the beguine status.[80] Although the fate of beguines was by no means the only matter of church business discussed at the council (the case of the Knights Templar, for instance, was a major issue), the council eventually produced two confusing and contradictory decrees targeting beguines in general while offering ambiguously worded exceptions for "faithful women." The second decree, *Ad nostrum*, listed eight "errors" allegedly espoused by beguines and their male counterparts, beghards, who according to the decree constituted an "abominable sect." Like the first decree, *Cum de quibusdam*, this second decree condemned the beguine status but specifically targeted communities in German lands.[81] *Cum de quibusdam* had a more direct effect on Parisian beguines and is quoted here in full:

Since certain women commonly known as beguines neither promise obedience to anyone, nor renounce personal property, nor profess any approved rule, they are by no means considered religious, although they wear a so-called beguine habit and attach themselves to certain religious to whom they are drawn by special affection. Reports have come to us from trustworthy sources that some of them, as if having been led into insanity, dispute and preach about the highest Trinity and the divine essence and introduce opinions contrary to the Catholic faith concerning the articles of the faith and the sacraments of the church. They lead many simple people who are deceived in such things into various errors, and they do and commit much else under the veil of sanctity that occasions danger to souls. Having frequently heard from these and from others about their perverse opinions, on account of which they have merited suspicion, we, with the approval of the sacred council, declare that their status ought to be perpetually prohibited and completely abolished from the church of God. We expressly enjoin upon these and all other women under pain of excommunication, which we wish those who do otherwise incur automatically, that they no longer follow this way of life in any way whatsoever, regardless of whether they adopted it some time ago or whether, having once lived it, they take it up anew. Moreover, we strictly forbid under the penalty of similar excommunication, which they shall immediately incur if they act otherwise, those previously mentioned religious, who are said to have favored those women and to have induced them to take up this way of life in the beguinage, to admit any woman who formerly adopted the status in question or who perhaps wish to take it up again, or to give to these sectarians any counsel, aid, or favor; no privilege availing against the above. Of course by the preceding we in no way intend to forbid any faithful women, whether or not they promise chastity, from living honestly in their dwellings, doing penance, and serving the Lord in a spirit of humility, this being allowed to them as the Lord inspires them.[82]

Cum de quibusdam, which affected lay religious women in cities and towns all over northern Europe, clearly evokes the actions and behavior Parisian clerics attributed to the beguines to whom they ministered. Indeed, the "reports" that had come to the council regarding the behavior of beguines could easily have come from the Parisian clerics in attendance. More broadly, the decrees suggest the difficulties clerical and secular authorities experienced defining and controlling female religious expression. Marguerite's life and work reflected widely held notions about beguines as actively engaged in theological discussion. At the same time, her ideas (misunderstood as antisacerdotal and antinomian) and contentious relationship with ecclesiastical authority refracted back upon living communities of lay religious women.

CHAPTER 7

The King's Beguines

Even as church authorities condemned the beguine status at the Council of Vienne in 1311–1312, the French kings took charge of rehabilitating the reputation of the beguinage, calling attention to the community's sainted founder and tying their own support of the beguines to their place in this saintly line. After almost a decade of confused, selective, or opportunistic implementation of Vienne's contradictory legislation against beguines, which left lay religious women all over northern Europe vulnerable to harassment, loss of property, or worse, King Charles IV (r. 1322–1328) issued a new set of statutes for the Paris beguinage. The preface to the statutes unequivocally affirmed royal support of the community by recalling "Saint Louis [who] among other works of mercy that he did during his life, had acquired an enclosure of houses in Paris located near the Barbel gate, and he placed there good and honest beguines to serve our Lord chastely."[1] Louis IX's sanctity, as manifested in his personal behavior and deeds, which included his foundation of the beguinage, was actively promoted by his successors in the creation of a "cult of kingship."[2] Just as narratives, such as the life and deeds of Saint Louis, and symbols, ceremonies, shrines, and public works served to communicate the link between Capetian lineage and sanctity, the beguinage was one of the symbols by which French kings projected and preserved an image of themselves as "the Most Christian Kings."[3]

Louis's foundation of a beguinage in Paris, then, had long-term significance for religious laywomen in Paris. Although Louis's successors did not necessarily exhibit the intense humility and charity of their sainted forebear, the concept of the royal family as a holy lineage—or *beata stirps*—meant that Louis's successors recognized the importance of supporting his foundations, including the beguinage. Louis's biographies, which highlight his religious and charitable foundations, were read at court, ensuring that his successors were aware of the connections between the royal beguinage and its residents and their sainted ancestor.[4] In recognition of the community's significance to the royal image and reputation, the French kings carefully preserved the original mission and, as far as possible, the structure and organization of Louis's foundation, which they kept under strict royal control.[5]

Royal support for the beguinage was particularly important in the early decades of the fourteenth century. Despite the beguinage's reputation as a royal foundation, chronicle accounts indicate that even the king's beguines were not unaffected by the accusations leveled in the Vienne decrees. Indeed, Parisian beguines may have been among the decrees' primary targets. As we have seen, sermons and vernacular literature composed and circulated in Paris associated beguines with preaching and teaching. Paris, moreover, was the city in which Marguerite Porete publicly met her end for writing and circulating a book deemed heretical and, as the records of her trial report, sharing her ideas with "many other simple people."[6] In many ways, she represented the zealous beguine (as celebrated in Robert of Sorbon's writings) gone too far.

Nevertheless, the beguines of Paris, though not above suspicion, benefited from their association with Louis's memory. The French kings continually expressed their affection for the beguines of Paris through requests for the beguines' prayers, testamentary bequests, and consistent material support. Indeed, French royal support of the beguine life was so widely known that the beguines of Ghent emphasized Louis's admiration of their beguinage in their attempts to defend their way of life against detractors.[7] Although university clerics might have become wary of closely associating themselves with the beguinage of Paris, the French kings responded to the Vienne decrees with a forceful argument for the orthodoxy of "their" beguines, sustaining the beguinage as a viable option for women who wished to pursue a religious life in the world. Indeed, in spite of the ravages of the fourteenth century, when plague, war, and economic crisis posed serious challenges to the survival of many a religious community, the beguinage endured into the late fifteenth century, when, through royal initiative, the house was transformed into a convent for Observant Poor Clares.

In Memory of Saint Louis: Royal Patronage of Beguines

Charity, as Xavier de La Selle has argued, was a virtue essential to medieval conceptions of good kingship.[8] Accordingly, charitable giving was enormously important for the Capetian public image. The French kings had long allocated funds for specific religious houses, hospitals, and communities. During his reign, Philip Augustus (r. 1180–1223) established a formal system of royal almsgiving, delegating the task of distributing royal charity to a special officer, the almoner.[9] In 1260, Louis IX expanded the number of recipients of royal alms, adding more houses, many of which he himself founded, and increasing the amounts given as gifts in money and kind.[10] Louis's successors followed the precedents established by their saintly forebear by means of the royal almonry. During his reign, Philip IV initiated a significant reorganization and rationalization of the royal system of charity.[11] Ending the more casual distributions of food for which his grandfather was celebrated, Philip systematized the allocation of ordinary alms in money and kind.[12] One of the best-documented categories of royal alms was the "ordinary" disbursement of Lenten alms. These disbursements, however, were highly irregular and became increasingly unreliable over the course of the fourteenth century.[13] Nevertheless, the French kings seem to have gone to considerable effort to continue to recognize the various beneficiaries of royal alms originally favored by Louis IX.

Yet royal foundations, such as the Quinze-Vingts and the beguinage, as well as royally favored institutions, such as the Hôtel-Dieu and Filles-Dieu, were not among the recipients of Lenten alms. For these institutions, Louis's successors organized separate, more reliable systems of royal support. The Quinze-Vingts, for example, collected its annual alms directly from the royal treasury rather than receive these disbursements from the almonry.[14] The beguines received regular payments for the support of individual beguines, communal expenses, and building maintenance through a separate account administered by the canons of Sainte-Chapelle.[15]

The beguines, as we have seen, held special importance for Saint Louis, and during his life members of the royal family already exhibited interest in supporting the king's foundation for beguines. In 1265, not long after Louis founded the Paris beguinage, his brother Alphonse of Poitiers (d. 1271) gave one hundred sous tournai in alms to the community.[16] Alphonse remembered the beguines again in his will, drawn up in 1270, with ten livres tournois.[17] After Louis's death in 1270, his successors tied themselves to their holy predecessor's legacy by supporting his foundations and emulating—as far as possible—the forms of support he had offered to various religious and charitable institutions in Paris and throughout the kingdom. In this, Louis's testament, which meticulously listed the various recipients of his generosity, served as the template.[18] Louis, it will be remembered, bequeathed substantial funds for the maintenance of the Paris beguinage, as well as a smaller amount to support the poorer members of the community.[19] In addition, "poor beguines" throughout the kingdom received one hundred livres, to be distributed as certain "good men" saw fit.[20] Louis also requested that his successors respect and maintain the provisions, specifically the pensions, that he had instituted for "honest women called beguines" living throughout the realm. These pensions, alluded to in the testament and described in greater detail in the vita of William of Saint-Pathus, were apparently offered to an unspecified number of beguines, poor scholars, and converted Jews, attesting to Louis's commitment to supporting all three groups.[21]

Testaments and royal account books demonstrate that Louis's successors modeled their personal charitable acts, as well as a more official system for disbursing royal alms and subsidies, on Louis's example. In 1282, Louis's son Pierre d'Alençon bequeathed one hundred sous to the Paris beguinage and sixty sous to various houses located in the more established centers of beguine life in the Low Countries, with a request for masses and prayers.[22] Louis's successor, Philip III, who died in October 1285, left six hundred livres tournois to the Paris beguinage, strong evidence that it had become a religious institution of considerable importance to the French kings.[23] Like his father, Philip also left one hundred livres to "the other poor beguines in our lands."[24]

Philip IV, who employed Louis's memory to his advantage during his clashes with Pope Boniface VIII, carried on his grandfather's support for beguines and beguine houses by designating royal funds for the various small beguine convents throughout the kingdom.[25] In 1308, Philip gave the beguines of Senlis alms for the purpose of purchasing clothing and wood.[26] The royal accounts also list payments of what appear to be pensions for six beguines of Senlis.[27] Likewise, nine beguines of Orleans each received pensions in the amount of seven sous and four deniers per week.[28] Beguine convents throughout the kingdom are also listed in the accounts as recipients of royal support.[29] Finally, the account books note payments to individual beguines in the realm, possibly indicating a more personal relationship with residents of these royally sponsored beguine houses.[30] Like beguine convents in the Low Countries and Germany, these houses were generally quite small, ranging from seven to twelve beguine residents. Royal support for these houses, distributed on a regular basis, underline the French kings' support for lay religiosity in a variety of forms and contexts.

The pattern of royal patronage of beguines seems to have been based on Louis's example. Although incomplete and fragmentary, royal account books affirm that Louis's successors faithfully paid pensions for individual beguines in Paris and throughout the kingdom while also allocating specific funds for the upkeep of the Paris beguinage and its buildings. Royal support for beguines was not, however, administered by the almoner. Sometime in the 1280s, Philip III established a special account for allocating royal funding to the beguinage, an account that was shared with poor scholars, converted Jews, and special building projects around the royal residences in Paris and Vincennes.[31] Evidence for this separate account, largely overlooked in the scholarly literature, is found in the various published account books from the reigns of Philip III and his successors.[32] The account was managed by a royal appointee, who was sometimes described as a "payer of pensions for scholars and beguines."[33] In every reference to this particular account, the appointee can be identified as a canon of Sainte-Chapelle.[34]

The choice of the canons is significant from a religious and practical perspective. Louis IX founded the college of canons in 1246 to watch over the Passion relics in Sainte-Chapelle.[35] The college initially consisted of a master chaplain and seven principal chaplains. In 1314 Philip IV added four canons, and in 1318 his son, Philip V, added a twelfth and final prebend. The canons' houses were located alongside administrative buildings such as the Chambre des Comptes, the Chambre des Monnaies, the Chancellerie, and the Chambre aux Deniers. It is little wonder, then, that so many canons of Sainte-Chapelle served in an administrative capacity at some point during their careers.[36] Indeed, over the course of the fourteenth and fifteenth centuries, the canons came to dominate royal administrative posts associated with the royal purse. The personnel of the Chambre des Comptes was commonly drawn from the canons of Sainte-Chapelle, and the French kings frequently designated a canon of Sainte-Chapelle as royal almoner.[37] Testaments and property records reveal that some canons maintained close ties with individual beguines. These ties may have developed as a result of the canons' regular dealings with the beguinage, or the canons may have used their influence to acquire a spot in the beguinage for a close female relative or family friend.[38] While existing evidence does not reveal the full nature of these ties between beguines and the canons, it is clear that the canons' attachment to the beguinage was not limited to their administrative responsibilities.[39]

Significantly, royal account books list payments to beguines in the kingdom as a public work. For example, one of the first extant entries concerning royal disbursements to the beguinage of Paris is listed under the heading "concerning the works of the king."[40] After "poor scholars" and converted Jews, the beguines of Paris are included as recipients of pensions amounting to twenty-nine livres and eight sous.[41] The relatively complete rolls of the *Journaux du Trésor*, which cover the reign of Philip the Fair (r. 1285–1314) and for which several consecutive years of entries survive, show that each month one canon of Sainte-Chapelle received several hundred livres, and sometimes even one thousand livres, "for the works of the king and other things."[42] Often, these entries specify that these "other things" were allocations for beguines, scholars, and converted Jews.[43] Given the importance of the university and the realm's cherished reputation as "Most Christian," it is no surprise that university scholars and converted Jews were among the recipients of the kings' support, and that the pensions of scholars and converted Jews would be maintained as part of the works of the kingdom. That the beguines were grouped alongside these two groups suggests that the French kings perceived support of beguines to be an equally important part of their duty as rulers.[44]

Details relating to these pensions are frustratingly difficult to uncover. We are not told, for example, if they were intended for certain favored or senior members of the community (the mistress, for example) or for its neediest members. The royal account books rarely specify the number of pensioners, and the amount of the pension is only occasionally cited for a handful of individuals. Moreover, the criteria for determining beneficiaries are not specified in the available sources. A register from the fifteenth century detailing disbursements of royal funds to the beguine convent in Orleans, which was also founded by Louis IX, provides some interesting clues, however. The register reports that the royal almoner delivered funds to the mistress and beguines of the Orleans beguinage, which was composed of thirteen women at the time, and specifies the amounts to which each beguine was entitled. The amounts seem to have been based on hierarchical divisions within the community, but perhaps also on economic need. According to the register, "the mistress should have two sous per week and 40 sous per year for her clothing." Another six beguines of the community were entitled to eighteen deniers per week and twenty sous per year for clothing. The remaining six received slightly less: twelve deniers per week and twenty sous per year for clothing.[45]

A handful of entries reveal that the French kings honored the precedents set by Louis by allocating funds for beguines deemed needy. Royal accounts categorized these allocations as "alms," payments that conveyed the royal family's charitable concern for individual beguines living in the beguinage.[46] Like the payments to the beguine convent at Orleans described above, the payments to the Paris beguinage reveal that a specific number of beguines benefited from these disbursements. For example, in March and May 1284, the canon Pierre de Condé delivered fourteen livres and eight sous to sixteen beguines.[47] Similar entries suggest that this disbursement for needy beguines was allocated on a regular basis.[48] They do not, however, specify the criteria for determining the amount to which each beguine was entitled, or if the number of beguine recipients of these alms was fixed at sixteen.

Some entries specifically name the recipients of royal pensions and the purposes for which the funds were intended. For May 1332, an entry in the *Journaux* states that the canon of Sainte-Chapelle in charge of the account, Jean de La Chapelle, was given sixteen livres and nineteen sous, which he was to deliver to "Emeline de Blangy and Emeline Vandes, beguines, for un-paid pensions and clothing that the said beguines take possession of from the alms of the king." This amount, apparently, represented moneys owed to the two women since May 1320.[49] Another beguine received several disbursements from the royal almoner from 1293 to 1305 for clothing.[50] In 1334, a beguine identified only as "Alice la beguine" was granted eighteen deniers tournois every week.[51] An account from 1349 records the names of several beguines who were to receive disbursements between four to six deniers per day from the royal treasury.[52] It is unclear whether the individual beguines who benefited from these pensions were needy in the economic sense. The royal account books rarely identify beguines by name, and, as yet, no information about the property holdings and relative wealth of the individual beguines who bene-fited from these alms has been uncovered.

Records concerning payments made by the canons of Sainte-Chapelle show that the French kings paid the seigneurial dues the beguinage owed the abbey of Tiron at least until 1327.[53] The canons also compensated the mistress of the beguinage for expenses related to maintenance of the enclosure. In 1299, the canons paid the mistress a little more than four livres to repair a hearth and windows in the beguinage.[54] That same year, a canon delivered thirty-six livres to the mistress of the beguinage in recompense "for certain houses that they [the beguines] acquired."[55]

The Dominican Prior and the Administration of the Beguinage

In addition to providing material support for the beguines in Paris and throughout the realm, Louis's successors endeavored to maintain good rela-tions between the beguines and the parochial and seigneurial authorities in whose jurisdictions the beguinage was located. They also took care to ensure that the beguinage was soundly administered. While the evidence does not allow for an in-depth look at the beguinage's administration, it is clear that it was a matter of great importance to the beguines' royal patrons. Philip IV took an active role administering the beguinage, protecting its residents' reputations, and providing the beguines with consistent pastoral care. In the late thirteenth or early fourteenth century, Philip appointed the prior of the Dominican order as guardian of the beguines for the sake of "the good government and estate of the beguinage."[56]

Although the beguines themselves seem to have cultivated close ties with the Dominicans early in their history, there is much to suggest that it was Philip IV who decided to assign to the Dominican prior the task of overseeing the administration of the beguinage. This would be in keeping with his marked reliance on the Dominicans, particularly those of the convent of Saint-Jacques in Paris, as confessors and administrators.[57] It is certain that Philip was behind the decision to place beguinages in other regions under Dominican governance. For example, in 1299, Philip gave the local Dominican prior charge of regularly visiting the beguinage of Saint Elizabeth in Lille in order to monitor the beguines' morality and religious orthodoxy.[58] Philip likely had the same expectations of the Dominican prior assigned to the Paris beguinage. Famously concerned about squelching all forms of heretical activity in his realm, Philip may have considered Dominican oversight of the beguinage as the best measure to ensure that *his* beguines remained above suspicion.

Most of what is known about the Dominican prior's responsibilities can be gleaned from the statutes of the beguinage issued in 1327 under King Charles IV. The preface notes that since the time of Philip IV the Dominican prior was responsible for ensuring "good governance" at the beguinage. The prior's responsibilities were largely administrative, namely, maintaining a close eye on the community's finances, visiting the beguinage on a regular basis, and advising the mistress on important matters.[59] The prior also chose, in consultation with the mistress, three or four senior beguines to assist her in governing the community.[60]

Although the statutes are silent on the issue of pastoral care, as in other beguine communities, the Dominican prior may have been assigned the task of appointing the chaplain of the Paris beguinage, perhaps in consultation with the mistress and with the approval of the king.[61] Assigning the governance of the beguinage to the Dominican prior, however, may have been what prompted the parish priest of Saint-Paul to renegotiate the arrangement settled under Louis IX concerning pastoral care of the beguines. Although details are sparse, in 1290 Philip IV issued an accord stating that the parish priest was obliged to say Mass at the beguinage chapel at least once a year.[62] Account books show that the Crown continued to pay the priests of Saint-Paul about fifteen livres per year "for the chapel of the beguinage" into the fifteenth century.[63]

Philip's material support of the beguines, as well as the care with which he attended to the governance of their house, gains special significance when we consider the growing climate of suspicion surrounding lay religious women in medieval Paris, suspicion which could only have intensified with the trial and execution of Marguerite Porete in 1310 and the subsequent condemnation of the beguine status at the Council of Vienne. Marguerite's fate, in fact, has been directly linked to Philip IV's concerns about maintaining his public image as a pious and just king. Because Marguerite's arrest, trial, and execution coincided with inquisitorial proceedings against the Templars, and because William of Paris, the Dominican inquisitor who presided over both trials, served as Philip IV's confessor, scholars have suggested that the king's personal interests played a significant role in determining Marguerite's fate.[64] Specifically, Robert Lerner has argued that Philip IV, anxious to maintain his reputation as defender of the faith, seized the opportunity to pursue the case against Marguerite, a case in which, Lerner asserts, "no questionable motives could be found at a time when the crown was pressing controversial proceedings against the Templars, against Guichard, bishop of Troyes, and against the memory of Boniface VIII."[65] Whether or not we accept this interpretation, there is little doubt that Philip was enormously concerned about preserving his public image as a pious king and redoubtable opponent of heresy. This image, however, was enhanced through his grandfather, Louis IX, who famously supported beguine communities throughout his realm.

Indeed, these concerns might be discerned in Philip's decision to place the beguinage under the guardianship of the Dominican prior. The Dominicans, along with the mistress—who was most likely selected because of her connections with the court—chose who might be admitted into the beguinage. It can be assumed that all parties did their utmost to protect the house's reputation, particularly in the wake of Marguerite's execution and the Council of Vienne. Whatever his concerns about the orthodoxy of beguines in general, Philip faithfully maintained royal support for the beguines of Paris. In his testament, composed in 1311 and unchanged at the time of his death in 1314, Philip bequeathed twenty livres to the "poor" beguines of Paris and one hundred livres to the beguine communities throughout the realm.[66]

The Clementine Decrees

Concerns about the beguinage's reputation must have become increasingly acute by 1311 when an ecumenical council met in Vienne to discuss, among other things, the orthodoxy of beguines. As we have seen, the council determined that the estate of "women commonly known as beguines" should be abolished, expressing this decision in two decrees. Of the two, the first, *Cum de quibusdam*, had a more direct effect on the beguines of Paris, since it targeted the status itself. Specifically, *Cum de quibusdam* objected to the beguines' assumption of religious dress and close ties with certain clerics (probably friars), both of which made the beguines appear "religious" in the strict sense although they followed no approved rule, swore obedience to no one, and did not give up their personal property.[67] More troubling was the decree's condemnation of the beguines' behavior. Echoing some of the ideas about beguines expressed in sermons and preaching material circulating in Paris, *Cum de quibusdam*, as we have seen, specifically accused beguines of engaging in theological speculation and preaching. According to the decree, the beguines' public preaching and disputations had the pernicious effect of leading "simple people" into error, an inversion of earlier praise for the beguines' zealous exhortation of their fellow Christians.

Although the council met in 1311-1312, its decisions did not have an immediate effect on beguines and their communities.[68] Pope Clement V apparently ordered all copies of the canons to be destroyed sometime in 1312, after which he made what may have been substantial revisions.[69] He published his revised version on 21 March 1314, calling it *Liber Septimus* (following Boniface VIII's *Liber Sextus* of 1298). The pope's death on 20 April, however, prevented the formal promulgation of the decrees. His successor, John XXII, took charge of further revising the Vienne decrees and published them anew under the title *Constitutiones Clementinae*. By October 1317, the Clementine decrees were circulating in Paris.[70]

Cum de quibusdam posed several difficulties for secular and ecclesiastical authorities attempting to determine what implications it had for the "women commonly known as beguines" living in their own regions. The decree reads as a blanket condemnation of the beguine status ("We, with the approval of the sacred council, declare that their status ought to be perpetually abolished from the church of God") but ends with a curious so-called escape clause permitting "faithful women" to live "honestly in their dwellings."[71] Jacqueline Tarrant has argued that the decree actually targeted only "some" or "certain" beguines, that is, the beguines who disputed and preached about doctrinal matters. Nevertheless, evidence regarding contemporary reaction to and implementation of the decrees shows that few authorities recognized the distinction.[72] The Parisian chronicler Jean of Saint-Victor, in fact, described the decree as a condemnation of the beguine status "without any distinction."[73] Canon lawyers, for their part, tended to interpret the decree as a blanket condemnation of the beguine status without any sort of exemption for certain "types" of beguines. Johannes Andreae, the author of the standard gloss to the Clementine decrees, argued that the only lay religious women *not* implicated in the decrees were Franciscan tertiaries, who, the canonist noted, "promise obedience and have a rule."[74]

The issue for many, it seems, was the ways in which beguine convents and beguinages gave their residents the appearance of living as true "religious" in the sense of members of an approved order. In other words, the beguines' communal organization misled people into believing that they were "truly" religious, although they were not. In his commentaries on the decree, the canonist Alberic of Metz (d. 1354), for example, suggested that the last clause in *Cum de quibusdam*, which exempted women living "honestly in their dwellings," referred to beguines living chaste lives privately in their own homes.[75] Later canonists argued more forcefully in defense of women privately following a life of chastity and good works in their own homes. On the other hand, they interpreted *Cum de quibusdam* as an unequivocal denunciation of beguines— "good" or "bad"—who lived in common dwellings, such as convents or beguinages.[76] Local authorities were even less certain than canon lawyers about how to interpret and implement the Clementine decrees. Almost immediately after the publication of the *Clementinae* in late 1317, the bishop of Strasbourg, John of Dürbheim, wrote a letter to Pope John XXII asking for clarification.[77] Several clerics expressed dismay over local authorities seizing upon the ambiguities in the decrees to persecute tertiaries or other women who lived chastely in their own, or their parents', homes.[78] Ultimately, enforcement largely depended upon local attitudes of bishops, secular authorities, and clerics (both secular and religious) toward friars, beguines, and tertiaries. In some regions, such as Strasbourg, the secular clergy seem to have acted on the decrees out of resentment toward the mendicant orders, whom they accused of unlawfully protecting the condemned beguines.[79] In Strasbourg, the bishop had to contend with local animosity toward friars and the women with whom they were closely associated, and he was under considerable pressure to carry out the stipulations against lay religious women indiscriminately.[80]

The confusion was such that John XXII issued the bull *Ratio recta* in August 1318 in an effort to clarify *Cum de quibusdam*, particularly the final clause. The bull returned to the issue of the beguines' residence and behavior, stating, "In many parts of the world there are those women who are also called beguines but who live in their own homes, in those of their parents, or sometimes in community, but who lead lives beyond reproach. If those beguines do not engage in preaching or disputation about doctrine, and if they attend church regularly, submitting to the authority of local clergy, they must not be molested and should be allowed to retain both their habits and their way of life."[81] While the bull attempted to provide some guidelines for ecclesiastical authorities charged with the task of distinguishing the "bad" beguines targeted by the Vienne decrees and the good beguines who were to be left unmolested, it too left room for interpretations that would negatively affect all religious laywomen. Specifically, *Ratio recta* stated that although these "upright beguines" ought not to be harassed by local clergy, by saying this the pope in no way approved the beguine estate, nor was the bull intended to contradict earlier rulings.[82] Thus, the pope continued to draw attention to the beguines' lack of official approbation, allowing local authorities ironically to reference *Ratio recta* in their own prohibitions of the beguine status.[83] In short, the bull did nothing to clarify the papal position on the beguinages of northern Europe, including the Paris beguinage.

While the anti-beguine legislation targeted "bad" beguines who engaged in theological speculation, it also implied disapproval of the beguines' communal organization, which gave the women the semblance of belonging to an official religious order. Indeed, beguinages or beguine convents, the very institutions medieval and modern observers credited with protecting beguines from charges of heresy, seem to have been the chief concern for many churchmen, particularly because they approximated convents, and thus deprived "approved" religious communities of patronage. They also frequently stood apart from parish authority, with its residents enjoying privileges more appropriate to the properly "religious" (such as exemption from certain taxes) while still being able to hold and dispose of property in the manner of laypeople.[84]

In December 1320, John XXII attempted further clarification on the matter of beguines, addressing *Cum de mulieribus*, a summary of earlier papal and curial statements, to bishops in Tournai, Cambrai, and Paris. In all likelihood, the bull was a response to appeals from the various beguine communities—particularly beguinages—targeted by the *Clementinae*. Bishops in areas with heavy concentrations of beguine houses had up to this point hesitated to move on the anti-beguine legislation, seemingly unsure about whether or not the decrees applied to "their" beguines.[85] Local authorities, however, exhibited no such qualms and demanded that the bishops take decisive action. In some areas, secular authorities invoked the decrees in order to confiscate the beguinages' holdings or to force beguines to observe parochial authority.[86]

Similar in content to *Ratio recta*, *Cum de mulieribus* acknowledged that beguines "who, driven by necessity and for closer observance of chastity, dwell together in the several beguinages" might be included among the "faithful beguines" exonerated in the final clause of *Cum de quibusdam*.[87] Having included residents of beguinages among those exempted from the ban on the beguine status, the bull enjoined the bishops to investigate the beguinages in their respective dioceses either themselves or through their representatives to ensure that the beguines were not engaging in illicit disputations or preaching about matters of doctrine.[88]

These investigations, however, did not immediately vindicate the beguinages and their residents, and they often proved a welcome opportunity for urban officials or religious orders hostile to the beguines to seize beguinage properties or compel the beguines to take on the rule of the Third Order of Saint Francis. According to Walter Simons, the beguinages of the Low Countries were in "disarray" as a result of these investigations, which took place throughout the 1320s and prompted local advocates and patrons of the beguinages to commission letters to the pope defending the beguines' reputations and manner of life.[89] In some cities, women of these communities were careful to no longer describe themselves as beguines.[90] Some even discarded their distinctive habits and dressed in ordinary secular clothing or adopted the rule of the Third Order of Saint Francis.[91] In 1323, Franciscans and Dominicans negotiated a plan to dissolve the beguinage in Bruges and co-opt beguines into their third orders.[92]

Clearly the fallout from the Clementine decrees was different everywhere, depending on who stepped in (or did not) and to what effect. While local bishops intervened to defend the beguines in some areas, others were under considerable pressure to interpret the decrees as blanket condemnations of the beguine status. Local authorities tended to respond to these various, internally contradictory papal decrees—and subsequent attempts to clarify them—in accordance with local conditions. In some regions, local clergy moved on the legislation to condemn communities they opposed (friars, beguines, or both). In other areas, savvy bishops or secular patrons could interpret the decrees in ways that exonerated local beguines and preserved their privileges.[93] On the other hand, beguines might end up on the defensive once again should they find themselves under new bishops or secular powers with less sympathy for their way of life. Without ecclesiastical status, beguines depended upon their patrons, sympathetic bishops, and parochial authorities to maintain their privileges and protect them from the accusations and attacks of those less favorably disposed to their way of life. As Elizabeth Makowski has astutely observed, beguines enjoyed privileges "on an *ad hoc* basis," since they "possessed no canonical bulwark against the vicissitudes of popular and ecclesiastical opinion."[94]

The Vienne Decrees and the Beguinage of Paris

In Paris, the response to the publication of the Clementine decrees was reportedly swift and severe. The continuator of Guillaume de Nangis's chronicle observed that the publication of the Clementine decrees at the Parisian schools led to the condemnation of beguines, further confirmation that the initial reaction to the decrees, at least among university clerics, was unfavorable.[95] The Parisian canon John of Saint Victor reports in his chronicle that the beguines were "deprived of their beguinage and their order was condemned." The beguines, the chronicler tells us, no longer sang or read.[96] Given the ambivalent, and even negative, views university clerics held with regard to beguines, this reaction is hardly surprising. As we have seen, Parisian scholars and masters recognized beguines as women who actively exhorted one another and their fellow Christians, both by their examples and their words. While some clerics clearly valued the beguines' exercise of an active lay apostolate, others expressed concerns about women arrogating to themselves the role of preacher. Certainly, the response to Marguerite Porete and her book, as well as the specific accusations leveled in *Cum de quibusdam,* indicates that beguines who "disputed and preached" were of grave concern to Parisian clerics.

Sometime in 1318, not long after the *Clementinae* first circulated in Paris, but well before Pope John XXII issued *Cum de mulieribus* (1320), which ordered the bishops to conduct official inquiries into beguine communities,

King Philip V (r. 1316–1322) instructed the provost of Paris to assess the beguinage's holdings.[97] The intent and outcome of this royally initiated investigation is not known; it is likely, however, that it was related to the circulation
of the Vienne decrees. If the beguines of Paris were, in fact, deprived of their
beguinage (as the chroniclers report), then certainly the king would have
played a major, if not central, role in this process. The French kings carefully
controlled their image as Most Christian Kings and could hardly ignore heresy accusations, particularly if they were leveled at women living in a royally
sponsored beguinage. It should be noted that the bishop of Paris's position on
the beguines is entirely unknown, although he was surely among the parties
interested in the beguinage's fate. His involvement in the matter, however, is
suggested by John XXII's reference to the bishop of Paris in his bull *Cum de
mulieribus*, which directed episcopal authorities to conduct inquiries into the
beguinages of their dioceses. Whatever the perspectives of royal and ecclesiastical authorities might have been, local authorities could not have helped but
discern connections between Marguerite Porete, a beguine publicly executed
in their city, and the beguines residing in the Paris beguinage. It is clear that,
for at least a few years, the residents of the beguinage faced inquiries and suspicion. Forced out of the beguinage, they returned to their families (if possible)
or found alternate accommodations. Some may have joined the Haudriettes
or the Bonnes Femmes of Sainte-Avoye. Although there is no evidence of inquisitorial activity in Paris during these years, the effects of the Vienne decrees
on the city's communities of lay religious women should not be minimized.

At some point, the local Dominican and Franciscan friars intervened on
behalf of the beguines; at least this is what the chronicles report.[98] The Paris beguinage was under the guardianship of the Dominican prior, who surely had a
stake in defending the women for whose reputations he was responsible. The friars, as intimates of the royal court, were in a good position to influence the king.
Little is known of the king's stance on the beguines, however, until the reign
of Charles IV, who succeeded Philip V in February 1322. Royal account books
confirm that the beguinage received its monetary disbursements as early as
March of that year. Although no source indicates when, or under what circumstances, women were readmitted into the enclosure, any disruptions in
royal support for the beguinage were evidently temporary.[99] Nevertheless, the
beguinage's troubles seem to have prompted the abbey of Tiron to pursue its
seigneurial rights over justice concerning the beguinage community in April
1327. One month later, Charles IV, in consultation with the Dominicans in his
circle, affirmed the community's orthodoxy and issued a new set of statutes.[100]

Whatever the motivation of the abbey, the timing is certainly suspect and suggests that anti-beguine legislation in Paris—as elsewhere—opened the door for various groups to pursue their political or economic interests.

During the months and years following the publication of the Vienne decrees, beguines without such powerful patrons might have been particularly vulnerable. Unfortunately, nothing is known of the fate of the beguines living outside the royal beguinage. The last extant tax roll is for the year 1313, four years before the circulation of the Vienne decrees in Paris. Nevertheless, pious foundations and donations offer some clues. The early fourteenth century saw the establishment of alternative communities for lay religious women, ones that did not employ the term "beguine." These communities may have developed organically from the clusters of lay religious women living and working together throughout the city of Paris. Some chapel-based, others located in areas where work opportunities for unmarried women were more abundant, these communities of women attracted wealthy patrons seeking ways to secure intercession for their souls and memorialize their family lines.[101]

Indeed, the early decades of the fourteenth century witnessed a veritable explosion of foundations for lay religious women. The houses founded by Étienne Haudry (the Haudriettes) and Constance of Saint-Jacques (the Bonnes Femmes of Sainte-Avoye) were established in the first decade of the fourteenth century, before the circulation of the Vienne decrees but during the years when suspicions may have been high. In 1334, Jean Roussel, a wealthy merchant, established a community for forty-eight "bonnes femmes" on the rue des Poulies, a street bordering the Paris beguinage.[102] An almoner's roll dating from 1342 lists eleven different communities of "bonnes femmes," a term that had become a popular descriptor for lay religious women.[103] Without denying the charitable impulses behind these foundations, they were fueled at least in part by the need to accommodate lay religious women. In the absence of concrete evidence regarding the fate of beguines living outside the beguinage, it cannot be claimed with certainty that these foundations absorbed the households of lay religious women dotting the streets of Paris in the late thirteenth century. Nevertheless, these new foundations, regulated by house rules, bound by promises secured with property, and known by a less controversial name, suggest something about the nature of Parisian responses to anti-beguine inquiries. Just as beguine communities in the Low Countries and German lands responded to controversies surrounding the term "beguine" in the aftermath of the Council of Vienne by consciously avoiding the label, Parisian lay religious communities seem to have offered women opportunities to live a "beguinish" life without risking association with the controversial name.[104] Asserting its members' upright and innocent behavior during a time when "beguine" signified a possible association with heresy, communities of bonne femmes represented an effort to deal with the tricky problem of labels without changing the fundamental characteristics of life as a lay religious woman.[105]

While evidence of the immediate aftermath to the circulation of the Vienne decrees is extremely fragmentary, a set of statutes issued for the beguinage of Paris in May 1327 under Charles IV makes clear that an ecclesiastical inquest had by then been conducted at the beguinage and that the status of the Parisian beguines had received both royal and papal approbation. The preamble to the rule provides important insight into the French kings' role in protecting the beguinage's status as a royal foundation, as well as its residents, and deserves to be quoted here in full.

> We make known to all present and to come that my lord Saint Louis, among other works of mercy that he did during his life, had acquired an enclosure of houses in Paris located near the Barbel gate, and he placed there good and honest beguines to serve our Lord chastely, and they have and hold the said houses as their own, the property of the place safe and maintained by him. And our very dear lords father and brothers, the kings Philip [IV], Louis [X], and Philip [V], recently deceased, may God save him, for the sake of good governance and estate of the said dwelling of the beguinage, had committed the care of the administration of the beguines to the prior of the Preaching Friars of Paris, who by virtue and authority of his commissions composed certain statutes and ordinances according to which the said beguines should live and comport themselves. Since our Holy Father the Pope, by a council that met in Vienne, because some beguines outside our kingdom behaved badly and on account of certain excesses and evil deeds that they had committed and done, eradicated and abolished all in the said estate, and because, as much by inquest as by common rumor and report, the beguines living in the said dwelling were found innocent and not guilty of the said misdeeds, it pleased our said Holy Father to reestablish and summon them to their estate and their place. We, desiring always to follow the good works of our predecessors, who by their power raised the status of the Holy Church, and of persons established in the service of Our Lord, at the humble request of

some of the said beguines, charged and ordered by our letters to our beloved brothers Pierre de La Palu, of the Order of the Preaching Friars, Master in Divinity, to Master Richard des Champs and Master Jean Justice, our clerks, that they should diligently consider and examine the said statutes and ordinances, and if there were any rules that were intolerable and too harsh for the beguines that they should moderate and amend them in whatever way necessary. And with the counsel of the mistress and the most senior beguines of the dwelling and of the community, they modified the rules and added certain declarations, just as we have seen to be contained in a letter bearing the seal of their office. Moreover, for the greater confirmation of those ordinances and declarations we have since shown them to our beloved brother Gilbert, our confessor, and to Master Michel de Mauconduit and others of our council, who have seen them and have thoroughly and diligently inspected them just as we have reported. Having heard their statement and report, and having deliberated with our council, we have made and ordered the statutes and ordinances of the said beguinage in the form and in the manner that follows.[106]

Several points in Charles IV's preface to the statutes are of interest here. Charles opens with a discussion of the beguinage's saintly founder, who, the king asserts, established the beguinage out of charity. By prefacing his defense of the beguinage with this reference to Saint Louis, Charles insisted that the beguinage was a royal and saintly foundation worthy of the Crown's continued support. Moreover, like the hagiographical descriptions of Louis IX's role in founding and populating the beguinage, Charles's preface draws attention to the saintly king's role in choosing the "good and honest women beguines" who came to reside there. Charles's defense of the beguinage underscores the importance of the beguinage as a royal institution, specifically a "good work" undertaken by his esteemed predecessors, who "by their power raised the status of the Holy Church." The beguines, moreover, are recognized as "persons established in the service of Our Lord," thereby affirming the value of the beguines to the realm.

These "bonnes et preud'femmes beguines," the preamble noted, owned their own houses, which were protected and maintained by royal authority. The reference to beguines living in their own (royally protected) homes no doubt aimed to evoke the "faithful women" living honestly in their own dwellings referred to in the final clause of *Cum de quibusdam*. Further defending the beguines' reputations, Charles emphasizes the role of the Dominican prior as guardian of the beguinage. As we have seen, the kings of France since Philip IV had charged the prior with overseeing administrative matters "for the sake of good governance." It was the prior, too, who composed the statutes for the beguines, which were apparently not the first set of statutes followed at the beguinage. In commissioning the Dominican prior as guardian of the beguinage, the French kings demonstrated their commitment to the preservation of the beguines' reputations and the foundation's stability.

The various revisions the statutes underwent as a result of several rounds of consultation before being published in their final form are also illustrative of the care with which the French kings approached the matter of the beguinage's governance and reputation. Charles reports that some of the beguines requested that the king's men—which included Pierre de La Palu, a Dominican master in theology—examine the statutes provided to them by the Dominican prior to ensure that they were not unduly harsh or burdensome. These men amended the statutes in consultation with the mistress and senior beguines, indicating that the women themselves played a role in the composition of their own rule. After these modifications, the statutes underwent yet another round of inspection, being read and ultimately approved by members of the king's own council, including his Dominican confessor. The confessor, it turns out, was Gilbert Louvel, whose name must have carried some weight. Gilbert had also served as the confessor of Philip IV and had been the inquisitor of France, taking over from William of Paris, the Dominican inquisitor who had presided over Marguerite Porete's trial.[107]

Most notably, Charles insisted that the beguines in Paris were not among those targeted by the Council of Vienne. According to Charles, the *Clementinae* concerned beguines *outside* the French kingdom. Acknowledging the Vienne decrees' abolishment of "all in the said estate," Charles's preamble to his statutes recognized the thorny problem of names, which had had the unfortunate consequence of lumping the good beguines with the bad. Asserting that the French kingdom harbored no heretics—and by implication that its rulers were particularly scrupulous in rooting them out—Charles hoped to clarify matters for Parisian authorities with regard to the beguines. Since the heretical beguines against whom the decrees were aimed did not reside within his realm, no such confusion about "good" or "bad" beguines should arise within his kingdom. According to Charles, the beguines of Paris were found innocent of "the said misdeeds . . . as much by inquest as by common rumor and report," and the pope restored to the beguines their estate—likely a reference to papal restoration of the beguines' privileges and property.[108] Case closed.

Royal patronage, then, went a long way in protecting the beguines of Paris. But it was more than simply the authority the Capetians wielded that mattered during the post-Vienne period. The French kings, desirous of maintaining a link between themselves and the most celebrated example of their sacred lineage, continued to support the beguinage of Paris as a tangible symbol of its founder's—and by extension Capetian—sanctity. In other regions of northern Europe, bishops and secular patrons supportive of the beguine life might be succeeded by authorities hostile or indifferent to the status. Moreover, religious and charitable foundations often lost their association with their original founders as later patrons' contributions—whether material or administrative in nature—reshaped or even radically changed the purpose of the house and corporate identity of the residents.[109] The Paris beguinage, however, remained a royal institution strictly under the kings' patronage and control. Louis's successors consciously emulated their sainted ancestor, materially providing for the beguinage and its residents while actively preserving its reputation as a royal foundation. They also, significantly, stuck with the name "beguine." Among the eleven houses of "bonnes femmes" listed in the almoner's roll in 1342, the residents of the royal beguinage stand out as "Les beguines de Paris."[110] No attempt was made to drop the label, so important for identifying the women as the very same community founded by Saint Louis and supported by his successors.

Royal Patronage, Post-Vienne

Royal account books indicate that the beguinage did not suffer any significant disruption in patronage as a result of the Clementine decrees. While chronicle reports of the beguines being deprived of their beguinage suggest that the immediate response to the *Clementinae* was negative, suspicions about the Paris beguinage and the orthodoxy of its residents must have been sufficiently dispelled by 1322. No account books survive for the short reign of Philip V (r. 1316–1322), whose reign coincided with the initial circulation of the *Clementinae* in 1317. References to Philip V's testament, however, attest to the king's support for individual beguines.[111] Account books for the reign of Philip V's successor, Charles IV, as we have seen, show that the canons of Sainte-Chapelle delivered royal disbursements to the beguinage from the very first fiscal term of Charles's reign, suggesting that there was no significant break in royal patronage as a result of the Clementine decrees.[112]

Charles IV's successor, Philip VI (r. 1328-1350), publicized his support for the beguinage, underscoring the importance this royal foundation held for the Valois king, who hoped to bolster his own claims to the French throne and Capetian sanctity by emphasizing his descent from Saint Louis.[113] In 1340, Philip VI gave the beguinage an annuity worth eight livres out of "the affection and devotion that we have for the prayers of our beloved mistress and the community of beguines of the beguinage of Paris, which Saint Louis founded."[114] The following year, he confirmed the statutes of the beguinage, which had undergone further revision since 1327.[115] Other members of the Valois family conveyed their support for the Paris beguinage through testamentary bequests, further attesting to the endurance of royal patronage well into the fourteenth century. In a testament drawn up in May 1329, Philip VI's first wife, Jeanne of Burgundy (d. 1348), designated ten livres for the beguines of Paris.[116] Philip VI's second wife, Blanche of Navarre (d. 1398), bequeathed twelve gold francs to the beguinage in her testament, which she composed in 1396.[117] Similarly, Philip VI's half sister Isabelle of Valois, the Duchess of Bourbon (d. 1385) left ten gold francs to the beguinage, with the request that the beguines pray for her soul.[118] Philip's daughter-in-law, Blanche, the Duchess of Orleans, also remembered "the poor beguines of Paris," leaving them forty sous parisis in her testament.[119] The Valois family's connection with beguines is also evident in the fact that an intimate of the Valois court, the noblewoman Jeanne de La Tour, lived as a beguine in the Paris beguinage sometime before 1432. The duchess Isabelle of Valois bequeathed to Jeanne, who in another document is identified as a "demoiselle de la roine," a generous bequest of two hundred gold francs.[120] Clearly, the Valois were committed to supporting the beguinage as a community of lay religious women and as a symbol of French royal identity.

From Beguine to Sister to Nun

Local support for Paris's beguines remained strong throughout the fourteenth century, underscoring the ways in which local circumstances dictated the extent to which anti-beguine legislation was put into practice. In the early fifteenth century, the beguinage continued to serve as a refuge for women from diverse backgrounds. Widows of Parisian elites lived out their final years in the beguinage. Noblewomen took up residence in the community while maintaining a presence at court. Beguines worked and prayed within the enclosure, bought and sold annuities on urban properties, and served in Parisian households and hospitals. Royal councilors and members of Parlement continued to leave bequests to the beguinage, seeking the beguines' prayers and acknowledging the women's intercessory powers. The beguinage school continued to educate local girls. Although beguines never obtained papal recognition as a religious order, to Parisians they were "religious women."

While this positive recognition helped beguine communities in Paris weather the years of inquiry and investigation following the circulation of the Vienne decrees, it must be acknowledged that these years were marked by fear and uncertainty for lay religious women. Uncloistered and unprofessed, beguines were vulnerable. The French kings who decreed that the beguines of Paris had not espoused heretical teachings came to this conclusion only after carrying out an investigation of the women in the enclosure. During these years, some women undoubtedly were evicted from the beguinage. Others may have voluntarily left the beguine life in fear for their reputations and safety. Beguines living outside the enclosure may have changed their clothing and lifestyle to avoid being taken for one of the "bad" beguines targeted in the Clementines.

By the late fifteenth century, the beguinage's powerful sources of support had deteriorated under the pressures of plague, war, and economic decline. While a thorough evaluation of the confluence of factors that led to the decline of the Paris beguinage is beyond the scope of this book, several points merit a brief sketch here. Having weathered heresy accusations, Paris's beguines had a much harder time enduring the social, economic, and political upheavals of the early fifteenth century. Although few account books for the late fourteenth and early fifteenth century have survived, it is evident that royal support of the hospitals and religious houses of the realm declined over the course of the later Middle Ages, particularly as the Hundred Years' War (1337–1453) drained royal energies and funds.[121]

Houses of lay religious women, which relied on familial, occupational, and social networks, declined in the late fourteenth century when violence and commercial decline forced many merchants and artisans out of the city.[122] The extant evidence shows that Paris's houses for lay religious women, including the beguinage, suffered greatly as a result of the political and economic crises of the later Middle Ages.[123] The civil wars of the late fourteenth and early fifteenth centuries made Paris a particularly violent environment, and there are hints that the beguinage, like most institutions, had trouble collecting its urban rents during the late fourteenth and fifteenth centuries.[124] Like the beguinages in the southern Low Countries, Paris's beguinage may have sought to relieve the strain on its resources by charging substantial entrance fees to women entering it, a move that may have affected recruitment into the community.[125] The Black Death, which decimated the Parisian population in the mid-fourteenth century, made it increasingly difficult for individual Parisians, as well as the city's religious and charitable institutions, to collect the annuities on which they relied for revenue.[126] While records for this period are sparse, it is reasonable to assume that, as was the case for religious houses all over the realm, the Black Death set the beguinage on a course of demographic and economic decline nearly impossible to reverse.

In addition, the beguinage's social value was seriously diminished with the closure of its school in the mid-fifteenth century. In 1442, the cathedral chapter of Notre Dame brought a case before Parlement against the beguinage, claiming that the beguines operated a school for girls without proper licensing. Although the beguines defended their activities by pointing out that they received permission to teach from the almoner of the king, the cathedral chapter eventually won their case, indicating that support for the school (and the beguinage) had eroded significantly by this date. In 1457 the cathedral chapter brought suit against a beguine named Renaude la Fuchine for running a school for beguines without permission from the chapter.[127] The loss of the school was probably a major blow to the beguine community.

The beguines' lack of strict enclosure also increasingly affected patronage, as Parisian elites, whose religious and social sensibilities shifted to fall increasingly in line with those of the nobility, sought to place their daughters in convents or contract a favorable marriage.[128] Important too were changes in urban property laws, which accompanied the gradual development of family strategies aiming to preserve wealth and status among urban elites.[129] As Martha Howell has shown in her work on late medieval Douai, propertied elites over time "chose more lineal marital property regimes when preservation of wealth seemed more urgent than its acquisition, when social place seemed harder to acquire and more difficult to protect, when social mobility felt less like opportunity and more like risk."[130] Parisian elites increasingly employed such strategies to preserve economic and cultural capital in ways that favored men, thereby weakening women's ability to support themselves outside the conjugal household.[131] At the same time the beguinage experienced a decline in royal support and difficulty collecting revenues from its urban properties, fewer elite Parisian women, it seems, had the resources necessary to enter the beguinage.

With less control over property, the daughters, wives, and widows of Parisian bourgeois families were less likely to join or patronize such foundations.

All evidence points to a general neglect of the beguinage and its residents over the course of the fifteenth century. By 1470, the buildings of the beguinage had reportedly fallen into ruin, and only two women remained as residents.[132] The decline in population occurred perhaps only gradually. Certainly, the testament of Martine Canu (composed in 1408) suggests a bustling institution with a school, hospital, and community of women of all ages and backgrounds.[133] The following decades, however, were tumultuous times for Parisians, as the city suffered through the civil war between the Burgundians and the Armagnacs and later came under siege by French forces.[134] During the first two decades of the fifteenth century, troops loyal to either the Burgundians or the Armagnacs staged bloody massacres of their opponents' supporters in the city, plunging Paris into frequent cycles of fear and chaos. The city was eventually handed over to the English in 1419, who occupied it until 1436.[135] The first few years of the English occupation were relatively peaceful for the city as the Dauphin—the future Charles VII—struggled to gather an effective military force against the English. Between 1429, when the French led the initial assault against the capital, and 1436, when the French managed to recover the city, however, life in Paris was extraordinarily difficult as blockades cut the city off from its food supplies, leading to famine and revolt.

It was during this period of war that the beguinage ceased to enforce the property laws dictated in the house rules. As we saw in the dispute over a house that had been in the possession of a beguine named Jeanne de La Tour, the mistress herself had allowed a non-beguine to purchase and claim full ownership over the house upon Jeanne's death in 1385.[136] Tellingly, the beguinage did not pursue the matter until 1432—almost fifty years after the initial sale—when it finally brought the case before the Châtelet. While the documents recording the outcome of the case show that the beguinage was able to assert its rights successfully, they show that the beguinage had long turned a blind eye to violations of the property regulations that protected the corporate integrity of the enclosure. That the beguinage chose to assert its rights over the property in the 1430s, when the beguines were also pursuing property claims against the confraternity of Saint Sépulcre, might indicate concerns about the financial solvency of the community.[137] Significantly, the beguines pursued the property claim via the royal almoner and confessor, Pierre Cauchon (d. 1432), best known for presiding over the trial of Joan of Arc.[138] Citing the rules of the beguinage, Pierre vigorously defended the community's property rights, referring to the authority of the guardians of the beguinage, alongside the mistress, to manage the rents and revenues belonging to the community, as well as the rights of the king (in this case, Henry VI of England) over the property within the enclosure.[139]

Over the course of the fifteenth century, and well after King Charles VII's entry into Paris in November 1437, the Paris beguinage seems to have fallen into decay. While property disputes from the 1430s indicate that the community had the support necessary to pursue legal claims in court, little is known of the fate of the beguines during Charles VII's reign (1422–1461). It can be surmised that Charles did little to maintain the community, being far too preoccupied with driving the English out of France, dealing with rebellious noble factions, including one centered on his own son (the future King Louis XI), and asserting royal control over the French clergy. Important too was a lack of support for the beguines' spiritual welfare. While university clerics in the thirteenth century took an active interest in the pastoral care of the city's beguines, by the fourteenth century they evidently took little interest in the women's spiritual needs. The political upheavals and religious crises with which the University of Paris grappled in the fourteenth and fifteenth centuries discouraged the dialogue and collaboration evident in the sermon collections compiled during the first decades of the Sorbonne. The university of the later Middle Ages was one in which male clerics increasingly emphasized the authority of scholarly consensus over divine inspiration, competition over humility, the prud'homme over the beguin. Indeed, by the late fifteenth century, university clerics seem to have purposely avoided becoming involved in the care of lay religious women. The only clerics involved in the pastoral care of beguines—other than the special chaplains retained by the beguinage—were the parish priests of Saint-Paul.[140] With the decline in the beguinage's revenues over the course of the fifteenth century, the community most likely found it impossible to maintain their chaplains, eventually leading to an end to religious services at the beguinage.[141]

Finally, in 1471 the French king Louis XI (r. 1461–1483) transferred the beguinage to a group of Franciscan tertiaries. Significantly, it took some time for Louis to find new residents for the buildings. The king's wars in Flanders and Hainaut, which devastated convents and religious houses throughout those regions, resulted in a flood of displaced women making their way to Paris to take refuge in the beguines' former enclosure.[142] The proposal to bring women from these regions to start up a new community in Paris— reminiscent of Louis IX's efforts to establish the original beguine community in the 1260s—suggests a renewed commitment among the French kings to preserve the original mission of the beguinage. In the letters patent concerning the transfer, the king stated that he wished to turn over the enclosure to the tertiaries so that the house would once again be inhabited by good and holy women and divine services would be celebrated once more.[143] The document also reveals that the king's efforts were part of a broader campaign to restore the convents of his kingdom, including the house and convent of the beguines.[144] For Louis, the best way to restore the house to its original purpose was to invite tertiaries from outside Paris to take up residence in the buildings of the beguinage, which he vowed to repair. Taking the name Filles de l'Ave Maria, the community would welcome lay religious women from all over the realm. Louis XI, like religious and secular observers across Europe, evidently understood tertiaries as a "type of beguine," perceiving the difference between the two groups to be one of name alone.[145] Significantly, the last two beguine residents of the enclosure, who were permitted to remain in the community and to follow their former way of life, did not cooperate with the opponents of the king's plan. Indeed, the women ended up living among the new residents, whose way of life, after all, differed little from their own.[146]

Yet local conditions once again determined the fate of this religious community. Conflict between the Conventual and Observant wings of the Franciscan order created problems for the new community as the local mendicant orders opposed the installation of tertiaries in Paris. Because the tertiaries were under the oversight of Observant friars, the Franciscan convent in Paris (Conventuals) opposed the move, since they had no wish for the Observants to gain a foothold in Paris. The nuns of Longchamp, delegates representing the four mendicant orders, the University of Paris, the parish priest of Saint-Paul, and Anne de Beaujeu, daughter of the king, supported the Parisian friars in contesting the king's plan.[147] The Parlement of Paris eventually ruled that the tertiaries were permitted to set up a house at the former site of the beguinage, but they were not to be under Observant control.[148] Nevertheless, royal intervention eventually settled the matter in favor of the Observants. Determined to install an Observant Clarissan convent in Paris, Queen Charlotte of Savoy (d. 1483) invoked a papal bull permitting her to establish monasteries under Observant obedience throughout the realm.[149] By 1485, the former beguinage of Paris was home to a convent for Observant Poor Clares.[150] The nuns, who kept the name Filles de l'Ave Maria saw no need to preserve the history of the enclosure's previous occupants, and memory of the beguines of Paris soon faded. Indeed, the rue des Béguines, just south of the enclosure, eventually came to be called the rue de l'Ave Maria, the name by which this street in the Marais is known today.

The beguine life combined action and contemplation to fulfill women's religious aspirations while accommodating the social and economic realities of life in a medieval city, characteristics that made the beguine status attractive to women as an alternative to marriage or the cloister and appealing to townspeople as a new and socially engaged expression of urban piety. Hardly peripheral to the city in which they prayed and worked, beguines were part of the very fabric of medieval Paris. Paris's silk industry took off just as beguines were flocking to the trade in the late thirteenth century. Robert of Sorbon founded his college for secular clerics at the same time beguines set up households along the streets of the Left Bank and his friend and king, Louis IX, founded a community for "honest women who are called beguines." Clerics found inspiration in the beguine life, which served as a model for their own religious lives in the midst of urban temptations and university conflicts. Bourgeois and royal patrons viewed the beguines as powerful intercessors for their souls and valued providers of social services. Paris's property laws enabled women to support themselves—and use their resources to support one another—thereby facilitating the growth of beguine communities both formal and informal. In short, beguine communities were all things to all people: havens for the spiritually inspired, refuges for the unmarried, retirement communities for the elderly. The beguine status was certainly viewed negatively by some, but its practical and religious value was important to the groups who possessed the influence and authority to make or reject such views.

Beguines Whose Occupations Are Known

I have traced each woman across the extant tax rolls in an effort to glean as much information on her as possible. I have identified each beguine by her surname if this information is available. In most cases, however, only the woman's religious identity is noted in the tax records.

BEGUINES DESCRIBED AS SILK SPINNERS (18)

Adeline la Beguine ("Adeline la beguine, fileresse de soie"; AN KK 283, fol. 258)

Agnes la Beguine[1] ("Anes la beguine, fillatre Symon de Grey"; BnF fr. 6220, fol. 9)

Agnes de Senliz, beguine[2] ("Agnes de senliz, fileresse de soie"; AN KK 283, fol. 51v)

Ameline la Beguine ("Ameline la beguine, fileresse de soie"; AN KK 283, fol. 221)

Ameline la Navete, beguine[3] ("Ameline, fileresse de soie"; AN KK 283, fol. 243)

Basile la Beguine ("Basile la beguine, fileresse de soie"; AN KK 283, fol. 259)

Basilette la Beguine ("Basilette la beguine, fileresse de soie"; AN KK 283, fol. 181v)

Gile de Galardon ("Gile de galardon, fileresse de soie"; AN KK 283, fol. 220v)

Isabelle la Beguine ("Isabelle la beguine, file soie"; AN KK 283, fol. 231v)

Isabelle de Limeuil ("Isabelle de lymueil, fileresse de soie"; AN KK 283, fol. 220v)

Jeanne la Beguine ("Jehanne la beguine, fileresse de soie"; AN KK 283, fol. 79v)

Jeanne la Beguine ("Jehanne la beguine, fileresse de soie"; AN KK 283, fol. 91)

Jeanne la Beguine ("Jehanne la beguine, fileresse de soie"; AN KK 283, fol. 243)

Juliote la Beguine ("Juliote la beguine, file soie"; AN KK 283, fol. 126v)

Maheut aus Cholez[4] ("Mahaut aus cholez, fileresse de soie" AN KK 283, fol. 220v)

Maheut de La Croiz, la beguine[5] ("Maheut, fileresse de soie"; AN KK 283, fol. 64v)

Thomasse la Beguine ("Thomasse la beguine, fileresse de soie"; AN KK 283, fol. 64v)

Thomasse la Normande[6] ("Thomasse la beguine, fileresse de soie"; AN KK 283, fol. 292v)

BEGUINES DESCRIBED AS ENGAGED
IN THE PRODUCTION OF SMALL SILK GOODS (9)

Alice de Saint-Joce[7] ("Aalis de saint-joce, qui fet ausmonieres"; AN KK 283, fol. 235v)

Alison la Beguine ("Alison la beguine, crespiniere"; AN KK 283, fol. 70v)

Ameline la Beguine ("Ameline et Basile, beguines, font chapiax a pelles"; AN KK 283, fol. 259)

Basile la Beguine ("Ameline et Basile, beguines, font chapiax a pelles"; AN KK 283, fol. 259)

Jeanne la Beguine[8] ("Jehanne qui fet laz de soie"; AN KK 283, fol. 231)

Marie la Beguine ("Marie, la beguine, crespiniere"; AN KK 283, fol. 133)

Marie la Beguine ("Marie la beguine, qui fait tissu"; AN KK 283, fol. 279)

Marie la Beguine ("Laurette et sa soeur Marie la beguine, crespinieres"; AN KK 283, fol. 187)

Marie des Cordeles[9] ("Marie la beguine, fabricante de couvre-chef"; AN KK 283, fol. 256)

BEGUINES DESCRIBED AS *OUVRIERE DE SOIE* (5)

Adeline de Mauregart ("Adeline de Mauregart, beguine, ouvriere de soie"; AN KK 283, fol. 292)

Benoite la Beguine ("Benoite la beguine, ouvriere de soie"; AN KK 283, fol. 9)

Jeanne la Beguine ("Jehanne la beguine, ouvriere de soie"; AN KK 283, fol. 222)

Jeanne la Beguine ("Jehanne la beguine, ouvriere de soie"; AN KK 283, fol. 243)

Thomasse la Beguine ("Thomasse la beguine, ouvriere de soie"; AN KK 283, fol. 111)

BEGUINES DESCRIBED AS SILK MERCHANTS (5)

Isabelle d'Oroer[10] ("Ysabel d'oroer, vendeur de soie"; AN KK 283, fol. 186v)

Isabelle de Cambrai[11] ("Isabiau de cambrai, merciere"; AN KK 283, fol. 112v)

Jehanne du Faut[12] ("Jehanne du fauc, mercier"; AN KK 283, fol. 17)

Marguerite de Troyes ("Marguerite de troies, merciere"; AN KK 283, fol. 266v)

Maria Osanne[13] ("Marie Osane, mercier"; AN KK 283, fol. 268)

BEGUINES WHO DID NOT WORK WITH SILK (5)

Alice la Feutrière, beguine ("Aalis la feutriere, beguine";[14] AN KK 283, fol. 30v)

Ameline la Beguine ("Ameline la beguine, aveniere";[15] AN KK 283, fol. 118v)

Jehannete la Chanevacière ("Jehannette et perrete, dites les cuillieres,[16] beguines"; AN KK 283, fol. 235 v)

Marie la Beguine ("Marie la beguine, regratier";[17] AN KK 283, fol. 282v)

Perrenelle la Chanevacière ("Jehannette et perrete, dites les cuillieres, beguines"; AN KK 283, fol. 235v)

NOTES

INTRODUCTION

Epigraph: "En riens que Beguine die, N'entendeiz tuit se bien non: Tot es de religion, Quanque hon trueve en sa vie. Sa parole est prophetie; S'ele rit, c'est compaignie; S'el pleure, devocion; S'ele dort, ele est ravie; S'ele songe, c'est vision; S'ele ment, n'en creeiz mie. Se Beguine se marie, C'est sa conversacions: Ses veulz, sa prophecions, N'est pas a toute sa vie. Cest an pleure et cest an prie, Et cest an pannra baron: Or est Marthe, or est Marie, Or se garde, or se marie; Mais n'en dites se bien non: Li roix no sofferoit mie." Rutebeuf, "Li diz des beguines," *Oeuvres complètes,* ed. Michel Zink, vol. 1 (Paris: Garnier, 1989), 240. All translations are my own unless otherwise indicated.

1. "Domum insuper Parisius honestarum mulierum, quae vocantur beguinae, de süo adquisivit et eisdem assignavit." As reported in Geoffrey of Beaulieu, "Vita ludovici noni," *Recueil des historiens des Gaules et de la France* (henceforth *RHF*), ed. Martin Bouquet et al., vol. 20 (Paris, 1840), 12.

2. For official, canonical interpretations of the beguine status, see Elizabeth Makowski, *"A Pernicious Sort of Woman": Quasi-Religious Women and Canon Lawyers in the Later Middle Ages* (Washington, DC: Catholic University of America Press, 2005).

3. On the varied interpretations of the story of Mary and Martha through the Middle Ages, see Giles Constable, "The Interpretation of Mary and Martha," in *Three Studies in Medieval Religious and Social Thought* (Cambridge: Cambridge University Press, 1995), 3–141.

4. "Et apud nos mulieres aliae, de quibus nescimus, utrum debeamus eas vel saeculares vel moniales appelare, partim enim utuntur ritu saeculari, partim etiam regulari." Gilbert of Tournai, *Collectio de Scandalis Ecclesiae,* ed. Autbertus Stroick, "*Collectio de Scandalis Ecclesiae:* Nova editio," *Archivium Franciscanum Historicum* 24 (1931): 58.

5. Jennifer K. Deane, "Beguines Reconsidered: Historiographical Problems and New Directions," *Monastic Matrix* (2008), Commentaria 3461.

6. A single article published in 1893 by the French historian Léon Le Grand remains the definitive publication on Parisian beguines. Le Grand's article is an institutional history of the royal beguinage, focusing on the establishment, organization, and administration of the community. Thus, Le Grand's study examines the Paris beguinage strictly as a royal foundation and reveals very little about the women and their place in urban society. See

Léon Le Grand, "Les béguines de Paris," *Mémoires de la société de l'histoire de Paris et de l'Ile-de-France* 20 (1893): 295–357.

7. On the attraction Paris held for migrants of all backgrounds, see Sharon Farmer, *Surviving Poverty in Medieval Paris: Gender, Ideology, and the Daily Lives of the Poor* (Ithaca, NY: Cornell University Press, 2002), 11–38.

8. On Marguerite Porete's trial and condemnation see now Sean L. Field, *The Beguine, the Angel, and the Inquisitor: The Trials of Marguerite Porete and Guiard of Cressonessart* (Notre Dame, IN: University of Notre Dame Press, 2012). Other useful historical treatments include Paul Verdeyen, "Le procès d'inquisition contre Marguerite Porete et Guiard de Cressonessart," *Revue d'histoire ecclésiastique* 81 (1986): 47–94; and Edmund Colledge, "Introductory Interpretive Essay," in Margaret Porette, *The Mirror of Simple Souls*, trans. Edmund Colledge, J. C. Marler, and Judith Grant (Notre Dame, IN: University of Notre Dame Press, 1999). But see Field (pp. 3–6) for a summary of the errors that crop up in the many fine studies on Marguerite and her book.

9. For the Latin text and English translation, see Norman P. Tanner, ed., *Decrees of the Ecumenical Councils: Nicaea I–Lateran V* (Washington, DC: Georgetown University Press, 1990), 1: 374. The translation here is found in Makowski, *"A Pernicious Sort of Woman,"* 23–24.

10. Tanner, *Decrees of the Ecumenical Councils*, 1: 383–384. On the "abominable sect" mentioned in *Ad Nostrum*, see Robert E. Lerner, *The Heresy of the Free Spirit in the Later Middle Ages* (1973, repr. Notre Dame, IN: University of Notre Dame Press, 1991).

11. I suggested some of these links in "What's in a Name? Clerical Representations of Parisian Beguines (1200–1328)," *Journal of Medieval History* 33, no. 1 (2007): 60–86. Sean Field has recently analyzed the trials of Marguerite Porete and Guiard of Cressonessart in extraordinary detail, illuminating the multiple interests and concerns that converged at the trials and how they played out at the Council of Vienne. See Field, *The Beguine, the Angel, and the Inquisitor.*

12. Robert Lerner's *Heresy of the Free Spirit* and Richard Kieckhefer's *Repression of Heresy in Medieval Germany* (Philadelphia: University of Pennsylvania Press, 1979) in particular have contributed significantly to our knowledge of the persecutorial activity inspired by the Vienne Decrees in German lands. For an overall assessment of the fate of beguine communities in the years after the publication of the Vienne decrees, see also Ernest W. McDonnell, *The Beguines and Beghards in Medieval Culture, with Special Emphasis on the Belgian Scene* (New Brunswick, NJ: Rutgers University Press, 1954), 421–556, and Walter Simons, *Cities of Ladies: Beguine Communities in the Medieval Low Countries, 1200–1565* (Philadelphia: University of Pennsylvania Press, 2001), 133–137.

13. For a concise overview of beguine scholarship over the last century, see Simons, *Cities of Ladies*, ix–xii.

14. For a useful discussion of the scholarship on medieval women inspired by Grundmann's study, see *New Trends in Feminine Spirituality: The Holy Women of Liège and Their Impact*, ed. Juliette Dor, Lesley Johnson, and Jocelyn Wogan-Browne (Turnhout: Brepols, 1999).

15. Herbert Grundmann, *Religious Movements in the Middle Ages: The Historical Links Between Heresy, the Mendicant Orders, and the Women's Religious Movement in the Twelfth*

and Thirteenth Century, with the Historical Foundations of German Mysticism, trans. Stevan Rowan (Notre Dame, IN: University of Notre Dame Press, 1995), 1.

16. Lerner, *Heresy of the Free Spirit,* and Kieckhefer, *Repression of Heresy in Medieval Germany.*

17. For an insightful overview of the ways in which this narrative of persecution has shaped scholarship on beguines, especially in German lands, see Jennifer Deane, "Beguines Reconsidered: Historiographical Problems and New Directions," *Monastic Matrix* (2008), Commentaria 3461, available at http://monasticmatrix.org/commentaria/article.php?textId=3461

18. McDonnell, *Beguines and Beghards.*

19. McDonnell asserts that while "the Belgian beguinage held aloof from the heterodox forces at work in the Rhineland, the German sisters, not so well claustrated, were sometimes led astray by usurping the office of preaching, by discussing the doctrine of the Trinity and divine essence, and by casting aspersion on the sacraments." *Beguines and Beghards,* 412.

20. Simons puts to rest theories about the origins of the term "beguine" and the existence of a beguine "founder." He also tackles the oft-cited but erroneous four-stage model of beguine organization described in L. M. J. Philippen's 1918 study *De Begijnhoven, Oorsprong, Geschiedenis, Inrichting* (Antwerp: Veritas, 1918). See Simons, *Cities of Ladies.*

21. See Joanna Ziegler, "The *Curtis* Beguinages in the Southern Low Countries: Interpretation and Historiography," *Bulletin van het Belgisch Historisch Instituut te Rome/Bulletin de l'Institut Historique Belge de Rome* 57 (1987): 31–70. Recent scholarship on German beguines has shown that this narrative of persecution and suppression does not work for much of the region. See Deane, "Beguines Reconsidered."

22. In his study of beguines and beghards in the Rhineland, Jean-Claude Schmitt argues that the beguines who were attached to a stable community were less likely to be associated with heresy than the unattached, "unstable" beguines. Jean-Claude Schmitt, *Mort d'une hérésie: L'Église et les clercs face aux béguines et aux béghards du Rhin supérieur du xive au xve siècle* (Paris: Mouton, 1978), 44–50. Ziegler implies that the beguines in German lands, who did not live in court beguinages, were poor, vulnerable, and lacking in "corporate identity." Ziegler, "The *Curtis* Beguinages," 35.

23. McDonnell, *Beguines and Beghards,* 367.

24. The quote is from Robin O'Sullivan's otherwise insightful article on beguine education, "The School of Love: Marguerite Porete's Mirror of Simple Souls," *Journal of Medieval History* 32 (2006): 145. Joanna Ziegler portrays the beguinages after the Council of Vienne as places where the exuberant, Christocentric piety of beguines was domesticated. See Joanna E. Ziegler, "Reality as Imitation: The Dynamics of Imagery Among the Beguines," in *Maps of Flesh and Light: New Perspectives on the Religious Experience of Late Medieval Women,* ed. Ulrike Wiethaus (Syracuse: Syracuse University Press, 1993), 118–119.

25. The classic study on female spirituality is Caroline W. Bynum's *Holy Feast, Holy Fast: The Religious Significance of Food to Medieval Women* (Berkeley: University of California Press, 1987). On beguine spirituality more specifically and the ways in which clerics sought to shape, harness, or benefit personally from the beguines' privileged access to God,

see Jo Ann McNamara, "Rhetoric of Orthodoxy: Clerical Authority and Female Innova-tion in the Struggle with Heresy," in *Maps of Flesh and Light*, ed. Wiethaus, 9–27; André Vauchez, "Prosélytisme et action antihérétique en milieu féminin au XIIIe siècle: La Vie de Marie d'Oignies (d. 1213) par James of Vitry," in *Propagande et contre-propagande religieuses*, ed. Jacques Marx (Brussels: Éditions de l'Universitaire, 1987), 95–110; John W. Coakley, "Gender and Authority of the Friars: The Significance of Holy Women for Thirteenth-Century Franciscans and Dominicans," *Church History* 60 (1991): 445–460; "Friars as Con-fidants of Holy Women in Medieval Dominican Hagiography," in *Images of Sainthood in Medieval Europe*, ed. Renate Blumenfeld-Kosinski and Timea Szell (Ithaca, NY: Cornell University Press, 1991), 222–246; and most recently, *Women, Men, and Spiritual Power: Female Saints and Their Male Collaborators* (New York: Columbia University Press, 2006). See too the essays in *Gendered Voices: Medieval Saints and their Interpreters*, ed. Catherine Moody (Philadelphia: University of Pennsylvania Press, 1999).

26. Dyan Elliott, *Proving Woman: Female Spirituality and Inquisitional Culture in the Later Middle Ages* (Princeton, NJ: Princeton University Press, 2004).

27. In a critique of Joanna Ziegler's argument that beguinages sought to control or render "ordinary" beguine spirituality, Penelope Galloway argues that this "ordinary" spirituality was not imposed but rather created by the beguines themselves; see Penelope Galloway, "Neither Miraculous Nor Astonishing: The Devotional Practice of Beguine Communities in French Flanders," in *New Trends in Feminine Spirituality*, ed. Juliette Dor et al., 107–127.

28. O'Sullivan, "The School of Love."

29. I owe this observation to Jennifer Deane. See Deane, "Beguines Reconsidered." Jennifer Deane is currently working on several projects that grapple with these issues, with particular focus on beguine houses in German-speaking lands.

30. I benefited in particular from access to the archive of copious notes and unpub-lished work on the Parisian bourgeoisie left by Anne Terroine, housed at the Institut de Recherche et d'Histoire des Textes in Paris. I am indebted to Caroline Bourlet for allowing me access to these precious materials.

31. Sharon Farmer is currently writing a study that deals with the topic, entitled *The Origins of the Paris Silk Industry in the Thirteenth Century* (forthcoming). Parts of this larger project are published in Farmer, "Medieval Paris and the Mediterranean: The Evidence from the Silk Industry," *French Historical Studies* (forthcoming). I thank Sharon Farmer for sharing her unpublished research with me.

32. The scholarship on laywomen and clerics is vast. In addition to the works cited above in note 25, see Elizabeth Petroff, "Male Confessors and Female Penitents: Possibili-ties for Dialogue," in *Body and Soul: Essays on Medieval Women and Mysticism* (New York: Oxford University Press, 1994), 139–160; John Coakley, "Friars, Sanctity, and Gender: Men-dicant Encounters with Saints, 1250–1325," in *Medieval Masculinities: Regarding Men in the Middle Ages*, ed. Clare Lees (Minneapolis: University of Minnesota Press, 1994), 91–110; Catherine Mooney, "The Authorial Role of Brother A. in the Composition of Angela of Foligno's Revelations," *Creative Women in Medieval and Early Modern Italy*, ed. E. Ann Matter and John Coakley (Philadelphia: University of Pennsylvania Press, 1994), 34–63.

33. See Sean L. Field, "The Master and Marguerite: Godfrey of Fontaines's Praise of *The Mirror of Simple Souls*," *Journal of Medieval History* 35 (2009): 136–149.

34. Alcuin Blamires, "Women and Preaching in Medieval Orthodoxy, Heresy and Saints' Lives," *Viator* 26 (1995): 135–152, and Clare M. Waters, *Angels and Earthly Creatures: Preaching, Performance, and Gender in the Later Middle Ages* (Philadelphia: University of Pennsylvania Press, 2004).

35. Michel Lauwers, "*Praedicatio—Exhortatio:* L'Église, la réforme, et les laïcs (XIe et XIIe siècles)," in *La parole de prédicateur, Ve–XVe siècle* (Nice: Centre d'Études Médiévales, 1997), 187–232, and Nicole Bériou, "The Right of Women to Give Religious Instruction in the Thirteenth Century," in *Women Preachers and Prophets Through Two Millennia of Christianity*, ed. Beverly M. Kienzle and Pamela J. Walker (Berkeley: University of California Press, 1998), 134–145.

36. Recent scholarship on beguines has stressed the religious aspect of the beguine life while recognizing the beguines' importance to their urban context. Walter Simons's study on beguines in the Low Countries is particularly valuable in its approach, which stresses the history of beguines "first as a religious 'movement' of the laity; second, as a movement shaped and promoted by urban conditions; and third . . . as a movement characterized by the gender of its participants." *Cities of Ladies*, xii. See also recent scholarship on German beguines by Jennifer Kolpacoff Deane, "From Case Studies to Comparative Models: Würzburg Beguines and the Vienne Decrees," in *Labels, Libels, and Lay Religious Women in Northern Medieval Europe*, ed. Letha Böhringer, Jennifer K. Deane, and Hildo van Engen (Turnhout: Brepols, forthcoming).

37. I borrow this phrase from John W. Baldwin's study of religious and social thought in medieval Paris, *Masters, Princes and Merchants: the Social Views of Peter the Chanter and his Circle* (Princeton, NJ: Princeton University Press, 1970).

38. On this view, see John Van Engen, who discusses "conversion" in the Middle Ages as a "deliberate reconfiguring of life toward an envisioned perfect form." John Van Engen, *Sisters and Brothers of the Common Life: The Devotio Moderna and the World of the Later Middle Ages* (Philadelphia: University of Pennsylvania Press, 2008), 14.

CHAPTER 1. THE *PRUD'HOMME* AND THE BEGUINES

1. "Et propter quasdam mulieres juvenes, quas appellant beguinas per totum regnum iam diffusas." Johann Lorenz Mosheim, *De Beghardis et Beguinabus commentarius*, ed. G. H. Martini (Leipzig, 1790), 26–27. On William of Saint-Amour, see Michel-Marie Dufeil, *Guillaume de Saint-Amour et la polémique universitaire parisienne, 1250–1259* (Paris: J. Picard, 1972).

2. Geoffrey of Beaulieu, "Vita ludovici," *RHF*, vol. 20, 12.

3. As a number of studies have shown, lay religious women—whether identified in the sources as *beguinae, mulieres religiosae, sorores*, or by some other name—lived together in a variety of settings, formal or otherwise. For the Low Countries, see McDonnell, *Beguines and Beghards*, 8–70; Simons, *Cities of Ladies*, 36–48. On German houses of lay religious

women, see Jennifer K. Deane, "*Geistliche Schwestern:* The Pastoral Care of Lay Religious Women in Würzburg," in *Partners in Spirit: Women, Men and Religious Life in Germany, 1100–1500,* ed. Fiona Griffith and Julie Hotchin (Turnhout: Brepols, 2013), 164–188. Fiscal records attest to the presence of beguine communities around the Franciscan and Dominican convents in the late thirteenth century, and such communities may have existed for several decades. See Sharon Farmer, "Down and Out and Females in Thirteenth-Century Paris," *American Historical Review* (1998) 345–372.

4. "Rex devotissimus Ludovicus, in tantum amplectitur virginae dignitatis pudicitiam consectantes, ut Parisiis collegerit Beghinarum maximam multitudinem. . . ." Thomas of Cantimpré, *Bonum Universale de Apibus,* ed. Georgius Colvenerius (Douai: B. Belleri, 1627). Thomas dedicated the work to Humbert of Romans, whom he addressed in the dedicatory letter as master-general of the Dominican order, a post Humbert resigned in May 1263. On the dating of this work, see Simone Roisin, "La méthode hagiographique de Thomas de Cantimpré," in *Miscellanea Historica in Honorem Alberti de Meyer* (Louvain: Bibliothèque de l'Université, 1946), 1: 548–549. See also Robert Sweetman, "Dominican Preaching in the Southern Low Countries, 1240–1260: *Materiae Praedicabiles* in the *Liber de natura rerum* and *Bonum universale de apibus* of Thomas of Cantimpré" (Ph.D. dissertation, University of Toronto, 1988).

5. "Domum insuper Paris . . . in qua religiose et honeste conversantur circiter quadringentæ." *RHF*, vol. 20, 12.

6. We can assume that Geoffrey was a reliable source on this matter. As Louis IX's confessor, he occasionally performed administrative tasks for the king, including the distribution of alms to houses like the beguinage. Moreover, Geoffrey himself preached at the beguinage in 1272 and therefore probably had a good sense of how many women lived within the enclosure (Paris, Bibliothèque nationale de France, Lat. 16481, fol. 27vb). The figure of four hundred, it should be noted, represents a tiny fraction of Paris's population, which scholars have estimated to have been about 210,000 in 1328. On the population of Paris, see Raymond Cazelles, "La population de Paris avant la peste noire," *Académie des Inscriptions et Belles Lettres: Comptes Rendus* (Paris, 1260), 539–554 and David Herlihy, *Opera Muliebria: Women and Work in Medieval Europe* (New York: McGraw-Hill, 1990), 128–131. By way of comparison, court beguinages in the southern Low Countries housed hundreds, and in some cases over a thousand women. See Simons, *Cities of Ladies,* 48–60.

7. In his testament, which he composed in February 1270, Louis made arrangements to expand the beguinage. See *Layettes du trésor des Chartes* (henceforth *Layettes*), ed. Alexandre Teulet and Joseph de Laborde (Paris: 1863–1875), vol. 4, 419–421.

8. William Chester Jordan has highlighted the ways in which Louis brought together the spiritual and practical as king and crusader, as well as the tensions between his religious ideals and kingly duties. See William C. Jordan, *Louis IX and the Challenge of the Crusade: A Study in Rulership* (Princeton, NJ: Princeton University Press, 1979), and "The Case of Saint Louis," *Viator* 19 (1988): 209–218. Jacques Le Goff sees less tension between religious ideals and kingship, arguing that Louis embodied the ideal Christian king: "In Saint Louis's case, the individual and his ideal models were historically unified. Thus . . . studying Saint Louis's models of sainthood amounts to studying the 'real' Saint Louis." Jacques Le Goff,

Saint Louis, trans. Gareth E. Gollard (Notre Dame, IN: University of Notre Dame Press, 2009), 608. As will be seen in this treatment of Louis, I am inclined to believe that Louis had to negotiate between two somewhat conflicting codes of behavior, frequently having to stand his ground against objections to aspects of his piety.

9. On Louis's support for the various mendicant orders, particularly his efforts to establish houses in Paris and throughout the kingdom, see Richard W. Emery, *The Friars in Medieval France: A Catalogue of French Mendicant Convents, 1200–1550* (New York: Columbia University Press, 1962). On the lesser-known mendicant orders, see Frances Andrews, *The Other Friars: The Carmelite, Augustinian, Sack and Pied Friars in the Middle Ages* (Woodbridge: Boydell Press, 2006).

10. Le Grand, "Les béguines de Paris," 303–305, and McDonnell, *Beguines and Beghards*, 224–226. William Jordan mentions Louis's support for beguines as "part of a broader program of charity for vulnerable segments of society," *Louis IX and the Challenge of the Crusade*, 185.

11. Jordan argues that the crusade was the defining event in Louis's life. Le Goff, on the other hand, sees this as an exaggeration, arguing that the crusade, while an important religious experience, was just one manifestation of Louis's image and identity as a saintly king. Jordan, *Louis IX and the Challenge of the Crusade*, 127–129.

12. Louis's expansion and restructuring of the system of royal almsgiving is evident in surviving royal account books. For an overview, see Xavier de La Selle, *Le service des âmes à la cour: Confesseurs et aumôniers des rois de France du XIIIe au XVe siècle* (Paris: École des Chartes, 1995), and Robert-Henri Bautier (with François Maillard), "Les aumônes du roi aux maladreries, maisons-dieu, et pauvres établissements du royaume: Contribution à l'étude du réseau hospitalier et de la fossilisation de l'administration royale de Philippe Auguste à Charles VII," in *Assistance et assistés jusqu'à 1610, Actes du 97e Congrès national des Sociétés Savantes: Nantes 1972* (Paris: Bibliothèque nationale, 1979), 37–105.

13. Jordan, *Louis IX and the Challenge of the Crusade*, 152.

14. Ibid., 182–213.

15. Louis's foundation of the Paris beguinage is mentioned in most accounts of Louis's life, but has not received much sustained discussion other than the older treatment in Le Grand, "Les béguines de Paris," from which most of McDonnell's brief discussion is drawn. See *Beguines and Beghards*, 224–233.

16. See note 5, above. Geoffrey of Beaulieu wrote his hagiographical account (entitled *Vita et sancta conversatio*) at the request of Pope Gregory X. It was begun in 1272 and completed sometime before Geoffrey's death in 1275.

17. "[Et] pluribus exceptis, maxime pauperibus nobilibus, quamdiu viverent, de sustentatione quotidiana providit. Similiter in pluribus aliis regni sui civitatibus atque castris dictis Beguinis domos ad habitandum providit." *RHF*, vol. 20, 12.

18. John of Joinville, *The Life of St. Louis*, trans. René Hague from the text edited by Natalis de Wailly (New York: Sheed and Ward, 1955), 210.

19. On Isabelle, see Sean L. Field, *Isabelle of France: Capetian Sanctity and Franciscan Identity in the Thirteenth Century* (Notre Dame, IN: University of Notre Dame Press, 2006).

20. Ibid., 2–4. On Isabelle's influence on Louis, see also Jordan, *Louis IX and the Challenge of the Crusade,* 9–12, and more recently, "Isabelle of France and Religious Devotion at the Court of Louis IX," in *Capetian Women,* ed. Kathleen Nolan (New York: Palgrave Macmillan, 2003), 209–223.

21. Jordan, *Louis IX and the Challenge of the Crusade,* 9–12, and Field, *Isabelle of France,* 27–31.

22. Field, *Isabelle of France,* 37–59.

23. "Quae soli Deo vacans, adeo contemplationi deditur et virtuti, ut nulla ei cura in ullis transitoriis videatur." Thomas of Cantimpré, *Bonum Universale de Apibus,* II.29.40. I have followed the translation in Field, *Isabelle of France,* 45.

24. "Sed et ipsius frater, quem diximus, Rex devotissimus Ludovicus, in tantum amplectitur virgineae dignitatis pudicitiam consectantes, ut Parisiis collegerit Beghinarum maximam multitudinem, ut se in humilitatis obsequiis exerceat et salute." Ibid. Translation in Field, *Isabelle of France,* 45–46.

25. Field, *Isabelle of France,* 46.

26. Grundmann, *Religious Movements,* 81–82; Simons, *Cities of Ladies,* 121–125.

27. On this conflict, see Decima L. Douie, *The Conflict Between the Seculars and the Mendicants at the University of Paris in the Thirteenth Century* (London: Blackfriars, 1954); Michel-Marie Dufeil *Guillaume de Saint-Amour et la polémique,* and Dufeil "Le roi Louis dans la querelle des mendiants et des séculiers," in *Septième centenaire de la mort de saint Louis: Actes des colloques de Royaument et de Paris (21–27 mai 1970)* (Paris: Les Belles Lettres, 1976), 281–289.

28. I discuss the significance of Louis's dress later in this chapter.

29. Women making a public claim to sanctity were subject to intense efforts to prove the veracity of their claims. See Dyan Elliott, *Proving Woman: Female Spirituality and Inquisitional Culture in the Later Middle Ages,* and Nancy Caciola, *Discerning Spirits: Divine and Demonic Possession in the Middle Ages* (Ithaca, NY: Cornell University Press, 2006).

30. Penn R. Szittya, *The Antifraternal Tradition in Medieval Literature* (Princeton, NJ: Princeton University Press, 1986). Szittzya notes that secular masters, in their letters to the pope and other ecclesiastical authorities protesting the extension of mendicant privileges, also associated the friars with the false prophets forewarned in scripture. See ibid., 21. Guy Geltner has recently published a Latin edition, along with an English translation and short introduction, of William's treatise: *William of Saint-Amour: De periculis novissimorum termporum,* ed. and trans. G. Geltner, Dallas Medieval Texts and Translations 8 (Louvain: Peeters, 2007).

31. 2 Tim. 3:1–6.

32. William of Saint-Amour, *De periculis,* 66.

33. Ibid., 68.

34. Indeed, preaching and pastoral care were central issues in the secular-mendicant conflict. See Chapter 4.

35. William of Saint-Amour, "Les '*Responsiones*' de Guillaume de Saint-Amour," ed. Edmond Faral, *Archives d'histoire doctrinale et littéraire du moyen âge* 18 (1950–1951), 337–394 (henceforth, *Responsiones*), 343–344.

36. "Quasdam mulieres juvenes, quas appellant Beguinas, per totum regnum Franciae

jam diffusas: qui omnes cum sint validi ad operandum, parum aut nihil volunt operari, sed vivere volunt de elemosinis in otio corporali sub praetextu orandi." Ibid., 342.

37. Ibid.

38. William of Saint-Amour, "Collectiones catholicae et canonicae scripturae," in *Guillielmi de S. Amore Opera omnia* (Constance [Paris]: Alitophilos, 1632), 268–269. Some of William's insinuations regarding beguines and friars are discussed in Szittya, *The Antifraternal Tradition*, 57–60.

39. On suspicions surrounding unmarried women, see Ruth Mazo Karras, "Sex and the Singlewoman," in *Singlewomen in the European Past, 1250–1800*, ed. Judith M. Bennett and Amy M. Froide (Philadelphia: University of Pennsylvania Press, 1999), 127–145.

40. "Beguinarum amator." William of Saint-Amour, "Collectiones," 271; Szittya, *The Antifraternal Tradition*, 59–60.

41. On Rutebeuf's sympathies, which had once been with the mendicants, see Edmond Faral, "Pour le commentaire de Rutebeuf: Le dit des 'règles,'" *Studi Medievali* 16 (1943–1950): 176–211.

42. "L'Ordre aus beguines est legiere, / Si vous dirai en quel maniere: / L'en s'en ist bien por mari prendre. / D'autre part, qui besse la chiere / Et a robe large et pleniere / Si est beguine sanz li rendre." Rutebeuf, "Les ordres de Paris," *Oeuvres complètes,* 2 vols., ed. Michel Zink (Paris: Garnier, 1989), 1: 227.

43. Compare this understanding of *religio* with that of Robert of Sorbon in Chapter 4.

44. "Beguines avons mont / Qui larges robes ont; / Desouz les robes font / Ce que pas ne vous di." Rutebeuf, "La Chanson des ordres,"*Oeuvres completes,* 1: 332. Beguines were a frequent target in French literature; see Renate Blumenfeld-Kosinski, "Satirical Views of the Beguines in Northern French Literature," *New Trends in Feminine Spirituality: The Holy Women of Liège and Their Impact,* ed. Juliette Dor, Lesley Johnson, and Jocelyn Wogan-Browne (Turnhout: Brepols, 1999), 237–249.

45. "Tantost Astenance Constrainte / Vest une robe cameline / E s'atourne come beguine," *Le roman de la rose* par Guillaume de Lorris et Jean de Meun, 5 vols., ed. Ernest Langlois (Paris: Édouard Champion, 1914–1924), vol. 3, 226.

46. Ibid.

47. As Guy Geltner has noted in his recent edition and translation of *De periculis novissimorum temporum*, the fact that Louis was one of the main targets in William's writings during the conflict has not received much attention in the scholarly literature on the secular-mendicant conflict. See William of Saint-Amour, *De periculis,* 11.

48. As William Jordan has shown, most of the mendicant houses Louis founded predate the Seventh Crusade. See *Louis IX and the Challenge of the Crusade,* 232–235.

49. De La Selle, *Le service des âmes à la cour,* 98–106. Indeed, friars soon came to dominate ecclesiastical positions at all levels. See R. F. Bennett, *The Early Dominicans: Studies in Thirteenth-Century Dominican History* (Cambridge: Cambridge University Press, 1937).

50. See Jordan, *Louis IX and the Challenge of the Crusade,* 53–54, 153.

51. Lester K. Little, "Saint Louis' Involvement with the Friars," *Church History* 33, no. 2 (1964): 124–148.

52. Joinville, *Life of Saint Louis,* 196.

53. Ibid. LeGoff points out inconsistencies in some of these portrayals of Louis's simplicity, which show that Louis was cognizant of his elevated position and avoided excessive displays of piety that might embarrass his company or station.

54. Dufeil, *Guillaume de Saint-Amour et la polémique universitaire parisienne*, 152–153.

55. On the French kings' support for the university, see Stephen C. Ferruolo, *The Origins of the University: The Schools of Paris and Their Critics, 1100–1215* (Stanford: Stanford University Press,1985), 13–15.

56. Dufeil, "Le roi Louis dans la querelle des mendicants et des séculiers."

57. William of Saint-Amour, *De periculis*, chapters 11, 13, and 14.

58. "Fi! fi! deusses tu estre roi de France? Mout miex fust que un autre fust rois que tu; car tu es tant seulement des freres Meneurs, des freres Preescheurs et des prestres et des clers." William of Saint-Pathus, "Vie de Saint Louis," *RHF*, vol. 20, 106. See also the discussion in Le Goff, *Saint Louis*, 522 and 675. In fact, Louis's clothing, like the beguines', seems to have been a flashpoint around which debates about clothing, rank, and piety revolved. The king's dress was a much-discussed issue in William of Saint-Amour's writings (see *Responsiones*, 347–348). Jean of Meun also addresses clothing as a marker of status in the *Roman de la Rose*. On this point in general, see Dyan Elliott, "Dress as Mediator Between Inner and Outer Self: The Pious Matron of the High and Later Middle Ages," *Mediaeval Studies* 53 (1991): 279–308.

59. William of Saint-Pathus, "Vie de Saint Louis," 106.

60. Grundmann, *Religious Movements*, 163–164.

61. On the ways in which the meaning of term *religio* broadened to include those who lived a religious life outside the cloister, see Peter Biller, "Words and the Medieval Notion of 'Religion,'" *Journal of Ecclesiastical History* 36, no. 3 (1985): 351–369.

62. James of Vitry, *Historia occidentalis*, cited in Giles Constable, *The Reformation of the Twelfth Century* (Cambridge: Cambridge University Press, 1996), 293. A product of the Parisian schools and a student of Peter the Chanter, James supported and promoted new conceptions of *religio* while strenuously upholding the sacerdotal authority of the ordained clergy. See Jessalyn Bird, "The Religious's Role in a Post-Fourth-Lateran World: Jacques de Vitry's Sermones ad status and Historia occidentalis," in *Medieval Monastic Preaching*, ed. Carolyn Muessig (Leiden: Brill, 1998), 209–229.

63. While famed as the founder of the Sorbonne, Robert has not received much attention in the scholarly literature outside studies on the University of Paris. See Palémon Glorieux, *Aux origines de la Sorbonne*, volume 1, *Robert de Sorbon, l'homme, le collège, les documents* (Paris: J. Vrin, 1965–1966); Astrik L. Gabriel, *The Paris Studium: Robert of Sorbonne and His Legacy: Interuniversity Exchange Between the German, Cracow and Louvain Universities and that of Paris in the Late Medieval and Humanistic Period: Selected Studies* (Notre Dame, IN: University of Notre Dame Press, 1992); and Nicole Bériou, "Robert de Sorbon," in *Dictionnaire de spiritualité: Ascétique et mystique, doctrine et histoire*, ed. André Vauchez, 13 (1988): cols. 816–824.

64. Robert is listed among several clerics associated with the king's household in 1256. He is listed alongside William of Chartres (at the time a secular cleric), the bishops of Bourges and Senlis, John of Saint-Amand, and several other important members of the court. See *Johannis Sarraceni tabulae ceratae*, in *RHF*, vol. 21, 360.

65. See Glorieux, *Aux origines,* 28. Robert's friendship with the king is evident in the various property transactions in which the two men partnered, including those that eventually led to the creation of the Sorbonne. See *Aux origines,* 29–35.

66. Ibid., 33–38.

67. Although this claim has been disputed, Robert was certainly a trusted associate of the king. Ibid., 28.

68. Joinville, *Life of Saint Louis,* 30.

69. Nicole Bériou, "Robert de Sorbon, le prud'homme et le béguin," *Comptes Rendus de l'Académie des Inscriptions et Belles Lettres* (Paris: 1994), 474–482.

70. See Chapter 4.

71. Joinville, *Life of Saint Louis,* 30.

72. On Robert's sermons comparing the prud'homme with the beguin, see Bériou, "Robert de Sorbon, le prud'homme et le béguin." For an examination of these terms in the context of the secular-mendicant conflict of the thirteenth century, see Tanya Stabler Miller, "Mirror of the Scholarly (Masculine) Soul: Thinking with Beguines in the Colleges of Medieval Paris," in *Negotiating Clerical Identities: Priests, Monks, and Masculinity in the Middle Ages,* ed. Jennifer Thibodeaux (New York: Palgrave Macmillan, 2010), 238–264.

73. On Robert's praise of the beguines and explicit comparison of the status with that of the prud'homme, see Chapter 4.

74. William Jordan argues that Louis's response, which historians have frequently taken seriously, should be read as ironic. See Jordan, "The Case of Saint Louis," 215.

75. Jordan makes a similar point in "The Case of Saint Louis."

76. Even Louis's wife, Margaret of Provence, famously disapproved of her husband's simple clothing. Robert of Sorbon related an exemplum about an exchange between Louis and Margaret, in which the queen asked Louis to dress in clothing more appropriate to his position. Louis agreed to dress to please Margaret if she would, in turn, wear clothing more pleasing (i.e., more simple) to him. Predictably, Margaret let the matter drop. See also "Vie de Saint Louis," *RHF,* vol. 20, 106.

77. Jordan, "The Case of Saint Louis," 217.

78. See Chapter 4.

79. Jordan argues that this criticism must have bothered Louis, asserting that "his sense of his own rightness was undoubtedly unsettled by close friends and learned pious scholars making such remarks. Still, he refused (or was incapable of) changing." Jordan, "The Case of Saint Louis," 212.

80. Geltner claims that Louis must have found *De periculis* deeply offensive, yet Louis took no action initially against William. See Geltner, "Introduction," in William of Saint-Amour, *De periculis,* 12.

81. For the sermon, *Si quis diligit me,* see *The Opuscula of William of Saint-Amour: The Minor Works of 1255–1256,* ed. Andrew G. Traver (Münster: Aschendorff, 2003).

82. *Chartularium Universitatis Parisiensis,* ed. H. S. Denifle and E. Chatelain, 4 vols. (Paris, 1889–1891), vol. 1, 281.

83. Geltner, "Introduction," William of Saint-Amour, *De periculis,* 13.

84. See Chapter 4.

85. "Mais n'en dites se bien non: / Li Rois no sofferroit mie." Rutebeuf, "Li diz des beguines," *Oeuvres complètes*, ed. Michel Zink, vol. 1 (Paris: Garnier, 1989), 240.

86. In a letter dated September 1216, James reported that he had obtained oral permission from Pope Honorius III on behalf of "religious women" not only in the diocese of Liège but in the kingdom of France and imperial territories to live in common and incite one another to live good Christian lives. See *Lettres de Jacques de Vitry*, ed. R. B. C. Huygens (Leiden, 1960), 74.

87. On the beguinage "school" in Paris, see Chapter 5. On beguines and hospital work, see McDonnell, *Beguines and Beghards*, 271–272 and Simons, *Cities of Ladies*, 76–79. On beguines and education, see Penelope Galloway, "'Life, Learning and Wisdom': The Forms and Functions of Beguine Education," in *Medieval Monastic Education*, ed. George and Carolyn Muessig Ferzoco (London: Leicester University Press, 2000), 153–167.

88. William Jordan has traced Louis's itinerary from the port of Hyères, where he and his entourage disembarked in July 1254, through eastern Languedoc and their arrival in Paris in August 1254; see Jordan, *Louis IX and the Challenge of the Crusade*.

89. Field, *Isabelle of France*, 93; Jordan, *Louis IX and the Challenge of the Crusade*, 232–33; Little, "Saint Louis' Involvement with the Friars."

90. The accounts of Jean Sarrasin list a donation of forty livres to the beguines of Senlis "pro domo empta" by Louis's Dominican confessor Geoffrey de Beaulieu. See *RHF*, vol. 21, 356.

91. "Rich. de Bec, pro beguinis et metresses menare Turones et Aurelianum, et reducere a Roan, a Caan, Verneuil, 20 livres." *RHF*, vol. 21, 356. On Louis's foundation of the beguinage at Rouen, see *RHF*, vol. 23, 353. The beguine convent at Tours is also mentioned in Edgar Boutaric, ed., *Actes du Parlement de Paris (1254–1328)*, vol. 1. (Paris: H. Plon, 1863), no. 961.

92. *RHF*, vol. 21, 372; "Item magistra beguinarum de Cambrey, quando rediit, Parisius, per Petrum Marcel, X L"; ibid., 356.

93. *RHF*, vol. 21, 325.

94. While the number of women living in a beguine convent fluctuated over time, the beguine house in Orleans, which credited Louis IX as its founder, fixed the number of beguines at thirteen, including the mistress. "Le beguignage et les beguignes d'Orleans, fonde par saint Louis, et doibvent estre XIII beguignes." Paris, Bibliothèque Nationale de France (henceforth BnF) nov. acq. 1440. Walter Simons calculates the average number of women in beguine convents to be 14.7. Convent beguinages were by far the most common type of beguine institution. According to Simons, 221 out of the 298 (74.2 percent) beguine houses established before 1566 were convents. See *Cities of Ladies*, 50–51. Such houses were the norm in German lands, housing anywhere between two and twenty women, with the apostolic number of twelve being common. Jennifer Deane's forthcoming book will provide a useful overview of the German scene. See also Erica Gelser, "Lay Religious Women and Church Reform in Late Medieval Münster: A Case Study of the Beguines" (Ph.D. dissertation, University of Pennsylvania, 2008), and Günter Peters, "Die Bremer Beginen im Mittelalter: Entstehung und Struktur einer städtischen Frauengemeinschaft," *Niedersächsisches Jahrbuch für Landesgeschichte* 64 (1992): 143.

95. See Bernard Delmaire, "Les béguines dans le Nord de la France au premiere siècle de leur histoire (vers 1230–vers 1350)," in *Les religieuses en France au XIIIe siècle*, ed. Michel Parisse (Nancy: Presses Universitaires de Nancy, 1985), 121–162 and Simons, *Cities of Ladies*, 50–51.

96. Jean Béthune, *Cartulaire du Béguinage de Sainte-Elizabeth à Gand* (Bruges: Aimé de Zuttere, 1883), 73–76, no. 106.

97. Ibid., 76.

98. Ziegler, "The *Curtis* Beguinages"; Walter Simons, "The Beguine Movement in the Southern Low Countries: A Reassessment," *Bulletin van het Belgisch Historisch Instituut te Rome/Bulletin de l'Institut Historique Belge de Rome* 59 (1989), and *Cities of Ladies*.

99. On the dispute, see Charles A. Duvivier, *La querelle des d'Avesnes et des Dampierre jusqu'à la mort de Jean d'Avesnes (1257)* (Brussels: Librairie européenne C. Muquardt, 1894).

100. Duvivier, *La querelle*, vol. 2, 397–400.

101. Agnes's name indicates that she was from Orchies, a small town in French Flanders. There was a beguine convent in Orchies, but Agnes's sermons suggest that she was from Douai. See Nicole Bériou, "La prédication au béguinage de Paris pendant l'année liturgique 1272–1273," *Recherches augustiennes* 13 (1978): 194. Bériou also suggests that Louis had a direct hand in selecting the first mistress.

102. See Chapter 5.

103. "Vie de Saint Louis," *RHF*, vol. 20, 71 and 88.

104. See Field, *Isabelle of France*, 98.

105. "Monseigneur saint Loys, entre les autres oeuvres de misericorde que il fist en son vivant, eust acquis une enceinte de maisons à Paris assis delez la porte Barbeel, et illec eust mis bonne et preude fames beguines pour servir Nostre-Seigneur chastement." Archives Nationales (henceforth, AN) JJ 64, no. 475, fol. 256v, ed. Le Grand, "Les béguines de Paris," 342.

106. The confirmation states: "Stephanus, etc. abbas de Tyronio, totusque eiusdem loci conuentus saltem in domino . . . concessimus et quittauimus in manu mortua, tenendum in perpetuum domino regi Francorum Ludouico et eius successoribus, et ab eisdem causam habentibus quicquid acquisitum est Parisius titulo emptionis uel alio modo ad opus Beguinarum, et quicquid de cetero acquirent, uel aliquis nomine earumdem, in uico qui incipit a porta dictarum Beguinarum usque ad falsam posternam Sancti Pauli in censiue nostra sito, uidelicet in parte dicti uici contigua domibus dictarum Beguinarum, altera parte dicti uici ex opposite nobis prout prius nichilominus remanente, pro centum libris turonensium. . . . In cujus rei testimonium sigilla nostra presenti pagine ducentesimo sexagesimo quarto, mense nouembri." AN J 151/A.

107. Most beguine communities have left few traces in the archives, and foundation charters have survived for only a handful of beguinages. See Delmaire, "Les béguines dans le Nord de la France," 121–162. Even the better-preserved archives of the Quinze-Vingts, King Louis's other major foundation, do not contain a foundation charter. See Mark P. O'Toole, "Caring for the Blind in Medieval Paris" (Ph.D. dissertation, University of California, Santa Barbara, 2007).

108. AN S 6213, no. 149. Perhaps Gervais's generous donation was given out of enthusiasm for the king's new project.

109. On the dating of the *Bonum universale*, see note 4 above. On the dating of Rute-beuf's poem see *Oeuvres completes*, ed. Michel Zink, vol. 1 (Paris: Garnier, 1989), 226.

110. Records from April 1265 show that the beguines already held houses on the rue des Fauconniers. The document records a sale of a rent (annuity) worth twenty sous parisis in exchange for eleven livres parisis. The house is described as held by the beguines of Paris: "Nous feisonz à savoir que par devant nos vint Alixandre de Cristuel et afferma qu'il avoit et poursivoit chascun an aus quatre termes acoustumés à Paris vint souz de parisis de crois de cens ou de rante seur une meson seant à Paris en la rue aus Fauconniers, entre la meson feu Mabile la Boisteuse et la meson feu Thomas Paumier, en la censive de Tyron, si comme il disoit, et laquelle meson les Beguines tienent à Paris." AN J 153, no. 3. Cited in *Layettes,* 130.

111. Most court beguinages were built outside city walls. According to Walter Simons's analysis of fifty court beguinages for which documentation mentioning location has sur-vived, only eight (16 percent) were built inside city walls. See Simons, *Cities of Ladies*, 51 and 180, note 95.

112. The history of German beguine communities illustrates this point particularly well. For an overview of the German beguine houses, see Frank-Michael Reichstein, *Das Beginenwesen in Deutschland: Studien und Katalog* (Berlin: Verlag Dr. Köster, 2001), and more recently Deane, *"Geistliche Schwestern."*

113. Louis's efforts to negotiate with seigneurial and parish authorities were paralleled in Flanders, where the Countesses Joan and Margaret negotiated several competing inter-ests to ensure the stability and spiritual care of the beguinages they founded in Ghent and Lille. See Penelope Galloway, "The Origins, Development and Significance of the Beguine Communities in Douai and Lille, 1200–1500" (Ph.D. dissertation, University of Oxford, 1998). The same balancing act of various authorities was, of course, trickier for beguine communities with less exalted founders and patrons.

114. Grundmann, *Religious Movements in the Middle Ages,* 142.

115. See Chapter 5.

116. In his testament, Louis requested that all of his religious and charitable founda-tions celebrate anniversary masses every year in remembrance of their royal patron. See *Layettes*, vol. 4, 420.

117. See Chapter 4.

118. See Chapter 5.

119. The archives of the Quinze-Vingts, unlike those of the Paris beguinage, have survived largely intact. On the Quinze-Vingts, see Léon Le Grand, "Les Quinze-Vingts depuis leur fondation jusqu'à leur translation au faubourg Saint-Antoine," *MSHP* 13 (1886): 105–260, and "Les Quinze-Vingts depuis leur fondation jusqu'à leur translation au fau-bourg Saint-Antoine (Suite)," *MSHP* 14 (1887): 1–208, and O'Toole, "Caring for the Blind in Medieval Paris."

120. Le Grand, "Les Quinze-Vingts,"130–131, and O'Toole, "Caring for the Blind in Medieval Paris," 109.

121. Le Grand, "Les Quinze-Vingts," 130.

122. Clerics and secular patrons often cited the residents' physical safety and moral reputations as the motivation for erecting chapels within beguine enclosures.

123. In her testament, composed in 1408, the mistress of the beguinage, Martine Canu, refers to herself as a "parishioner" of Saint-Paul. See Alexandre Tuetey, ed., *Testaments enregistrés au Parlement de Paris sous le règne de Charles VI, Collection de documents inédits, Mélanges historiques, III* (Paris: 1880), 226 (henceforth *Testaments*). Moreover, the parish priests themselves asserted their pastoral rights over the Paris beguinage in the fifteenth century.

124. The accord is described in an inventory of documents (the original apparently lost) preserved in the archives of the Filles de l'Ave Maria. The accord stated that the parish priest was "obliged, among other things, to say one mass annually as long as there are beguines there." AN S 4642. A case from the late fourteenth century reveals that, by that time, the parish priest of Saint-Paul said mass at the beguinage chapel every Sunday and administered baptism. AN S 4642 (judgment dated 2 September 1482.) Of course, by the late fourteenth century, there were very few women living at the beguinage and the parish priests obligations had probably changed over the course of the Middle Ages.

125. These chaplains are mentioned in testaments dating from the fourteenth century. For example, the testament of Alice Cournon states: "Item, capellanis et clericis ipsarum beguinarum qui predictum servicium divinum pro salute anime sue facient octo s. p." *Testaments*, 261.

126. In 1284: "Capellanus Sancti Pauli, pro capella beguinarum, pro medietate, X livres," *RHF*, vol. 22, 624. In 1285: "Capellanus Sancti Pauli pro capella beguinarum pro medietate, 7 livres, 10 sous," ibid. In 1298: "Capellanus Sancti Pauli, pro capella beguinarum, pro medietate: 7 livres; et de dono Regis, pro medietate: 40s," *Comptes royaux (1285–1314)*, ed. Robert Fawtier (Paris: Imprimerie nationale, 1953–1956), vol. 3, no. 217. In 1299: "Capellanus Sancti Pauli, pro capella beguinarum, pro medietate: 7 l. 10 s; et de dono Regis, pro medietate: 40 s," ibid, no. 549. In 1305: "Capellanus Sancti Pauli, pro capella beguinarum, pro medietate: 7 livres; et de dono Regis, pro medietate: 40 s," ibid., no. 3597. The French kings continued to compensate the chaplains of Saint Paul throughout the fourteenth and fifteenth centuries. In 1471, when Louis XI proposed to turn over the beguinage to a group of Franciscan tertiaries, the priest at Saint Paul joined the four mendicant orders in opposing the king's plan, citing the annuity he was accustomed to receiving from the Crown. AN S 4642.

127. See Chapter 7.

128. The Dominicans played a prominent role as guardians of beguinages. See Marie-Dominique Chapotin, *Histoire des Dominicains de la Province de France: Le siècle des fondations* (Rouen: Impr. Cagniard, 1898), and Galloway, "The Origins, Development and Significance of the Beguine Communities in Douai and Lille."

129. Béthune, *Cartulaire du Béguinage de Sainte-Elizabeth à Gand*, 66, no. 92.

130. On pastoral care and beguines, see Deane "*Geistliche Schwestern*."

131. Geoffrey of Beaulieu, *RHF*, vol. 20, 12.

132. William of Saint-Pathus seems to see a direct connection between the two groups. After describing the mechanisms of the financial support Louis offered to poor scholars studying at the Sorbonne, namely, housing and weekly subsidies, William states: "In this manner, he provided for several beguines." "Derechief, li benoiet rois fist acheter mesons qui sont en deux rues assises a Paris devant le palès de Termes, esqueles il fist fere mesons

bonnes et granz, pource que escoliers estudianz a Paris demorassent ilecques a tozjors; esqueles esoliers demeurent, qui a ce sont receu par cels qui ont lautorité dels recevoir; et encores de ces mesons sont aucunes loees a autres escoliers, desqueles le pris ou le louage est converti au benoiet roy, si comme len croit, quatre mile livres de tornois. Derechief, li sainz rois fesoit donner chascune semaine deniers a moult de poures clers por leur bourse, lesquex il pourveoit aus escoles; cest a savoir a aucuns deux sous, a aucuns trois sous, et a aucuns douze deniers, et a aucuns dix-huit; et en ceste maniere il porveoit a aucunes beguines." William of Saint-Pathus, "Vie de Saint Louis," *RHF*, vol. 20, 93. There seems to have been a tiered system of financial support for scholars. The extant evidence suggests that this was also the case at the beguinage.

133. On this arrangement, see Chapter 7.

134. "Item legamus ad aedificandum et ampliandum locum beguinarum parisiensium centum libras." *Layettes*, vol. 4, 420.

135. "Et ad sustentationem pauperiorum ex ipsis vinginti libras." *Layettes,* vol. 4, 420.

136. "Item legamus pauperibus mulieribus beguinis in regno Francie constitutis centum libras, per bonos viros quos ad hoc executores nostri viderent ordinandos distribuendas." *Layettes,* vol. 4, 420. The king also gave forty livres to the beguines of Cantimpré. Ibid.

137. "Volumus insuper et praecipimus ut provisionem quam fecimus quibusdam honestis mulieribus quae beguinae dicuntur, in diversis civitatibus et villis religiose degentibus, servet et teneat heres noster qui nobis succedet in regno, et eam servari faciat et teneri, quamdiu vixerit earum quaelibet, quae videlicet assignatae non fuerint alias competenter." *Layettes*, vol. 4, 421.

138. On Capetian policies toward Jews, see William Chester Jordan, *The French Monarchy and the Jews: From Philip Augustus to the Last Capetians* (Philadelphia: University of Pennsylvania Press, 1989).

139. See Chapter 7.

CHAPTER 2. THE WORLD OF THE BEGUINAGE

1. Parisian customary law allowed women to inherit, manage, and bequeath substantial properties. Paris's property regime permitted and even encouraged women to take an active role in managing property, whether as single women preparing for or rejecting marriage; as wives consenting to their husbands' economic activities or pursuing their own commercial transactions independently; or as widows managing their deceased spouses' workshops. Such a context meant that independent action was not unusual among Parisian women, which may have encouraged some women to delay or forgo marriage. On Parisian women's control over property, see François Olivier-Martin, *Histoire de la coutume de la prévôté et vicomté de Paris*, 2 vols. (Paris: E. Leroux, 1926), 2: 184–277. For an excellent discussion of Parisian women's independent management of home workshops, see Janice Archer, "Working Women in Thirteenth-Century Paris" (Ph.D. dissertation, University of Arizona, 1995). On environment and rates of singlehood, see Judith Bennett and Amy M. Froide, *Singlewomen in the European Past, 1250–1800* (Philadelphia: University of Pennsylvania Press, 1999). The

range of economic and administrative activity in which propertied, elite Parisian women were able to engage is sketched in Sharon Farmer, "Merchant Women and the Administrative Glass Ceiling in Thirteenth-Century Paris," in *Women and Wealth in Late Medieval Europe*, ed. Theresa Earenfight (New York: Palgrave Macmillan, 2010), 89–108.

2. Similar patterns of mutual support are evident in beguine communities all over northern Europe. On the Low Countries, see Simons, *Cities of Ladies*, 115–117. German houses typically permitted beguines to maintain private control of property, which they could use to support themselves and their fellow beguines. See Gelser, "Lay Religious Women and Church Reform in Late Medieval Münster," 66 and 75 (Münster) and Andreas Wilts, *Beginen im Bodenseeraum* (Sigmaringen: Thorbecke, 1994), 13 (Lake Constance area). On independent beguine gatherings in Paris, see Chapter 3. On women's networks and associations in general, see Farmer, "Down and Out and Female in Thirteenth-Century Paris."

3. Recent scholarship on beguines in the Low Countries and German lands has also noted this compatibility with local economic and social interests. For the Low Countries in general, see Simons, *Cities of Ladies*, especially chapter 4. For Holland and Zeeland, see Florence W. J. Koorn, *Begijnhoven in Holland en Zeeland gedurende de middeleeuwen* (Assen: VanGorcum, 1981). Scholarship arguing for the marginality of beguine in German lands notwithstanding, recent publications have shown that these ties sustained German communities. See Peters, "Die Bremer Beginen im Mittelalter," and Gelser, "Lay Religious Women and Church Reform in Late Medieval Münster," especially chapter 2.

4. On early German scholarship that understood beguine institutions as poor houses, see the discussion in McDonnell, *Beguines and Beghards*, 81–85. This view is also espoused in Dayton Phillips, *The Beguines in Medieval Strasburg: A Study of the Social Aspect of Beguine Life* (Ann Arbor, MI: Edwards, 1941).

5. Karl Bücher, *Die Frauenfrage im Mittelalter*, 2nd ed. (Tubingen: H. Laupp, 1910). For a brief overview of how the *Frauenfrage* shaped beguine scholarship, see the discussion in Simons, *Cities of Ladies*, 90–91, and McDonnell, *Beguines and Beghards*, 81–85.

6. According to Grundmann, such women joined these communities out of sincere religious conviction, not economic need. Grundmann, *Religious Movements in the Middle Ages*, 85–88, 148–149.

7. In the prologue to his *Life of Mary of Oignies*, James reported that there were "many holy maidens" living together in the diocese of Liège. James's characterization of the women is significant: they were from wealthy families, yet they rejected the riches and temptation of the world, preferring the love of their "heavenly bridegroom." James of Vitry, *The Life of Mary of Oignies*, trans. Margot King, in *Mary of Oignies: Mother of Salvation*, ed. Anneke Mulder-Bakker (Turnhout: Brepols, 2006), 42.

8. See Chapter 3.

9. Ernest McDonnell's influential work on beguine communities of the southern Low Countries argues that over time, beguinages attracted fewer elites. McDonnell, *Beguines and Beghards*, 92–93. Jean-Claude Schmitt has suggested that, as beguine communities admitted increasingly large numbers of poor women, the beguine life gradually declined in status. See *Mort d'une hérésie*, 42–43.

10. Simons argues that over time beguines were recruited increasingly from lower and middle classes. *City of Ladies*, 91.

11. Michael Connally's study of women's religious communities in medieval Paris, with particular focus on the Haudriettes, a house for widows, makes a compelling case for the importance of reputation and social networks in determining recruitment into lay religious communities. Michael Connally, "Les 'Bonnes Femmes' de Paris: Des communautés religieuses dans une société urbaine du bas Moyen Âge" (doctoral thesis, University of Lyon, II, 2003). Erica Gelser's recent analysis of house rules in Münster indicate that reputation was a major concern for beguine communities in German lands, too. Gelser, "Lay Religious Women and Church Reform in Late Medieval Münster," chapter 2. Given that beguines enjoyed their privileges with the blessing of local authorities and not through papal recognition as an official religious order, the emphasis on reputation is not at all surprising.

12. The earliest extant rules of the beguinage, compiled in 1327, include references to the need to secure windows that could provide access to the interior of the enclosure, indicating that the periphery of the enclosure was composed of adjacent buildings. AN JJ 64, fol. 256v, n. 475, edited by Le Grand, "Les béguines de Paris" (henceforth *Beguinage Statutes*), art. 12. References to the "beguines of the rue des Fauconniers" suggest that these houses were along the western periphery of the beguinage. AN KK 5, fol. 367.

13. On the beguinage school, see Chapter 5.

14. Guillaume de Saint-Pathus, *Les miracles de Saint Louis,* ed. Percival B. Fay (Paris: Honoré Champion, 1931), no. 44, 135–137.

15. "Christus verus amicus noster vult nobiscum loqui, solo ad solum, et vult quod ubicumque vadas, sive ad ecclesiam, sive ad sermonem, vel ad res publicas, quod totum propter suum honorem facias." BnF 16481, fol. 71ra.

16. "Sed seculares sicut beguine et alie sunt tote declause, ita quod ex omni parte possunt invadi." BnF 16482, fol. 21va. See also Bériou, "La prédication au béguinage," 181.

17. "Ideo beginae et ceterae mulieres bonae deberunt esse multum clause et in habitu et in aliis." BnF 16481, fol. 140va. See also Bériou, "La prédication au béguinage," 181.

18. See Chapter 6.

19. *Beguinage Statutes*, art. 1.

20. Ibid., art. 3.

21. Ibid., art. 5.

22. This possibility is suggested by Hedwig Röckelein, "Hamburger Beginen im Spatmittelalter—'Autonome' oder 'fremdbestimmte' Frauengemeinschaft?" *Das Mittelalter* 12 (1996): 73–88, at 53. Beguine communities in German lands had similar flexibility regarding extended stays outside the beguinage. Indeed, it seems to have been fairly common practice and did not in any way affect the beguines' reputations for chastity, always of significant concern for beguine communities.

23. This rule is directed at the women living in the convent, indicating that some beguines had welcomed male visitors, perhaps even priests, into their rooms. The rule doesn't prohibit male guests, but it specifies that beguines should speak with them only in the public areas of the enclosure. "Item, que celles qui sont en couvent ne mainent nul homme en leur dortoir, mès parlent ou lieu ou elles menguent, ou en la chapelle." *Beguinage Statutes,*

art. 6. Article 10 reiterates the prohibition against being alone with a man: "Item, se l'en puet trouver fame qui se encloe seule avec homme, espécialment s'il y a aucune soupeçon de mal, soit mise hors."

24. See my discussion later in this chapter.

25. Including expelling beguines; see *Beguine Statutes*, arts. 16 and 26.

26. These three or four senior beguines were, by the early fourteenth century, chosen in consultation with the Dominican prior. *Beguinage Statutes,* art. 16.

27. See *Beguinage Statutes,* arts. 4 and 5.

28. *Beguinage Statutes,* art. 19. The "guardian and governor" referenced in the statutes was the Dominican prior, as specified in the preamble to the statutes.

29. The rules, as they were revised under King Philip VI in 1341, specify that the proceeds from the sale of beguinage property should be used to maintain the other houses within the enclosure or be applied to the needs of the community in general. "Et voult et ordena que touz le tiers du pris que les maisons seront vendues ou chargiés appartiengne au commun pour les autres maisons soustenir, ou pour les besongnes du lieu faire, et soi tenue la mestresse à rendre compte touz les ans en la présence du prieur et du commun des béguines." *Beguinage Statutes*, art. 19.

30. See Chapter 7.

31. At least three of the beguinage's mistresses were interred in the Dominican chapel. The sepulchers are described in Piganiol de La Force, *Description historique de la ville de Paris et de ses environs*, vol. 5 (Paris, 1765), 455–456. De La Force speculates that this area of the chapel, located in the nave, was a burial place for the beguines of Paris, though only these three sepulchers are known. On the importance of these sepulchers as a mark of distinction, see Michel Lauwers, *La mémoire des ancêtres, le souci des morts: Morts, rites et société au moyen âge (diocèse de Liège, XIe–XIIIe siècles* (Paris: Beauchesne, 1996), 127–128. For Agnes of Orchies's tombstone, see figure 3.

32. On these sermon collections, see Chapter 4. The residents of the beguinage were obliged to attend the sermons preached in the chapel. See *Beguinage Statutes,* art. 24.

33. For a thorough discussion of the relationship between the Sorbonne and the beguinage, see chapter 4. The mistress's sermons are discussed in Chapter 5.

34. Jeanne composed her will in 1330. Her relationship to Roland can be discerned through her generous bequests, which included several to Roland's nieces. Jeanne not only made Roland an executor to her will but also entrusted him with saying three masses per week for the health of Jeanne's soul. Archives de l'Assistance Publique (henceforth AAP) fonds St. Jacques, reg. 1, pièce 31.

35. "Testament et Codicille de Jeanne d'Eu: Comtesse d'Étampes et Duchesse d'Athènes, 1388–1389," ed. Louis Sandret, *Revue Historique, Nobiliaire et Biographique* 17 (1880) : 273–300.

36. AN L 665/A no. 5. Pierre Chagrin's ties to lay religious women are described in Connally, "Les 'Bonnes Femmes' de Paris," chapter 3.

37. "Une lettre soubz le seel de lofficial donne mil CCC xxiiii le samedi apres lascension par laquelle il appert que Henri le Bourguigon vendi a Perrette la mairesse et ses hoirs iiii livres par de rente a prendre chascun an sur une maison en la rue Michel le Comte." AN S* 4634, fol. 145v (lll). See also a copy of the transaction in the Censive de Saint-Martin

des Champs (AN S*1461/1) in which Henry is identified as "procureur du prieur des freres prescheurs" and Perrette is identified as a beguine (fol. 329). Perrette lived within the enclosure of the beguinage. Her house is mentioned in a testament from 1330). AAP, fonds St.-Jacques, reg. 1, pièce 31.

38. AN KK 330/A. See my discussion later in this chapter.

39. For further consideration of these ties, see my discussion later in this chapter.

40. *Beguinage Statutes,* art. 13.

41. The statutes refer to a common dining area. *Beguinage Statutes,* arts. 2 and 5.

42. Bourges de Mortieres is described as living with her niece, Jeanne. AN KK 330/A. The mistress of the beguinage in 1408 lived with her niece, Agnes. *Testaments,* 228. In a property dispute from the early fifteenth century, two beguines are described as living together in a house belonging to the beguinage community. "Tenant dune part a un hostel appelle lostel des escoliers dudit beguinage et dautre part a une maison appartenir a la communaulte desdces beguines ou demeurs a present Perrette de Leans et Jehanne la Corelle." AN S 4642. The act is not numbered.

43. By 1341, it seems that the practice of allowing servants and young girls to reside in the beguinage had become a problem. The revised statutes included a new rule requiring beguines to obtain the mistress's permission before allowing other women or young girls to live with them in their residence. Young girls were also required to pay twelve deniers as an entrance fee. Older women were required to pay more. See *Beguinage Statutes*, art. 13.

44. "Item, que nulle jueune fame ne soit souveraine en chambre, se elle ne passe trente ans." *Beguinage Statutes*, art. 11.

45. "Item, que nulle jueune fame ne demeure seule en chambre, et se aucune en y a qui soit seule, que ladite matresse, par le conseil de trois ou de quatre anciennes que elle jujera en sa conscience, et cuidera qui plus ayment l'onnesteté de léens, li doint compaignie convenable dedens trois jours." *Beguinage Statutes*, art. 9.

46. In this respect, beguines in Paris had more in common with beguines in the Low Countries than with those of German lands. Walter Simons has shown that beguines in the Low Countries were heavily involved in textile work. See *Cities of Ladies*, 85–87. There is evidence of beguines in some northern German cities engaged in spinning and weaving. See Peters, "Norddeutsches Beginen," 82–85, and Rockelein,"Hamburger Beginen," 84. It seems that most beguines who joined German convents were independently wealthy and subsisted largely on annuities. See Peters, "Bremer Beginen," 152, and Gelser, "Lay Religious Women and Church Reform in Late Medieval Münster," 224.

47. Constance Berman has suggested that tensions existed within the Cistercian abbey of Saint-Antoine-des-Champs, as the practice of endowing individual nuns increased over the course of the Middle Ages. See Constance H. Berman, "Dowries, Private Income, and Anniversary Masses: The Nuns of Saint-Antoine-des-Champs (Paris)," *Proceedings of the Western Society for French History* 20 (1993): 3–20.

48. See Chapter 1.

49. Béthune, *Cartulaire du Béguinage de Sainte-Elizabeth à Gand*, no. 106, 74.

50. On royal patronage of the beguines of France after the death of Louis IX, see Chapter 7.

51. "De hoc dixit michi unum mirabile verbum quedam domina nobilis, quando ei predicabam quod esset begina. 'Hoc non facerem, nec sic nec sic, quia faciunt sic et sic.'" BnF Lat. 16482, fols. 167va–167vb. Part of this sermon has been edited by Nicole Bériou in "La prédication au béguinage," 182. I discuss this sermon in greater detail in Chapter 6.

52. I elaborate on this point in Chapter 6.

53. BnF Lat. 16481, fol. 274rb. Several sermon manuscripts contain exempla about proud beguines who, while professing humility and virtue, become indignant when publically called out on their imperfections. See Paris, BnF, Lat. 14947 and Lat. 15005, cited in Barthélémy Hauréau, *Notices et extraits de quelques manuscrits latins de la Bibliothèque nationale* (Paris: Librairie Klincksieck, 1891), 4: 234.

54. "Sicut liber non reputatur alicuius valoris, nisi sit illustratus et illuminatus; sed quando ibi sunt littere 'dazur' et de auro 'tornees au pincel,' tunc liber est pulcher. Sed aliqui sunt sicut libri beguinarum vel dominarum, qui sunt extra noviter depicti, intus vero maculati et deleti; qui vellet eos emere, cito posset decipi." BnF Lat. 14799, fol. 168, col. 4, cited in Hauréau, *Notices et extraits*, 4: 96.

55. One of the statutes warns women not to wear habits that are greater than the one appropriate to their estate. "Et que ycelles qui sont et seront ainsi receues oudit béguinage soient tenues de porter l'abit honneste et convenable acoustumé à porter, et se aucunes en y avoit portassent greigneur habit que leur estat ne requiert, nous voulons et ordenons que la matresse leur monstre." *Beguinage Statutes*, art. 16.

56. Article 6 of the *Beguinage Statutes* mentions beguines who lived "en couvent."

57. "Item, nostre très chier seigneur et cousin le roy Charles, notre prédécesseur des-susdit, pour oster toutes doubtes ou temps avenir, ordena, et nous aussi ordenons que les béguines à qui les maisons ont esté baillées franchement, ne n'i ont fait édifices notables, combien que elles les aient retenues pour leur aisement, ne les puissent de rien chargier, mès viegnent franchement au commun." The reference to the king and the desire to "remove all doubts" suggests that the mistress or perhaps the residents of the beguinage had tried to charge rent to these specially selected beguines. Ibid., art. 19.

58. Ibid., art. 22.

59. "Item pauperibus mulieribus commorantibus retro domum beguinarum parisius, 100 solidos Parisienses in communi." AN S 938/A, no. 46. It is possible that Jeanne was referring to an independent community of lay religious women on the street running parallel to the beguinage. An almoner's list from 1336, which mentions several recipients of royal alms, includes an unspecified number of "bonnes femmes," a term frequently used to describe lay religious women, on the rue des Fauconniers.

60. "Item domui dei seu hospitali pauperum beguinarum parisius viginti solidos." AN S 938/A, no. 58.

61. In his testament, Jean gave two gold francs to "the poor women of the hospital" of the beguinage and two francs to "the poor women of the beguinage." "Item il lessa aux povres femmes de lospital et aux povres femmes du dit beguinage, 2 frans dor. Item a la court du dit beguinage au pourffit de tout le lieu especial de la dicte chappelle vi frans dor." AN KK 330/A.

62. Examples include the testaments of Martine Canu and Alice Cournon. See *Testaments*, 226–230 (Martine Canu) and 252–264 (Alice Cournon).

63. During the Middle Ages, however, "poor" did not necessarily refer to the destitute or impoverished. Indeed, the term could refer to a person who voluntarily adopted an apostolic life, who was unable to live up to his or her status, or who was vulnerable in some way, not necessarily economically. Certainly, many of the beguinage's residents fit this definition of "poor." Michael Connally has argued in his work on the Haudriettes (a hospice for widows) that women without men could be regarded as "poor" in the sense that they did not have male protection. Connally, "Les 'Bonnes Femmes' de Paris." See also Richard Trexler, "Charity and the Defense of Urban Elites in the Italian Communes," in *The Rich, the Well Born, and the Powerful: Elites and Upper Classes in History*, ed. Frederic Cople Jaher (Urbana: University of Illinois Press, 1973), 64–109. On ideas about "deserving poor" see Farmer, *Surviving Poverty in Medieval Paris*.

64. Ernest McDonnell and Nicole Bériou, following Le Grand, have claimed that the almoner was involved in the selection of the mistress (McDonnell, *Beguines and Beghards*, 224, and Bériou, "La prédication au beguinage," 194). Le Grand, however, based his assertion on a late fourteenth-century document (BnF nouv. acq. fr. 1440), which lists the beguinage as an institution over which the almoner played a supervisory role. The king's almoner's responsibilities did indeed expand by the late fourteenth century, but it seems that prior to this time the almoner did not have a direct supervisory role in any of Paris's hospitals or religious institutions. On the almoner's role by the late fourteenth century, see De La Selle, *Le service des âmes à la cour*, 207.

65. *Beguinage Statutes*, art. 16.

66. See my discussion later in this chapter.

67. *Layettes*, vol. 4, 210.

68. *Les Journaux du Trésor de Philippe IV le Bel*, ed. Jules Marie Eduard Viard (Paris: Imprimerie Nationale, 1940), no. 1927 (henceforth *Journaux*).

69. Isabelle entrusted Jeanne with the task of acquiring linens and other household materials, reimbursing Jeanne for linens and cushions she had purchased for Isabelle's household. AN P 1378^2 nos. 92 and 638.

70. On these families and their influence, see Boris Bove, *Dominer la ville: Prévôts des marchands et échevins parisiens de 1260 à 1350* (Paris: Editions du CTHS, 2004). Although names are not always reliable indicators of origins, it seems that several residents of the Paris beguinage hailed from the northern regions of France, including Emeline Vandieres, Emeline de Blangy, Marie de Saint-Amand, and Jeanne de Laigny. The beguine Jeanne du Faut, who resided in the beguinage for a number of years, may have been from Rouen. In her testament, Jeanne left a bequest to the beguines of Rouen, suggesting a possible tie to that city.

71. Perrenelle is identified as mistress in 1306 in a document recording the purchase of an annuity. See AN J 740, no. 6. In 1312, Perrenelle is recorded, along with her brother Jean, selling some family property (AN S 65, no. 12). By the late thirteenth century, the Chanevacier family had established ties with several of Paris's wealthy and politically connected merchant families. Jean Chanevacier married into the Marcel family in 1315, making him a relative of the future *prévôt des marchands* Étienne Marcel. See "La Famille d'Étienne Marcel, 1250–1397," *Mémoires de la société de l'histoire de Paris et de l'Île-de-France*, 30 (1903):

209–210. Perrenelle's father was probably the wealthy draper Pierre Chanevacier, who served as a supplier to the Count of Artois, Robert II, in 1292. See *Inventaire-sommaire des Archives départementales antérieures à 1790* (Pas-de-Calais: Archives civiles—Série A. Ed. Jules-Marie Richard), vol. 1, 155.

72. *Testaments,* 226.

73. On Isabelle de Tremblay, see Bove, *Dominer la ville,* 76. More recently, Sharon Farmer has discussed Isabelle and her connections with the French court. See Farmer, "Merchant Women and the Administrative Glass Ceiling in Thirteenth-Century Paris," in *Women and Wealth in Late Medieval Europe,* ed. Theresa Earenfight (New York: Palgrave Macmillan, 2010) 89–108.

74. In a badly damaged document related to a property transaction initiated by a certain Jean of Ghent, a neighboring property is described as belonging to "Jehanne levroude mestress des beguines." AN S 60, no. 4. On the Arrode family, see Bove, *Dominer la ville,* 12, 492–494.

75. For the 1292 entry, see BnF fr. 6220, fol. 17v, published in Hercule Géraud, ed., *Paris sous Philippe-le-Bel, d'après des documents originaux et notamment d'après un manuscrit contenant "Le Rôle de la Taille" imposée sur les habitants de Paris en 1292, 1837,* reprint, with introduction and index by Caroline Bourlet and Lucie Fossier (Tübingen: Max Niemeyer, 1991), 40. The 1296 tax roll is housed in the Archives Nationales, see AN KK 283, fol. 7r, published in Karl Michaëlsson, ed., *Le livre de la taille de Paris, l'an 1296* (Göteborg: Almquist and Wiksell, 1958). For the tax years 1297–1300, I cite the manuscript folio.

76. 1297: AN KK 283, fol. 40r; 1298: AN KK 283, fol. 100r.

77. 1300: AN KK 283, fol. 237v.

78. 1296: AN KK 283, fol. 2v; 1297: AN KK 283, fol. 39r; 1298: AN KK 283, fol. 99r; 1299: AN KK 283, fol. 156; 1300: AN KK 283, fol. 235v.

79. See the discussion later in this chapter and in Chapter 3.

80. King Charles V bought Jean's house in order to house the archbishop of Sens, whose residence in the parish of Saint Paul had been confiscated by the king during the building of the royal residence in that parish. See Fernand Bournon, "L'Hotel royal de Saint-Pol," *Mémoires de la Société de l'histoire de Paris et de l'Ile-de-France* 6 (1879): 67. Among the belongings Jean stored in Bourge's house were weapons, including two crossbows; several cushions, covers, and bolts of cloth; numerous chests and purses filled with currencies of all types; and other household utensils and furnishings. In all, the movable wealth Jean stored in Bourge's home was worth more than seven hundred livres tournois, demonstrating the extent to which Jean trusted Bourges. Moreover, when Jean made his will in 1380, he left Bourges and her niece, Jeanne, one hundred gold francs for an anniversary mass at the beguinage's chapel, as well as a silver-gilded chalice with an enamel plaque bearing the arms of Flanders. AN KK 330/A. Bourges is described as Jean's *chambrière* in a document recording his funeral expenses (AN L 617). The document was edited by Douët D'Arcq. See "Des frais d'enterrement dans Paris au XIVe siècle," *Mémoires de la Société de l'histoire de Paris et de l'Île-de-France* 4 (1877), 138.

81. "Il quitta Jehanne la mareschalle beguine de toutes chozes quelzconques dont illui pourroient faire demande de tout le temps passe iusques." AN KK 330/A.

82. AN S 931/B, no. 4. Pierre also requested intercessory lights be maintained on his soul's behalf.

83. "Aux Beguines, pour ce que Richarde y avoit sa devocion, pour y avoir vigils et messe à note pour elle et pour moy, vint solz *Parisis*." *Testaments*, 297.

84. "Item, aux six bonnes femmes des Beguines . . . a chascun une paire de draps." Ibid., 194.

85. "Item, je lesse a l'ostel de Sainte Avoye, a la chappelle Estienne Haudry et aux Beguines, a chascun des dis hostelz deux frans." Ibid., 274.

86. Like Pierre du Châtel, Robert lumped the beguines with other Parisian communities of lay religious women. " Item, je donne et laisse aux Filles Dieu de Paris, aux Beguines, a celles de Saincte Avoye, a celles de la Chapelle Haudry, a l'ostel du Saint Esperit en Greve, a chascun pour unes vigiles et messe xx solz Parisis." Ibid., 361.

87. "Item, collegio seu domui beguinarum Parisiensium viginti s. p. ut vigilias mortuorum in novem psalmis et novem lectionibus una cum commendaciis et una missa de requiem pro salute anime sue dicere valeant." Ibid., 261.

88. "Item, capellanis et clericis ipsarum beguinarum qui predictum servicium divinum pro salute anime sue facient octo s. p." Ibid. Finally, Alice gave eight sous to Guillamette, the beguine in charge of the beguinage chapel's upkeep.

89. Indeed, had the record-keeping practices of the early fifteenth century been in place in the thirteenth, many more such testaments, with presumably many more such bequests for beguines, would undoubtedly exist.

90. The French kings gave the beguinage annuities (see Chapter 7), as did the Parlementary official Pierre Michel and others who hoped to benefit from the beguines' prayers. The records for two other hospitals in medieval Paris, the Quinze-Vingts and the Haudriettes, whose archives (unlike the beguinage's) have survived largely intact, include dozens of references to annuities and properties located throughout the city. Given the loss of the Paris beguinage's archive, it is impossible to evaluate the community's income from annuities. The few documents that remain in the archives of the Ave Maria community (the Observant Franciscan nuns who took control of the beguinage enclosure in the late fifteenth century) primarily concern property located around the beguinage. When the house was at its height in the late thirteenth century, the community probably possessed a significant number of urban properties.

91. *Beguine Statutes,* art. 19.

92. Ibid., art. 13. This article was not in the 1327 statutes but was added in the revised rules of Philip VI. Beguine communities in the southern Low Countries began collecting entrance fees in the late fourteenth and early fifteenth centuries. See Simons, *Cities of Ladies*, 99. This seems to have been a practice followed in German houses as well. See Peters, "Bremer Beginen," for Bremen.

93. Historians of beguine communities in the southern Low Countries have long recognized the beguines' participation in the textile industries. Many, if not most, of the beguines in the *curtis* beguinages of the Southern Low Countries worked in the textile industries. Simons, "The Beguine Movement in the Southern Low Countries: A Reassessment," 72–73, 85. Bernard Delmaire has shown that elite families in Arras were closely

involved in the foundation of beguine communities, which functioned as textile centers. See Bernard Delmaire, *Le diocèse d'Arras de 1093 au milieu du XIVe siècle*, vol. 1 (Arras: Commission départementale d'histoire et d'archéologie du Pas-de-Calais, 1994), 324–332.

94. The school within the beguinage is cited in documents from the late fourteenth century. The porteress is mentioned in a gift from Alphonse of Poitiers to the beguinage in 1267, and a marguillier is referred to in a fifteenth-century testament.

95. Martine Canu, mistress of the beguinage in 1408, gave generous gifts to a certain Marguerite de Stain, "en recompensacion des bons et agreables services qu'elle lui a fais ou temps passé," indicating that Marguerite had served the mistress in some capacity. *Testaments*, 227.

96. See "Des frais d'enterrement dans Paris au XIVe siècle," 138.

97. *The Goodman of Paris (Le Ménagier de Paris): A Treatise on Moral and Domestic Economy by A Citizen of Paris, c.1393*, trans. Eileen Power (London: G. Routledge, 1928).

98. "Item il laissa a Jehanne la mareschalle beguine quatre livres parisis de rente chacun an a la vie d'elle seullement." AN S 930/A, no. 2.

99. Documents related to the execution of Isabelle's testament refer to Jeanne de La Tour as lady of the court in 1385. AN P 1378², 3098. According to a property dispute over Jeanne's house in the beguinage, by 1385 Jeanne had been a resident of the beguinage for twelve years. AN S 4642.

100. Simons, *Cities of Ladies*, 115.

101. Sharon Farmer, "Biffes, Tiretaines, and Aumonieres: The Role of Paris in the International Textile Markets of the Thirteenth and Fourteenth Centruries," in *Medieval Clothing and Textiles* 2, ed. Robin Netherton and Gale R. Owen-Crocker (Woodbridge: Boydell and Brewer, 2006), 73–89. The introduction of the heavy loom in the twelfth century and the importance of woolen cloth to the economies of northern European cities increased the demand for cheap laborers to spin wool and perform other tasks in the process of finishing cloth.

102. Jean-François Belhoste, "Paris, Grand centre drapier au moyen âge," *Fédération des Sociétés historiques et archéologiques de Paris et de l'Ile-de-France, Mémoires* 51 (2000) : 36–37.

103. On the relationship between textile work and the growth of beguine communities, see Delmaire, *Le diocèse d'Arras de 1093 au milieu du XIVe siècle*, vol. 1, 332.

104. On this miracle story, see Farmer, "Down and Out and Female in Thirteenth-Century Paris," 360–361.

105. François Maillard, *Comptes Royaux (1314–1328)*, 2 vols., *Recueil des historiens de la France: Documents financiers, v. 4* (Paris: Imprimerie nationale, 1961), no. 14187.

106. This connection was not as pronounced in German lands, where beguine houses tended to be smaller and to reflect the interests and concerns of elite burgher families, who seemed to have not wanted the women to have to support themselves. See Letha Böhringer, "Beginen als Konkurrentinnen von Zunftgenossen? Kritische Bemerkungen am Beispiel Kölner quellen des späten Mittelalters," in *Vielfalt der Geschichte—Lernen, Lehren und Erforschen vergangener Zeiten, Festgabe für Ingrid Heidrich zum 65 Geburtstag*, ed. Sabine Happ and Ulrich Nonn (Berlin: Wiss. Verl. Berlin, 2004), 182–197, and "Beginen und Schwestern

in der Sorge um Kranke, Sterbende und Verstorbene: Eine Problemskizze," in *Organisierte Barmherzigkeit: Armenpflege und Hospitalwesen in Mittelalter und Früher Neuzeit*, ed. Artur Dirmeier (Regensburg: Pustet, 2010), 127–155. I thank Jennifer Deane for these references.

107. See Chapter 3.

108. Connally, "Les 'Bonnes Femmes' de Paris," 148.

109. I owe this observation to Connally, ibid., 155.

110. The hospital founded by the wealthy cloth merchant Étienne Haudry—the Haudriettes—was limited to forty widows. The Bonnes Femmes of Saint-Avoye was a community of lay religious women founded by a wealthy Parisian widow named Constance de Saint-Jacques and a curé of Saint Merry. It too was limited to forty women, all of whom had to be older than fifty, poor, and widowed. See Le Grand, "Les béguines de Paris," 335.

111. The Haudriettes required those admitted to the community to give their property to the community. See Connally, "Les 'Bonnes Femmes' de Paris," 351. The women in the community of Saint-Avoye also had to give themselves and their property to the community. See Le Grand, "Les béguines de Paris," 338. This gift "of self and of goods" is based on the notion of "conversion" in the sense of turning from the world to God, a life turn. As Michael Connally has argued, these property arrangements made the bonnes femmes seem to approximate nuns, thereby avoiding some of the criticisms leveled at beguines. Connally, "Les 'Bonnes Femmes' de Paris," chapter 5. On the significance of laymen and women rendering self and goods to a religious community, see Charles de Miramon, *Les donnés au Moyen Âge: Une forme de vie religieuse laïque, v. 1180–v. 1500* (Paris: Cerf, 1999).

112. A useful survey of women's control of property in medieval Paris can be found in Archer, "Working Women in Thirteenth-Century Paris," 60–70. For an excellent examination of women's control of property in fourteenth-century Ghent see Shennan Hutton, *Women and Economic Activities in Late Medieval Ghent* (New York: Palgrave Macmillan, 2011).

113. A document concerning the donation reports that Perrenelle lived at the beguinage for about seventeen years. Since she was dead by 1394, it seems that she entered the beguinage upon her husband's death. AN L938B, no. 95.

114. AN L938B, no. 93.

115. S 3973B, no. 21.

116. The first was an urban rent worth twenty-eight sous and four deniers on a house located on the rue Saint-Denis. The second was a rent on a piece of land located outside the city, worth an annual income of thirty-three sous and four deniers. AN S 931/A, doss. 2, no. 1.

117. AN S 931/A, doss. 2, no. 2.

118. AN S 931/A, doss. 2, no. 3.

119. Ernest Coyecque, ed., *L'Hôtel-Dieu de Paris au moyen âge: Histoire et documents*, vol. 1 (Paris: Chez H. Champion, 1889), 240.

120. "Item il laissa a Jehanne la mareschalle beguine quatre livres parisis de rente chastun an a la vie delle seullement a lui estre assis par ses executeurs en la terre du roy nostre sire et en propriete les laissa a la dite eglise du sepulcre et que tantost la dicte Jehanne trespasse la dicte eglise en joisse des ore en avant a tous jours." AN S 930, no. 2.

121. On the bonds among single women, see Farmer, "Down and Out and Female in

Thirteenth-Century Paris." I discuss workshops composed of beguines in more detail in Chapter 3.

122. See Chapter 3.

123. This was a common feature of beguine communities across Europe. Statutes for several beguinages in the southern Low Countries required wealthy beguines to provide for their poorer sisters in their testaments. Many beguinages established a fund for poorer beguines called the Table of the Holy Spirit, which provided destitute beguines food, clothing, and shelter. The wealthier beguines of the community were required to contribute to this fund. Simons, *Cities of Ladies*, 97.

124. "Et nous aussi ordenons que les béguines à qui les maisons ont esté baillées franchement, ne n'i ont fait édifices notables, combien que elles les aient retenues pour leur aisement, ne les puissent de rien chargier, mès viegnent franchement au commun." Ibid., art. 19. See also *Beguine Statutes*, art. 22.

125. I discuss this testament and its gifts to beguine silkworkers in greater detail in Chapter 3.

126. "Domino praedicta testatrix proprio labore et industria acqui fierat fideliter." AAP fonds St.-Jacques, reg. 1, pièce 31.

127. In other words, Jeanne insists that the property she bequeathed to Beatrice was not family property, which would have had to devolve to Jeanne's relatives. Of course, the properties mentioned in Jeanne's testament should not be thought of as all of the property she owned at the time she composed her testament. On reading wills, see Clive Burgess, "Late Medieval Wills and Pious Convention: Testamentary Evidence Reconsidered," in *Profit, Piety, and the Professions in Later Medieval England*, ed. Michael Hicks (Gloucester: Alan Sutton, 1993), 14–33; Martha C. Howell, "Fixing Movables: Gifts by Testament in Late Medieval Douai," *Past and Present* 150 (1995): 3–45.

128. "Item legauit dicta testatrix Micheli dico Baudri, Guillelmo Baudri, fratribus et Theophanie liberis Luce Baudri quondam fratrus de testatricis, Gauffrido, Nicolas et Johanne fratribus liberis quondam Radulphi Baudri quondam fratrus dicta testatricis cuilibet eorum octo libras parisiensis sub tali conditione que . . . nichil contradicerent in occulto nichil apperto quouis modo." AAP, fonds St.-Jacques, reg. 1, pièce 31.

129. *Testaments*, 226–230.

130. Ibid., 228.

131. Ibid.

132. *Beguine Statutes*, art. 19.

133. *Testaments*, 229.

134. "Elle laissa à la dicte Marguerite de Stain, à tousjours, pour elle, ses hoirs et aians cause, la maison où icelle testaterresse demeure en hault, avecques une maison en bas que l'en appelle le Conven, ainsi comme elle se comporte. Avec ce, lui laissa . . . une maison . . . en la rue des Escouffles." Ibid.

135. "Et est assavoir que la dicte testaterresse a voulu et ordené que les dictes deux messes que sera tenue faire la dicte Marguerite de Stain, après le trespas du dit frere Robert [le] Canu, à cause de la dicte maison ou dit Beguinage, emprès le puis, que ycelles deux messes soient chantées à note ou dit Beguinage." Ibid.

136. "La dicte testaterresse fist, nomma et esleut ses executeurs et feaulx commissaires, le dit Jehan de Combes, la dicte Margeurite de Stain, messire Phelippe le Pigaut, prestre, et Jehan le Blanc." Ibid., 230.

137. See Chapter 3.

138. Penelope D. Johnson, *Equal in Monastic Profession: Religious Women in Medieval France* (Chicago: University of Chicago Press), 18–25.

139. Boris Bove, "Espace, piété et parenté à Paris aux XIIIe–XIVe siècles d'après les fondations d'anniversaires des familles échevinales," in *Villes et religion: Mélanges offerts à Jean-Louis Biget*, ed. P. and J. Chiffoleau Boucheron (Paris: Publications de la Sorbonne, 2000), 255–258; Anne Terroine, "Recherches sur la bourgeoisie parisienne au XIIIe siècle," (doctoral thesis, École des Chartes, 1940), vol. 3, 133–166. Moreover, it probably cost less to place daughters in convents than to contract a marriage. Johnson, *Equal in Monastic Profession*, 23–24.

140. The statutes of the beguinage are explicit on this point. "Et se le cas avenoit que aucunes d'icelles eussent amendé ou édifié le lieu de leur habitacion, et elles de vousissent marier ou issir hors dudit béguinage de leur volenté et sanz délit. *Beguinage Statutes*, art. 19.

141. The beguine Marguerite la Quarreliete, for example, sold her share of a house to the widow of her deceased brother. AN S* 5594 I. 62v. Agatha la Petite brought a case to the royal court when her daughter Emmeline sold part of Agatha's property, apparently without her permission. See *Les olim ou Registres des arrêts rendus par la Cour du roi: Sous les règnes de Saint Louis, de Philippe le Hardi, de Philippe le Bel, de Louis le Hutin et de Philippe le Long*, ed. Arthur Beugnot, vol. 3 (Paris: Impr. royale, 1839–1848), 654. Perrenelle la Chanevacière, mistress of the beguinage in 1306, is mentioned alongside her brother, Jean, in an act recording the sale of a house. AN S 65, no. 12.On beguines outside the beguinage, see Chapter 3.

142. AN S 931/A, doss. 6, no. 2.

143. On Jeanne du Faut: AAP Fonds St.-Jacques, reg. 1, pièce 31. On Martine Canu, see *Testaments*, 226–230.

144. AN L938B, no. 93.

145. "Le XIX jour dudit mois, on doibt dire vegiles et chanter messe pour Perrenelle de Vemars (P. Rose) et pour seur Perrenele Auberde, sa niepce. . . . Pour ce faire avons receu de la ditte Perrenele 210 livres parisis et de saditte niepce nous est escheu après son deceps XXVIII livres de rente à Paris et 1 muy de blè à Tremblay." *Obituaires de la province de Sens*, ed. Auguste Molinier, vol. 1 (Paris: Academie des Inscriptions et Belles-Lettres, 1902), 660.

146. On female relatives joining the community together, see Walter De Keyser, "Aspects de la ville béguinagle à Mons aux XIIIe et XIV siècles," in *Autour de la ville en Hainaut: Mélanges d'archéologie et d'histoire urbains offerts à J. Dugnoille et à René Sansen: Études et documents du cercle royal d'histoire et d'archéologie d'Ath et de la région et musées athois* (Ath: CRHAA, 1986), 205–226.

147. AN KK 330/A, fol. 2r.

148. See Chapter 3.

149. *Beguinage Statutes*, art. 19.

150. Ibid.

151. Ibid.

152. "Et l'abitacion d'icelles tant seulement, et l'amendement nous avons octroyé et octroions aus personnes qui bien et honnestement demourront oudit béguinage, tandis comme elles vourront estre obéissans et garder nos ordenances et persévérer en bonnes et saintes euvres." Ibid.

153. AN S 4642 (no number). Although Filles de l'Ave Maria did not maintain the archives of the beguinage, they did preserve this particular document. The dispute and its outcome were frequently cited in documents concerning the convent and its buildings. It is likely that the sisters referred to this case in order to claim that the properties of the community belonged not to the women themselves but to the king.

154. "Lan mil ccc quatre vins et cinq a feue damoiselle Jehanne de la Tour a son vivant beguine et demourant audit lieu de beguinage laquelle damoiselle Jehanne qui en son vivant avoit este noble et de noble lignee et du sang royal ainsi que len disoit avoit joy de ladicte maison et icelle possider par tres long temps." Ibid.

155. "Ensuivant la voulente de ladicte damoiselle, yceulx executeurs apres le trespassement dicelle damoiselle entre autres choses dont ilz avoient dispose, avoient dispose de ladicte maison et . . . vender, ceder, et transporter a une femme nommer Alips la Malaisie en son vivant bourgoise de paris pour elle et pour ses hoirs et ayans cause moyennant certaine somme de deniers." Ibid.

156. "Ladicte maison et ses appartenances avoit competee et appartenue a la dicte damoiselle Jehanne de la tour et depuis a la dicte Alips la Malaisie et quelles en avoient joyes et possidees par longue espace de temps, cest assavoir la dicte damoiselle Jehanne de la Tour par lespace de douze ans et la dicte Malaisie par lespace de vint ans ou environ et que apres le trespassement de la dicte Malaisie icelle maison estoit venue et escheue a deux filles cestassavoir a la dicte Alips vesve dudit feu Robin de Brueil et a Alips femme de feu Jehan Crest, lesquelles en avoient joy et use au veu et sceu de la dicte maistresse dames et gens du roy et autres qui favoir lavoient voulu, et expres elles, lesdiz defendeurs a juste tiltre et de bonne foy par longue espace de temps, et mesurement depuis lan CCCC vint et deux." Ibid.

157. "Que ladicte maison avoit este vendue par ladicte maistresse et dames a la dicte feue damoiselle Jehanne de la Tour et non pas seulement a la vie delle mais pour ses hoirs." Ibid. In the Low Countries, individual beguines could purchase "living rights," which they could pass on, or even sell, to another party for a limited period, usually only for two generations. See Simons, *Cities of Ladies*, 73. No evidence exists that this was the practice in Paris, where the king was explicit about his rights over the property within the enclosure.

158. "Les dictes beguinees et celles qui avoient lesdictes maisons n'estoient point proprietairesses dicelles mais en appartenoit la propriete au roy nostre sire qui ycelle avoit retenue et reservee en faisant ladicte fondacion a lui et a ses successeurs car esdictes maisons lesdictes beguines et autres qui pretendoient droit avoir en icelles n'y avoient fors seulement droit dabitacion. . . . [A]voit aussi compectuee et appartenuee aux personnes qui bien et honnestement demourroient ou dit beguinage et qui porteroient labbit dicellui tandiz quelle y vouldroit demoures estre obeissans et garder les dictes ordonnances et personnes en bonnes ouvres." AN S 4642.

159. AAP, reg. 1, pièce 31. La Grande was a common nickname. The fact that both Guillamette and Beatrice shared it does not mean the two women were related.

160. We know about Jeanne's executors' efforts to sell the house in the beguinage because the case came before Parlement in March 1334. "Lite mota in curia nostra inter executores defuncte Johanne du faut ex una parte et procuratorem nostrum ex altera, super eo quod executores virtutes cuiusdam gracie a nobis facte dicebant quando domum situatam in beguinagio parisius ultra portam de barbell sibi licet vendere et pretium dicte vendiciones in utilitatem execucionis dicte defuncte." AN X 1a, 7, fols. 35–36. Documents dating from October 1334 that record the executors' attempts to carry out Jeanne's will state that Beatrice had also died by then. "Quos quidem sexaquinta solidos parisus annui redditus seu census, dicti exequtores nomine exequtoris predicto, ob remedium et salutem animarum defunctarum praedictae Johanne et Beatricis magne quondam puelle et dilecte dicte Johanne." AAP, reg. 20, no. 1254.

161. "Dicta testatrix legavit, dedit, et concessit perpetuo Beatrici dicte la grant cum suis juribus et pertinenciis domum praedictam et appendenciis universiis per eandem Beatricem et heredes suos tenendam et possidendam perpetuo pacifice et quiete." AAP, reg. 1, pièce 31.

162. "Dictum beguinagium fundatum existat a predecessoribus nostris et in fundacione dicti beguinagii retenta fuerit nobis proprietas dicti loci sola habitacione et usu beguinis concessa et licet dicta Johanna dum vivebat domum ibi edificaverit vel edificatum nobiliter emendaverit tamen dictam domum alienare non poterit nec in alium transferre presertim visis quibus ordonacionibus regis super alienacionibus domorum dicti beguinagii dudum factis plures alias raciones." AN X1a 7, fols. 35–36. The decision of the court was confirmed in December of that year. AN X 1a 7, fol. 89v.

163. Martine Canu, the mistress of the beguinage until her death sometime after 1408, loaned fifty crowns to a certain Nicholas le Riche. *Testaments*, 466. Jeanne du Faut loaned substantial amounts of money to other women, probably silk workers. See Chapter 3.

CHAPTER 3. BEGUINES, SILK, AND THE CITY

1. Jeanne kept her house in the beguinage, bequeathing the property to her silkworkers, which indicates that she had not been evicted from the enclosure. Women who were evicted from the beguinage lost ownership of their houses or other property in the beguinage. See *Beguinage Statutes*, art. 19.

2. Although Jeanne du Faut is never identified in the tax assessments with the term "beguine," there is substantial evidence to suggest that she continued to live as a lay religious woman after leaving the beguinage. Her testament, for example, portrays a woman of deep piety. Moreover, Jeanne continued to live with and among other women (some of whom the assessors described as beguines), remaining unmarried until her death sometime before 1334.

3. For a broad discussion of the multiple forms and contexts in which lay female religiosity appeared in medieval Europe, see Deane, " 'Beguines Reconsidered.' "

4. See Chapter 5.

5. This was the case in beguine communities all over northern Europe, in which the enjoyment of certain privileges as well as access to spiritual care (beyond the routine pastoral care provided by the parish priest) was contingent upon residence in a formal community. See Bernard Delmaire, "Les béguines dans le Nord de la France," 128; McDonnell, *Beguines and Beghards,* 138–139; and Zeigler, "The Curtis Beguinages," 56–57.

6. I discuss these variable understandings of the term 'beguine' in "'Love Is Beguine': Labeling Lay Religiosity in Thirteenth-Century Paris," in *Labels and Libels: Naming Beguines in Northern Medieval Europe*, ed. Letha Böhringer, Jennifer K. Deane, and Hildo van Engen (Turnhout: Brepols, 2014).

7. See Chapter 2.

8. William of Saint-Amour, *Responsiones,* 342.

9. Grundmann, *Religious Movements in the Middle Ages,* 144. These social tensions are especially emphasized in Schmitt, *Mort d'une hérésie.*

10. Thomas of Eccleston, *Tractatus de adventu Fratrum Minorum in Angliam*, ed. A. G. Little (Manchester: Manchester University Press, 1951), 98–99.

11. Béthune, ed. *Cartulaire du beguinage de Sainte Élisabeth à Gand*, 74.

12. For a useful discussion of "high-status labor," see Martha C. Howell, *Women, Production, and Patriarchy in Late Medieval Cities* (Chicago: University of Chicago Press, 1986).

13. Farmer, "Medieval Paris and the Mediterranean."

14. The tax was levied in livres tournois but collected in livres parisis. Eight livres parisis was equal to ten livres tournois.

15. Two of the five rolls from this levy, 1296 and 1297, were published by Karl Michaëlsson, ed., *Le livre de la taille de Paris, l'an 1296* (Göteborg: Almquist and Wiksell, 1958), and *Le Livre de la taille de Paris l'an 1297* (Göteborg: Almquist and Wiksell, 1962). The unpublished rolls from 1298, 1299, and 1300 are housed at the Archives Nationales in Paris (AN KK 283) Copies of the unpublished manuscripts are available at the Institut de Recherche et d'Histoire des Textes (IRHT) in Paris. I benefited greatly from the computerized database created by Caroline Bourlet at the IRHT. I thank her for providing me with access to these data, which were instrumental in helping me to locate beguines and silk workers across the tax rolls. In addition to examining data printouts of names of Parisians identified as silk workers, I consulted the published editions and the unpublished manuscripts.

16. Hercule Géraud edited and published the 1292 list in 1837. It was then reprinted by Caroline Bourlet and Lucie Fossier, who added an index in 1991. Hercule Géraud, ed., *Paris sous Philippe-le-Bel, d'après des documents originaux et notamment d'après un manuscrit contenant "Le Rôle de la Taille" imposée sur les habitants de Paris en 1292, 1837,* reprint, with introduction and index by Caroline Bourlet and Lucie Fossier (Tübingen: Max Niemeyer, 1991) (henceforth *1292*). On the purpose of the 1292 roll, see Archer, "Working Women in Thirteenth-Century Paris," 78–79, and Caroline Bourlet, "L'anthroponymie à Paris à la fin du XIIIème siècle d'après les rôles de la taille du règne de Philippe le Bel," in *Genèse médiévale de l'anthroponymie moderne*, ed. Monique Bourin and Pascal Chareille (Tours: Publication de l'université de Tours, 1992), 10. Jean Guerot's "Fiscalité, topographie, et démographie à Paris au Moyen Âge (à propos d'une publication recente de rôles d'impôt),"

Bibliothèque de l'École des Chartes 130 (1972) : 383–465 is also useful. The manuscript is housed at the Bibliothèque Nationale de France (BnF fr. 6220).

17. Michaëlsson published the 1313 roll, which is located in the Bibliothèque Nationale de France (BnF fr. 6736). Karl Michaëlsson, ed., *Le livre de la taille de Paris, l'an de grace 1313* (Göteborg: Almquist and Wiksell, 1951) (henceforth *1313*).

18. Indeed, Janice Archer estimates that the 1292 register only lists about a quarter of Parisian households. See Archer, "Working Women in Thirteenth-Century Paris," 83.

19. Twelve denier was equal to one sou; twenty sous was equal to one livre. Estimates come from Bronislaw Geremek, *The Margins of Society in Late Medieval Paris*, trans. Jean Birrell (Cambridge: Cambridge University Press, 1987), 68. Janice Archer has argued persuasively that the tax was most likely based on the value of a person's business inventory (tools and merchandise) combined with revenue. See Archer, "Working Women in Thirteenth-Century Paris," 84.

20. Farmer, *Surviving Poverty*, 32.

21. Caroline Bourlet has examined naming patterns in these sources. See "L'anthroponymie à Paris."

22. Unfortunately, the highest degree of inconsistency is in the recording of an individual's second name. The assessors' descriptions seem to have become more specific over time. Caroline Bourlet has found that in the earliest years of the assessments, the assessors tended to include fewer details (providing only a name and possibly a surname) than in later years, when they included names, surnames, and often the taxpayer's profession. See Bourlet, "L'anthroponymie à Paris," 15.

23. Jeanne is identified as a beguine in a property dispute between the executors of her will and the beguinage. AN X/IA, 7, fols. 35–36.

24. "La béguine de son hostel, 24s," *1292*, 30

25. I have traced each individual beguine across all seven assessments, paying close attention to how a beguine is identified as well as the location of her household in the neighborhood. This is important for gathering as much information as possible (since tax assessors include or exclude details in different rolls) as well as for avoiding counting individual beguines more than once.

26. "Marie, la fille dame Osane, 7 liv 10s," *1292*, 91.

27. "Marie la beguine, merciere, 11 liv, 10s," AN KK 283, fol. 113v (1298); "Marie Osane, merciere, 10 liv, 10s," AN KK 283, fol. 191v (1299). We cannot assume that the assessors mentioned Marie's religious identity because she had recently converted to the beguine life. The assessors might note that the woman lived as a beguine one year, fail to include the term the next, only to mention it again in a subsequent roll.

28. Women made up 13.8 percent of taxpayers listed in the 1297–1300 rolls (the rolls that are most comparable, since they were part of the eight-year levy imposed by Philip IV). See Archer, "Working Women in Thirteenth-Century Paris," 110.

29. Archer, "Working Women in Thirteenth-Century Paris," 127.

30. AN KK 283, fol. 3 (1296); fol. 39 (1297).

31. BnF fr. 6736, 2v.

32. "Perronnelle la béguine—ses compagnes, 3s," *1292*, 113.

33. "Ysabiau de cambrai et beguines qui sont aveques li," AN KK 283, fol. 16.

34. "Ses compaignes beguines," AN KK 283, fol. 190.

35. "Les béguines chiés Lorenz de Saint-Marcel," *1292*, 62.

36. See Appendix.

37. "Aalis de Saint-joce, ouvriere de soie, 24s," AN KK 283, fol. 99. The term *ouvrière de soie* is a generic label that might be used to refer to someone who wove cloth. It could also, however, refer to someone who "worked" cloth, perhaps as an embroiderer. In the case of Alice of Saint-Joce, it is evident that she "worked" cloth, since she is later described as someone who made alms purses. See Farmer, "Medieval Paris and the Mediterranean."

38. "Aalis de saint-joce, fabricante d'aumonieres, 24s," AN KK 283, fol.156v.

39. Archer asserts that the ouvrières de soie were silk weavers. Archer, "Working Women in Thirteenth-Century Paris," 174. Recent research suggests that some ouvrières were embroiderers of silk cloth. I thank Sharon Farmer for her insight on how to understand the term "ouvrier/ouvrière."

40. "Marie des cordeles, ouvriere de soie," AN KK 283, fol. 178v (1299); "Marie la beguine, fabricante de couvre-chef," AN KK 283, fol. 256 (1300).

41. "Isabelle d'oroer, fileresse de soie, 42s," AN KK 283, fol. 111v (1298); "Ysabel d'oroer, vendeur de soie, 36s," AN KK 283, fol. 186v (1299); "Isabelle d'ouroer, fileresse de soie, 62s," AN KK 283, fol. 263v (1300).

42. Isabelle's tax assessments, which averaged forty-eight sous, were far above that paid by silk spinners on average (4.84 sous) and three times larger than the highest tax paid by any other silk spinner (sixteen sous) listed in the rolls. I have drawn the average tax for silk spinners from Sharon Farmer, "Women in the Parisian Textile Industries in the Late Thirteenth and Early Fourteenth Centuries," unpublished conference paper, Forty-first International Congress on Medieval Studies, Kalamazoo, MI. I thank Sharon Farmer for her permission to use her data.

43. Sharon Farmer has calculated the average tax for non-Lombards and non-Jews (groups the assessors treated separately) in 1292 as 14.6 sous. See Farmer, *Surviving Poverty*, 98. Additional evidence that Isabelle worked as a mercer is found in the censive of Saint-Merry, which identifies Isabelle as a "doreur" or someone who specializes in embellishing mercery items. See Léon Cadier and Camille Couderc, "Cartulaire et censier de Saint-Merry de Paris," *Mémoires de la Société de l'histoire de Paris*, 18 (1891): 204.

44. Most of the residents of this street were engaged in silk work. Agnes's neighbor from 1292 to 1300 (Agnes does not appear in the 1313 register) was the mercer Thibaut de Flori. See map 3. Agnes lived in the middle of what Sharon Farmer has helpfully identified as the "Quicampoix mercery," where 27 percent of all taxed mercers resided. For these zones, see map 3. I thank Sharon Farmer for allowing me to use her labeling system in my own maps.

45. According to Archer's calculations, female mercers paid an average tax of about 52.83 sous. See "Working Women in Thirteenth-Century Paris," 316. Sharon Farmer's calculations are a bit lower (42 sous), because she counted each woman only once (tracking individuals through the rolls), rather than take the average from all female mercers in the four complete consecutive rolls (1297–1300) as Archer did. I am grateful to Sharon Farmer for sharing her calculations with me.

46. See map 3. Based on my own analysis of silk workers listed in the tax rolls from 1296 to 1300 (graciously provided to me by Caroline Bourlet), about 40 percent of all taxed silk workers lived in these parishes.

47. See map 1. Indeed, as Sharon Farmer has recently noted, this section of the city around the Franciscan houses was, in the late thirteenth and early fourteenth centuries, home to about 5 percent of all of the taxed silk workers. See Farmer, "Medieval Paris and the Mediterranean."

48. Of course, I do not wish to claim an exclusive association between unenclosed beguines and silk work. There is some evidence to suggest that the beguines who lived in the beguinage worked with wool, and there is at least one example of a resident who worked with silk. Moreover, it is important to acknowledge that the tax rolls do not list all of the "unenclosed" beguines living in medieval Paris. Beguines too poor to pay the taille probably worked in a range of crafts that escaped the notice of tax assessors.

49. AAP, fonds St.-Jacques, reg. 1, pièce 31. I discuss Jeanne's will in detail later in this chapter.

50. G. B. Depping, *Ordonnances sur le commerce et les métiers rendues par les prévôts de Paris depuis 1270 jusqu'à l'an 1300.* Vol 3 of *Réglemens sur les arts et métiers de Paris rédigés au xiiie siècle* (Paris: Crapelet, 1837), 379–382.

51. Specifically, royal account books from the fourteenth century mention beguine silk workers. See, for example, Louis Douët-d'Arcq, *Comptes de l'Argenterie des rois de France au XIVe Siècle* (Paris: Renouard, 1851), 296. I discuss specific examples of beguines supplying silk garments to noble households later in this chapter.

52. Jules Labarte, *Inventaire du mobilier de Charles V, roi de France* (Paris: Imprimerie Nationale, 1879), 144.

53. Map 3 shows this striking overlap between religious identity and work identity.

54. Indeed, none of the beguines listed in the tax rolls is ever described as a widow. This strongly suggests that these beguines were lifelong single women, since the tax assessors often identified widows in relation to their deceased husbands or living children.

55. Archer, "Working Women in Thirteenth-Century Paris"; Simone Roux, "Les femmes dans les métiers parisiens: XIIIe–XVe siècles," *CLIO* 3 (1996): 13–30. Drawing on the *Livre des Métiers*, Diane Frappier-Bigras notes that the statutes for thirty-three of the 101 guilds evince the presence of women in the métier. Judicial records and the tax rolls show that, in practice, women were involved in as many as sixty-two of the craft associations mentioned in the *Livre des Métiers*. See Frappier-Bigras, "La famille dans l'artisanat parisien du XIIIe siècle," *Le moyen âge* 95 (1989), 60. The *Livre des Métiers* has been edited by René de Lespinasse and François Bonnardot. See *Le Livre des métiers d'Etienne Boileau* (henceforth *LDM*) (Paris: Imprimerie nationale, 1879).

56. On the privileges enjoyed by the wives and widows of Parisian masters, see Frappier-Bigras, "La famille dans l'artisanat parisien." Frappier-Bigras argues that it was in becoming a widow that women attained greatest autonomy. "La famille dans l'artisanat parisien," 61. The crucial connection between marital status and labor status has been recognized by historians of women and work in other medieval cities. See Martha C. Howell,

Women, Production, and Patriarchy and Judith Bennett, *Ale, Beer, and Brewsters in England: Women's Work in a Changing World, 1300–1600* (Oxford: Oxford University Press, 1999).

57. As Archer has shown in her study of the tax rolls, widows managed these workshops not as a stopgap but in their own right. See "Working Women in Thirteenth-Century Paris," 127–130.

58. *LDM* title 50.

59. Scholars have deduced that Paris's estimated 450 wool weavers would have required at least seventeen hundred wool spinners to supply them with spun wool. Tax records, however, list an average of only seven wool spinners per year, all of whom were women. The small number of taxed wool spinners indicates that the vast majority of Paris's wool spinners were either married, making them invisible to the tax assessors, or simply too poor to pay the taille. Moreover, some of the wool yarn for the Paris wool industry was spun by workers in the local countryside and imported into the city. See Belhoste, "Paris, Grand centre drapier au moyen âge," and Farmer, "Women in the Parisian Textile Industries in the Late Thirteenth and Early Fourteenth Centuries." On the upper end of the wool industry were the drapers. While it was extremely unusual for women to work in this profession (less than 2 percent of the Parisian taxpayers identified as drapers were women), Sharon Farmer has made the point that many of the women from alderman families (whose members dominated the draper profession) listed in the rolls were probably drapers. These women likely broke into this industry through their position in the family. See Farmer, "Merchant Women and the Administrative Glass Ceiling in Thirteenth-Century Paris," 94–95.

60. The statutes claim that this was because young women, if allowed to join the guild independently, would set up their shops only to live lives of debauchery. Once they had spent all of their money, the statutes assert, these women would return home, to the shame of their parents. Thus, the statutes assume that women will fall into sin—and squander their inheritances—unless they married within the métier, where their fathers and husbands could better supervise them. *LDM,* 87:16.

61. While it is important to recognize that women married to dependent laborers were also unable to gain entry into the guilds and had limited resources and support, single women as a group faced greater limitations because of their marital status. See Ruth Mazo Karras, "Sex and the Singlewoman."

62. E. Jane Burns, *Sea of Silk: A Textile Geography of Women's Work in Medieval French Literature* (Philadelphia: University of Pennsylvania Press, 2009), 73.

63. Archer, "Working Women in Thirteenth-Century Paris," 117.

64. *LDM,* nos. 35, 36, 38, 44, 45, 95.

65. One of these female-dominated crafts, the *fesseresses de chapeaux d'orfrois,* was absorbed by the mercers' guild by the late thirteenth century. The guild regulations for the fesseresses de chapeaux d'orfrois suggest that this craft was very similar to that of the small-scale mercers. Like the mercers who specialized in embellishing hats, belts, and purses, the makers of embroidered hats made luxury accessories, primarily for women. Lespinasse notes that the only mention of the fesseresses de chapeaux d'orfrois is in Étienne Boileau's compilation of the guild statutes, which dates around 1268. See René de Lespinasse, *Les*

métiers et corporations de la ville de Paris XIVe–XVIIIe siècle (Paris: Imprimerie Nationale, 1886), vol. 2, 232, n.2.

66. Seventy-three percent of the *crépinières* and eighty-nine percent of the *aumônières* in the tax rolls were female. Archer, "Working Women in Thirteenth-Century Paris," 317. Frappier-Bigras suggests that female crépinières were trained in the métier by their husbands. However, the fact that almost all of the crépinères mentioned in the tax rolls, as well as in the list of guild members, were female indicates that women were able to practice this métier in their own right.

67. G. B. Depping, *Réglemens sur les arts et métiers de Paris rédigés au XIIIe siècle* (Paris: Crapelet, 1837), 382–386.

68. Ibid., 379–382.

69. Indeed, as the guild statutes suggest and tax rolls confirm, many silk women lived with female apprentices who learned the trade over an extended period of training in residence.

70. "Des fillaresses de soie à grans fuiseaus," *LDM*, 35:2. "Des fillaresse de soie à petiz fuiseaus," ibid., 36:3.

71. "Ouvrières de tissuz de soie," ibid., 38:2. "Fesseresses des ceuvre-chefs de soie," ibid., 45:4.

72. Although the guild regulations for the spinners' guilds mention formal contracts for apprenticeship, it seems that none of these contracts has survived. Carol Loats has examined hundreds of apprenticeship contracts involving women from the sixteenth century; see Carol L. Loats, "Gender, Guilds, and Work Identity: Perspectives from Sixteenth-Century Paris," *French Historical Studies* 20, no. 1 (1997): 5–30. Both of the silk spinners' guilds required that apprentices train with a mistress for at least seven years and a ten-sou fee, or for eight years with no fee (*LDM*, 35:2 and 36:3). Apprentices for weavers of silk *tissu* were required to serve for at least six years with a four-livre fee, eight years with a forty-sous fee, or ten years with no fee (*LDM*, 45:4).

73. While historians of women and work in northern Europe have rightly noted the ways in which marital status and life-cycle determined women's participation in the local economy as well as their access to high-status occupations, such factors were not necessarily applicable to women engaged in many of the crafts related to Paris's silk industry. On women, work, marital status, and life-cycle, see Judith Bennett, *Ale, Beer, and Brewsters in England*; Martha C. Howell, "Women, the Family Economy, and the Structures of Market Production in the Cities of Northern Europe During the Late Middle Ages," in *Women and Work in Pre-Industrial Europe*, ed. Barbara Hanawalt (Bloomington: Indiana University Press, 1986) and *Women, Production, and Patriarchy*; Merry Wiesner, "Spinsters and Seamstresses: Women in Cloth and Clothing Production," in *Rewriting the Renaissance: The Discourses of Sexual Difference in Early Modern Europe,* ed. Maureen Quilligan, Margaret W. Ferguson, and Nancy J. Vickers (Chicago: University of Chicago Press, 1986).

74. *LDM*, 37:5 (crépinières) and *LDM* 38:8 (*ouvrières de tissuz de soie*). *LDM* title 38:8 states that, should any of the guild's members violate the association's rules, they would be fined eight sous. One of these sous was to go to their *confrerie*. "Et quiconque mesprendra

en auqun des articles desus diz, elle poiera viii souz de parisis . . . desquex viii souz li Rois aura v sous, et la confrarie du mestier xii deniers."

75. *LDM*, 36:7.

76. Ibid., 38:8.

77. Ibid., 44:5 and 8. The female guild officers were also paid to perform this task.

78. Lespinasse includes the names of a few female jurés in his *Les métiers et corporations de la ville de Paris*. Specifically, he lists four jurés for the silk spinners (pages 72 and 75) and two for the weavers of silk head coverings (page 84). I have checked the names in Lespinasse against my own list of beguine silk workers. On women and work indentity, see Natalie Zemon Davis, "Women in the Crafts in Sixteenth- Century Lyon," *Feminist Studies* 8 (Spring 1982): 47–80; Judith M. Bennett and Maryanne Kowaleski, "Crafts, Guilds, and Women in the Middle Ages: Fifty Years After Marian K. Dale," in *Sisters and Workers in the Middle Ages,* ed. Judith Bennett, Elizabeth A. Clark, Jean F. O'Barr, and B. Anne Vilen (Chicago: University of Chicago Press, 1989), 11–25; and Loats, "Gender, Guilds, and Work Identity," who argues convincingly that women developed a strong work identity outside the guild structure.

79. Bennett and Kowaleski, "Crafts, Guilds, and Women in the Middle Ages," 481.

80. Farmer, "Women in the Parisian Textile Industries in the Late Thirteenth and Early Fourteenth Centuries."

81. "Quiconques veut ester fillaresse de soie a grans fuiseaus à Paris . . . estre peut franchement, pour tant qu'il œuvre aus us et aus coustumes du mestier." *LDM* 35:1. The fact that the statutes for both silk spinners' guilds include references to workers from outside Paris who wish to take up the métier serves as further evidence that Parisian authorities sought to attract silk workers to Paris. "Se aucune ouvrière de dohors Paris vient à Paris, et voelle ouvrer du mestier devant dit, elle doit jurer pardevant ii des jurez qui gardent le mestier, au mains, que elle le mestier devant dit fera bien et loiaument, et que ele se contendra aus us et as coustumes du mestier." Ibid., 36:8.

82. As Sharon Farmer has noted in her work on the migration of silk workers to medieval Paris, "the introduction of silk technology was almost always accompanied by the immigration of workers who understood that technology." Farmer, "Medieval Paris and the Mediterranean."

83. The process of spinning raw silk into thread was a communal task—requiring the cooperation of at least two workers—and was based in the home workshop. An examination of the silk spinners' statutes provides some detail on the process of making silk textiles and the relationships these tasks could potentially foster among workers. The *Livre des Métiers* states that the silk spinners were responsible for "reeling, spinning, folding, and twisting" the silk, tasks that required at least two workers. For details on these processes, see John Munro, "Silk," in *Dictionary of the Middle Ages*, ed. Joseph R. Strayer (New York: Charles Scribner's Sons/Macmillan, 1988), 293–294.

84. The *Livre des Metiers* is full of regulations attesting to the mercers' dominance of the silk industry in Paris. In order to assure the quality of the silk and silk-made goods they marketed, the mercers' guild sought to maintain tight control over silk workers. The

mercers' guild regulations contain numerous restrictions on the materials mercers could use in the silk luxury goods they marketed. By the early fourteenth century, the mercers had gained a tremendous amount of control over the various associations of silk workers, especially the silk spinners' guilds. Lespinasse, *Les métiers et corporations de la ville de Paris XIVe–XVIIIe siècle*, vol. 2, 377–378.

85. Bove, *Dominer la ville*, 71–74. Female mercers, of course, did not exercise official political power.

86. As Sharon Farmer has argued, this was not quite a "putting out" system of production. Silk workers owned the materials they purchased from the mercers, which they then sold back to the mercers as finished products. See "Medieval Paris and the Mediterranean."

87. Most of the mercers' regulations in the *Livre des Métiers* concern the type of materials mercers were permitted to use in certain pieces. Mercers could not sell silk head coverings, purses, or any cloth with a warp of linen or "flourin," which was probably an inferior silk (*LDM*, 75:3). They could not use false pearls (ibid., 75:6) or sell alms purses in which cotton is mixed with the silk "since this is a deception to those who do not know it" (ibid., 75:10).

88. Mercers were fined twelve sous for each violation and the cloth or article in question was cut up. Ibid., 75:14.

89. According to my own analysis of the data, 40 percent of taxed mercers lived in the same parishes populated by silk workers, namely, the parishes of Saint-Joce, Saint-Jacques, and Saint-Merry. See map 3. This area was adjacent to the neighborhood in which Italian merchants tended to settle. Italian merchants supplied raw silk for spinning as well as Italian and eastern silks, which Parisian mercers purchased to sell at Parisian and regional markets and fairs. Lucchese merchants brought silk to the Champagne fairs in the twelfth and thirteenth centuries. By the second half of the thirteenth century, Italian merchants set up permanent branches in England, Bruges, and Paris, where they sold fine Italian and eastern silks to nobles and local merchants. Florence Elder de Roover, "Lucchese Silks," *Ciba Review* 80 (1950): 2912.

90. "Et beguines qui sont avecques li," KK 283, fol. 16.

91. Although identified as a mercer in 1298 (KK 283, fol. 112v), Isabelle is described as "Dame Isabel de cambrai, fet cuevrechies" in 1300 (fol. 266v), suggesting that her workshop primarily produced small silk items.

92. "Marguerite de troies compagne Isabelle de cambrai, 16s," KK 283, fol. 51v.

93. Isabelle paid twelve sous in 1297, whereas Marguerite was assessed sixteen sous.

94. KK 283, fol. 112v.

95. "Ysabiau de cambray et ses compaignes, beguines, 16s," KK 283 fol. 190r.

96. KK 283, fol. 190r.

97. KK 283, fol. 266v.

98. "Anes d'orliens, beguine," AN KK 283, fol. 17v.

99. Possibly because the other rolls did not list apprentices and valets, whereas the 1292 roll occasionally did. I owe this observation to Janice Archer, "Working Women in Thirteenth-Century Paris," 112.

100. I discuss Jeanne's relationship with her female employees later in this chapter.

101. Isabelle consistently appears in the tax assessments, paying a relatively high tax (average fifty sous). Each year, she was taxed next to silk workers, particularly Sanceline la Royne, a silk worker (ouvrière de soie). Just across the rue de Temple lived the beguine sisters and crépinières Laurette and Maire. AN KK 283, fol. 187.

102. Ameline and Basile lived on the rue Quicampoix, a street dominated by silk workers.

103. "Les béguines chiés Lorenz de Saint-Marcel." *1292,* 63.

104. These companions were sometimes blood relatives, such as sisters, aunts, or mothers, or other beguines. In a few cases, these relatives are also identified as beguines. The rolls include three pairs of sisters, all of whom are identified as beguines. Seven beguines lived with sisters, who may or may not have identified as beguines; four beguines lived with their mothers, and two lived with nieces.

105. Sharon Farmer has examined this cluster of woman as evidence of "non-economically motivated female clustering," although not in connection with silk work. Farmer, "Down and Out and Female in Thirteenth-Century Paris," 366–367.

106. KK 283, fol. 30v ("Martine la beguine et Jehanne sa compagne, 48s"); fol. 64v ("Martine la beguine et Jehanne sa compagne, 48s"); fol. 220v ("Martine de Manle et Jehanne sa compagne, 62s"); fol. 292v ("Martine de manle, beguine et Jehanne sa compaigne, 62s").

107. On these mercery zones, see Farmer, "Medieval Paris and the Mediterranean." For the locations of these zones, see map 1.

108. See Chapter 4 on the relationship between beguines and the University of Paris.

109. Farmer, "Medieval Paris and the Mediterranean."

110. Particularly on the rue Raoul Roissole at the intersection where the rue au Conquillier (also called the ruèle au Curé de St. Eustache) met the rue du Four. See map 4.

111. In 1297, a certain "Alison la beguine" appeared on the rue Raoul Roissole. In 1298, Alison appears in the same location on the rue Raoul Roissole, as well as a silk spinner "Juliote la beguine," perhaps the same Juliote mentioned in the 1292 register. By 1299, Juliote's sister Jeanette reappears in the same location as the primary taxpayer. On the other side of the street, a similar pattern of beguine clustering appears. KK 283, fol. 126v.

112. KK 283, fol. 7 (1296) and fol. 42v (1297).

113. Intriguingly, the cross that stood at this intersection (Croix Neuve) was sometimes called the Croix Jean Bigue, suggesting a possible connection with lay religiosity. See *1292,* 219.

114. On Bernard of Pailly, see Anne Terroine, *Un bourgeois parisien du XIIIe siècle: Geoffroi de Saint-Laurent, 1245?–1290,* ed. Lucie Fossier (Paris: CNRS, 1992), 34. On Bernard's role at the Haudriettes, see Connally, "Les 'Bonnes Femmes' de Paris," 82–84.

115. Connally, "Les 'Bonnes Femmes' de Paris," 84.

116. *1313,* 33.

117. In 1292, several clusters appear: one around the beguine Ade and her sister, Marguerite, and another around the beguine Juliote (1292, fol. 5v). Jeanne "la beguine" also set up a household on the same street. Beguines turn up on this street throughout the 1290s, suggesting that the street was a magnet for lay religious women. Michael Connally has surmised that this cluster of beguines eventually transformed into the "bonnes femmes de la rue du Coq," who were mentioned in the testament of a Parisian counselor Jean Crété.

See Connally "Les 'Bonnes Femmes' de Paris." For Jean Crété's will, see *Testament,* 433. I discuss this possibility in more detail in chapter 6. For the locations of these houses for lay religious women, see map 1.

118. These studies have shown that some members of lay religious communities took on the role of entrepreneurs and merchants, employing their coreligious as spinners, weavers, or dyers. See Sally M. Brasher, *Women of the Humiliati: A Lay Religious Order in Medieval Civic Life* (New York: Routledge, 2003); Simons, *Cities of Ladies.*

119. "Item legavit dicta testatrix Guillamete dicte la grant fillatrici de serico quamdiu vita duxitur in humanis dumtaxat domum suam quam habet dicta testatrix in beguinagio parisiensis," AAP, fonds St.-Jacques, reg. 1, pièce 31.

120. *Beguinage Statutes,* 20.

121. Olivier-Martin, *Histoire de la coutume de la prévôté et de la vicomté de Paris,* 2: 268.

122. Latin records in other northern European towns sometimes referred to an individual beguine as *puella.* See Gelser, "Lay Religious Women and Church Reform in Late Medieval Münster," 190.

123. "Beatrice dicta la grant factor et impensor," AAP, fonds St.-Jacques, reg. 1, pièce 31. Silk merchants often employed factors. See de Roover, "Lucchese Silks."

124. "Et post easdem Guillamete decessum dicta testatrix legavit, concessit, perpetuo Beatrici dicte la grant ad cum suis juribus et pertinenciis domum praedictam et appendenciis universiis per eandem Beatricem et heredes suos tenendam et possidendam perpetuo pacifice et quiete." AAP, fonds St.-Jacques, reg. 1, pièce 31.

125. "Item legavit, dedit, et concessit coram dictis juratis et commissis nostris dicta testatrix praeface Beatrici dicte la grant in puram et perpetuam elemosinam suisque heredibus et tamen ab ipsas habentibus et habituris totum residuum omnium et singulorum bonorum suorum mobilium et immobilium quondcunque ubicumque existecium absque aliqua excepcione de eisdem vel parte eorundem facienda tacite vel expresse." Ibid.

126. "Item legavit dedit et concessit perpetuo et hereditabiliter praedicta testatrix coram praedictis juratis et commissis nostris in puram et perpetuam elemosinam necnon et in recompensacionem et remunerationem gratorum servitiorum eidem testatrici pluribus temporibus retroactis ab eadem testatrice receptor et a Beatrice dicta la grant factor et impensor." Ibid.

127. "Personaliter constituti domii Rolandus Hellomyni et Robertus Godefredi presbyteri et Reginaldus Paonnier, civis parisis, exequtores testamenti seu ultime voluntatis defuncte Johanne quondam dicte du faut civis et mercerie parisiensi ab eadem electi nominati et facti una cum Beatrice dicta la grant nunc defuncta." AAP, fonds St.-Jacques, reg. 1, pièce 1154.

128. "Quos quidem sexaquinta solidos parisus annui redditus seu census, dicti exequtores nomine exequtoris predicto, ob remedium et salutem animarum defunctarum praedictae Johanne et Beatricis magne quondam puelle et dilecte dicte Johanne." AAP, fonds St.-Jacques, reg. 1, pièce 1154.

129. The other women mentioned in the will owed between twenty-three and forty-two sous. Unfortunately, the women's occupations are not mentioned and I was unable to find their names in the tax rolls. AAP, fonds St.-Jacques, reg. 1, pièce 31.

130. "Noveritis quod in nostra presentia constituti Robertus dictus milles bouclerius et Johanna eius uxor, recognoverunt coram nobis se vendidisse et, nomine vendicionis ex nunc perpetuo quitavisse et concessisse, Agneti de Cauda et Johanne du Fauc eius socie merceriis parisis et earum heredibus pro precio duodecim liberos parisis." AAP, fonds St.-Jacques, reg. 1, pièce 1163.

131. "Devant nous vindrent en jugement Thomas le convers barbier et Marguerite sa fame . . . avoient et ont tiennent et poussuient paisiblement, une meson sicomme elle se comporte scant a paris en rue neuve saint merri en la censive saint merri chargiee tant seulement et sus le tout soissant et quatre soulz paris tant de cens comme de crois de cens ou de rente. . . . Les devant nommez Thomas et Marguerite sa fame . . . recognurent en droit eus chascun pour le tout avoir vendu et par non de pure vente quittie, otroie et delessie desorendroit a touz jours mes heriablement a Jehanne de Faut merciere bourgoise de paris." AAP, fonds St.-Jacques, reg. 1, pièce 1166.

132. While we do not know the total value of all of Jeanne du Faut's assets—only those mentioned in her testament and surviving documents—she was clearly quite wealthy. She owned at least three houses and received annual rents worth more than twenty-two livres annually.

133. Jeanne named Regnaut le Paonnier, mercer and governor of the confraternity of Saint-Jacques, as one of the executors of her testament and gave ten *sous* to the hospital established by a mercer neighbor, Imbert de Lyons. See AAP, fonds St.Jacques, reg. 1, pièce 31.

134. Very little has been published on the confraternity of Saint-Sépulcre. A recent article by Béatrice Dansette briefly sketches the history of the confraternity, describing its foundation in the context of renewed interest in crusade and pilgrimage in the early fourteenth century. Béatrice Dansette, "Les pèlerins occidentaux du moyen âge tardif au retour de la Terre sainte: Confréries du Saint-Sépulcre et paumiers parisiens," in *Dei gesta per Francos: Études sur les croisades dédiées à Jean Richard*, ed. Benjamin Z. Kedar, Michael Balard, and Jonathan Riley-Smith (Aldershot, U.K.: Ashgate, 2001), 301–314.

135. Ibid., 306.

136. The inventory was published in 1882. See Émile Molinier, "Inventaire du trésor de l'église du Saint-Sépulcre à Paris," *Mémoires de la Société de l'histoire de Paris* IX (1882) : 239–286.

137. Jeanne du Faut bequeathed twenty sous to support the maintenance of the church of Saint-Sépulcre as well as an annuity of nine sous with the request that the confraternity celebrate an annual mass for her soul. AAP, fonds St.-Jacques, reg. 1, pièce 31. Jeanne la Maraschalle, a silk worker and a beguine, gave the confraternity of Saint-Sépulcre an annuity worth 52 sous. AN S 931A, doss. 2.

138. See Farmer "Biffes, Tiretaines, and Aumonières."

139. Jules-Marie Richard, *Une petite nièce de Saint Louis: Mahaut, comtesse d'Artois et de Bourgogne* (Paris: H. Champion, 1887).

140. Richard, *Une petite nièce de Saint Louis*, 199, 200, 204–205.

141. Marie de Val was a member of the Countess of Flanders's household. "Adonc a Marie fille dame Ossanne par damisele marie de la val pour 2 dousaines de coeffes et pour 1 dousaine de springletes donc damisele marie a les pieces." Ghent, Rijksarchief, Inventaire

Gaillard 52, membrane 3. I am very grateful to Sharon Farmer for sharing with me photographs of this manuscript.

142. "Jehanne des Granches, beguine, pour un orfrois à ladicte chasuble avec un parement pour nappes d'autel, tout baillé au dit Pierre Marie, 22 livres, 10 sous." Douët-d'Arcq, *Comptes de l'Argenterie des rois de France au XIVe Siècle*, 296.

143. The account of the argentier Étienne Lafontaine states: "Jehanne des Granches beguine, pour la soye et facon de deux brayes de cendal, lu pour le comte d'Anjou, lautre pour le comte d'Estampes." Ibid., 94.

CHAPTER 4. MASTERS AND PASTORS

I have personally consulted all of the manuscripts cited in this chapter. In several cases, I have followed Nicole Bériou's expert transcriptions and have cited her editions wherever appropriate.

1. Richard H. Rouse, "The Early Library of the Sorbonne," *Scriptorium* 21 (1967), 45.

2. BnF Lat. 15972, fols. 174–177r. Very little has been written about this manuscript. Delisle simply identified it as "material for the use of preachers." See Léopold Delisle, "Inventaire des manuscrits latins de la Sorbonne, conservés à la Bibliothèque impériale sous les numéros 15176–16718 du fonds latin," *Bibliothèque de l'École des Chartes* 31 (1870), 32. Madeleine Mabille identified the hand as that of Stephen of Abbeville, a student of the Sorbonne. See Madeleine Mabille, "Les manuscrits d'Étienne d'Abbeville conservés à la Bibliothèque Nationale de Paris," *Bibliothèque de l'École des Chartes* 132 (1974), 262. On Pierre de Limoges's scholarly contributions, including the copying of books useful to preachers, see Louis J. Bataillon, "Comptes de Pierre de Limoges pour la copie de livres," in *La production du livre universitaire au Moyen Âge*, 265–273.

3. *Benigna* was a common spelling variant of the term *beguina*. See the discussion later in this chapter.

4. "Notam que nullus est bonum predicator vel confessor nisi velit sustinere beginagium," BnF Lat. 15972, fol. 174r. The miscellany is a kind of preaching aid typical of the types of texts found at the Sorbonne library in the Middle Ages. On the manuscripts found in the medieval library of the Sorbonne, see Delisle, *Le cabinet des manuscrits de la Bibliothèque Nationale*, II (Paris, 1874), 142–208, and "Inventaire des manuscrits latins." Richard Rouse's study is also particularly useful for the early history of the Sorbonne library, "The Early Library of the Sorbonne."

5. BnF Lat. 16481. This manuscript has received extensive treatment in several studies by Nicole Bériou, "La prédication au béguinage de Paris pendant l'année liturgique 1272–1273," *Recherches augustiniennes* 13 (1978): 105–229, and *L'avènement des maîtres de la Parole: La prédication à Paris au XIIIe siècle* (Paris: Institut d'études augustiniennes, 1998).

6. BnF Lat. 16482. Bériou lists the folios of these extracts in *L'avènement*, 220. The sermons attributed to the mistress of the beguinage are examined in Chapter 5.

7. See Chapter 1.

8. The library of the Sorbonne has been a topic of great interest to intellectual historians as well as those interested in manuscripts. See note 2 above.

9. Richard H. Rouse and Mary A. Rouse, *Preachers, Florilegia, and Sermons: Studies on the* Manipulus Florum *of Thomas of Ireland*, Studies and Texts, 47 (Toronto: PIMS, 1979).

10. In her masterful study of Parisian sermons and preaching culture, Nicole Bériou notes that the manuscripts produced by Sorbonne clerics suggest a close tie between the two institutions. See *L'avènement*, 219. Bériou further illustrates the connection in "Robert de Sorbon: Le prud'homme et le béguin," *Comptes-rendus de l'Académie des inscriptions et belles-lettres* (1994): 469–510.

11. On this point, see especially Elliott, *Proving Woman*.

12. Much has been written on this dynamic. See John W. Coakley, *Women, Men, and Spiritual Power: Female Saints and Their Male Collaborators* (New York: Columbia University Press, 2006) and the essays in *Gendered Voices: Medieval Saints and their Interpreters*, ed. Catherine M. Mooney (Philadelphia: University of Pennsylvania Press, 1999.)

13. This has been remedied somewhat in recent years with studies on nuns and their spiritual advisors. See Jeffrey Hamburger, *The Visual and the Visionary: Art and Female Spirituality in Late Medieval Germany* (New York: Zone Books, 1998), and Fiona Griffiths, *The Garden of Delights: Reform and Renaissance for Women in the Twelfth Century* (Philadelphia: University of Pennsylvania Press, 2007). On beguines and pastoral care, see Jennifer Deane, "*Geistliche Schwestern:* The Pastoral Care of Lay Religious Women in Wuerzburg," in *Partners in Spirit: Women, Men and Religious Life in Germany, 1100–1500,* ed. Fiona Griffiths and Julie Hotchin (Turnhout: Brepols, 2013).

14. On this point, two influential studies are Josef Greven, *Die Anfänge der Beginen: Ein Beitrag zur Geschichte der Volksfrömmigkeit und des Ordenswesens im Hochmittelalter* (Münster: Aschendorffsche Verlagsbuchhandlung, 1912), and Herbert Grundmann, *Religious Movements in the Middle Ages*.

15. Grundmann, *Religious Movements in the Middle Ages*, 142–143.

16. McDonnell, *Beguines and Beghards*, 170–186.

17. Fiona Griffiths, "'Men's Duty to Provide for Women's Needs': Abelard, Heloise, and their Negotiation of the *Cura Monialium*," *Journal of Medieval History* 30 (2004), 3.

18. Griffiths's argument is, of course, supported by scholarship on individual male clerics who forged spiritual friendships with religious laywomen. See note 12 above.

19. The exception is Nicole Bériou. See *L'avènement*, 219–220.

20. Ruth Karras has argued persuasively that university clerics largely ignored women in *quodlibetal* discussions. Ruth Mazo Karras, "Using Women to Think with in the Medieval University," in *Seeing and Knowing: Women and Learning in Medieval Europe, 1200–1550,* ed. Anneke B. Mulder-Bakker (Turnhout: Brepols, 2004), 21–34. See also Ruth Mazo Karras, *Boys to Men: Formations of Masculinity in Late Medieval Europe* (Philadelphia: University of Pennsylvania Press, 2003), 85–95.

21. See Chapter 1.

22. Waters, *Angels and Earthly Creatures*, 33–35.

23. The literature on lay religious movements and heresy is vast. The classic study remains Grundmann, *Religious Movements in the Middle Ages*. See also Malcolm Lambert,

Medieval Heresy: Popular Movements from the Gregorian Reform to the Reformation, 3rd edition (Malden, MA: Blackwell, 2001). Jennifer Deane has recently published a useful overview of the topic. See Jennifer K. Deane, *A History of Medieval Heresy and Inquisition* (New York: Rowman and Littlefield, 2011).

24. On the relationship between religious dissidence and the project of developing new techniques and tools for university-trained preachers, as well as clerical efforts to define preaching as the exclusive prerogative of trained clerics, see Philippe Buc, "*Vox clamantis in deserto?* Pierre le Chantre et la prédication laïque," *Revue Mabillon* 65 (1993): 5–47; Lauwers, "*Praedicatio–Exhortatio*," 187–232; and Bériou, *L'avènement*, especially chapter 1.

25. John W. Baldwin, *Masters, Princes and Merchants: The Social Views of Peter the Chanter and His Circle* (Princeton, NJ: Princeton University Press, 1970); Bériou, *L'avènement*, 1–10; Stephen C. Ferruolo, *The Origins of the University: The Schools of Paris and Their Critics, 1100–1215* (Stanford: Stanford University Press, 1985).

26. Franco Morenzoni, *Des écoles aux paroisses: Thomas de Chobham et la promotion de la prédication au début du XIIIe siècle* (Paris: Institut d'études augustiniennes, 1995).

27. *Verbum Abbreviatum*, PL, 205, 25, trans. in Beryl Smalley, *The Study of the Bible in the Middle Ages*, 3rd edition (Oxford: Blackwell, 1983), 208.

28. Buc, "*Vox clamantis*," 14–24.

29. Buc, "*Vox clamantis*," 26–27; Lauwers, "*Praedicatio–Exhortatio*," 213.

30. Lauwers, "*Praedicatio–Exhortatio*," 216–217.

31. Ibid., 217–223.

32. Ibid., 225

33. Of course, in doing so, preachers risked weakening claims to possess personal authority or charisma. For a fascinating study that addresses this point, among others, see Waters, *Angels and Earthly Creatures*.

34. Lauwers, "*Praedicatio–Exhortatio*." Thus, rather than seeing the diversity of opinions or tolerance argued in Buc's "*Vox clamantis*," Lauwers sees the church defining lay speech with the label *exhortatio* in order to limit and contain it while maintaining their own monopoly on preaching.

35. Lauwers, "*Praedicatio–Exhortatio*," 226.

36. Indeed, as Lauwers argues, the debate regarding lay preaching often centered on women. By evoking prohibitions on female preaching, clerical commentators argued against the notion of a lay apostolate. See Lauwers, "*Praedicatio–Exhortatio*," 210. See also Waters, *Angels and Earthly Creatures*.

37. I borrow the phrase "quintessential laypersons" from Dyan Elliott, *Proving Woman*, 48. On women and preaching, see Michel Lauwers, "Noli me tangere: Mary Magdeline, Marie d'Oignies et les pénitentes du XIIIe siècle," in *Mélanges de l'École française de Rome (Moyen Âge)*, 104/1 (1992): 209–268; Nicole Bériou, "The Right of Women to Give Religious Instruction in the Thirteenth Century," in *Women Preachers and Prophets Through Two Millennia of Christianity*, ed. Beverly Kienzle and Pamela Walker (Berkeley: University of California Press, 1998), 134–145. Blamires, "Women and Preaching in Medieval Orthodoxy, Heresy and Saints' Lives."

38. Baldwin, *Masters, Princes, and Merchants*, 6.

39. On the rapid growth of the mendicant orders in France (more than four hundred houses had been established in the kingdom by the 1270), see Emery, *The Friars in Medieval France*, 1–17.

40. Hastings Rashdall, *Universities of Europe in the Middle Ages* 1, ed. F. M. Powicke and A. B. Emden (Oxford: Clarendon Press, 1936), 371–372, and Monika Asztalos, "The Faculty of Theology," in *A History of the University in Europe*, vol. 1, ed. Hilde De Ridder-Symoens (Cambridge: Cambridge University Press, 1992), 409–441.

41. Rosalind B. Brooke, *The Coming of the Friars* (London: George Allen and Unwin, 1975). On mendicant preaching, see David d'Avray, *The Preaching of the Friars: Sermons Diffused from Paris Before 1300* (Oxford: Oxford University Press, 1985). See also Marian Michèle Mulchahey, *First the Bow Is Bent in Study: Dominican Education Before 1350* (Toronto: Pontifical Institute of Medieval Studies, 1998).

42. On this conflict, see Decima L. Douic, *The Conflict Between the Seculars and the Mendicants at the University of Paris in the Thirteenth Century* (London: Blackfriars, 1954); Michel-Marie Dufeil, *Guillaume de Saint-Amour et la polémique universitaire parisienne, 1250–1259* (Paris: J. Picard, 1972).

43. De La Selle, *Le service des âmes à la cour: Confesseurs et aumôniers des rois de France du XIIIe au XVe siècle* (Paris: 1995).

44. D'Avray, *Preaching of the Friars*, 50.

45. See Chapter 1.

46. M. Peuchmaurd, "Mission canonique etprédication: Le prêtre ministre de la parole dans la querelle entre mendiants et séculiers au XIIIe siècle," *Recherches et Théologie Ancienne et Médiévale* 30 (1963): 122–144 and 251–276.

47. Douie, *The Conflict Between the Seculars and the Mendicants*, and Szittya, *The Antifraternal Tradition in Medieval Literature*, 44–46. See also Yves M.-J. Congar, "Aspects ecclésiologiques de la querelle entre mendiants et séculiers dans la seconde moitié du XIIIe et le début du XIVe," in *Archives d'histoire doctrinale et littéraire du moyen âge* 28 (1961–1962): 35–151.

48. On Robert of Sorbon and the mission of his college, see Palémon Glorieux, *Aux origines de la Sorbonne*, volume 1, *Robert de Sorbon, l'homme, le collège, les documents* (Études de philosophie médiévale 53) (Paris: J. Vrin, 1966), 39–40, and Astrik L. Gabriel, *The Paris Studium*, 63–79.

49. Glorieux, *Aux origines de la Sorbonne*, 29.

50. Glorieux argues quite forcefully that Robert did not establish the Sorbonne in order to compete with the mendicants, *Aux origines de la Sorbonne*, 27. Nevertheless, the timing and purpose of the foundation suggest that Robert was concerned about the secular clergy's ability to properly minister to the laity with resources and lay support increasingly funneled to the friars.

51. Gabriel, *Paris Studium*, 85.

52. For a survey of these treatises and their contents, see Glorieux, *Aux origines de la Sorbonne*, 1: 54–60.

53. Gabriel, *The Paris Studium*, 80, and "The Ideal Master of the Medieval University," *Catholic Historical Review* 60 (1974): 1–40.

54. Gabriel, *The Paris Studium*, 80.

55. "Ordinatum est quod illi qui steterunt in domo cum expensis domus, quatinus provideant sibi ut infra breve tempus se preparent et disponent ad proficiendum in sermonibus publicis per parrochias, in disputationibus et lectionibus in scolis; alias beneficiis domus totaliter privabuntur." Glorieux, *Aux origines de la Sorbonne*, 1:195.

56. Francis Rapp, "Rapport introductif," in *Le clerc séculier au Moyen Âge: Actes du XXIIème Congrès de la Société des historiens médiévistes de l'enseignement supérieur public*, Amiens, 1991 (Paris: Publications de la Sorbonne, 1993), 9–25.

57. Katherine L. Jansen, *The Making of the Magdalen: Preaching and Popular Devotion in the Later Middle Ages* (Princeton, NJ: Princeton University Press, 2000).

58. In many ways, then, Robert's praise of beguine exhortatio was reminiscent of Peter the Chanter's praise for lay ministry.

59. See Chapter 1.

60. "In hoc beginario fuit Christus," BnF Lat. 15971, fol. 72vb.

61. "Oportet quod sciat istos punctos ordinis qui ordinis huius vult monachus fieri ut sciat scilicet pacientiam et benignitatem." Ibid.

62. "Qui hunc ordinem caritatis intrauerit tandem ordinabitur cum sanctis in gloria, ubi simus." Ibid. This view is evident too in sermons delivered at the beguinage, in which Robert asserts that anyone, in whatever status they might be, are able to be a beguine. ("Quilibet in quocumque statu sit potest esse beguinus.") BnF Lat. 16471, fol. 99vb.

63. "Paulus dicit caritas paciens est, benigna est idest begina. . . . Qui hunc ordinem caritatis intrauerit tandem ordinabitur cum sanctis in gloria." BnF Lat. 15971, fol. 72vb.

64. "Sic sit tu vides socium tuum vel quemcumque cadere in ignem infernalem, cum scilicet luxuriatur et huiusmodi facit, et non aportas aquam sancte monitionis vel orationis . . . crudelis es." Ibid.

65. "Begina dicitur quasi bene ignita. Ignis omnia trait in sui natura, sic qui caritatis est monachus trait alios as hunc ordinem, etiam inimicos." Ibid.

66. BnF 16471, fols. 99va–105ra. Robert's personal version of the sermon is edited in Bériou, "Robert de Sorbon: Le prud'homme et le béguin," appendix II, 496–508.

67. Godfrey of Fontaine's copy of the sermon (BnF Lat. 16507) is also edited in Bériou, "Robert de Sorbon: Le prud'homme et le béguin," appendix I, 486–495.

68. BnF Lat. 16496, fols. 48v–50v. On the manuscrits Jean of Essômes donated to the Sorbonne, see Madeleine Mabille, "Les manuscrits de Jean d'Essômes conservés à la Bibliothèque Nationale de Paris," in *Bibliothèque de l'École des Chartes* 130 (1972): 231–234.

69. BnF Lat. 16507, fol. 421a, ed. Bériou, "Robert de Sorbon: Le prud'homme et le béguin," 486.

70. "Sed campus Christi de quo facit mentionem euangelium colitur per contritionem et confessionem, seminatur autem semine verbi diuini." BnF Lat. 16507, fols. 322a–322b, ed. Bériou, "Robert de Sorbon: Le prud'homme et le béguin," 489.

71. "Sed qui sunt in beguinagio ponuntur in publiquo ut succurrant aliis spiritualiter," BnF Lat. 16507, fols. 322a–322b, ed. Bériou, "Robert de Sorbon: Le prud'homme et le béguin," 490.

72. Robert claims that the beguines labored more for the conversion of their fellow Christians than others (presumably the "great masters" he refers to throughout the sermons). "Et specialiter uidetur iste thesaurus esse absconditus in beguinagio, quia inter alios ipsi et ipse habent feruens desiderium ad Deum et feruentiores sunt in conuersione peccatorum quam ceteri, unde plus laborant ad salute et conuersionem peccatorum quam alii." BnF Lat. 16507, fol. 322b, ed. Bériou, "Robert de Sorbon: Le prud'homme et le béguin," 490.

73. "Item uidetur plus habere de gratia Dei quam alii, quia unus alium incitat ad habendum et ad benefaciendum, et accipit unus in alio bonum quantum sancte uite." BnF Lat. 16507, fol. 322b, ed. Bériou, "Robert de Sorbon: Le prud'homme et le béguin," 490.

74. "Et iste thesaurus in predicto agro in tantum est absconditus quod pauci aut nulli possunt ibi illud inuenire, etiam magni magistri, immo dicunt: Fi de beguinagio. Dicunt enim: Bene uolo esse probus homo, sed nequaquam beguinus." BnF Lat. 16507, fol. 322b, ed. Bériou, "Robert de Sorbon: Le prud'homme et le béguin," 490.

75. "Et tamen aliqui illum thesaurum bene cognoscunt et in predicto agro bene inueniunt, unde uerificatum est illud euuangelii dictum a Domino [Matthew 11:25]: *Confiteor tibi, Pater celi et terre, quia abscondisti hec a sapientibus et reuelasti ea paruulis*. . . . Et que est causa quare isti magni magistri et sapientes mundani hoc non possunt cognoscere nec istum thesaurum in beguinagio inuenire? Hec est ratio, quia non per studium nec per rationem potest iste thesaurus inueniri, sed per gratiam." BnF Lat. 16507, fol. 322b, ed. Bériou, "Robert de Sorbon: Le prud'homme et le béguin," 491.

76. "Et tamen, ut iam prius dictum est, plus ceteris uilipenduntur, et ideo sunt ibi quasi contraria simul, scilicet esse probum hominem et esse despectum. Item ibi inuenitur ignis, scilicet karitatis et dilectionis, in aqua, scilicet tribulationum ut derisionum et uituperiorum, unde quantumcumque fuerit homo honoratus, si intrat beguinagium et fiat beguinus uilipenditur plus ceteris." BnF Lat. 16507, fol. 322b, ed. Bériou, "Robert de Sorbon: Le prud'homme et le béguin," 491.

77. "Vnde aliqui simplices qui in hoc se cognoscunt non uellent esse reges et non esse beguinos, uel uoluntatem et propositum non habere ut essent. Pro me dico, dicebat predicator." Ibid.

78. Robert refers to Stephen as a guardian of "mulieres sanctae et religiosae," loosely basing this assertion on a passage in the Acts of the Apostles, in which it is stated that the apostles entrusted Stephen with ministering to widows. BnF Lat. 16507, fol. 322b, ed. Bériou, "Robert de Sorbon: Le prud'homme et le béguin," 488.

79. "Unde non dicet: 'Simile est regnum celorum thesauro abscondito' in turre uel in castro uel in claustro uel in orto, sed in agro, quod est contra multos qui occultant se, et ita quod ad eos est difficilis uel forte nullus accessus, et qui subtrahunt se a necessitatibus proximorum in consilio, auxilio, et exemplo, contra quos Gregorius: 'Qui uita et scientia predicti uitam solitarium sibi eligunt tot animarum rei sunt quot ad publicum uenientes prodesse potuerunt.'" BnF Lat. 16471, fol. 99vb, ed. Bériou, "Robert de Sorbon: Le prud'homme et le béguin," 497.

80. "Item ager cultus et seminatus fructum multiplicem reddit, et qui sunt qui magis sunt culti aratro confessionis et penitentie et seminati verbo Dei quam beguine et beguini,

unde trahunt ad sermonem et confessionem quam multi magni clerici, sicut patet demonstratione ad oculum." BnF Lat. 16471, fol. 100ra, ed. Bériou, "Robert de Sorbon: Le prud'homme et le béguin," 497.

81. Suzanne LaVere, "From Contemplation to Action: The Role of the Active Life in the Glossa ordinaria on the Song of Songs," *Speculum* 82, no. 1 (2007): 54–69.

82. "*Quesiui* sponsum, idest Christum, in religiosis et secularibus qui uolunt uocari probi homines et honorari et nolunt propter Christum uituperari, *et non inueni*," BnF Lat. 16471, fol. 103ra, ed., Bériou, "Robert de Sorbon: Le prud'homme et le béguin," 492.

83. "Nec tamen adhuc cessat querere, sed interrogat predicatores unde sequitur: *Inuenerunt me uigiles qui custodiunt ciuitatem,* Glosa: 'predicatores.' *Num quem diligit anima mea uidistis?* Glosa: 'interrogat uigiles cum predicatorem intente suscipit et in ea bonorum operum exhibitione fructificat.' Et qui magis hoc faciunt quam beguini et beguine?" BnF Lat. 16471, fol. 103rb, ed. Bériou, "Robert de Sorbon: Le prud'homme et le béguin," 504.

84. "Unde sequitur: *Paululum cum pertransissem, inueni quem diliget anima mea,* idest postquam adimpleui consilia in religion uel precepta in seculo et frequentaui sermones et quesiui a predicatoribus ubi inuenirem dominum Ijesum Christum, qui tamen non responderunt michi." BnF Lat. 16471, fol. 103rb, ed. Bériou, "Robert de Sorbon: Le prud'homme et le béguin," 504.

85. Waters, *Angels and Earthly Creatures,* 58.

86. Ibid., 62.

87. Ibid., 64–66.

88. On the evolution of the sermon form and its intimate connection with the university context, see Rouse and Rouse, *Preachers,* Florilegia, 65–90, and Bériou, *L'avènement.* On the influence of the mendicant orders on this development, see d'Avray, *Preaching of the Friars,* 163–211, and Marian Michèle Mulchahey, "Preaching Aids: Collections, Florilegia, *Exempla,* and *Artes,*" in *First the Bow Is Bent in Study,* 400–479.

89. Rouse and Rouse, *Preachers,* Florilegia, 3–42.

90. Baldwin, *Masters, Princes, and Merchants,* and Phyllis B. Roberts, "Sermons and Preaching in/and the Medieval University," in *Medieval Education*, ed. Ronald B. Begley and Joseph W. Koterski (New York: Fordham University Press, 2005), 83–98.

91. Glorieux, *Aux origines de la Sorbonne,* vol. 1, 56.

92. For a list of sermons attributed to Robert of Sorbon, see Johannes-Baptist Schneyer, *Repertorium der lateinischen Sermones des Mittelalters für die Zeit von 1150–1350,* vol. 5 (Münster: Aschendorffsche Verlagbuchhandlung, 1973), 224–330. For corrections, see Bériou, "Robert de Sorbon," in *Dictionaire de Spiritualité* 13 (Paris, 1988), cols. 816–824.

93. Delisle, "Inventaire des manuscrits latins de la Sorbonne," and Rouse, "Early Library of the Sorbonne."

94. Glorieux, *Aux origines de la Sorbonne,* 2: 354–355. Gerard's donation substantially improved the library's holdings, both quantitatively and qualitatively. See Rouse, "The Early Library of the Sorbonne," 47–51.

95. Delisle, *Cabinet des Manuscrits,* vol. 2, 173.

96. Delisle, *Cabinet des Manuscrits,* vol. 2, 168–208. See Bériou, *L'avènement,* 193, on admiration for Guiard of Laon's sermons.

97. Mabille, "Les manuscrits de Jean d'Essômes conservés à la Bibliothèque Nationale de Paris."

98. The *Manipulus Florilegium* survives in more than 180 copies, attesting to its usefulness to university preachers and scholars. See Rouses, *Preachers,* Florilegium, x.

99. Rouse, "The Early Library of the Sorbonne," 45.

100. We know little about Raoul other than the fact that he was a student of theology and resided at the Sorbonne. He died in 1286, leaving money and manuscripts to the Sorbonne. See Bériou, *L'avènement,* 86.

101. BnF Lat. 16481. This manuscript is composed of 216 sermons, the contents of which are listed in Bériou, *L'Avènement,* appendix 11.

102. This related manuscript—BnF Lat. 16482—is organized alphabetically by theme and contains distinctions, sermons, sermon excerpts, and collations. See Bériou, *L'avènement,* appendix 12. The three sermons mentioned here do not include the sermons preached by the mistress of the beguinage. See Chapter 5.

103. On this point, see Chapter 5.

104. Richard and Mary Rouse have discussed Raoul's collection as a prime example of sermons preached in the "modern" style. See *Preachers,* Florilegia*, and Sermons.* In her magisterial study of these collection, Nicole Bériou has noted that Raoul was especially careful toward the beginning of the collection, recording the venue, name of the preacher, occasion. In cases where he fails to note these details, Bériou was frequently able to draw on clues in the text to supply them. See Bériou, *L'avènement,* 223.

105. Raoul's sermon collections include only a few sermons preached at the university, and many of these are attested in other manuscripts. In all likelihood, Raoul relied on these copies. See Bériou, *L'avènement,* 218–219.

106. The project may even have been related to similar endeavors carried out by Raoul's fellow Sorbonnist Pierre of Limoges, who eventually gained possession of the manuscript sometime after Raoul's death in 1286.

107. Of the 243 sermons in this collection, nearly half (119) were preached by Dominicans. Raoul recorded fifty sermons by Franciscan preachers, sixty-six by secular clerics, and eight by regular canons. Raoul records sermons by fifty-three different mendicant preachers (thirty Dominicans, eighteen Franciscans, and five "frères") but only seventeen secular clerics and three regular canons. See Bériou, *L'avènement,* 243. For a thorough description of these collections, see her appendices 11 and 12. Like Robert of Sorbon, Raoul had a great deal of admiration for mendicant preaching and went out of his way to attend sermons by certain Dominican preachers, especially Giles of Orleans, who features prominently in Raoul's collection of *reportationes* as well as his *distinctiones.* We would know nothing about him were it not for the sermons in these two manuscripts, which together contain twenty-eight sermons or extracts of sermons preached by Giles (these are reported in Schneyer, RLS, I, 53–56).

108. Bériou, *L'avènement,* appendix 11.

109. Bériou, *L'avènement,* 223.

110. Bériou observes that on the second Sunday of advent, Raoul copied a sermon preached at Saint Magloire, where Gerard de Reims (who seems to have been a master of

Raoul's) was preaching. On another Sunday in 1273, Raoul attended a sermon at the convent of the Sachets, where he rarely seems to have gone, in order to hear his friend Pierre of Limoges preach. See Bériou, *L'avènement*, 225.

111. Of the fifty-six sermons recorded at the beguinage for which a preacher is identifiable, twenty were preached by Dominicans, eighteen by secular clerics, fifteen by Franciscans, and three by regular canons. See Bériou, "La prédication au béguinage," 162.

112. In reaching this conclusion, I have benefited greatly from Bériou's dating of the sermons in the manuscript. Bériou, *L'avènement*, appendix 11.

113. Of the twenty-three sermons Raoul recorded between 2 July and 1 October, ten took place at the beguinage. The other places were: Saint-Germain-l'Aurrexois (1); Hôtel-Dieu (3); Saint-Gervais (3); Sainte-Chapelle (1); Champeaux (1); Saint-Paul (1), Saint -Antoine (1). The location of the other two sermons was not recorded. Nearly all of the sermons Raoul recorded between 20 August and 24 September were preached at the beguinage.

114. BnF Lat. 15972, fols. 174r–177v.

115. Madeleine Mabille, "Les manuscrits d'Étienne d'Abbeville conservés à la Bibliothèque nationale de Paris," 262.

116. BnF Lat. 15972, fol. 177v. Paul Meyer dates the script to the later thirteenth century. The French is of the Picardian dialect. See Paul Meyer, "Les propriétés des béguinages," *Bulletin de la Société des anciens textes français* 38 (1912): 98–99. Meyer did not identify the text as the work of Stephen of Abbeville, and Mabille does not mention the French verses on beguines. But it is known that Stephen had been a canon in Amiens, and thus "Les 32 propriétés" was probably written by—or copied at the behest of—Stephen or someone from his circle in Amiens.

117. BnF Lat. 15972, fol. 176vb This same manuscript includes a lengthy description of the beguines' humility and religious devotion, followed by the familiar claim that beguines draw their neighbors to confession and sermons through their good words and example.

118. On women's affective spirituality, see Sarah McNamer, *Affective Meditation and the Invention of Medieval Compassion* (Philadelphia: University of Pennsylvania Press, 2010).

119. "Et quia vos multa specula in sacra scriptura vidistis et ibi respexistis et affectum vostrum retardastis." BnF Lat. 15972, fol. 176vb.

120. The sermons preached in the 1220s and 1230s at the Cistercian convent of Saint-Antoine, located just beyond the city walls, indicate that there was some precedent in Paris for combining pastoral care of women with the instruction of male clerics. The chapel of Saint-Antoine, for example, served as a venue for university preaching almost from its foundation as a Cistercian convent in 1204. Saint-Antoine was originally founded as a house for reformed prostitutes in 1198 by Foulques de Neuilly. It became a Cistercian convent in 1204. Sermons recorded at the chapel of Saint-Antoine and addressed specifically to scholars (*ad scolares*), include several intriguing references to nuns in the audience. See Bériou, *L'avènement*, 120. On Saint-Antoine, see Constance H. Berman, "Cistercian Nuns and the Development of the Order: The Abbey of Saint-Antoine-des-Champs Outside Paris," in *The Joy of Learning and the Love of God: Essays in Honor of Jean Leclercq, OSB*, ed. E. Rozanne Elder (Kalamazoo, MI: Cistercian Publications, 1995), 121–156.

121. James of Vitry, *The Life of Marie d'Oignies*, 98–99. Useful recent studies on these

themes in the *vita* include Michel Lauwers, "Entre béguinisme et mysticisme: La vie de Marie d'Oignies (1213) de Jacques of Vitry ou la définition d'une sainteté féminine," *Ons geestelijk erf* 66 (1992): (pg) 46–69 and Coakley, *Women, Men, and Spiritual Power*, especially chapter 4.

122. *The Life of Marie d'Oignies*, 99.

123. *The Life of Marie d'Oignies*, 99 and 104–105. For a thorough discussion of Mary's role in aiding James's pastoral work, see Coakley, *Women, Men, and Spiritual Power*, chapter 4.

124. *The Life of Marie d'Oignies*, 98–99.

125. Coakley, *Women, Men, and Spiritual Power*, 82–86.

126. Sharon Farmer, "Persuasive Voices: Clerical Images of Medieval Wives," *Speculum* 61 (1986): 517–543.

127. Ibid., 542.

128. Ibid., 539, and Waters, *Angels and Earthly Creatures*, 73–74.

129. BnF Lat. 15955, fol. 307va.

130. "Et nota quod quandoque plus proficient in parochia bonae mulieres quam etiam presbiteri, vel magistri in theologia regendo Parisius, per earum bona opera et exempla et bona verba." BnF, Lat. 15955, fol. 307va.

131. "Exemplum de begina quae venit Parisius emptum Summam de viciis et virtutibus; quae cum monraretur in quadam civitate ad quam saepe veniebant presbiteri subditi illi civitati, accommodabat eis per quaternos huiusmodi Summam, praequirendo si erant ociosi, ante quam missam celebraverant, ita quod per totam regionem illam multiplicavit eam." BNF Lat. 15955, fol. 307va–307vb.

CHAPTER 5. RELIGIOUS EDUCATION AND SPIRITUAL COLLABORATION AT THE BEGUINAGE OF PARIS

1. Gilbert de Tournai, *Collectio de scandalis ecclesiae,* in P. Autbertus Stroick, "Collectio de scandalis ecclesiae: Nova editio," *Archivum Franciscanum Historicum* 24 (1931): 58. See my discussion of this passage in Chapter 6.

2. Sara S. Poor, *Mechthild of Magdeburg and Her Book: Gender and the Making of Textual Authority* (Philadelphia: University of Pennsylvania Press, 2004) .

3. Robin O'Sullivan discusses the didactic aim of Marguerite Porete's *Mirror of Simple Souls*, arguing that scholars must understand the book against the backdrop of a religious and intellectual culture of informal communities of women. While this is an important observation, O'Sullivan overlooks the fact that this sort of interaction occurred in all sorts of configurations of the beguine life. See Robin O'Sullivan, "The School of Love: Marguerite Porete's *Mirror of Simple Souls,*" *Journal of Medieval History* 32 (2006): 143–162. Suzanne Kocher argues that the *Mirror*, which contains passages addressed to groups of people at different stages in their spiritual progress, seems to have been intended for a mixed audience. See Suzanne Kocher, *Allegories of Love in Marguerite Porete's* Mirror of Simple Souls (Turnhout: Brepols, 2009), 49–54.

4. See Kocher, *Allegories of Love,* 42–43. For a compelling and convincing analysis

of the evidence surrounding Marguerite Porete's activities and behavior leading up to her execution in 1310, see Sean L. Field, *The Beguine, the Angel and the Inquisitor: The Trials of Marguerite Porete and Guiard of Cressonessart* (Notre Dame, IN: University of Notre Dame Press, 2012).

5. Herbert Grundmann was among the first to posit a direct relationship between the rise of popular religious enthusiasm, especially among women, and vernacular literature. He argues that religious writings in the vernacular were a direct result of the popular religious movements of the thirteenth century, which involved laypeople without knowledge of Latin who demanded access to religious teachings. See Grundmann, *Religious Movements in the Middle Ages*. See too the useful overview in Bernard McGinn, *The Flowering of Mysticism: Men and Women in the New Mysticism 1200–1350* (New York: Crossroad, 1998). On women and the production of vernacular devotional literature in Italy, see Katherine Gill, "Women and the Production of Religious Literature in the Vernacular, 1300–1500," in *Creative Women in Medieval and Early Modern Italy* (Philadelphia: University of Pennsylvania Press, 1994), 64–104. Ursula Peters has also written extensively on the subject of religious women and the production of devotional literature. See *Religiöse Erfahrung als literarisches Faktum: Zur Vorgeschichte und Genese frauenmystischer Texte des 13. und 14. Jahrhunderts* (Tübingen: Niemeyer, 1988).

6. Barbara Newman "La mystique courtoise: Thirteenth-Century Beguines and the Art of Love," *From Virile Woman to Womanchrist: Studies in Medieval Religion and Literature* (Philadelphia: University of Pennsylvania Press, 1995), 143.

7. Ibid., 138–139, and Kocher, *Allegories of Love,* 69–70.

8. *The Vernacular Spirit: Essays on Medieval Religious Literature,* ed. Renate Blumenfeld-Kosinski, Duncan Robertson, and Nancy Bradley Warren (New York: Palgrave, 2002), 2.

9. Bernard McGinn has argued for the usefulness of conceiving the relationship between women and their clerical advisors as an "overheard conversation," rather than characterized by confrontation. See *The Flowering of Mysticism*, 17. See also the points relayed by Jeffrey Hamburger in his discussion of the relationship between nuns and their advisers, which he describes as spanning "the entire spectrum from antagonism to admiration, from friendship to hostility." *The Visual and the Visionary: Art and Female Spirituality in Late Medieval Germany* (New York: Zone Books, 1998), 22.

10. This dynamic is examined in great detail, but from different perspectives, in Elliott, *Proving Woman,* and Coakley, *Women, Men, and Spiritual Power.*

11. See Chapter 1.

12. Galloway, "'Life, Learning and Wisdom,'" 155; Simons, *Cities of Ladies,* 82.

13. *The Life of Beatrice of Nazareth,* 1200–1268, ed. and trans. Robert De Ganck (Kalamazoo, M.I.: Cistercian Publications, 1991), 24.

14. Goswin of Bossut, *Send Me God: The Lives of Ida the Compassionate of Nivelles, Nun of La Ramee, Arnulf, Lay Brother of Villers, and Abundus, Monk of Villers,* ed. and trans. Martinus Cawley (Turnhout: Brepols, 2003), 31–32.

15. Anneke Mulder-Bakker notes that medieval observers recognized that formal training, contrary to modern understanding, was not the only means of obtaining knowledge. Anneke B. Mulder-Bakker, "Introduction," in her edited volume *Seeing and Knowing,*

2–3, and "The Metamorphosis of Woman: Transmission of Knowledge and the Problems of Gender," *Gender and History* 12, no. 3 (2000): 114–115.

16. The practice of meeting in common for the purpose of prayer, reading, and religious instruction fits a pattern of beguine education to which scholars have only recently focused their attention. See Anneke Mulder-Bakker's introductory chapter in *Seeing and Knowing*, 1–19. See also Penelope Galloway's article on beguine education, "'Life, Learning and Wisdom,'" 153–167.

17. The beguine rule references the beguines' obligation to attend chapter meetings. *Beguinage Statutes,* art. 25. Statutes for beguine communities in the Low Countries, including that of Ghent, on which the beguinage of Paris was modeled, mandated daily recitation of the Marian psalter. See Judith Olivier, "Devotional Psalters and the Study of Beguine Spirituality," *Vox Benedictina* 9, no. 2 (1992): 199–225. On prayer routines of beguines, see Galloway, "Neither Miraculous nor Astonishing."

18. On this sermon collection, see Chapter 4.

19. Several sources mention a *schola* (choir) at the Paris beguinage, and testamentary evidence refers to beguines performing the Divine Office. See the discussion later in this chapter.

20. Extant documentation referring to the beguinage's *l'ostel escoliers* or *schola* suggests that the residents of this house were members of the beguine choir—a select group of beguines trained in chant. On the term and its usage in reference to choirs, see Walter Simons, "Beguines, Liturgy and Music in the Middle Ages: An Exploration," in *Beghinae in cantu instructae: Musical Patrimony from Flemish Beguinages (Middle Ages–Late Eighteenth Century),* ed. Pieter Mannaerts (Turnhout: Brepols, 2009), 21.

21. The mistress's authority over the choir is cited in a document concerning the property and administration of the beguinage. ("Et une maistresse qui estoient proposez . . . par le roy nostre dit seigneur pour le gouvernement et administracion tant dudit beguinage et des beguines et escoliers estans en icellui.") AN S 4642.

22. On Jean's relationship with Bourges, who worked as his *chambrière* and stored Jean's valuables in her home in the beguinage, see chapter 2. "Item il lessa a Bourges de Mortieres et a Jehanne sa niepce beguines du dit beguinage, 100 frans dor pour paier par leur main de une partie des frans dessus diz un anuel que elles feront chanter et faire en la dicte chappelle des beguines ou ailleurs a leur voulente." It is interesting that Jean allowed the beguines some discretion as to where this anniversary mass might take place. AN KK 330/A, fol. 2r.

23. "Il lessa aux Beguines escolieres qui font le service messes en la chappelle des dictes Beguines en la dicte paroisse de saint pol pour avoir unes vegilles et une messe de requiem, 2 frans dor pour ce." Ibid.

24. "Aux Beguines, pour ce que Richarde y avoit sa devocion, pour y avoir vigiles et messe a note pour elle et pour moy, vint solz Parisis." *Testaments*, 297.

25. "Item, je donne et laisse aux Filles Dieu de Paris, aux Beguines, a celles de Saincte Avoye, a celles de la Chapelle Haudry, a l'ostel du Saint Esperit en Greve, a chascun pour unes vigiles et messe xx solz Parisis." Ibid., 361.

26. "Novem psalmis et novem lectionibus, una cum commendaciis et una missa de Requiem, pro salute anime sue dicere valeant," Ibid., 261.

27. In his testament, Louis requested that all of his religious and charitable foundations celebrate anniversary masses every year in remembrance of their royal patron. See *Layettes*, vol. 4, 420.

28. "Dont lors les Beguines furent privées de beguinage et leur ordre dampns; ne n'i-chantoit on, ne n'i-lisoit on." *RHF*, vol. 21, 666.

29. Beguine education could be quite similar to monastic liturgical instruction, in which "reading, singing, and writing were fully integrated." See Susan Boynton, "Training for the Liturgy as a Form of Monastic Education," in *Medieval Monastic Education*, ed. George Ferzoco and Carolyn Muessig (London: Leicester University Press, 2000), 7–20.

30. Bériou, "La prédication au béguinage de Paris," 181.

31. BnF 16481, fol. 80vb. William's advice echoes the rule for the beguinage of Ghent, which distinguishes between beguines who were able to read their Psalters and those who could not. Those unable to read were to recite the Paternoster and Ave Maria. See Béthune, *Cartulaire du Béguinage de Sainte-Elizabeth à Gand*, 75. Several other beguinages had regulations with similar distinctions between literate and illiterate beguines. See Simons, "'Staining the Speech of Things Divine': The Uses of Literacy in Medieval Beguine Communities," in *The Voice of Silence: Women's Literacy in a Men's Church*, ed. Thérèse de Hemptinne and María Eugenia Góngora, Medieval Church Studies, 9 (Brepols: 2004), 106–107.

32. Very little is known about Paris's beguinage school. As Walter Simons has noted, it is not always clear from the sources whether the *scholae* refer to choirs or schools focused on a more general curriculum of reading and writing (*Cities of Ladies*, 193, note 142). Of course the scholae of chant would also teach reading. A suit brought by the cathedral chapter of Notre Dame in 1442 indicates that there was indeed a school within the enclosure (*scola filiarum*), which the cathedral chapter of Notre Dame sought to close, claiming that the beguines operated a school for girls without proper licensing. Le Grand briefly alludes to the case, preserved at the AN (LL 115, fol. 263). See also "Les béguines," 333.

33. On beguinage schools in the Low Countries, see Simons, *Cities of Ladies*, 80–85, and "'Staining the Speech of Things Divine.'" For a more general discussion of beguine education that includes references to schools in the beguinages of northern France, see Galloway, "'Life, Learning and Wisdom.'"

34. Nicole Bériou cites several sermons in which the preacher assumes some theological knowledge on the part of the beguines. See *L'avènement*, 235–236.

35. "Personnes qui bien et honnestement demourront oudit béguinage, tandis comme elles vourront estre obéissans et garder nos ordenances et persévérer en bonnes et saintes euvres." *Beguinage Statutes*, art. 19.

36. "Le dit beguinage avoit este fonde en lonneur de dieu et pour y recevoir femmes de devocion qui facent et meinent bonnes et saintes ouvres." AN S 4642.

37. Scholars of beguine communities throughout Northern Europe have often noted beguines' involvement in charitable works, in particular hospital work. I have uncovered a few references to beguines working in Parisian hospitals. More research into the extant records for these institutions would probably uncover more. Documents concerning rents and properties of the beguine Mahaut la Clavière refer to her as "des aveugles," suggesting that she worked at the Quinze-Vingts, the city's hospital for the blind. Quinze-Vingts

(QV), box A 24, ms 1354. I am grateful to Mark O'Toole for sharing his transcription of this manuscript with me. Similarly, in 1360, the records of the Hôtel-Dieu list a certain Jeanne la Beguine as a sister of the community. See *L'Hôtel-Dieu de Paris au moyen âge*, vol. 2: *Délibérations du Chapitre de Nôtre-Dame de Paris relatives à l'Hôtel-Dieu (1326–1539)* (Paris: H. Champion, 1891), 6.

38. The beguines' role in the care of the poor and the ill and their instruction of children is well attested for beguine communities in cities throughout northern Europe. On hospitals, see McDonnell, *Beguines and Beghards*, 270; Simons, *Cities of Ladies*, 77–78. On the beguines' administration of a hospital in Liège, see Madeleine Pissart, "L'Administration du béguinage de Saint–Christophe à Liège," *Bulletin de la Société Royale "Le Vieux Liège"* 97 (1952): 113–130.

39. *Testaments*, 228.

40. AAP, fonds St.-Jacques, reg. 1, pièce 31.

41. "Sed aliqui sunt sicut libri beguinarum vel dominarum, qui sunt extra noviter depicti, intus vero maculati et deleti; qui vellet eos emere, cito posset decipi." BnF 14799, fol. 168, col. 4, cited in Hauréau, *Notices et extraits*, vol. 3, 96.

42. Simons, "'Staining the Speech of Things Divine,'" 101.

43. *Testaments*, 228.

44. On girdle books, see Margit Smith, "The Medieval Girdle Book Project" (with Jim Bloxam), *International Journal of the Book* 3, no. 4 (2006): 15–24.

45. Ibid., 19.

46. Geneviève Hasenohr, "D'une 'poésie de béguine' à une 'poétique des béguines': Aperçus sur la forme et la réception des textes (France, XIIIe–XIVe siècles)," *Comptes rendus des séances de l'Académie des inscriptions et belles-lettres* 150, no. 2 (2006): 913–943.

47. Tony Hunt, ed., *Les Cantiques Salemon: The Song of Songs in MS Paris BNF fr. 14966* (Turnhout: Brepols, 2006); Barbara Newman, "Conversion: The Literary Traditions of Marguerite Porete," in *Medieval Crossover: Reading the Secular Against the Sacred* (Notre Dame, IN: University of Notre Dame Press, 2013), 111–165. I thank Barbara Newman for sharing this chapter with me prior to publication.

48. BnF 15972, fol. 178vb. Indeed, Joann Ziegler has argued that the model of comportment expressed in the *vita* of Mary of Oignies served as the basis of beguine rules. See Joann Ziegler, "Reality as Imitation: The Dynamics of Imagery Among the Beguines," in *Maps of Flesh and Light: New Perspectives on the Religious Experience of Late Medieval Women*, ed. Ulrike Wiethaus (Syracuse, NY: Syracuse University Press, 1993), 112–126.

49. "Vechii les XXXII propriétés de beguinage. Bouche orant, eul plorant, ceur desirant, petit aller, bas regarder, en haut penser, droite entencion, douche pacience, ceur croissant, entendement cherubinal, sentement ceraphinal, aler en seant, parler en taisant, plourer en riant, estre fort en enfleivant, riche en apovriant, sage en taisant, pensees coulees, paroles enmelees, euvres ordenees, foi enluminee, esperance eslevee, amour embrasee, angelique entendement, courtoisie espirituel, devins sentemens, dormir en vellant, vellier en dormant, morir en vivant, vivre en morant, juner en maignant, maignier en junant." BnF Lat. 15972, fol. 177v. The use of paradoxes in this text led Léon le Grand to believe that "The 32 Properties of the Beguinage" was intended as a satire of the beguine life. Le Grand, "Les

béguines de Paris," 309–310. Paradoxes, of course, were a feature of mystical writing. See Michael Sells, *Mystical Languages of Unsaying* (Chicago: University of Chicago Press, 1994).

50. "Li ordres des fins amans est beginaiges. Par xii signes connoist on les fin amans." "*La règle des fins amans*: Eine Begininregel aus dem Ende des XIII. Jahrhunderts," ed. Karl Christ, in *Philologische Studien aus dem romanische-germanischen Kulturkreise: Festschrift für Karl Voretzsch*, ed. B. Schädel and W. Mulertt (Halle, 1927), 195. Barbara Newman refers to the *Règle* as "a typical or representative statement of a beguinal ethos that by 1300 was widely shared." See Newman, "La mystique courtoise," 139.

51. Christ, "*La Règle des fins amans*," 183.

52. Newman, "La mystique courtoise," 143. Clerics studying at the Sorbonne would have been familiar with the *Roman de la Rose*. Huot notes that the *Rose* was among the few vernacular texts among the chained books stored in the library of the Sorbonne in the early fourteenth century. Sylvia Huot, *The* Romance of the Rose *and Its Medieval Readers: Interpretation, Reception, Manuscript Transmission* (Cambridge: Cambridge University Press, 1993), 84.

53. Léopold Delisle, *Cabinet des manuscrits de la Bibliothèque nationale*, 3: 107. See also Pierre-Yves Badel, *Le Roman de la Rose au XIVe siècle: Étude de la réception de l'oeuvre* (Geneva: Droz, 1980), 57.

54. "Beguine, chou est benigne, autretant beguine comme bon feus," *Règle*, 196.

55. As Barbara Newman has shown, the *Règle* draws on the same courtly themes and language found in beguine poetry and in the writings of Hadewijch of Brabant, Mechthild of Magdeburg, and Marguerite Porete. Newman, "La mystique courtoise," 143–158.

56. "Cis pilers porte tout, cis pilers garde tout et fait tout." *Règle*, 199.

57. As Andreas Capellanus famously stated, jealousy "is the very substance of love." *Andreas Capellanus on Love*, ed. and trans. P. G. Walsh (London: Duckworth, 1982), 146–148. Ellen Babinsky examined these connections in "A Beguine in the Court of the King: The Relation of Love and Knowledge in 'The Mirror of Simple Souls' by Marguerite Porete," Ph.D. dissertation, University of Chicago, 1991, 80–89.

58. *Règle*, 194.

59. "Li xj. Est avoir dolour del damaige son ami. Li xij. Est estre apareillies de faire de cuer et de cors et d'avoir quanque ses amis veut et commande. Cist xij. Signe sont tous jours en vraie amor et en fins amans." *Règle*, 194. In the margin of the text, these gifts that the beguine owes her lover are described as "devotes orisons, piue meditations, jemissement de ce que on est si loing de son ami, soingneus et desirreus et covoitens d'estre avec lui, larmes poingnans, souspirs atraians." *Règle*, 194, note 59. On affective piety and its association with women, see Sarah McNamer, *Affective Meditation and the Invention of Medieval Compassion* (Philadelphia: University of Pennsylvania Press, 2009).

60. *Règle*, 201.

61. McNamer, *Affective Meditation*, 80.

62. Over the course of the Middle Ages, these practices became increasingly democratized as devotional writers began to produce manuals and guides to the attainment of visionary experience aimed at religious laywomen. The practices outlined in such manuals, as Barbara Newman has recently argued, were part of a "specialized religious subculture" that

embraced various methods for interpreting and facilitating visions. See Barbara Newman, "What Did It Mean to Say 'I Saw'? The Clash Between Theory and Practice in Medieval Visionary Culture," *Speculum* 80 (2005): 2.

63. The phrase is from Suzanne Kocher's discussion of Marguerite Porete's preference for *Amour* over *Charité* in her mystical treatise. See *Allegories of Love*, 72. The notion that nuns and anchoresses engaged in affective meditation in order to reinforce their status as Christ's "true" brides is discussed in McNamer, *Affective Meditation*, especially chapter 1.

64. "Les beguines les ont plus vraiement que les autres gens. Car eles les ont esperitueuement. Quele merveille, se eles ainment plus vertueument et plus fermement et miex sevent amer que nule autre, qu'eles sont de l'ordre as amans, si comme fu la Madelainne qui Jhesucrist ama si ardamment!" *Règle*, 195.

65. "Premiere on doit prïer chou que on doit, c'est a dire ses matines, ses eures et ce qu'on a de penance en commandement." *Règle*, 201.

66. "On doit prïer pour toute sainte eglise et pour les pecheours que diex les convertisse, et pour les mors qui merci atendent que diex leur aliege leur tormens et haste leur gloire." *Règle*, 201. On the beguines' "Purgatorial piety," see Robert Sweetman, "Thomas of Cantimpré, 'Mulieres Religiosae,' and Purgatorial Piety: Hagiographical 'Vitae' and the Beguine 'Voice,'" in *A Distinct Voice: Medieval Studies in Honor of Leonard E. Boyle, O.P*, ed. Jacqueline Brown and William P. Stoneman (Notre Dame, IN: University of Notre Dame Press, 1997), 606–628.

67. *Règle*, 201. Barbara Newman notes the *Règle*'s focus on community, a theme in courtly romances. The beguines, an "Order of Perfect Lovers," relied upon the encouragement and companionship of the like-minded women in their circle. "La mystique courtoise," 142.

68. *Règle*, 201.

69. Ibid., 201.

70. "Jalousie si vint avant et dist i mot: 'Douce amie, li cloistriés l'ont enclos. Alons i, je le vos lo! Venez i, si entrons en leur gardin.'" Christ, *"La règle des fins amans,"* 205. Barbara Newman identified the *Règle*'s reference to the *Roman de la Rose*. See "La mystique courtoise," 143.

71. "S'il i est, si l'en traions fors." *Règle*, 205.

72. Ibid.

73. "Bons feus enluminez rent clarité a cues qui sont loing et si eschaufe cues qui sont pres. Sa nature est monter en haut et si demeure après le bon feu cendre et charbon, Ausi fait beguinaiges. Il enlumine cues qui sont loing de claret et de flamme, de bonne renommé et de bon example de vie qu'eles monstrent." Ibid., 196.

74. On James of Vitry's role in promoting the beguines, see Brenda Bolton, "Vitae matrum: A Further Aspect of the Frauenfrage," in *Medieval Women: Dedicated and Presented to Professor Rosalind M. T. Hill on the Occasion of Her Seventieth Birthday*, edited by Derek Baker (Oxford: Basil Blackwell, 1978), 253–273. See also Michel Lauwers, "Expérience béguinale et récit hagiographique: À propos de la 'Vita Mariæ Oigniacensis' de Jacques de Vitry (vers 1215)," *Journal des savants* (1989): 61–103 and "Entre béguinisme et mysticisme."

75. On the long-term influence of the "Vita Mariæ Oigniacensis," see André Vauchez, "Prosélytisme et action antihérétique en milieu féminin au XIIIe siècle: La Vie de Marie d'Oignies (d. 1213) par James of Vitry," in *Propagande et contre-propagande religieuses*, ed. Jacques Marx (Brussels: Editions de l'Universitaire, 1987): 95–110. The vita circulated widely across northern France and the Low Countries in both Latin and the vernacular and was probably well known within clerical circles by the late thirteenth century. The vita seems to have circulated especially in Latin, suggesting that Mary was "not so much a role model for women as an example for learned men." See Suzan Folkerts, "The Manuscript Transmission of the Vita Mariae Oigniacensis in the Later Middle Ages," in *Mary of Oignies: A Mother of Salvation*, ed. Anneke B. Mulder-Bakker (Turnhout: Brepols, 2006), 221–241.

76. On these (and other) features of female spirituality, see Bynum, *Holy Feast, Holy Fast*. Much has been written about James of Vitry's agenda in composing his vita of Mary of Oignies. It has been noted, for example, that James dedicated the work to Bishop Fulk of Toulouse (c. 1155–1231), who had come to Liège seeking support for the Albigensien Crusade. The portrait James offers of Mary's sanctity was designed to serve as a useful model of orthodoxy, sacramental piety, and obedience to the clergy during a time when the "Good Men and Women" of Fulk's lands seemed to surpass the representatives of the hierarchical church in their commitment to the vita apostolica. Dyan Elliott has forcefully argued for the propagandistic aim of the beguine vitae in *Proving Woman*, especially chapter 2. See also McNamara, "Rhetoric of Orthodoxy." Thomas of Cantimpre's writings, too, have clear pastoral goals. See John W. Coakley, "Thomas of Cantimpré and Female Sanctity," in *History in the Comic Mode: Medieval Communities and the Matter of Person*, ed. Rachel Fulton and Bruce Holsinger (New York: Columbia University Press, 2007), 45–55. The *Lives* composed by Thomas have been recently edited. See *Thomas of Catimpré: The Collected Saint's Lives*, ed. Barbara Newman. Other hagiographers utilized the lives of holy women to pursue institutional agendas or to enhance the prestige of their orders. Simons, "Holy Women of the Low Countries: A Survey," in *Medieval Holy Women in the Christian Tradition: c. 1100–c. 1500*, ed. A. J. Minnis and Rosalynn Voaden (Turnhout: Brepols, 2010), 625–662. Amy Hollywood, too, argues for the need to consider gender and genre when reading hagiographical texts. See *The Soul as Virgin Wife: Mechthild of Magdeburg, Marguerite Porete, and Meister Eckhart* (Notre Dame, IN: University of Notre Dame Press, 1995).

77. Lauwers, "Entre béguinisme et mysticisme." Walter Simons also touches on some of these tensions in "Holy Women of the Low Countries: A Survey."

78. This discomfort with the unenclosed life is particularly evident in the fact that two-thirds of the women whose hagiographies compose the dossier became enclosed nuns. See Hollywood, *The Soul as Virgin Wife*, 40; Lauwers, "Expérience béguinale et récit hagiographique," 66–67. While many clerics considered work, when performed voluntarily by women, as a particularly meritorious form of penance, they viewed the contemplative life as more praiseworthy and suitable for religious women. On clerical tendencies to regard women's voluntary manual labor as penitential, see Farmer, *Surviving Poverty in Medieval Paris*, 117–130.

79. Lauwers, "Entre béguinisme et mysticisme," 50. For James of Vitry and Thomas of Cantimpré, manual labor was an important element of beguine life. Hugh of Floreffe's

vita of Juette of Huy (*AA SS* January, 2: 145–69), Gossuin of Bossuet's Ida of Nivelles (published in C. Henriquez, ed., *Quinque predentes virgins*, Antwerp, 1630), and an anonymous canon's vita of Juliana of Cornillon (*AA SS* April 1: 442–475) portray the women's manual labor as penitential.

80. "Wherefore, like someone who has retired from active duty and is freed from all manual labor, she lingered with the Lord in the liberation with which Christ had endowed his handmaid." *The Life of Marie d'Oignies*, 74.

81. Hollywood, *The Soul as Virgin Wife*, 41–42.

82. For this important insight, see Bynum *Holy Feast, Holy Fast* and "The Female Body and Religious Practice in the Later Middle Ages," in *Fragmentation and Redemption: Essays of Gender and the Human Body in Medieval Religion* (New York: Zone Books, 1991), 181–238.

83. Hollywood, *The Soul as Virgin Wife*, 49.

84. Jo Ann McNamara, "The Need to Give: Suffering and Female Sanctity in the Middle Ages," in *Images of Sainthood in Medieval Europe*, ed. Renate Blumenthal-Kosinski and Timea Szell (Ithaca, NY: Cornell University Press, 1991) 199–221 and Elliott, *Proving Woman*.

85. The special role beguines played as intercessors for souls—whether of the dead or of the living—may have been forged by the women themselves, however, suggesting mutual influence in the "beguine vitae." See Robert Sweetman, "Thomas of Cantimpré, 'Mulieres Religiosae,' and Purgatorial Piety: Hagiographical 'Vitae' and the Beguine 'Voice,' " in *A Distinct Voice: Medieval Studies in Honor of Leonard E. Boyle, O.P*, ed. Jacqueline Brown and William P. Stoneman (Notre Dame, IN: University of Notre Dame Press), 606–628. See also Bynum, *Holy Feast and Holy Fast*, 120–121, and Elliott, *Proving Woman*, 74–84.

86. Bériou, "La prédication au béguinage de Paris," 124.

87. Bnf Lat.16481, fol. 7va–8va. As Bériou points out, there was no consensus among preachers as far as what sort of penance beguines ought to perform. Most preachers mention fasting, but there was a range of opinions as to when and how often beguines should fast. "La prédication au béguinage de Paris," 189.

88. BnF Lat. 16482, fol. 162vb, ed. Bériou, "La prédication au béguinage de Paris," 159–160.

89. BnF Lat. 16481, fol. 139ra.

90. BnF Lat. 16481, fol. 183va.

91. "Et si sit res que te grauaret, sacerdos te libenter relaxabit, dum tamen non uoueris illud." BnF Lat.16481, fol. 60ra, ed. Bériou, "La prédication au béguinage de Paris," 159–160.

92. "Robe vestre quas vos portatis signant vitam quam debetis ducere. Non pro nichil vobis honeratus est talis habitus. Velum quo capita vestra teguntur signat humilitatem et obedientiam. Albedo eius signat castitatem et mundiciam. Roba que est rufa signat carnis mortificationem." BnF Lat. 16481, fol. 159ra–b, ed. Bériou, "La prédication au béguinage de Paris," 217–218.

93. BnF Lat. 16481, fol. 263va–265rb.

94. BnF Lat. 16481, fol. 323 rb–324vb.

95. BnF Lat. 15971, fol. 72vb.

96. BnF Lat. 16481, fol. 71ra.

97. "Christus verus amicus noster vult nobiscum loqui, solo ad solum, et vult quod ubicumque vadas, sive ad ecclesiam, sive ad sermonem, vel ad res publicas, quod totum propter suum honorem facias et quod quandoque in secreto orationis ei loquamur, et dicas quod tibi placuerit et requires, et ipse similiter tibi illuc reveles secreta sua." BnF Lat. 16481, fol. 71ra.

98. "Gratia Dei te visitat et in te descendit dum sic devote te applicas in oratione et contemplatione in loco solitario cum Deo. In tali enim loco solent amici invicem sibi revelare secreta sua. Putas tu quod quando tu tota die burdasti, descendet ad te iste amicus per suam gratiam? Certe non, sed quando vadis iuxta unum altare, vel ante ymaginem crucifixi vel beate Virginis, vel, si ad ecclesiam ire non potes, iuxta lectum tuum, flectis genibus et ad terram totus prostratus vel prostrata." BnF Lat. 16481, fol. 71rb.

99. "Seigneur je ne veux que vous, votre amour et votre acointance." BnF Lat. 16481, fol. 264vb.

100. BnF Lat. 16481, fol. 32 vb.

101. BnF Lat. 16481, fol. 55va.

102. BnF Lat. 16481, fol. 122rb.

103. BnF Lat. 16481, fol. 59rb–62va, ed. Bériou, "La prédication au béguinage de Paris," 202–210.

104. BnF Lat. 16482. On this manuscript, see Chapter 4.

105. On the evolution of the sermon form and its intimate connection with the university context, see Rouse and Rouse, *Preachers*, 65–90, and Bériou, *L'avènement*, chapter 1. On the influence of the mendicant orders on this development, see d'Avray, *Preaching of the Friars*, and Mulchahey, "Preaching Aids."

106. See my discussion of this term in Chapter 6.

107. On this poem and its influence on medieval and Renaissance devotional literature, as well as the inclusion of verses in a poem interpolated into versions of the *Roman de la Rose*, see Sylvia Huot, "Popular Piety and Devotional Literature: An Old French Rhyme About the Passion and Its Textual History," *Romania* 115 (1997): 451–494.

108. "Quatuor modis accusatur amor dei. Deus enim amando accusatur, in amando custoditur, et servat illos qui ipsum amant, et sufficit eis qui eum amant. Len aquert deu en amant, si l'en gadde un en se ke l'en eyme, et si garde sun amant, et suffit a cheus ke leyment." BnF Lat. 16482, fol. 3vb. Curiously, the Latin version of the poem uses the word *accusatur,* although the French version clearly indicates that the appropriate word would be "aquisitur." I thank Barbara Newman for her thoughts on this passage.

109. Katherine Gill discusses the ways in which women shaped the content of sermons and vernacular religious literature in "Women and the Production of Religious Literature in the Vernacular, 1300–1500," in *Creative Women in Medieval and Early Modern Italy,* ed. E. Ann Matter and John W. Coakley (Philadelphia: University of Pennsylvania Press, 1994), 64–104. This dynamic is also similar to what Sara Poor has noted in the work of the beguine Mechthild: "Mechthild's vernacular writings were used to instruct on the subject of the divine for different groups of religious (both lay and clerical)—for the composers of sermons and their listeners, for the devout reader, and for friars engaged in the pastoral care of beguines." *Mechthild of Magdeburg and Her Book,* 131.

110. BnF Lat. 16482, fol. 42ra.

111. BnF Lat, 16482, fol. 265vb–266ra.

112. Although Bériou asserts that the mistress's sermons are in line with those preached by university clerics, I see some evidence of resistance to clerical expectations of female spirituality. See "La predication au béguinage de Paris," 194.

113. BnF 16482, fol. 15ra. The sermon extract—filed under *Confessio*—opens with the statement "Confessio est minime pars penitentiae," an obvious play on Peter the Chanter's formulation "Confessio est maxima pars satisfactionis." *Verbum abbreviatum* 143, in *PL* 205, col. 342.

114. Indeed, Peter the Chanter and Thomas of Chobham had argued that auricular confession was the greatest part of satisfaction in part because the act induced such shame as to constitute the most burdensome aspect of exterior penance (satisfaction). See John W. Baldwin, "From the Ordeal to Confession: In Search of Lay Religion in Early Thirteenth-Century France," in *Handling Sin: Confession in the Middle Ages*, ed. Peter Biller and A. J. Minnis (Rochester, NY: York Medieval Press, 1998), 202–204.

115. Dyan Elliott, "Women and Confession: From Empowerment to Pathology," in *Gendering the Master Narrative: Women and Power in the Middle Ages*, ed. Mary C. Erler and Maryanne Kowaleski (Ithaca, NY: Cornell University Press, 2003), 34.

116. In this sense, the mistress's position was closer to Abelard's view. See Baldwin, "From the Ordeal to Confession," 201.

117. "Frater Johanes de Betune: In jure confessionis doit avoir v choses." BnF Lat.16482, fol. 15ra.

118. Filed under the rubric *Templum*, the sermon is labeled "Magistra beginarum, de dedication ecclesie." BnF Lat.16482, fols. 250 vb–251va. The sermon has been edited in Bériou, "La prédication au béguinage de Paris," 200–202. My transcription of this sermon varies slightly.

119. On this theme in church dedication sermons, see Ruth Horie, *Perceptions of Ecclesia: Church and Soul in Medieval Dedication Sermons* (Turnhout: Brepols, 2006).

120. "Quando uenitur ad dedicationem ecclesie materialis, episcopus accipit aquam benedictam et proicit eam tribus modis: primo inferius versus terram, secundo aliquantulum altius, mediocriter in aere, nec nimis alte, nec nimis basse, tertio altius quo potest, et hoc facit in signum puniendi tria genera peccatorum, scilicet peccatum ignorantie quod est minus, et licet peccet, secunda ad puniendum peccatum carnis vel corporis quod est gravius. Sed tertia fit propter puniendum peccatum malitie quod est grauissimum et altius puniendum." BnF 16482, fol. 251ra.

121. On this strategy, see Mary Carruthers, *The Craft of Thought, Meditation, Rhetoric, and the Making of Images, 400–1200* (Cambridge: Cambridge University Press), 198–199.

122. "In omnia ecclesia dedicata fiunt cruces, ab intra et extra, et sic ab episcopo aqua benedicta ubique, 'par toz senz,' ubi apparet 'peneence de foreine' ut ieiunare et simil. Est signum quod ipsa est ecclesia Deo dedicata. Et hee sunt cruces que fiunt extra. Intra, scilicet memoria passioquam in corde anima sancta simper debet habere." BnF Lat. 16482, fol. 251ra.

123. "Per canes intelligunter peccata detractionis, per porcellos, turpes et uiles cogitationes, que debent repelli ne eis consentiatur uel in eis delectatur, quia aliter non sunt peccatum." BnF Lat.16482, fol. 251rb.

124. "Abbas Nicholaus dicebat: 'Quid uobis calet si occurat uobis quod una uilitas, dum tamen ei non delectemini nec consentiatis?' Hoc dicebat propter aliquos et aliquas qui desolant propter istos occursus ymaginationum et fantasmatum: nec est uis facienda ex quo homo non consenti eis, non est nisi affirmatio huius de hoc." BnF Lat. 16482, fol. 251rb.

125. "Per mercationes intelligitur appetitus diuine laudis in quocumque bono opere, nichil aliud esset quam quedam mercatio." BnF Lat. 16482, fol. 251rb.

126. "Et quando uoluntas uult, ratio se accordat et memoria est pura, tunc hic ecclesia Deo dedicata et maritata." BnF Lat. 16482, fol. 251va.

127. Given canonical prohibition against female preaching in public, Bériou assumes that the mistress preached privately to the beguines of the enclosure. This is certainly a reasonable conclusion. It is interesting to speculate how these sermons came into Raoul's possession. Did the mistress provide him with a written copy? See Bériou, "La prédication au béguinage de Paris," 122, and L'avènement, 113, where Bériou surmises that Raoul had access to the mistress's notes as he did in the case of several other preachers.

128. "Magistra beginarum dicebat se audiuisse in pleno sermone a quodam predicatore magno." BnF Lat. 16482, fol. 42ra.

129. BnF Lat. 15971, fol. 72. Cited in McDonnell, Beguines and Beghards, 344.

CHAPTER 6. "THERE ARE AMONG US WOMEN CALLED BEGUINES"

1. On this points, see Lauwers, "Exhortatio–Praedicatio."

2. Bériou, "Right of Women to Give Religious Instruction," 137.

3. In addition to Bériou, see Blamires, "Women and Preaching"; Lauwers, "Noli me tangere"; and Waters, Angels and Earthly Creatures.

4. The trial is discussed later in this chapter.

5. In a sermon preached at the beguinage in 1273, an anonymous Franciscan preacher noted: "Non sis per unum annum vel duos in tuo bono proposito, et postea facis pactum cum alio a Christo, vel per malas cogitationes et locutiones cum viris suspectis." BnF Lat. 16482, fol. 245ra. See also Bériou, "La prédication au béguinage de Paris," 181.

6. Bériou, "La prédication au béguinage de Paris," 181.

7. Mary Suydam, "Women's Texts and Performances in the Medieval Southern Low Countries," in Visualizing Medieval Performance, Perspectives, Histories, Contexts, ed. Elina Gertsman (Aldershot, U.K.: Ashgate, 2008), 148.

8. The two versions of the chronicle account, Gesta Philippi tertii Francorum regis and Vie de Philippe III par Guillaume de Nangis are edited in RHF, vol. 20. The Latin version is on one side of the page (502) and the French on the other (503). A legal deposition concerning the case also exists. See J. de Gaulle, ed. "Documents historiques," in Bulletin de la société de l'histoire de France (1844): 87–100. This version of the story reports that Elizabeth was sought out because she had supposedly claimed that the king was involved in some unnatural vice, which she prophesied would result in the death of his children. The king sent an envoy to investigate Elizabeth's claims. She eventually denied these rumors and vouched

for the queen's innocence. For an interesting discussion of this case and how it relates to perceptions of beguines, see Nancy Caciola, *Discerning Spirits*, 113–125.

9. *RHF*, vol. 20, 502–503.

10. See Caciola, *Discerning Spirits,* 119–124.

11. *RHF*, vol. 20, 502.

12. Ibid., 503.

13. *RHF*, vol. 20, 590.

14. "De aliis conqueritur Dominus quia in eorum iardino non est flos nec fructus, sed loco dictorum florum bonorum, sunt ibi urtice mordentes, 'cuisenz'—urtica enim cuisit—, viole fetentes, et rose pungentes." BnF Lat. 16481, fols. 157ra–159rb, ed. Nicole Bériou, *La prédication de Ranulphe de la Houblonnière* (Paris: Études Augustiniennes), vol. 2, 106–107.

15. "Urtice pungentes: videbitis unam personam ut unam beginam, que videtur exterius ita humilis per habitum, et si dicatur sibi unum verbum modicum, quod sibi displiceat, statim accipiet urticam, id est unum verbum 'cuisant,' et proicit in faciem dicentis. Viole fetentes: videbitis unam beginam que extra per habitum ostendet quod sit ita sancta, pura et bona puella vel casta, attamen intra erit viola fetens, quia intra tota ardet luxuria et mala voluntate peccandi,—pro malis loquor. Tertio rose pungentes: videbitis unam beginam que apparet ita sapiens quod videtur quod qui eam bene verberaret, umquam plus quam ovis se revindicaret. Sed faciatis ei aliquid quod sibi displiceat, statim mordebit et punget fortiter. Sicut faciatis ei aliquid quod sibi displiceat, statim mordebit et punget fortiter. Sicut ovis quando mordet—sic morsura de begina est morsura 'de berbiz.'" BNF Lat. 16481, fols. 157ra–159rb, ed. ibid., 107.

16. "Contra pravas beginas et alias quecumque sint, sive in religione sive extra, que habent habitus provocantes homines ad peccatum, et contra illas que excultant homines, unde scandalizant alias probas mulieres et totum beginagium, quia statim dicunt qui talia semel vident 'O, tales sunt begine.' Ue illi per quem scandalum venit! [Matthew 18:7]." BnF Lat. 16482, fols. 167va–167 vb, ed. Bériou, "La prédication au béguinage," 182.

17. "De hoc dixit michi unum mirabile verbum quedam domina nobilis, quando ei predicabam quod esset begina. 'Hoc non facerem, nec sic nec sic, quia faciunt sic et sic.' Et ego ei 'Domina, vidistis vos umquam tam bonum pirum in vita vestra quin aliqua pira haberet verminosa? Non. Modo, dicatis michi, si illud pirum habeat duo vel tria pira verminosa, sciditurne propter hoc pirum? Constat quod non. Plus, non est nec fuit umquam in terra tam bona societas multorum in qua non esset aliquis malus. Etiam in societate Christi fuit unus verminosus, scilicet Iudas. Non tamen propter hoc bona religio est reprobanda. Non enim tam bonus monachus vel monacha, nec ita bene clausus quin bene cadat aliqua vice.'" BnF Lat. 16482, fols. 167va–167vb. Part of this sermon has been edited by Nicole Bériou in "La prédication au beguinage," 182.

18. "Et ipsa respondit michi mirabiliter. 'Non est mirum si una monacha vel nona cadat in peccatum et vadat ad malum pudorem.' Sancta Maria, dixi ego, quid dicitis vos? Et illa, 'Domine, ostendo vobis quid dicere volo. Ego habeo quatuor vel quinque filias. Non potero maritare eas secundum quod status meus et earum requirit, sed oportebit me eas maritarem ad sutores—chavetiers—si volo eas maritare.'" BnF Lat. 16482, fol. 167vb.

19. "Et cogitans quod hoc esset michi pudor secundum mundum, licet non secundum Deum, pono eas in religione ita quod nec Deus, nec mater sua, nec sancti eius invocabuntur ad introitum. Sed dabo abbatie centum libras vel ducentas, ita quod nec puer habet Deum pre oculis, nec ego, nec abbatissa, nec priorissa. Nec Deus est ibi invocatus, nec est ad introitum. Quid igitur mirum si malus sit eventus ex quo malus est introitus?" BnF Lat. 16482, fol. 167vb.

20. "Sed quando una begina vadit ad beginnagium, vadit ibi de propria voluntate, et ideo, ex quo de sua propria voluntate vadit inter alias sanctas et probas mulieres, deberet lapidari et 'flatir' quando facit rem inhonestam et facit magnum scandalam." BnF Lat. 16482, fol. 167vb.

21. On "conversion" as life turn, see John Van Engen, *Sisters and Brothers*, 14.

22. "Unde ego nescirem proprius vocare beguinam quam unctam. Begina enim idem est quod begnigna et begnigna idem est quod uncta." BnF Lat. 16482, fol. 119vb.

23. "Ut quando una sancta anima est ita bene uncta gratia Spiritus sancti que dicitur pietas, habet unum affectionem ad auxiliandum et subveniendum indigentiam omnium indigentium si posset. Appropriat enim sibi mala aliena per compassionem, et sua bona communicat aliis per caritatem." Ibid.

24. "Et si hoc debeat esse in qualibet anima sancta, precipue tamen in illis que portant nomen beginne, ut res sit cum nomine." Ibid.

25. "Ergo begina idem est quod bene uncta, scilicet oleo compassionis, et que hoc non habet non est begina, nisi secundum nomen solum, sed realiter quassatur quidquid ipsa facit, nisi sic benigna sit pro posse suo." Ibid.

26. The mistress of the beguinage referred to "Abbot Nicholas" in a sermon she gave on the occasion of the dedication of a chapel (perhaps that of the beguinage) (BnF 16482, fol. 251rb). The mistress refers to a certain "Nicholas de Douai" in a sermon excerpt Raoul included under the heading "Tribulatio" (BnF Lat. 16482, fol. 265vb). Raoul most likely acquired this statement via the mistress herself. On these sermons, see chapter 5.

27. "Si essem begina, non uellem esse pluris nominis nec minoris, 'de plus de num ne de meins,' quia minus importat scandalum, plus est occasio vane glorie." BnF Lat. 16482, fol. 64rb.

28. See Karras, *Boys to Men*, and Miller, "Mirror of the Scholarly (Masculine) Soul."

29. Coakley, "Gender and Authority of the Friars," 449–450.

30. Ibid. See also Coakley, *Women, Men, and Spiritual Power*, especially chapter 4.

31. "Notam exemplum de quaedam benigna fleute . . . quaesiuit quidam magnum magistrem qui dui fuerat parisius causam fletuum . . . respondens et dicens in trias causas fletus in hac ualle miseriae, scilicet, peccata propria, peccata aliena, oppressio pauperum . . . illo quaerente causam specialem sui fletus cum admiratione. Respondit quod flebat pro dilatione patrie et absenciam sui sponsi." BnF Lat. 15972, fol. 175v.

32. "Quaesiuit 'et quid cognoscis tu et scis de illo pro quo tam ploras'? Respondit ipsa parum scio de illo nisi quod passus pro nobis mortus et resurrexit . . . et cogitauit ille in corde suo quod multa plura sciebat de deo quam ipsa, nec tam afficiebatur ad ipsum ut diligebat . . . dixit 'ego dui studui ut multa scirem de deo, scilicet, ypostases unitatem essencio

et trinitem partiter, et ydeas etc, parum autem ad senciendum de ipsum laboraui.'" BnF Lat. 15972, fol. 175v.

33. "Job: paui sterilem et quae non parit, scilicet, intellectum qui non meretur et uiduae non bene feci, scilicet, affectui." Ibid.

34. "Cui illa respondit narrans exemplum de quodam animali, quod uocatur thygris . . . fetus uenatores raperee uolentes quaerunt eius absenciam et quia animal est uelox et ferox, timentes eius ferotitatem . . . recedunt ponunt specula in uia sua que thigris respitiens moratur et retardatur quia credit fetus suos reperisse propter sui apeciem et ymagiem quam uidet in speculo." Ibid.

35. "Sed quia uos multa specula in sacra scriptura uidistis et ibi respexistis et affectum uostrum retardastis." Ibid.

36. The master's book learning could easily be a detour in comparison to the more direct route to knowledge followed by inspired women. As a direct participant, the visionary saw and knew, rather than settling for "hearsay," as the book-educated scholastic. Her direct knowledge made the visionary free of error, giving her unquestionable authority. See Mulder-Bakker, "Introduction," *Seeing and Knowing*, 2–3.

37. "Unde de hoc dixit bonum uerbum quedam begineta. . . . Per quem locum intrauit Deus in uobis quem uos ita diligitis? 'Certe, domine per aurem quia uita amoris est per auditum et intrat per aurem.' Optime dixit. Si esset melior clericus de Parisius, non posset melius respondere." BnF 16482, fol. 97rb.

38. "Il fu uns maistres a Paris, si apiella un sein compaignon et le dist que il li amenast une beghine, et cils l'en amena une. Et li maistres li dist: 'Quels gens iestes vous et que faites vous?' 'Maistres,' fait elle, 'nous faisons che que li fols ne scet ne ne poet faire; car li fols poet vivre en pain et en yauwe et aler descaus et en laignes et viestir haire. Et se ne le scés, si l'apreng a faire.' 'Et que faites vous dont?' Che li a dit li maistres. 'Nous sçavons Dieu amer, confesser, nous warder, Dieu cognoistre, les VII sacremens, nos proimes amer et desevrer les vices et des virtus, avoir humilité sans orgoel, amour sans haÿne, pascienche en tribulation, clere cognissanche de Dieu et de saint eglise, et apparillies de tout souffrir pour Diu: tout chou est beghinages.'" Berlin, Staatsbibliothek, MS Gall. oct. 28., ed. Alfons Hilka, "Altfranzösische Mystik und Beginentum," *Zeitschrift für romanische Philologie* 47 (1927): 123.

39. "Quant li maistres l'oÿ, si dist: 'Dont savés vous plus de divinité que tout li maistres de Paris.'" Ibid.

40. Simons, *Cities of Ladies*, 84.

41. Carolyn Muessig, "Prophecy and Song: Teaching and Preaching by Medieval Women," in *Women Preachers and Prophets Through Two Millennia of Christianity*, ed. Beverly Kienzle and Pamela Walker (Berkeley: University of California Press, 1998).

42. Blamires, "Woman and Preaching," 142–145.

43. Ibid., 147.

44. Carolyn Muessig, "Prophecy and Song: Teaching and Preaching by Medieval Women," 147. Unfortunately, thus far no sermons preached on the feast day of Saint Catherine of Alexandria have been identified as being preached at the Paris beguinage.

45. "Li Barré sont prés des Beguines/ IX.XX. en ont à lor voisines, / Ne lor faut que

passer la porte, / Que par auctorités devines, / Par essamples et par doctrines / Que li uns d'aus à l'autre porte, / N'ont povoir d'aler voie torte." Rutebeuf, *Oeuvres complètes,* ed. Zink, vol. 1, 226.

46. On these theological debates, see Blamires, "Woman and Preaching" and Alastair J. Minnis, "*De impedimento sexus*: Women's Bodies and Medieval Impediments to Female Ordination," in *Medieval Theology and the Natural Body*, ed. Peter Biller and Alastair J. Minnis (York, U.K.: York University Press, 1997), 109–139.

47. Waters, *Angels and Earthly Creatures*, 13–30. Mary Sudyam discusses citational authority of women's written visionary experiences in "Women's Texts and Performances in the Medieval Southern Low Countries," in *Visualizing Medieval Performance: Perspectives, Histories, Contexts*, ed. Elina Gertsman (Aldershot, U.K.: Ashgate, 2008), 143–159.

48. "Iudicium multiplex reperitur in sacra scriptura. Primo, iudicium temeritatis. [Matthew 7:1:] 'Nolite iudicare et non iudicabimini,' scilicet a Deo, sicut alique moniales uel alie quedam persone religiose uel begine." BnF 16482, fol. 58ra.

49. "Ieronimus in epistola ad matrem et filiam in Gallis commorantes, 'Inconguum est latere corpore et lingua per totum orbem uagari.'" BnF 16482, fol. 58ra.

50. BNF 16482, fol. 58ra.

51. "Sicut peccat qui scit et non vult primum docere, sic qui nescit et vult magister esse." Bériou, *L'avènement*, 315. Both sermons have been edited and published in Jacques-Guy Bougerol, ed., *Sermones de diversis* (Paris: Éditions françaises, 1993), nos. 44 and 45.

52. "Sunt apud nos mulieres, quae Beghinae vocantur, et quaedam earum subtilitatibus vigent et novitatibus gaudent. Habent interpretata scripturarum mysteria et in communi idiomate gallicata, quae tamen in sacra Scriptura exercitatis vix sunt pervia. Legunt ea communiter, irreverenter, audacter, in conventiculis, in ergastulis, in plateis. Vidi ego, legi et habui bibliam gallicatum, cuius exemplar Parisiis publice ponitur a stationariis ad scribendum haereses et errores, dubietates et inconcinnas interpretationes." Gilbert de Tournai, *Collectio de scandalis ecclesiae*, 58. I thank Barbara Newman for sharing her translation of Gilbert's report with me and for pointing out that the line "Habent interpretata scripturarum mysteria et in communi idiomate gallicata" should be read to mean not that the beguines themselves had translated the scriptures (a common mistranslation) but that they had translated scriptures in their possession.

53. Sean Field has argued convincingly that Marguerite was "surrounded by books and in contact with like-minded men (and presumably women)." See *The Beguine, the Angel, and the Inquisitor*, 55. Robin O'Sullivan has argued that, despite the quietist strain in the *Mirror*, the book expresses "an outwardly directed, pedagogical concern." See "The School of Love," 146. On this portrayal of Marguerite, see also Kocher, *Allegories of Love*, 41–44.

54. Indeed, Marguerite asserted: "Beguines say I err." *The Mirror of Simple Souls*, chapter 122.

55. Margaret Porette, *The Mirror of Simple Souls*, trans. Marler, Colledge, and Grant, 28.

56. Ibid.

57. Ibid., 89.

58. Here I am following Sean Field's careful study of the trial documents, in which he argues for a date of sometime around 1300 for Marguerite's initial condemnation by

Bishop Guido. See *The Beguine, the Angel, and the Inquisitor,* 54. Field's appendix A contains a full translation of the trial documents in AN J 428, nos. 15–19bis. Field's translation follows the Latin in Paul Verdeyen's edition, noting errors therein. I have cited the Latin from Verdeyen's edition here, while following Field's translation. Paul Verdeyen, "Le procès d'inquisition contre Marguerite Porete et Guiard de Cressonessart," *Revue d'histoire ecclésiastique* 81 (1986): 47–94.

59. In an earlier article, "What's in a Name?" I stated that Marguerite *sent* the bishop a copy of her book. However, this is a supposition based on Marguerite's subsequent actions. None of the trial documents directly states that Marguerite sent the book to Guido of Collemezzo. See Field, *The Beguine, the Angel, and the Inquisitor,* 43.

60. Although the trial records state that Marguerite hailed from the county of Hainaut, by the time she and her book came to the attention of the bishop of Cambrai, she most certainly resided in the city of Valenciennes, since that was the city in which the bishop ordered her book to be publicly burned. Such an act would have had little effect if Marguerite and her book had not been well known in that city. Suzanne Kocher has also noted that one of the clerics from whom Marguerite sought approval for her book—John "of Querayn"—was probably from Querenaing, a town ten kilometers south of Valenciennes. See *Allegories of Love,* 22–23,

61. "A quo episcopo tibi fuit sub pena excommunicationis expresse inhibitum ne de cetero talem librum componeres vel haberes aut eo vel consimili utereris, addens et expresse ponens dictus episcopus in quadam littera suo sigillata sigillo, quod, si de cetero libro utereris predicto vel si ea que continebantur in eo, verbo vel scripto de cetero attemptares, te condempnabat tamquam hereticam et relinquebat iustitiandam iustitie seculari." AN J 428, n. 15, ed. Verdeyen, "Le procès d'inquisition," 82.

62. Sean Field's discussion of the evidence for Marguerite's revision of the original, condemned version is useful for its summary of previous scholarship and analysis of the trial documents, bringing much-needed clarity and new insights to the question of when and why Marguerite wrote and revised her book. See *The Beguine, the Angel, and the Inquisitor,* 47–49.

63. Field thoroughly addresses the scholarly debate regarding whether Marguerite sought the approval of these three eminent clerics before or after the book was condemned by Bishop Guido of Collemezzo. Although Verdeyen, Babinsky, and most recently Robert Lerner have expressed doubt that these clerics would have approved a book that had been condemned as heretical, there are good reasons to believe that Marguerite had acquired these statements of approval after revising and recirculating her book as part of what Field calls her "campaign for rehabilitation." Field, *The Beguine, the Angel, and the Inquisitor,* 277–278, note 31. Indeed, the actions of the two bishops of Cambrai make more sense if we accept that Marguerite obtained these written and/or oral statements of approbation after the condemnation of Guido of Collemezzo. Guido seems to have unhesitatingly burned Marguerite's book, a move that, as Field argues, might be considered quite brash if the *Mirror* had at that point earned the approval of three eminent churchmen. By contrast, Guido's successor followed quite a different procedure when dealing with Marguerite's revised *Mirror.* As Fields puts it, "Guy [Guido] could be decisive because he encountered no

opposing opinions, while Philip was necessarily cautious because the situation had been complicated by Godfrey's intervention." See Sean Field, "The Master and the Marguerite: Godfrey of Fontaines's Praise of *The Mirror of Simple Souls*," *Journal of Medieval History* 35 (2009): 143. In this illuminating article, Field goes on to argue that Godfrey had very publicly declared that it was permissible for theologians to depart from episcopal opinion on matters that had not been settled by pope or council or if the bishop had been in error. Thus, if Godfrey would be so bold as to declare certain episcopal condemnations—such as the condemnations of 1277—as unjust, then surely it is not a stretch to imagine him defending Marguerite's book, even after it had met with the extreme disapproval of the bishop of Cambrai. For a detailed and convincing exploration of these arguments, see "The Master and the Marguerite," 143–149.

64. Although Marguerite reportedly did not bother to defend herself during the course of William of Paris's questioning, a stance scholars have sometimes interpreted as motivated by an utter indifference to explaining herself and her work, the evidence for Marguerite's determined efforts to clarify and gain approval for her work suggests that the beguine did indeed hope to convey her ideas to others. Sean Field's reconstruction of the events leading up to her trial ably shows that by the time Marguerite was brought before William of Paris, she had run out of options. *The Beguine, the Angel, and the Inquisitor*, especially chapter 4.

65. See Chapter 4.

66. Bériou, "Robert de Sorbon," 470.

67. Field, *The Beguine, the Angel, and the Inquisitor*, 56–57.

68. Ibid., 60–61.

69. Ibid., 73.

70. Ibid., 93.

71. Only a few Parisian masters were not among these twenty-one. It is also important to note, as far as the terse records report, that William of Paris was keeping the matter of the book's orthodoxy separate from the issue of Marguerite's defiance of episcopal order. Again, Field's analysis lays out these details carefully. See ibid., 127–133.

72. I owe this point to Field, ibid., 132–133. The treatment Marguerite's book received—with extracts presented for review—was similar to how cases of intellectual heresy were typically pursued within the university. See J. M. M. H. Thijssen, *Censure and Heresy at the University of Paris, 1200–1400* (Philadelphia: University of Pennsylvania Press, 1998).

73. Translation in Field, *The Beguine, the Angel, and the Inquisitor*, 224.

74. AN J 428, n. 19 bis, ed. Verdeyen, "Le procès d'inquisition," 78, trans. Field, *The Beguine, the Angel, and the Inquisitor*, 226.

75. AN J 428, no. 19 bis, ed. Verdeyen, "Le procès d'inquisition," 79, trans. Field, *The Beguine, the Angel, and the Inquisitor*, 226.

76. AN J 428, n. 15, ed. Verdeyen, "Le procès d'inquisition," 82. "Margaretam, non solum sicut lapsam in heresim, sed sicum relapsam finaliter condempnamus et te relinquimus iusticie seculari."

77. Ibid., 89.

78. "Beguuina quaedem, quae libellum quondam adversus clerum ediderat," cited in Lerner, *The Heresy of the Free Spirit in the Later Middle Ages*, 206.

79. "Une beguine clergesse qui estoit appellée Marguerite Porée qui avait trespassée et transcendée l'escriture devine et les articles de la foy avoit erré, et du sacrement de l'autel avoit dit paroles contraires et prejudiciables. Et pour ce des maitres expers en theologie avoit esté condampnée." *Les grandes chroniques de France*, ed. Jules Viard (Paris: Société de l'Histoire de France, 1934), 8: 273.

80. Verdeyen, "Le procès d'inquisition," 54. Field, *The Beguine, the Angel, and the Inquisitor*, 193–194.

81. Tanner, ed., *Decrees of the Ecumenical Councils*, 1: 383–384. On the wave of inquiry and persecution spawned by *Ad nostrum*, see Lerner, *The Heresy of the Free Spirit in the Later Middle Ages*.

82. The Latin text can be found in Emil Frieberg, *Corpus iuris canonici* (1879–1881; repr. Graz: Akademische Druck-u. Verlagsanstalt, 1959), vol. 2, col. 1169. The above translation is from Makowski, *"A Pernicious Sort of Woman,"* 23–24.

CHAPTER 7. THE KING'S BEGUINES

1. "Monseigneur saint Loys, entre les autres oeuvres de misericorde que il fist en son vivant, eust acquis une enceinte de maisons à Paris assis delez la porte Barbeel, et illec eust mis bonne et preude fames beguines pour servir Nostre-Seigneur chastement." AN JJ 64, no. 475, fol. 256v., ed. Le Grand, "Les béguines de Paris," 318.

2. On the Capetian cult of kingship, see Joseph R. Strayer, "France: The Holy Land, the Chosen People, and the Most Christian King," in *Medieval Statecraft and the Perspectives of History: Essays by Joseph R. Strayer*, ed. J. F. Benton and T. N. Bisson (Princeton: Princeton University Press, 1971), 300–315; Gabrielle Spiegel, "The Cult of Saint-Denis and Capetian Kingship," *Journal of Medieval History* 1 (1975): 43–69; Elizabeth A. R. Brown, "The Religion of Royalty: From Saint Louis to Henry IV (1226–1589)," in *Creating French Culture: Treasures from the Bibliothèque Nationale de France*, ed. Marie-Hélène Tesnière and Prosser Gifford (New Haven, CT: Yale University Press, 1995).

3. On the development of symbols of sacred kingship, see Colette Beaune, *Birth of an Ideology: Myths and Symbols of Nation in Late-Medieval France*, trans. Susan Ross Huston, ed. Frederic L. Cheyette (Berkeley: University of California Press, 1991).

4. On the concept of a holy lineage (*beata stirps*) see Gàbor Klaniczay, *"Beata Stirps:* Sainteté et lignage en Occident aux XIIIe et XIVe siècles," in *Famille et parenté dans l'Occident médiéval*, ed. Georges Duby and Jacques Le Goff (Rome: École Française de Rome, 1977), 397–406, and *Holy Rulers and Blessed Princesses: Dynastic Cults in Medieval Central Europe*, ed. Lyndal Roper and Chris Wickham (Cambridge: Cambridge University Press, 2002); also Field, *Isabella of France*, 2–4.

5. For a similar example of royal efforts to preserve the mission and organization of Louis's foundations, see Mark O'Toole's research on the Quinze-Vingts. Mark P. O'Toole, "Caring for the Blind," 227–259.

6. AN J 428, n. 19 bis, ed. Verdeyen, "Le procès d'inquisition," 78.

7. This defense was composed by sympathetic clerics in the wake of the implementation

of the Vienne decrees. Jean Béthune, *Cartulaire du Béguinage de Sainte-Elizabeth à Gand* (Bruges: Aimé de Zuttere, 1883), 73–76, no. 106.

8. De La Selle, *Le service des âmes,* 31–36.

9. Ibid.

10. Ibid, 164.

11. For an overview, see Bautier and Maillard, "Les aumônes du roi," 57–59 and De La Selle, *Service des âmes*, 167–174.

12. Under Philip, the almoner distributed fixed amounts of money, food, and clothing on major feasts, and continued Louis's practice of distributing food for the poor during Lent. See Bautier and Maillard, "Les aumônes du roi," 57, and De La Selle, *Service des âmes*, 169–173.

13. Bautier and Maillard, "Les aumônes du roi," 42–43.

14. O'Toole, "Caring for the Blind," 236–239.

15. Although De La Selle has listed the Paris beguinage as one of the houses administered by the royal almoner, the almoners do not seem to have exercised this responsibility until the fifteenth century. Moreover, the canons of Sainte-Chapelle, not the royal almoner, are consistently named in the royal accounts as the agents through whom the beguinage received funding.

16. The act is dated March 1265. These alms were delivered by Gilles de Luzarchis. *Layettes*, vol. 4, 119. In April 1267, Alphonse donated another fifty sous, this time designating a certain "Aleidis," the porter of the Paris beguinage, to deliver the funds. See ibid., 210.

17. *Layettes*, vol. 4, 456. See also Edgard Boutaric, *Saint Louis et Alfonse de Poitiers: Étude sur la réunion des provinces du Midi et de l'Ouest à la couronne et sur les origines de la centralisation administrative d'après des documents inédits* (Paris: H. Plon, 1870), 461.

18. As William Jordan has observed, Louis's testament "set a pattern which the later Capetians slavishly followed perhaps to the detriment of their financial solvency." *Louis IX and the Challenge of Crusade*, 183.

19. "Item legamus ad aedificandum et ampliandum locum beguinarum parisiensium centum libras." *Layettes,* vol. 4, 420. Discussed in Chapter 1.

20. "Item legamus pauperibus mulieribus beguinis in regno Francie constitutis centum libras, per bonos viros quos ad hoc executores nostri viderent ordinandos distribuendas." Ibid.

21. See Chapter 1.

22. "Aus Beguines de Paris cent sous, et requerons messes et oroisons pour nous. Aus povres d'Avauterre, a Cambrai, a Nivelle, a Douai, et a Liege soissante lievres et leurs requerons devotement messes et oroisons pour nous," Johan Lorenz Mosheim, *De Beghardis et Beguinabus commentarius*, ed. G. H. Martini (Leipzig: Libraria Weidmannia, 1790), 47.

23. "As povres beguines de Paris, six cens livres tournois." Ibid. 47. Compare this amount, for example, with the fifty livres tournois Phillip III left to another royal foundation, the Quinze-Vingts. See Léon Le Grand, "Les Quinze-Vingts: Depuis leur fondation jusqu'à leur translation au Faubourg Saint-Antoine," *Mémoires de la Société de l'histoire de Paris et de l'Ile-de-France* 13 (1886): 141, n. 5.

24. "As autres povres beguines en nostre domaine, C livres tournois," *De Beghardis et Beguinabus commentarius*, 47.

25. On Philip's role promoting the cult of Saint Louis, see Elizabeth M. Hallam, "Philip the Fair and the Cult of Saint Louis," *Studies in Church History* 18 (1982): 201–214 and Cecilia Gaposchkin, "Boniface VIII, Philip the Fair, and the Sanctity of Louis IX," *Journal of Medieval History* 29, no. 1 (2003): 1–26.

26. *RHF*, vol. 22, 559.

27. These six beguines received seven sous, six deniers per week. *RHF*, vol. 22, 630.

28. *RHF*, vol. 22, 637.

29. The beguines of Caen received eight livres (*RHF*, vol. 22, 560); Chartres (ibid., 551); Crespy (ibid., 602); Mantes (ibid., 558); Melun (ibid., 560); Sens (ibid., 656).

30. A beguine named Alice of Saint-Quentin is listed as receiving certain payments from the royal treasury in the late thirteenth and early fourteenth centuries; see *RHF*, vol. 22, 625. Another beguine from Amiens also received royal support during Philip IV's reign. *RHF*, vol. 22, 634, 721, and 762.

31. This too may have been in emulation of Louis's support for beguines and poor scholars. As recounted by William of Saint-Pathus, Louis provided individual beguines with pensions in the same manner that he provided financial support to poor scholars of the Sorbonne. See Chapter 1.

32. In his preface to an edited version of the *Journaux du Trésor*, Jules Viard noted that the canons of Sainte-Chapelle delivered royal alms to the beguines, poor scholars, and converted Jews. He did not, however, offer an explanation as to why the kings grouped the three together nor why they were maintained separately from other recipients of royal alms. *Journaux du Trésor de Charles IV le Bel* (Paris: Imprimerie Nationale, 1917), lxx–lxxi.

33. "Dominus Johannes de Condeto, canonicus capelle regalis Parisiensis solutorque bursarum scolarium et biguinarum palacii regalis Parisiensis, pro denariis, per ejus litteram recognitoriam datam XVII hujus mensis, per eum receptis a Johanne Perier commissario deputato ad explectandum et recipiendum certum debitum supra episcopum Lingonensem, ratione cujusdam subsidii quondam in sua dyocesi domino Regi concessi, distribuendis personis predictis, 300 l. t. valent 240 l. p.; quiquidem Johannes Perier cum hoc tradidit compt. 48 l. p. in 30 l. dupl. tur. pro 2 d. t. cujuslibet." Jules Viard, ed., *Journaux du Trésor de Philippe VI de Valois* (Paris: Imprimerie Nationale, 1899), no. 1145.

34. Evidence for this shared account may be found in the inventory of the royal official Robert Mignon. After accounts for the almoners, panetiers, and argentiers, we find listed the "Compotus Galteri de Cantalupi de operibus regis Parisius, de bursis scholarium, beguinarum et conversorum," Charles-Victor Langlois, ed., *Inventaire d'anciens comptes royaux dressé par Robert Mignon sous le règne de Philippe VI de Valois, Recueil des historiens de la France,* vol. 1, *Documents financiers* (Paris: Imprimerie Nationale, 1899), no. 2221. Gautier de Chanteloup is identified as a canon of Sainte-Chapelle in earlier entries of the royal accounts. Mignon compiled the inventory in 1328 in conformity with a 1320 ordinance. A later inventory of royal accounts dating from the 1340s also lists disbursements to beguines, scholars, and converted Jews in a separate account, again managed by a canon

of Sainte-Chapelle. See Robert-Henri Bautier, "Inventaires de comptes royaux particuliers de 1328 à 1351," *Bulletin philologique et historique* (1960), 88. For a prosopographical study of the canons of Sainte-Chapelle in the Middle Ages, see Claudine Billot, "Le collège des chanoines de la Sainte-Chapelle de Paris (1248–1550)," in *L'état moderne et les élites XIIIe–XVIIIe siècles: Apports et limites de la méthode prosopographique*, ed. Jean-Philippe Genet and Günther Lottes (Paris: Publications de la Sorbonne, 1996), 291–307.

35. Information on the canons of Sainte-Chapelle is surprisingly sparse. Recent articles by Claudine Billot analyze the social, geographical, and educational backgrounds of a select group of canons but do not discuss the canons' administrative roles. See Billot, "L'insertion d'un quartier canonial dans un palais royal, problèmes de cohabitation: L'exemple de la Sainte-Chapelle de Paris," in *Palais royaux et princiers au Moyen Âge: Actes du colloque international tenu au Mans les 6–7 et 8 octobre 1994* (Le Mans: Publications de l'Université du Maine, 1996), 111–116. and "Le collège des chanoines."

36. On the careers of the men who served in the Chambre des comptes, see Danièle Prévost, *Le personnel de la chambre des comptes de Paris de 1320 à 1418* (Villeneuve-d'Ascq: Presses universitaires du septentrion, 2003).

37. In his study of royal almoners between the thirteenth and fifteenth century, Xavier de La Selle has found that ten of the thirty-eight almoners were canons of Sainte-Chapelle. De La Selle, *Service des âmes*, 131–132.

38. Similar patterns of patronage can be seen at the Haudriettes and beguinages in the southern Low Countries.

39. The canon Jean de Hetomesnil, for example, nurtured particularly close ties with several women living at the beguinage of Paris. See Chapter 2.

40. "Compotus domini Gregorii et Philippi Viarii de operibus regis." Léopold Delisle and Natalis de Wailly, eds., *Recueil des Historiens des Gaules et de la France*, vol. 22 (Paris: Victor Palmé, 1860), 665.

41. "Pro bursis beguinarum, XXIX L. VIII s." Ibid.

42. For example, Viard, ed., *JT Philippe IV*, nos. 398, 1597, 850, 2051, 751.

43. For example, *JT Charles IV*, nos. 193, 505, 1927; Viard, ed., *JT Philippe IV*, nos. 5845, 5896, 6069.

44. Because the canons' own accounts have been lost, we usually do not know precisely how the canons distributed these allocations from the treasury. Gaps in the *Journaux*, as well as delays in the disbursements make it difficult to determine if the disbursements were of a fixed amount. Moreover, the range of the canons' responsibilities, which sometimes included building projects around the royal residences in Paris and Vincennes, renders any attempt to determine how much the royal treasury allocated for the beguines in the Paris beguinage purely speculative. An entry dating from March 1300 illustrates the point: "Dominus J. de Capella et Johannes Poynlasne, pro fine compoti sui de operibus Regis, bursis scolarium, beguinarium, et conversorum et aliis, a dominica post Sanctum Lucam XCVII usque ad dominicam post Sanctum Martinum Yemalem, ultra 9,256 l. 17 s. p." Viard, ed., *JT Philippe IV*, no. 2751.

45. "Le beguignage et les beguignes d'Orleans, fonde par saint Louis, et doibvent estre XIII beguignes, desquelles la maistress doit avoir II sous pour sepmaine, et XL sous par an,

pour robe, et les autres six, chacune XVIII deniers par sepmaine et XX sous par an, pour robe, et les autres six, chacune XII deniers par sepmaine et XX sous par an, pour robe." BnF nov. acq. 1440.

46. Several entries in the royal account books record payments delivered to beguines that are categorized as "ad elemosinas." December 1284: "Beguine Paris. ad elomosinas, 12 l, 16s," Lalou, *Comptes sur tablettes*, 6 and December 1285: "De quibus Beguinae Parisienses, ad elemosinas, 12 l, 16 s," Delisle and de Wailly, eds., *Recueil des Historiens des Gaules et de la France*, 488.

47. "Beguine Parisienses XVI, ad elemosinas, 14 l, 8 s," Lalou, *Comptes sur tablettes*, 6. "*Ceratae P(etrus). de Condeto tabulae*: De quibus Beguinae Parisienses XVI, ad elemosinas, XIIII l. VIII s." Delisle and de Wailly, eds., *Recueil des Historiens des Gaules et de la France*, 470.

48. Several entries in the royal account books record payments delivered to beguines that are categorized as "ad elemosinas." "Beguine Paris. ad elemosinas, 12 l, 16s," Lalou, *Comptes sur tablettes*, 6. "De quibus Beguinae Parisienses, ad elemosinas, 12 l, 16 s," Delisle and de Wailly, eds., *Recueil des Historiens des Gaules et de la France*, 488.

49. Viard, ed., *JT Charles IV*, no. 3223.

50. Delisle, eds., *Recueil des Historiens des Gaules et de la France*, 751.

51. Viard, ed., *JT Philippe VI*, no. 810.

52. Ibid., nos. 809–14.

53. The abbey of Tiron retained certain rights of justice over the land. See Edgar Boutaric, ed., *Actes du Parlement de Paris (1254–1328)*, vol. 1 (Paris: H. Plon, 1863), no. 7044. In 1284 the king paid thirty-three sous, four denier per term. "Pro censu domus earum, pro duobus terminis, III l. VI s VIII d." Delisle and de Wailly, eds., *Recueil des Historiens des Gaules et de la France*, 665. In 1299: "Pro censu domorum beguinarum ibi, pro toto: 9 s. 2 d.," Fawtier, *Comptes royaux (1285–1314)*, no. 2237. In 1327: "Magistra beguinarum Parisius pro denariis sibi solutis qui eidem debebantur pro censibus domus sue inter debita tradita curie per dominum Johannem de Capella, pro finibus compotorum, 14 l. 9 s.," Viard, ed., *JT Charles IV*, no. 10287.

54. "Pro quodam camino et fenestris in domo beguinarum refectis: 4 l. 2 s," Fawtier, *Comptes royaux (1285–1314)*, no. 2273.

55. Viard, ed., *JT Philippe IV*, no. 1943.

56. "Nos très chers seigneurs pere et freres, les roys philippe, Loys, et Philippe derrain trespassé, que Dieu absoille, pour le bon gouvernement et estat dudit hostel de beguinage, eussent commis la garde et l'administracion d'ycelui au prieur de l'ordre des Freres prescheurs de Paris." AN JJ 64, no. 475, fol. 256v, ed. Le Grand, "Les béguines de Paris," 350.

57. De La Selle, *Service des âmes*, 262–267, and Gaposchkin, *The Making of Saint Louis*, 77.

58. Galloway, "The Origins, Development and Significance of the Beguine Communities in Douai and Lille," 164. Galloway cites several other similar examples of Philip IV's involvement in the administration of the beguinages of French Flanders.

59. *Beguinage Statutes*, arts. 19 and 21.

60. See in particular article 16 as well as arts. 3, 9, 15, and 21.

61. See Simons, *Cities of Ladies* and Galloway, "The Origins, Development and Significance of the Beguine Communities in Douai and Lille," 95. See also Jennifer Deane "*Geistliche Schwestern.*"

62. See Chapter 1.

63. In 1284: "Capellanus Sancti Pauli, pro capella beguinarum, pro medietate, X livres," Delisle and de Wailly, eds., *Recueil des Historiens des Gaules et de la France*, 624. In 1285: "Capellanus Sancti Pauli pro capella beguinarum pro medietate, 7 livres, 10 sous," Delisle and de Wailly, eds., *Recueil des Historiens des Gaules et de la France*, 624. In 1298: "Capellanus Sancti Pauli, pro capella beguinarum, pro medietate: 7 livres; et de dono Regis, pro medietate: 40s," Fawtier, *Comptes royaux (1285–1314)*, no. 217. In 1298: "Capellanus Sancti Pauli, pro capella Regis, pro medietate: 7 livres; et de dono Regis, pro medietate, 40 s," Fawtier, *Comptes royaux (1285–1314)*, no. 218. In 1299: "Capellanus Sancti Pauli, pro capella beguinarum, pro medietate: 7 l. 10 s; et de dono Regis, pro medietate: 40 s," Fawtier, *Comptes royaux (1285–1314)*, no. 549. In 1305: "Capellanus Sancti Pauli, pro capella beguinarum, pro medietate: 7 livres; et de dono Regis, pro medietate: 40 s," Fawtier, *Comptes royaux (1285–1314)*, no. 3597.

64. Both Robert Lerner and Paul Verdeyen have argued that Marguerite's trial was directly related to the Templars' trial. This connection is evident in the fact that the documents recording both trials were found together in the papers of two royal ministers. See Robert Lerner, "An 'Angel of Philadelphia' in the Reign of Philip the Fair: The Case of Guiard de Cressonessart," in *Order and Innovation in the Middle Ages: Essays in Honor of Joseph R. Strayer* (Princeton, NJ: Princeton University Press, 1976); Verdeyen, "Le procès d'inquisition," and Marler, Colledge, and Grant, "Introductory Interpretive Essay," in Margaret Porette, *The Mirror of Simple Souls.*

65. Lerner, "An 'Angel' of Philadelphia," 357–358. For a closer analysis of the trial that bears out Lerner's argument on this point, see Field, *The Beguine, the Angel, and the Inquisitor*, especially chapter 7.

66. "Item pauperibus beguinis Parisius viginti lib. tur. Aliis pauperibus beguines Domaniorum nostrorum , Centum lib. Tur. ad adbitrium Exequtorum nostrorum distribuendas." AN J 404 no. 17 (Dated 17 May 1311). These provisions for beguines were the same as those detailed in earlier versions of Philip's testament from 1288 (AN J 403 no. 12) and 1297 (AN J 403 no. 13). I thank Elizabeth A. R. Brown for sharing with me her transcriptions of these documents.

67. Tanner, ed., *Decrees of the Ecumenical Councils* 1: 374.

68. Jacqueline Tarrant has argued that the decree was not the work of the council at all but rather represents Clement's revisions of the original. See "The Clementine Decrees on the Beguines: Conciliar and Papal Versions," *Archivum historiae pontificae* 12 (1974): 300–302.

69. Chronicle accounts explain the delays as due to papal recognition that the decrees were too harsh. "Constitutiones Clementinae, per papam Clementem editae in concilio Viennensi, cum ad tempus suspensae fuissent quia nimis rigidae videbantur." *RHF,* vol. 21, 48. See also Tarrant, "Clementine Decrees," 300.

70. Ewald Müller, *Das Konzil von Vienne 1311–1312* (Münster: Aschendorff, 1934), 389. On the Clementine Decree's publication in Paris, see *RHF,* vol. 21, 48.

71. See the translation of the decree in Chapter 6.

72. As Tarrant herself acknowledges. See "Clementine Decrees," 308.

73. "Pro quo Beguinae specialiter sunt turbatae, quoniam, sine omni distinctione, statue beguinagii condempnatur," *RHF,* vol. 21, 666.

74. As cited in Makowski, *"A Pernicious Sort of Woman,"* 28.

75. As Makowski points out, Alberic changes the phrasing of the "escape clause" in *Cum de quibusdam,* altering the original wording from *in suis hospitiis* ("in their own dwellings") to *in domibus propriis* ("in their own homes"), thereby defending women who observed a life of chastity and good works privately in their own homes and distinguishing such women from others following a common life. See ibid., 37.

76. Ibid., 43.

77. Philips, *The Beguines in Medieval Strasbourg,* 201; Lerner, *Heresy of the Free Spirit in the Later Middle Ages,* 94–95; Van Engen, *Sisters and Brothers,* 40.

78. McDonnell, *Beguines and Beghards,* 529–531.

79. Phillips, *The Beguines in Medieval Strasbourg;* McDonnell, *Beguines and Beghards,* 533. See also the useful analysis in Van Engen, *Sisters and Brothers,* 40–43.

80. McDonnell, *Beguines and Beghards,* 537. See also Van Engen, *Sisters and Brothers,* 42.

81. Friedberg, *Corpus,* 2: 1279–1280, trans. in Makowski, *"A Pernicious Sort of Woman,"* 47.

82. Makowski, *"A Pernicious Sort of Woman,"* 47.

83. Van Engen, *Sisters and Brothers,* 39–40. As Elizabeth Makowski has pointed out, *Ratio recta* was not the subject of much commentary by canon lawyers, thereby mitigating its effect. Makowski, *"A Pernicious Sort of Woman,"* 48–50.

84. See the useful discussion of anti-beguine legislation in Van Engen, *Sisters and Brothers,* 37–40.

85. Simons, *Cities of Ladies,* 133.

86. As shown in Philips, *Beguines of Medieval Strasbourg,* 222–223; McDonnell, *Beguines and Beghards,* 537–538; Lerner, *Heresy of the Free Spirit,* 96–103; and Simons, *Cities of Ladies,* 133–135.

87. Frédéricq, *Corpus,* II, 81. Cited in McDonnell, *Beguines and Beghards,* 540.

88. Ibid.

89. Simons, *Cities of Ladies,* 134. See also McDonnell, *Beguines and Beghards,* 541–545.

90. Philips, *Beguines of Medieval Strasbourg,* 222–223; Simons, *Cities of Ladies,* 134.

91. Lerner, *The Heresy of the Free Spirit in the Later Middle Ages,* 94; Simons, *Cities of Ladies,* 134.

92. The plan, apparently, was never carried out. Simons, *Cities of Ladies,* 134.

93. Recent scholarship on beguines in German lands has emphasized this point. See Deane, "Beguines Reconsidered." See too Van Engen, *Sisters and Brothers,* 40–41.

94. Makowski, *"A Pernicious Sort of Woman,"* xxiii.

95. *RHF,* vol. 21, 48.

96. *RHF,* vol. 21, 666.

97. C. Leber, ed., "Compte de Caperel, prevost de Paris," *Collection des meilleurs dissertations, notices et traités particuliers relatifs à l'histoire de France* 19 (1938): 55.

98. The chronicles report that the beguines had been exonerated through the intervention of the mendicant orders. See *RHF*, vol. 21, 666.

99. "Dominus Johannes de Capella, canonicus capelle regalis, pro denariis sibi traditis pro bursis scolarium et beguinarum et conversorum, per litteram suam datam IIII Marcii CCCXXI, pro termino Candelose, 1,52 l. p. cont. per se, super Regem." Viard, ed., *JT Charles IV*, no. 193.

100. "Super peticione proprietatis quam abbas et conventus de Thironio fecerunt in curia nostra contra procuratorem nostrum pro nobis, racione justicie domus beguinarum Parisiensium, advocavit dictus procurator noster in garendum suum episcopum Parisiensem, facta secunda protestacione de ulterius procedendo, si dictum non possit habere garandum, as quem habendum et ulterius procedendum est assignata dies prepositure parisiensis nostri futuri proximo Parlamenti, datum die XXV aprilis." AN X^{ia} 8844, fol. 354v, ed. Boutaric, *Actes de Parlement,* no. 7044.

101. See Jacques Chiffoleau, *La comptabilité de l'au-delà: Les hommes, la mort et la religion dans la région d'Avignon à la fin du moyen âge (vers 1320–vers 1480)* (Rome: École française de Rome, 1980). For Paris specifically, see Bove, "Espace, piété et parenté à Paris," 47–64.

102. AN S 5074A2 (ancienne cote AN S 5073, no. 40). Cited in Connally, "Les 'Bonnes Femmes' de Paris." The houses were supposed to accommodate two women each, according to stipulations in Jean Roussel's will.

103. AN KK 5, fols. 367v–368r.

104. On these naming controversies and strategies, see the essays in *Labels, Libels, and Lay Religious Women in Northern Medieval Europe*, ed. Letha Böhringer, Jennifer K. Deane, and Hildo van Engen (Turnhout: Brepols, forthcoming).

105. There is no indication that any of the beguines of Paris became Franciscan tertiaries. Given the reaction of the mendicant orders to a later proposal to transform the beguinage into a community of tertiaries, it is possible that the Franciscans actively resisted any efforts to have beguines adopt the Third Rule of the Order of Saint Francis. See my discussion later in this chapter.

106. AN JJ 64, no. 475, fol. 256v., ed. Le Grand, "Les béguines de Paris," 318–319.

107. De La Selle, *Service des âmes*, 266.

108. Although papal confirmations of beguines' privileges in the wake of these investigations exist for some communities, none survive for Paris.

109. The Cistercian convent of Saint-Antoine, which was originally founded as a house for reformed prostitutes, is a case in point. See Constance Berman, "Cistercian Nuns and the Development of the Order: the Abbey of Saint-Antoine-des-Champs Outside of Paris," in *The Joy of Learning and the Love of God: Studies in Honor of Jean Leclerq*, ed. E. Rozanne Elder (Kalamazoo, MI: Cistercian Publications, 1995), 121–156. On the ways in which donors shaped the mission and organization of the Haudriettes, see Connally, "Les 'Bonnes Femmes' de Paris."

110. In his otherwise meticulously researched study of the "Bonnes Femmes" of Paris, Michael Connally overlooked the inclusion of the beguines in the almoner's list.

111. Viard, ed., *Trésor de Charles IV*, no. 1166.

112. See discussion above.

113. On the succession crisis ushered in by the dying out of the Capetian line in 1328, see Raymond Cazelles, *La société politique et la crise de la royauté sous Philippe de Valois* (Paris: Librairie d'Argences, 1958). On Philip's efforts to legitimize his claim to the throne by emphasizing his connections to Louis IX, see Anne D. Hedeman, "Valois Legitimacy: Editorial Changes in Charles V's Grandes Chroniques de France," *Art Bulletin* 66 (1984): 97–115.

114. AN JJ 75, no. 168, in *Documents parisiens du règne de Philippe VI de Valois (1328–1350)*, ed. Jules Viard, vol. 2 (Paris: Société de l'histoire de Paris, 1900), 232.

115. "Confirmation de la foundation faite par Saint Louis d'un couvent de Béguines à Paris, près la porte Barbel," AN JJ 73, fol. 52v, no. 71, in Le Grand, "Les béguines de Paris," 342–349. A copy of these statutes is preserved in the archives of the Filles de l'Ave Maria (AN S 4642).

116. Murielle Gaude-Ferragu, "Les dernières volentés de la reine de France," *Annuaire-bulletin de la société de l'histoire de France* (2007): 23–66.

117. "Testament de Blanche de Navarre: Reine de France," *Mémoires de la société de l'histoire de Paris et de l'Ile-de-France* 12 (1885): 14.

118. "Nous maistresse des beguines du beguinaige de paris confessons avoir eu et receu des executeurs de feu tres noble dame madame Ysabeau de valloys jadis duchesse de bourdon . . . pour prier dieu pour lame de feu madam dicte dame la somme de dix frans dor de la quelle somme nous maistress dessus dicte nous tenons pour bien contente." Testament executed August 1386. AN P 1378^2 no. 3098.

119. Blanche was married to Philip VI's son Philip, Duke of Orléans, and was the post-humous daughter of Charles IV, Philip VI's Capetian predecessor. For Blanche's testament, see Gaston Vignat, "Notes sur une des chapelles absidales de la basilique de Sainte-Croix d'Orléans," *Mémoires de la société archéologique de l'orléanais* 9 (1866): 100–144.

120. Isabelle also seems to have entrusted Jeanne with the task of acquiring linens and other household materials for Isabelle's household. AN P 1378^2 nos. 92 and 638. For more on Jeanne de La Tour, see Chapter 2.

121. De La Selle suggests the toll the wars took on royal charity. See *Le service des âmes*. John Henneman's book on French royal taxation during the first part of the Hundred Years' War demonstrates the financial toll of the war on the monarchy. See John Bell Henneman, *Royal Taxation in Fourteenth-Century France: The Development of War Financing, 1322–1356* (Princeton, NJ: Princeton University Press, 1971).

122. Henneman, *Royal Taxation in Fourteenth-Century France*.

123. On the fate of these houses in the fifteenth century, see Michael Connally, "Les 'Bonnes Femmes' de Paris," chapter 6.

124. Raymond Cazelles, *Nouvelle Histoire de Paris, de la fin du règne de Philippe Auguste à la mort de Charles V, 1223–1380* (Paris: Hachette, 1972), 150. As Michael Connally has shown in his extensive work in the archives of the Haudriettes, the disruptions of the fifteenth century led to a crisis in revenue as the community faced difficulty collecting rents on its urban properties.

The Paris beguinage probably faced a similar crisis.

125. For a documented example of this, see Simons, *Cities of Ladies*, 136–137.

126. Raymond Cazelles, *Nouvelle Histoire de Paris, de la fin du règne de Philippe Auguste à la mort de Charles V, 1223–1380*. Paris: Hachette, 1972.

127. The case, which is alluded to in the briefest of terms, reveals few details about the circumstances surrounding the cathedral chapters' complaint and the beguinage's inability to successfully defend their case. Le Grand briefly alludes to the case, preserved at the AN (LL 115, fol. 263). See also "Les béguines de Paris," 333.

128. On Parisian family strategies, see Barbara B. Diefendorf, *Paris City Councillors in the Sixteenth Century: The Politics of Patrimony* (Princeton, NJ: Princeton University Press, 1983).

129. Ralph E. Giesey, "Rules of Inheritance and Strategies of Mobility in Pre-Revolutionary France," *American Historical Review* 82 (1977): 271–289.

130. Martha C. Howell, *The Marriage Exchange: Property, Social Place, and Gender in Cities of the Low Countries, 1300–1550* (Chicago: University of Chicago Press, 1998), 218.

131. Ibid., 219. See also Sarah Hanley, "Engendering the State: Family Formation and State Building in Early Modern France," *French Historical Studies* 16, no. 1 (1989): 4–27, and Diefendorf, *Paris City Councillors*.

132. This is according to letters patent preserved in the inventory of the letters and titles concerning the foundation of the convent of the Ave Maria, who eventually took over the enclosure in the 1480s. "Le Roy, ayant recongneu que lesdictes maisons et monastere desdictes Beguines, par faulte d'estre habitées et les repparations faictes, alloient en decadence pour n'y avoir que deux relligieuses." AN S 4642.

133. *Testaments*, 226–230.

134. On this civil war, see C. A. J. Armstrong, *England, France, and Burgundy in the Fifteenth Century* (London: Hambledon Press, 1983), and Bernard Schnerb, *Armagnacs et Bourguigons, la maudite guerre* (Paris: Perrin, 1988).

135. Guy L. Thompson, *Paris and Its People Under English Rule: The Anglo-Burgundian Regime, 1420–1436* (Oxford: Clarendon Press, 1991).

136. See Chapter 2.

137. The mistress of the beguinage, Comine Nangeres, brought this case before the Châtelet in 1433. AN S 931/B, no. 5.

138. AN S 4642. On Pierre Cauchon's dual role as almoner and confessor of the king, see De La Selle, *Service des âmes*, 229.

139. AN S 4642.

140. Martine Canu refers to herself as a parishioner of Saint-Paul but does not mention the chaplains of the beguinage. See *Testaments*, 226. Alice Cournon, however, in her testament (composed in 1409) does mention the chaplain and clerics serving the beguinage, but she may have been referring to the parish priest and clerics at Saint-Paul. See ibid., 261. It seems that the parish priest was in charge of providing pastoral care to the remaining beguines at the time of the community's transfer to the tertiaries, as suggested in a summary of the case preserved in the Archives Nationales (AN 4642). See note 141, below.

141. Letters patent concerning the state of the beguinage in 1471 reveal that the

celebration of divine services had ceased within the enclosure (AN AN Xia, 8606). Nevertheless, the parish priest of Saint-Paul claimed that he had been accustomed to saying mass at the chapel once a year. AN S 4642 (judgment dated 2 September 1482). Beguinages in other regions experienced similar difficulties maintaining their chaplains. See, for example, the discussion in Galloway, "Neither Miraculous nor Astonishing."

142. Gratien de Paris, "La foundation des Clarisses de l'Ave Maria et l'établissement des frères mineurs de l'Observance à Paris (1478–1485)," *Études Franciscaines* 27 (1912): 20.

143. "Loys, par la grace de Dieu, Roy de France . . . comme nous avons été advertiz que la maison et monastère des Béguines assiz près les Célestins à Paris, lequel fut anciennement fondé par nos prédécesseurs roys de France, soit par faut d'estre habité et entretenu en réparacions, tourne en grant decadence et veu qu'il n'y habite de present que une seulle religieuse, pourroit venir à totalle ruyne de par nous n'en estoit autrement dispose et soit ainsi que nous avons esté advertiz que se nostre plaisir estoit ordonner et establir ladite maison et monastère pour les filles et femmes qui ont prins et vouldront prendre la tierce ordre penitence et observance de monsieur Saint François. . . . Et par ce moien pourroit icelle maison et monastère estre facilement réparé, restauré et entretenu, et le divin service icelle célèbre et continue à louenge de Dieu notre Créateur." AN Xia, 8606, ed. Gratien de Paris, "La foundation des Clarisses de l'Ave Maria," 19. I have checked my transcription of this document against that of Gratien de Paris.

144. "Désirant sur toutes choses la restauration et entretenement des maisons et monastères de notre royaume, et la continuacion, entretenement et augmentacion dudit divin service." Ibid.

145. On these issues of labels, see *Labels, Libels, and Lay Religious Women*, ed. Böhringer, Deane, and van Engen. For the assertion that a tertiary is a "type of beguine," see Brigitte Degler-Spengler, "Die religiöse Frauenbewegung des Mittelalters: Konversen—Nonnen—Beginen," *Rottenburger Jahrbuch für Kirchengeschichte* 3 (1984): 75–88.

146. These beguines, Guillamette Estarde and Michelle la Normande, had at one point opposed the installation of the tertiaries, but issued separate letters in 1380 stating that they no longer objected to the king's plan. Michelle la Normande's letters reveal that she had decided to take up the rule of the Third Order of Saint Francis. AN L 1058, no. 33. See also Gratien de Paris, "La foundation des Clarisses de l'Ave Maria," 21.

147. The objection was not to the tertiaries themselves but to their dependence on Observant friars. Significantly, the negotiations among the various interested parties shows the extent to which the parish priests of Saint Paul remained interested in upholding their rights. To allow the tertiaries to set up a house in Paris would mean allowing the Observants to gain a foothold in the city. The controversy, which is enormously complicated, is laid out in detail in Gratien de Paris, "La foundation des Clarisses de l'Ave Maria." Another useful overview is presented in Pierre Moracchini, "Les Cordeliers de l'Ave Maria de Paris, 1485–1792," *Revue Mabillon*, n.s., 6 (1995): 243–266. The objections laid out by representatives of the university are particularly interesting. The Observants are pseudo-prophets and have produced no Doctors for the church (unlike the Conventuals, who mention Alexander of Hales and Bonaventure as examples of their greater contributions). The Observants, they contend, are seducers of women. They do not preach or study

and thus will only diminish the alms that would more properly go to the Conventuals. AN S 4642.

148. This resolution is described in a document dated 2 September 1482. AN S 4642.

149. Gratien de Paris, "La foundation des Clarisses de l'Ave Maria," 40.

150. For a description of the complex negotiations that took place during these years as Queen Charlotte labored to establish the Observant nuns in Paris, see de Paris, "La foundation des Clarisses de l'Ave Maria," especially 40–52.

APPENDIX. BEGUINES WHOSE OCCUPATIONS ARE KNOWN

1. Agnes's high assessment (thirty-six sous) indicates that she was a silk spinner.

2. Agnes de Senliz is identified as a beguine in 1300, cf. AN KK 283, fol. 296.

3. Ameline's surname is provided in the 1298 roll (AN KK 283, fol. 102v).

4. In 1300, Maheut was taxed as an "ouvrière de soie" (AN KK 283, fol. 292v), a term used to describe silk weavers specifically or silk workers in general. The ambiguity of the term "ouvrière de soie" makes it impossible to know precisely what sort of silk work Maheut did. Based on the description in the 1299 assessment (silk spinner), it is possible that she diversified, weaving in addition to spinning silk in her workshop.

5. Maheut's surname is provided in the 1299 roll (AN KK 283, fol. 220v).

6. Like Maheut aus Cholez, Thomasse la Normande was described generically as a silk "worker" in one assessment (1299, AN KK 283, fol. 220v, which is also the roll that provides her surname) and a silk spinner in another (1300, AN KK 283, fol. 292v).

7. Alice of Saint-Joce was described generically as an "ouvriere de soi" (AN KK 283, fol. 99) in 1298 and more specifically as a maker of alms purses in 1300 (fol. 235v). Alice is described as a beguine in 1292 (BnF fr. 6220, fol. 8).

8. Jeanne is identified as "Jehanne la Beguine" in 1297 (AN KK 283, fol. 68). Tracking her location through the tax rolls, it is clear that "Jehanne qui fet laz de soie" (AN KK 283, fol. 231) is the same person. She has the same neighbors and same location on the rue Saint-Honoré.

9. Marie des Cordeles was described as an "ouvrière de soie" in 1299 (AN KK 283, fol. 178v). Her subsequent assessment in 1300 (AN KK 283, fol. 256), which describes her as a beguine and a maker of head coverings, indicates that here the term "ouvrière de soie" refers to someone who wove silk items.

10. Although Isabelle is described in 1298 as a "seller of silk" ("*vendeur de soie*," AN KK 283, fol. 186v), in both 1297 and 1300 she is labeled a silk spinner (fols. 50v and 263v). I have categorized Isabelle as a silk merchant because her tax assessments are on par with the mercers and are well above the average paid by silk spinners (she paid an average tax of forty-three sous). Moreover, her assessments indicate that she employed other beguines as workers, further support for the argument that she was on the entrepreneurial side of silk production. Finally, a censive for Isabelle's parish (Saint-Merry) describes Isabelle as "Ysabiau la beguine, doreur." The descriptor here indicates that Isabelle was known to engage in mercery work. A "doreur" was someone who applied gilt to different materials. See Léon

Cadier and Camille Couderc, "Cartulaire et censier de Saint-Merry de Paris," *Mémoires de la Société de l'histoire de Paris*, 18 (1891): 204.

11. In 1300, Isabelle of Cambrai shows up in the tax registers as "Dame Isabel de cambrai, fet cuevrechies" (AN KK 283 fol. 266v), indicating that her workshop wove silk goods. I have categorized Isabelle as a mercer, however, because she is described as such in 1298 and was at the center of a cluster of beguine silk workers, as was her beguine mercer neighbor and partner Marguerite de Troyes. Of more modest means than some of the other beguine mercers (she paid an average tax of 13.5 sous), Isabelle was most likely a mercer who organized the production of smaller, silk items such as head coverings.

12. On Jeanne du Faut's identity as a beguine, see Chapter 3.

13. On Marie Osanne's identity as a beguine, see Chapter 3.

14. Felt maker.

15. Oats seller.

16. Parchment maker.

17. Peddler.

BIBLIOGRAPHY

ARCHIVAL SOURCES

Paris, Archives de l'Assistance Publique
Fonds St.-Jacques, reg. 1 and reg. 20

Paris, Archives Nationales
J 740, no. 6
J 151 A, no. 16
JJ 64, no. 475
JJ 90, pièce 46
KK 5
KK 283
KK 330/A
L 665/A
L 938/B
P 1378^2
S 60
S 65
S 930
S 931/A
S 931/B
S 938/A
S 3973/B
S 4642
S* 4634
S* 5594 I. 62v
X 1a
X 4a

Paris, Bibliothèque Nationale de France
MS. nov. acq. 1440
MS. Lat. 15955

MS. Lat. 15971
MS. Lat. 15972
MS. Lat. 16481
MS. Lat. 16482
MS. Lat. 16496
MS. Lat. 16507

PRINTED PRIMARY SOURCES

Andreas Capellanus. *Andreas Capellanus on Love*. Edited and translated by P. G. Walsh. London: Duckworth, 1982.

Bautier, Robert-Henri. "Inventaires de comptes royaux particuliers de 1328 à 1351." *Bulletin philologique et historique* (1960): 773–837.

Bériou, Nicole. *La prédication de Ranulphe de la Houblonnière*. 2 vols. Paris, Études Augustiniennes, 1987.

Béthune, Jean. *Cartulaire du Béguinage de Sainte-Elizabeth à Gand*. Bruges: Aimé de Zuttere, 1883.

Bonaventure of Bagnoreggio. *Sermones de diversis*. Edited by Jacques-Guy Bougerol. Paris: Éditions françaises, 1993.

Bonnardot, René de Lespinasse, and François Bonnardot, eds. *Le Livre des métiers d'Étienne Boileau*. Paris: Imprimerie Nationale, 1879.

Bougerol, Jacques, ed. *Sermones de diversis*. Paris: Éditions Françaises, 1993.

Boutaric, Edgar, ed. *Actes du Parlement de Paris (1254–1328)*. Vol. 1. Paris: H. Plon, 1863.

Cadier, Léon and Camille Couderc, ed. "Cartulaire et censier de Saint-Merry de Paris." *Mémoires de la Société de l'histoire de Paris* 18 (1891): 101–271.

Chartularium Universitatis Parisiensis, edited by H. S. Denifle and E. Chatelain, 4 vols. Paris: Delalain, 1889–1891.

Colledge, Edmund, J. C. Marler, and Judith Grant, trans. *The Mirror of Simple Souls* by Margaret Porette [*sic*]. Forward by Kent Emery Jr. Notre Dame, IN: University of Notre Dame Press, 1999.

Comptes royaux (1285–1314), edited by Robert Fawtier and François Maillard. Recueil des Historiens de la France, Documents financiers, 3. 3 vols. Paris: Imprimerie Nationale, 1953.

Comptes royaux (1314–1328), edited by François Maillard. Recueil des Historiens de la France, Documents Financiers, 4. 2 vols. Paris: Imprimerie Nationale, 1961.

Corpus documentorum inquisitionis haereticae pravitatis neerlandicae. Edited by Paul Fredericq. 3 vols. Ghent: J. Vuylsteke, 1889–1906.

Coyecque, Ernest, ed. *L'Hôtel-Dieu de Paris au moyen âge: Histoire et documents*. Vol. 1. Paris: Chez H. Champion, 1889.

De Lespinasse, René. *Les métiers et corporations de la ville de Paris XIVe–XVIIIe siècle*. 3 vols. Paris: Imprimerie Nationale, 1886.

Delisle, Léopold, ed. *Cabinet des manuscrits de la Bibliothèque nationale*. 3 vols. Paris: Imprimerie Nationale, 1868–1881.

———. "Inventaire des manuscrits latins de la Sorbonne, conservés à la Bibliothèque impériale sous les numéros 15176–16718 du fonds latin." *Bibliothèque de l'École des Chartes* 31 (1870): 1–50.

———. "Testament de Blanche de Navarre: Reine de France." *Mémoires de la société de l'histoire de Paris et de l'Île-de-France* 12 (1885): 1–63.

Delisle, Léopold, and Natalis de Wailly, eds. *Recueil des Historiens des Gaules et de la France.* Vol. 22. Paris: Victor Palmé, 1860.

Depping, G. B., ed. *Réglemens sur les arts et métiers de Paris rédigés au xiiie siècle.* Paris: Crapelet, 1837.

Douët-d'Arcq, Louis. *Comptes de l'Argenterie des rois de France au XIVe siècle: Société de l'histoire de France.* Paris: Renouard, 1851.

———. "Des frais d'enterrement dans Paris au XIVe siècle." *Mémoires de la Société de l'histoire de Paris et de l'Ile-de-France* 4 (1877): 125–139.

Gaude-Ferragu, Murielle. "Les dernières volontés de la reine de France." *Annuaire-bulletin de la societe de l'histoire de France* (2007): 23–66.

Geoffrey de Beaulieu. "Vita Ludovici noni." In *Recueil des historiens des Gaules et de la France.* Edited by Pierre Daunou and Joseph Naudet. 1–27. Vol. 20. Paris: Imprimerie Royale, 1840.

Géraud, Hercule, ed. *Paris sous Philippe-le-Bel, d'après des documents originaux et notamment d'après un manuscrit contenant "Le Rôle de la Taille" imposée sur les habitants de Paris en 1292, 1837,* reprint, with introduction and index by Caroline Bourlet and Lucie Fossier. Tübingen: Max Niemeyer, 1991.

Gilbert of Tournai. *Collectio de scandalis ecclesiae.* In P. Autbertus Stroick, "Collectio de scandalis ecclesiae: Nova editio," *Archivum Franciscanum Historicum* 24 (1931): 33–62.

The Goodman of Paris (Le Ménagier de Paris): A Treatise on Moral and Domestic Economy by A Citizen of Paris, c.1393. Trans. Eileen Power. London: G. Routledge, 1928.

Goswin of Bossut. *Send Me God: The Lives of Ida the Compassionate of Nivelles, Nun of La Ramee, Arnulf, Lay Brother of Villers, and Abundus, Monk of Villers.* Edited and translated by Martinus Cawley. Turnhout: Brepols, 2003.

Guigniaut, J. D., and J. N. de Wailly, eds. *Recueil des Historiens des Gaules et de la France.* Vol. 21. Paris: Imprimerie impériale, 1855.

Guillaume de St.-Pathus. *Les miracles de saint Louis.* Edited by Percival B. Fay. Paris: H. Champion, 1931.

Humbert of Romans. "*De eruditione religiosorum praedicatorum,* book 2, tractatus I." In *Maxima bibliotheca veterum patrum et antiquorum scriptorum ecclesiasticorum,* edited by Marguerin de La Bigne, 456–506. Lyon, 1677.

Inventaire-sommaire des Archives départementales antérieures à 1790: Pas-de-Calais: Archives civiles—Série A. Edited by Jules-Marie Richard. 2 vols. Arras: Imprimerie de la Société du Pas-de-Calais, 1878–1887.

James of Vitry. *Lettres de Jacques de Vitry (1160/1170–1240) évêque de Saint-Jean d'Acre.* Edited by R. B. C. Huygens. Leiden: Brill, 1960.

———. *Vita B. Mariae Oigniacensis. AA SS, June, 5:547–72.* Translated by Margot King.

In *Mary of Oignies: Mother of Salvation*. Edited by Anneke Mulder-Bakker, 33–127. Turnhout: Brepols, 2006.

John of Joinville. *The Life of St. Louis*. Translated by René Hague. New York: Sheed and Ward, 1955.

Labarte, Jules. *Inventaire du mobilier de Charles V, roi de France*. Paris: Imprimerie Nationale, 1879.

Lalou, Elisabeth. *Les comptes sur tablettes de cire de la Chambre aux deniers de Philippe III le Hardi et de Philippe IV le Bel (1282–1309)*. Vol. 8, *Documents financiers*. Paris: Boccard, 1994.

Le Grand, Léon, ed. "Reglèment donné aux Quinze-Vingts par Michel de Brache, aumônier du roi Jean (1351–1355)." In "Les Quinze-Vingts," part 2. *Mémoires de la Société de l'histoire de Paris et de l'Île-de-France* 14 (1887): 154–164.

———. "Les règles de béguinage de Paris." *Memoires de la société de l'histoire de Paris et de l'Île-de-France* 20 (1893): 347–350.

Leber, C., ed. "Compte de Caperel, prevost de Paris." *Collection des meilleurs dissertations, notices et traités particuliers relatifs à l'histoire de France* 19 (1938): 52–56.

Life of Beatrice of Nazareth. Edited and translated by Robert De Ganck. Kalamazoo, MI: Cistercian Publications, 1991.

Longnon, Auguste M, ed. *Pouillés de la Province de Sens. Receuil des historiens de la France*. Pouillés, IV. Paris: Imprimerie Nationale, 1904.

Meyer, Paul, ed. "Les propriétés des béguinages." *Bulletin de la Société des anciens textes français* 38 (1912): 98–99.

Michaëlsson, Karl, ed. *Le livre de la taille de Paris, l'an 1296*. Göteborg: Almquist and Wiksell, 1958.

———. *Le livre de la taille de Paris l'an 1297*. Göteborg: Almquist and Wiksell, 1962.

———. *Le livre de la taille de Paris, l'an de grace 1313*. Göteborg: Almquist and Wiksell, 1951.

Mignon, Robert. *Inventaire d'anciens comptes royaux dressé par Robert Mignon sous le règne de Philippe VI de Valois*. Edited by Charles-Victor Langlois. Paris: Imprimerie Nationale, 1899.

Molinier, Auguste, ed. *Recueil des historiens de la France. Obituaires, I. Obituaires de la province de Sens*. 2 vols. Paris: Academie des Inscriptions et Belles-Lettres, 1902.

Molinier, Émile, ed. "Inventaire du trésor de l'église du Saint-Sépulcre à Paris." *Mémoires de la Société de l'histoire de Paris* 9 (1882):1–48.

Les Olim ou registres des arrêts rendus par la Cour du roi: Sous les règnes de Saint Louis, de Philippe le Hardi, de Philippe le Bel, de Louis le Hutin et de Philippe le Long. Edited by Arthur Beugnot. 4 vols. Paris: Imprimerie royale, 1839–1848.

"*La règle des fins amans*: Eine Beginenregel aus dem Ende des XIII. Jahrhunderts." Edited by Karl Christ, in B. Schädel and W. Mulertt, eds., *Philologische Studien aus dem romanische-germanischen Kulturkreise: Festgabe Karl Voretzsch*, Halle: Max Niemeyer, 1927.

Le roman de la rose par Guillaume de Lorris et Jean de Meun. 5 vols. Edited by Ernest Langlois. Paris: Édouard Champion, 1914–1924.

Sandret, Louis, ed. "Testament et Codicille de Jeanne d'Eu: Comtesse d'Étampes et Duchesse d'Athènes, 1388–1389." *Revue Historique, Nobiliaire et Biographique* 17 (1880): 273–300.

Tanner, Norman P., ed. *Decrees of the Ecumenical Councils: Nicaea I–Lateran V.* Washington, D.C.: University of Georgetown Press, 1990.

Terroine, Anne, and Lucie Fossier, eds. *Chartes et documents de l'Abbaye de Saint-Magloire.* Vol. 2 (1280 à 1330). Paris: Editions du CNRS, 1966.

"Testament de Blanche de Navarre: Reine de France." *Mémoires de la Société de l'Histoire de Paris et de l'Île-de-France* 12 (1885): 1–63.

Thomas of Cantimpré. *Bonum Universale de Apidus.* Edited by Georgius Colvenerius. Douai: B. Belleri, 1627.

Thomas of Eccleston. *Tractatus de adventu Fratrum Minorum in Angliam.* Edited by A. G. Little. Manchester: Manchester University Press, 1951.

Tuetey, Alexandre, ed. *Testaments enregistrés au Parlement de Paris sous le règne de Charles VI, Collection de documents inédits, Mélanges historiques, III.* Paris: Imprimerie Nationale, 1880.

Verdeyen, Paul, ed. "Le procès d'inquisition contre Marguerite Porete et Guiard de Cressonessart." *Revue d'histoire ecclésiastique* 81 (1986): 47–94.

Viard, Jules, ed. *Documents Parisiens du règne de Philippe VI de Valois (1328–1350).* 2 vols. Paris: H. Champion, 1899.

———. *Journaux du Trésor de Charles IV le Bel.* Paris: Imprimerie Nationale, 1917.

———. *Journaux du Trésor de Philippe IV le Bel.* Paris: Imprimerie Nationale, 1940.

———. *Journaux du Trésor de Philippe VI de Valois.* Paris: Imprimerie Nationale, 1899.

———. *Les grandes chroniques de France.* 10 vols. Paris: Société de l'Histoire de France, 1920–53.

Vidier, Alexandre. "Un tombier liégeois à Paris au XIVe siècle. Inventaire de la succession de Hennequin de Liège (1382–1383)." *Mémoires de la Société de l'histoire de Paris et de l'Île-de-France* 30 (1903): 281–308.

Vignat, Gaston. "Notes sur une des chapelles absidales de la basilique de Sainte-Croix d'Orléans." *Mémoires de la société archéologique de l'orléanais* 9 (1866): 100–144.

William of Saint-Amour. *De periculis novissimorum termporum.* Edited and translated by G. Geltner. Dallas Medieval Texts and Translations 8. Louvain: Peeters, 2007.

———. *The Opuscula of William of Saint-Amour: The Minor Works of 1255–1256.* Edited and translated by Andrew Traver. Münster: Aschendorff, 2003.

———. "Les '*Responsiones*' de Guillaume de Saint-Amour." Edited by Edmond Faral. *Archives d'histoire doctrinale et littéraire du moyen âge* 18 (1950–1951): 337–394.

SECONDARY SOURCES

Abels, Richard, and Ellen Harrison. "The Participation of Women in Languedocian Catharism." *Mediaeval Studies* 41 (1979): 215–251.

Andrews, Frances. *The Other Friars: The Carmelite, Augustinian, Sack and Pied Friars in the Middle Ages.* Woodbridge: Boydell Press, 2006.

Archer, Janice. "Working Women in Thirteenth-Century Paris." Ph.D. dissertation, University of Arizona, 1995.

Armstrong, C. A. J. *England, France, and Burgundy in the Fifteenth Century.* London: Hambledon Press, 1983.

Asztalos, Monika. "The Faculty of Theology," in *A History of the University in Europe*, vol. 1. Edited by Hilde De Ridder-Symoens, 409–441. Cambridge: Cambridge University Press, 1992.

Babinsky, Ellen. "A Beguine in the Court of the King: The Relation of Love and Knowledge in 'The Mirror of Simple Souls' by Marguerite Porete." Ph.D. dissertation, University of Chicago, 1991.

Badel, Pierre-Yves, *Le Roman de la Rose au XIVe siècle: Étude de la réception de l'oeuvre.* Geneva: Droz, 1980.

Baldwin, John W. *Masters, Princes, and Merchants: The Social Views of Peter the Chanter and His Circle.* Princeton, NJ: Princeton University Press, 1970.

———. "From the Ordeal to Confession: In Search of Lay Religion in Early Thirteenth-Century France." In *Handling Sin: Confession in the Middle Ages*, edited by Peter Biller and A. J. Minnis, 191–209. Rochester, NY: York Medieval Press, 1998.

Bataillon, Louis J. "Comptes de Pierre de Limoges pour la copie de livres." In *La production du livre universitaire au Moyen Âge: Exemplar et pecia. Actes du symposium tenu au Collège San Bonaventura de Grottaferrata en mai 1983*, textes réunis par Louis J. Bataillon, Bertrand G. Guyot, Richard H. Rouse, 265–273. Paris: CNRS, 1988.

Bautier, Robert-Henri, and François Maillard (collaborator). "Les aumônes du roi aux maladreries, maisons-dieu, et pauvres établissements du royaume: Contribution à l'étude du réseau hospitalier et de la fossilisation de l'administration royale de Philippe Auguste à Charles VII." In *Assistance et assistés jusqu'à 1610, Actes du 97e Congrès national des Sociétés Savantes, Nantes 1972, Section de philologie et d'histoire jusqu'à 1610*, 37–105. Paris: Bibliothèque Nationale, 1979.

Beaune, Colette. *The Birth of an Ideology: Myths and Symbols of Nation in Late-Medieval France.* Translated by Susan Ross Huston. Berkeley: University of California Press, 1991.

Belhoste, Jean-François. "Paris, Grand centre drapier au Moyen Âge." *Mémoires de la Fédération des Sociétés historiques et archéologiques de Paris et de l'Île-de-France*, 51 (2000): 31–48.

Bennett, Judith. *Ale, Beer, and Brewsters in England: Women's Work in a Changing World, 1300–1600.* Oxford: Oxford University Press, 1999.

Bennett, Judith, and Amy M. Froide. "A Singular Past." In *Singlewomen in the European Past, 1250–1800*, edited by Judith Bennett and Amy M. Froide, 1–37. Philadelphia: University of Pennsylvania Press, 1999.

Bennett, Judith, and Maryanne Kowaleski. "Crafts, Guilds, and Women in the Middle Ages: Fifty Years After Marian K. Dale." In *Sisters and Workers in the Middle Ages*, edited by Judith Bennett, Elizabeth A. Clark, Jean F. O'Barr, and B. Anne Vilen, 11–25. Chicago: University of Chicago Press, 1989.

Bériou, Nicole. *L'avènement des maîtres de la Parole: La prédication à Paris au XIIIe siècle*, 2 vols. Paris: Institut d'études augustiniennes, 1998.

———. "La prédication au béguinage de Paris pendant l'année liturgique 1272–1273." *Recherches augustiennes* 13 (1978): 105–229.

———. "The Right of Women to Give Religious Instruction in the Thirteenth Century" in *Women Preachers and Prophets Through Two Millennia of Christianity*. Edited by Beverly Kienzle and Pamela Walker, 134–145. Berkeley: University of California Press, 1998.

———. "Robert de Sorbon." In *Dictionnaire de spiritualité: Ascétique et mystique, doctrine et histoire*, edited by André Rayez, Marcel Viller, and Charles Baumgartner, 816–824. Paris: G. Beauchesne, 1988.

———. "Robert de Sorbon: Le prud'homme et le béguin." *Comptes rendus de l'Académie des inscriptions et belles-lettres* (Paris, 1994): 469–510.

Berman, Constance H. "Cistercian Nuns and the Development of the Order: The Abbey of Saint-Antoine-des-Champs Outside Paris," in *The Joy of Learning and the Love of God: Essays in Honor of Jean Leclercq, OSB*. Edited by E. Rozanne Elder, 121–156. Kalamazoo, MI: Cistercian Publications, 1995.

———."Dowries, Private Income, and Anniversary Masses: The Nuns of Saint-Antoine-des-Champs (Paris)." *Proceedings of the Western Society for French History* 20 (1993): 3–20.

Biller, Peter. "Words and the Medieval Notion of 'Religion.'" *Journal of Ecclesiastical History* 36, no. 3 (1985): 351–369.

Billot, Claudine. "Le collège des chanoines de la Sainte-Chapelle de Paris (1248–1550)." In *L'état moderne et les élites XIIIe–XVIIIe siècles: Apports et limites de la méthode prosopographique*, edited by Jean-Philippe Genet and Günther Lottes, 291–307. Paris: Publications de la Sorbonne, 1996.

———. "L'insertion d'un quartier canonial dans un palais royal, problèmes de cohabitation: L'exemple de la Sainte-Chapelle de Paris." In *Palais royaux et princiers au Moyen Âge: Actes du colloque international tenu au Mans les 6–7 et 8 octobre 1994*, 111–116. Le Mans: Publications de l'Université du Maine, 1996.

Bird, Jessalynn. "The Religious's Role in a Post-Fourth-Lateran World: James of Vitry's *Sermones as Status* and *Historia Occidentalis*." In *Medieval Monastic Preaching*, edited by Carolyn Muessig, 209–230. Leiden: Brill, 1998.

Blamires, Alcuin. "Women and Preaching in Medieval Orthodoxy, Heresy and Saints' Lives." *Viator* 26 (1995): 135–152.

Blumenfeld-Kosinski, Renate. "Satirical Views of the Beguines in Northern French Literature." In *New Trends in Feminine Spirituality: The Holy Women of Liège and Their Impact*, edited by Juliette Dor, Lesley Johnson, and Jocelyn Wogan-Browne, 237–249. Turnhout: Brepols, 1999.

Blumenfeld-Kosinski, Renate, Duncan Robertson, and Nancy Bradley Warren, eds. *The Vernacular Spirit: Essays on Medieval Religious Literature*. New York: Palgrave, 2002.

Bolton, Brenda M. "Mulieres Sanctae." In *Women in Medieval Society*, edited by Susan Mosher Stuard, 141–156. Philadelphia: University of Pennsylvania Press, 1976.

———. "Thirteenth-Century Religious Women: Further Reflections on the Low Countries 'Special Case.'" In *New Trends in Feminine Spirituality: The Holy Women of Liège and Their Impact*, edited by Juliette Dor, Lesley Johnson, and Jocelyn Wogan-Browne, 237–249. Turnhout: Brepols, 1999.

————. "Vitae matrum: A Further Aspect of the Frauenfrage." In *Medieval Women: Dedicated and Presented to Professor Rosalind M. T. Hill on the Occasion of her Seventieth Birthday*, edited by Derek Baker, 253–273. Oxford: Basil Blackwell, 1978.

Bourlet, Caroline. "L'anthroponymie à Paris à la fin du XIIIe siècle d'après les rôles de la taille du règne de Philippe le Bel." In *Genèse médiévale de l'anthroponymie moderne*, edited by Monique Bourin and Pascal Chareille, 9–44. Tours: Publication de l'Université de Tours, 1992.

Bournon, Fernand. "L'Hôtel royal de Saint-Pol." *Mémoires de la société de l'histoire de Paris et de l'Île-de-France* 6 (1879): 54–179.

Boutaric, Edgard. *Saint Louis et Alfonse de Poitiers: Étude sur la réunion des provinces du Midi et de l'Ouest à la couronne et sur les origines de la centralisation administrative d'après des documents inédits*. Paris: H. Plon, 1870.

Bove, Boris. "Espace, piété et parenté à Paris aux XIIIe–XIVe siècles d'après les fondations d'anniversaires des familles échevinales." In *Villes et religion: Mélanges offerts à Jean-Louis Biget*, edited by P. Boucheron and J. Chiffoleau, 253–281. Paris: Publications de la Sorbonne, 2000.

————. *Dominer la ville: Prévôts des marchands et échevins parisiens de 1260 à 1350*. Paris: Editions du CTHS, 2004.

Boynton, Susan. "Training for the Liturgy as a Form of Monastic Education." In *Medieval Monastic Education*, edited by George Ferzoco and Carolyn Muessig, 7–20. London: Leicester University Press, 2000.

Brasher, Sally M. *Women of the Humiliati: A Lay Religious Order in Medieval Civic Life*. New York: Routledge, 2003.

Bremond, Claude, Jacques Le Goff, and Jean-Claude Schmitt. *L'exemplum. Typologie des sources du moyen âge occidental*. Vol. 40. Turnhout: Brepols, 1982.

Brett, Edward T. *Humbert of Romans: His Life and Views of Thirteenth-Century Society*. Toronto: Pontifical Institute of Medieval Studies, 1984.

Brooke, Rosaline B. *The Coming of the Friars*. London: George Allen and Unwin, 1975.

Brown, Elizabeth A. R. "The Religion of Royalty: From Saint Louis to Henry IV (1226–1589)." In *Creating French Culture: Treasures from the Bibliothèque Nationale de France*, edited by Marie-Hélène Tesnière and Prosser Gifford, 130–149. New Haven: Yale University Press, 1995.

Buc, Philippe. "*Vox clamantis in deserto?* Pierre le Chantre et la prédication laïque." *Revue Mabillon* (1993): 5–47.

Bücher, Karl. *Die Frauenfrage im Mittelalter*. 2nd ed. Tubingen: H. Laupp, 1910.

Burgess, Clive. "Late Medieval Wills and Pious Convention: Testamentary Evidence Reconsidered." In *Profit, Piety, and the Professions in Later Medieval England*, edited by Michael Hicks, 14–33. Gloucester: Alan Sutton, 1990.

Burns, E. Jane. *Sea of Silk: A Textile Geography of Women's Work in Medieval French Literature*. Philadelphia: University of Pennsylvania Press, 2009.

Bynum, Caroline Walker. "'And Woman His Humanity': Female Imagery in the Religious Writing of the Later Middle Ages." In *Fragmentation and Redemption: Essays on Gender and the Human Body in Medieval Religion*. New York: Zone Books, 1992.

———. *Holy Feast and Holy Fast: The Religious Significance of Food to Medieval Women.* Berkeley: University of California Press, 1987.

———. "Women's Stories, Women's Symbols. A Critique of Victor Turner's Theory of Liminality." In *Fragmentation and Redemption: Essays on Gender and the Human Body in Medieval Religion.* New York: Zone Books, 1992.

Caciola, Nancy. *Discerning Spirits: Divine and Demonic Possession in the Middle Ages.* Ithaca, NY: Cornell University Press, 2006.

Cazelles, Raymond. *Nouvelle Histoire de Paris, de la fin du règne de Philippe Auguste à la mort de Charles V, 1223–1380.* Paris: Hachette, 1972.

———. "La population de Paris avant la peste noire," *Académie des Inscriptions et Belles Lettres: Comptes Rendus* (Paris, 1260): 539–554.

———. *La société politique et la crise de la royauté sous Philippe de Valois.* Paris: Librairie d'Argences, 1958.

Chapotin, Marie-Dominique. *Histoire des Dominicains de la Province de France: Le siècle des fondations.* Rouen: Impr. Cagniard, 1898.

Coakley, John. "Friars as Confidants of Holy Women in Medieval Dominican Hagiography." In *Images of Sainthood in Medieval Europe,* edited by Renate Blumenfeld-Kosinski and Timea Szell, 222–246. Ithaca, NY: Cornell University Press, 1991.

———. "Friars, Sanctity, and Gender: Mendicant Encounters with Saints, 1250–1325." In *Medieval Masculinities: Regarding Men in the Middle Ages,* edited by Clare Lees, 91–110. Minneapolis: University of Minnesota Press, 1994.

———. "Gender and Authority of the Friars: The Significance of Holy Women for Thirteenth-Century Franciscans and Dominicans." *Church History* 60 (1991): 445–460.

———. "Thomas of Cantimpré and Female Sanctity." In *History in the Comic Mode: Medieval Communities and the Matter of Person,* edited by Rachel Fulton and Bruce Holsinger, 45–55 New York: Columbia University Press, 2007.

———. *Women, Men, and Spiritual Power: Female Saints and Their Male Collaborators.* New York: Columbia University Press, 2006.

Colledge, Edmund, J. C. Marler, and Judith Grant. "Introductory Interpretive Essay." In *Margaret Porette: The Mirror of Simple Souls.* Notre Dame, IN: University of Notre Dame Press, 1999.

Congar, Yves M.-J. "Aspects ecclésiologiques de la querelle entre mendicants et séculiers dans la seconde moitié du XIIIe et le début du XIVe." *Archives d'histoire doctrinale et littéraire du moyen âge* 28 (1961–1962): 35–151.

Connally, Michael. "Les 'Bonnes Femmes' de Paris: Des communautés religieuses dans une société urbaine du bas Moyen Âge." Docoral thesis, University of Lyon, II, 2003.

Constable, Giles. "The Interpretation of Mary and Martha." In *Three Studies in Medieval Religious and Social Thought,* 1–141. Cambridge: Cambridge University Press, 1995.

———. *The Reformation of the Twelfth Century.* Cambridge: Cambridge University Press, 1996.

Dale, Marian K. "The London Silkworkers of the Fifteenth Century" In *Sisters and Workers in the Middle Ages,* edited by Elizabeth Clark, Judith Bennett, Jean F. O'Barr, and B. Anne Vilen, 26–38. Chicago: University of Chicago Press, 1989.

Dansette, Béatrice. "Les pèlerins occidentaux du moyen âge tardif au retour de la Terre sainte: Confréries du Saint-Sépulcre et paumiers parisiens." In *Dei gesta per Francos: Études sur les croisades dédiées à Jean Richard,* edited by Benjamin Z. Kedar, Michael Balard, and Jonathan Riley-Smith, 301–314. Aldershot, U.K.: Ashgate, 2001.

Davis, Natalie Zemon. "Women in the Crafts in Sixteenth- Century Lyon." *Feminist Studies* 8 (Spring 1982): 47–80.

D'Avray, David. *The Preaching of the Friars: Sermons Diffused from Paris Before 1300* (Oxford: Oxford University Press, 1985).

Deane, Jennifer K. "Beguines Reconsidered: Historiographical Problems and New Directions." *Monastic Matrix* (2008), Commentaria 3461, available at http://monasticmatrix.org/commentaria/article.php?textId=3461

———. "*Geistliche Schwestern:* The Pastoral Care of Lay Religious Women in Wuerzburg." In *Partners in Spirit: Women, Men and Religious Life in Germany, 1100–1500,* edited by Fiona Griffith and Julie Hotchin (Turnhout: Brepols, forthcoming).

———. *A History of Medieval Heresy and Inquisition.* New York: Rowman and Littlefield, 2011.

Dechesne, A. *Historiae Francorum Scriptores.* 5 vols. Vol. 5. Paris, 1636–1649.

De La Force, Piganiol. *Description historique de la ville de Paris et de ses environs.* Vol. 5. Paris: Les Libraires Associés, 1765.

De La Selle, Xavier. *Le service des âmes à la cour: Confesseurs et aumôniers des rois de France du XIIIe au XVe siècle.* Vol. 43, *Mémoires et documents de l'École des Chartes.* Paris: École des Chartes, 1995.

Delmaire, Bernard. "Les béguines dans le Nord de la France au premier siècle de leur histoire (vers 1230–vers 1350)." In *Les religieuses en France au XIIIe siècle,* edited by Michel Parisse, 121–162. Nancy: Presses Universitaires de Nancy, 1985.

De Miramon, Charles. *Les donnés au Moyen Âge: Une forme de vie religieuse laïque, v. 1180–v. 1500.* Paris: Cerf, 1999.

De Roover, Florence Elder. "Lucchese Silks." *Ciba Review* 80 (1950): 2902–2030.

Diefendorf, Barbara B. *Paris City Councillors in the Sixteenth Century: The Politics of Patrimony.* Princeton, NJ: Princeton University Press, 1983.

Douie, Decima L. *The Conflict Between the Seculars and the Mendicants at the University of Paris in the Thirteenth Century.* London: Blackfriars, 1954.

Dufeil, Michel-Marie. *Guillaume de Saint-Amour et la polémique universitaire parisienne, 1250–1259.* Paris: J. Picard, 1972.

———. "Le roi Louis dans la querelle des mendiants et des séculiers." In *Septième centenaire de la mort de Saint Louis: Actes des colloques de Royaument et de Paris (21–27 mai 1970),* 281–289. Paris: Les Belles Lettres, 1976.

Duvivier, Charles A. *La querelle des d'Avesnes et des Dampierre jusqu'à la mort de Jean d'Avesnes (1257).* Brussels: Librairie européenne C. Muquardt, 1894.

Elliott, Dyan. "Dress as Mediator Between Inner and Outer Self: The Pious Matron of the High and Later Middle Ages." *Mediaeval Studies* 53 (1991): 279–308.

———. *Proving Woman: Female Spirituality and Inquisitional Culture in the Later Middle Ages.* Princeton, NJ: Princeton University Press, 2004.

———. "Seeing Double: John Gerson, the Discernment of Spirits, and Joan of Arc." *American Historical Review* 107 (2002): 26–54.

Emery, Richard W. *The Friars in Medieval France: A Catalogue of French Mendicant Convents, 1200–1550*. New York: Columbia University Press, 1962.

Faral, Edmond. "Pour le commentaire de Rutebeuf: Le dit des 'règles.'" *Studi Medievali* 16 (1943–1950): 176–211.

Farmer, Sharon. "Biffes, Tiretaines, and Aumonières: The Role of Paris in the International Textile Markets of the Thirteenth and Fourteenth Centuries." In *Medieval Clothing and Textiles II,* edited by Robin Netherton and Gale R. Owen-Crocker, 73–79. Woodbridge: Boydell and Brewer, 2006.

———. "Down and Out and Female in Thirteenth-Century Paris." *American Historical Review* 103, no. 2 (1998): 345–372.

———. "'It Is Not Good That [Wo]Man Should Be Alone': Elite Responses to Singlewomen in High Medieval Paris." In *Singlewomen in the European Past, 1250–1800,* edited by Judith M. Bennett and Amy M. Froide, 82–105. Philadelphia: University of Pennsylvania Press, 1999.

———. "Merchant Women and the Administrative Glass Ceiling in Thirteenth-Century Paris." In *Women and Wealth in Late Medieval Europe,* edited by Theresa Earenfight, 89–108. New York: Palgrave Macmillan, 2010.

———. "Persuasive Voices: Clerical Images of Medieval Wives." *Speculum* 61 (1986): 517–543.

———. *Surviving Poverty in Medieval Paris: Gender, Ideology, and the Daily Lives of the Poor*. Ithaca, NY: Cornell University Press, 2002.

Ferruolo, Stephen C. *The Origins of the University: The Schools of Paris and Their Critics, 1100–1215*. Stanford: Stanford University Press, 1985.

Field, Sean L. *The Beguine, the Angel, and the Inquisitor: The Trials of Marguerite Porete and Guiard of Cressonessart*. Notre Dame, IN: University of Notre Dame Press, 2012.

———. *Isabelle of France: Capetian Sanctity and Franciscan Identity in the Thirteenth Century*. Notre Dame, IN: University of Notre Dame Press, 2006.

———. "The Master and Marguerite: Godfrey of Fontaines's Praise of *The Mirror of Simple Souls*." *Journal of Medieval History* 35 (2009): 136–149.

Folkerts, Suzan. "The Manuscript Transmission of the Vita Mariae Oigniacensis in the Later Middle Ages." In *Mary of Oignies: A Mother of Salvation,* edited by Anekke B. Mulder-Bakker, 221–241. Turnhout: Brepols, 2006.

Frappier-Bigras, Diane. "La famille dans l'artisanat parisien du XIIIe siècle." *Le moyen âge* 95 (1989): 47–74.

Freed, John. "Urban Development and the 'Cura Monialium' in Thirteenth-Century Germany." *Viator* 3 (1972): 311–327.

Frémaux, Henri. "La Famille d'Étienne Marcel, 1250–1397." *Mémoires de la société de l'histoire de Paris et de l'Île-de-France* 30 (1903): 175–242.

Gabriel, Astrik L. "The Ideal Master of the Medieval University." *Catholic Historical Review* 60 (1974): 1–40.

———. *The Paris Studium: Robert of Sorbonne and His Legacy: Interuniversity Exchange*

Between the German, Cracow and Louvain Universities and That of Paris in the Late Medieval and Humanistic Period: Selected Studies. Texts and Studies in the History of Mediaeval Education 10. Notre Dame, IN: United States Subcommission for the History of Universities, University of Notre Dame Press, 1992.

Galloway, Penelope. "'Life, Learning and Wisdom': The Forms and Functions of Beguine Education." In *Medieval Monastic Education*, edited by George Ferzoco and Carolyn Muessig, 153–167. London: Leicester University Press, 2000.

———. "Neither Miraculous nor Astonishing: The Devotional Practice of Beguine Communities in French Flanders." In *New Trends in Feminine Spirituality: The Holy Women of Liège and Their Impact*, edited by Juliette Dor, Lesley Johnson, and Jocelyn Wogan-Browne, 107–127. Turnhout: Brepols, 1999.

Gaposchkin, Cecilia. "Boniface VIII, Philip the Fair, and the Sanctity of Louis IX." *Journal of Medieval History* 29, no. 1 (2003): 1–26.

Gelser, Erica. "Lay Religious Women and Church Reform in Late Medieval Münster: A Case Study of the Beguines." Ph.D. dissertation, University of Pennsylvania, 2008.

Geremek, Bronislaw. *The Margins of Society in Late Medieval Paris.* Translated by Jean Birrell. Cambridge: Cambridge University Press, 1987.

Giesey, Ralph E. "Rules of Inheritance and Strategies of Mobility in Pre-Revolutionary France." *American Historical Review* 82 (1977): 271–289.

Glorieux, Palémon. *Aux origines de la Sorbonne.* Vol. 1, *Robert de Sorbon, l'homme, le collège, les documents.* Études de philosophie médiévale 53. Paris: J. Vrin, 1966.

Gourmelon, Roger. "L'industrie et le commerce des draps à Paris du XIIIe au XVIe siècle." Doctoral thesis, École des Chartes, 1950.

Greven, Josef. *Die Anfänge der Beginen: Ein Beitrag zur Geschichte der Volksfrömmigkeit und des Ordenswesens im Hochmittelalter.* Münster: Aschendorffsche Verlagsbuchhandlung, 1912.

Griffiths, Fiona. *The Garden of Delights: Reform and Renaissance for Women in the Twelfth Century.* Philadelphia: University of Pennsylvania Press, 2007.

———. "'Men's Duty to Provide for Women's Needs': Abelard, Heloise, and Their Negotiation of the *Cura Monialium.*" *Journal of Medieval History* 30 (2004): 1–24.

Grundmann, Herbert. *Religious Movements in the Middle Ages: The Historical Links Between Heresy, the Mendicant Orders, and the Women's Religious Movement in the Twelfth and Thirteenth Century, with the Historical Foundations of German Mysticism.* Translated by Stevan Rowan. Notre Dame, IN: University of Notre Dame Press, 1995.

Guerot, Jean. "Fiscalité, topographie, et démographie à Paris au Moyen Âge (à propos d'une publication recente de rôles d'impôt)." *Bibliothèque de l'École des Chartes* 130 (1972): 32–129, 383–465.

Hallam, Elizabeth M. "Philip the Fair and the Cult of Saint Louis." *Studies in Church History* 18 (1982): 201–214.

Hamburger, Jeffrey. *The Visual and the Visionary: Art and Female Spirituality in Late Medieval Germany.* New York: Zone Books, 1998.

Hanawalt, Barbara, ed. *Women and Work in Preindustrial Europe.* Bloomington: University of Indiana Press, 1986.

Hanley, Sarah. "Engendering the State: Family Formation and State Building in Early Modern France." *French Historical Studies* 16, no. 1 (1989): 4–27.

Hasenohr, Geneviève, "D'une 'poésie de béguine' à une 'poétique des béguines': Aperçus sur la forme et la réception des textes (France, XIIIe–XIVe siècles)." *Comptes rendus des séances de l'Académie des inscriptions et belles-lettres*, 150, no. 2 (2006): 913–943.

Hedeman, Anne. "Valois Legitimacy: Editorial Changes in Charles V's Grandes Chroniques de France." *Art Bulletin* 66 (1984): 97–117.

Henneman, John Bell. *Royal Taxation in Fourteenth Century France: The Development of War Financing, 1322–1356*. Princeton, NJ: Princeton University Press, 1971.

Herlihy, David. *Opera Muliebria: Women and Work in Medieval Europe* (Philadelphia: Temple University Press, 1990).

Hilka, Alfons. "Altfranzösische Mystik und Beginentum." *Zeitschrift für romanische Philologie* 47 (1927): 121–170.

Hollywood, Amy. *The Soul as Virgin Wife: Mechthild of Magdeburg, Marguerite Porete, and Meister Eckhart*. Notre Dame, IN: University of Notre Dame Press, 1995.

Horie, Ruth. *Perceptions of Ecclesia: Church and Soul in Medieval Dedication Sermons*. Turnhout: Brepols, 2006.

Howell, Martha C. "Fixing Movables: Gifts by Testament in Late Medieval Douai." *Past and Present* 150 (1995): 3–45.

———. *The Marriage Exchange: Property, Social Place, and Gender in Cities of the Low Countries, 1300–1550*. Women in Culture and Society. Chicago: University of Chicago Press, 1998.

———. *Women, Production, and Patriarchy in Late Medieval Cities*. Women in Culture and Society. Chicago: University of Chicago Press, 1986.

———. "Women, the Family Economy, and the Structures of Market Production in the Cities of Northern Europe During the Late Middle Ages." In *Women and Work in Pre-Industrial Europe*, edited by Barbara Hanawalt, 198–222: Bloomington: Indiana University Press, 1986.

Hunt, Tony, ed. *Les Cantiques Salemon: The Song of Songs in MS Paris BNF fr. 14966*. Turnhout: Brepols, 2006.

Huot, Sylvia. "Popular Piety and Devotional Literature: An Old French Rhyme About the Passion and Its Textual History." *Romania* 115 (1997): 451–494.

———. *The* Romance of the Rose *and Its Medieval Readers: Interpretation, Reception, Manuscript Transmission*. Cambridge: Cambridge University Press, 1993.

Hutton, Shennan. *Women and Economic Activities in Late Medieval Ghent*. New York: Palgrave Macmillan, 2011.

Jansen, Katherine L. *The Making of the Magdalen: Preaching and Popular Devotion in the Later Middle Ages*. Princeton, NJ: Princeton University Press, 2000.

Johnson, Penelope D. *Equal in Monastic Profession: Religious Women in Medieval France*. Women in Culture and Society. Chicago: University of Chicago Press, 1991.

Jordan, William Chester. "The Case of Saint Louis." *Viator* 19 (1988): 209–218.

———. *The French Monarchy and the Jews: From Philip Augustus to the Last Capetians*. Philadelphia: University of Pennsylvania Press, 1989.

————. "Isabelle of France and Religious Devotion at the Court of Louis IX." In *Capetian Women*, edited by Kathleen Nolan, 209–223. New York: Palgrave Macmillan, 2003.

————. *Louis IX and the Challenge of the Crusade: A Study in Rulership*. Princeton, NJ: Princeton University Press, 1979.

Karras, Ruth Mazo. *Boys to Men: Formations of Masculinity in Late Medieval Europe*. Philadelphia: University of Pennsylvania Press, 2003.

————. "Sex and the Singlewoman." In *Singlewomen in the European Past, 1250–1800*, edited by Judith M. Bennett and Amy M. Froide, 127–145. Philadelphia: University of Pennsylvania Press, 1999.

————. "Using Women to Think with in the Medieval University." In *Seeing and Knowing: Women and Learning in Medieval Europe 1200–1550*, edited by Anneke B. Mulder-Bakker, 21–34. Turnhout: Brepols, 2004.

Keyser, Walter De. "Aspects de la ville béguinale à Mons aux XIIIe et XIV siècles." In *Autour de la ville en Hainaut: Mélanges d'archéologie et d'histoire urbains offerts à J. Dugnoille et à René Sansen. Études et documents du cercle royal d'histoire et d'archéologie d'Ath et de la région et musées athois*, 205–226. Ath: CRHAA, 1986.

Kittell, Ellen E. "Testaments of Two Cities: A Comparative Analysis of the Wills of Medieval Genoa and Douai." *European Review of History* 5, no. 1 (1998): 47–82.

Klaniczay, Gàbor. "*Beata Stirps*: Sainteté et lignage en Occident aux XIIIe et XIVe siècles." In *Famille et parenté dans l'Occident médiéval*, edited by Georges Duby and Jacques Le Goff, 397–406. Rome: École Française de Rome, 1977.

————. *Holy Rulers and Blessed Princesses: Dynastic Cults in Medieval Central Europe*. Translated by Éva Pálmai. Cambridge: Cambridge University Press, 2002.

Kocher, Suzanne. *Allegories of Love in Marguerite Porete's Mirror of Simple Souls*. Turnhout: Brepols, 2009.

Koorn, Florence W. J. *Begijnhoven in Holland en Zeeland gedurende de middeleeuwen*. Assen: Van Gorcum, 1981.

Lacey, Kay. "The Production of 'Narrow Ware' by Silkwomen in Fourteenth and Fifteenth Century England." *Textile History* 18, no. 2 (1987): 187–204.

Lambert, Malcolm. *Medieval Heresy: Popular Movements from the Gregorian Reform to the Reformation*. 3rd edition. Malden, MA: Blackwell, 2001.

Lauwers, Michel. "Entre béguinisme et mysticisme: La vie de Marie d'Oignies (1213) de Jacques of Vitry ou la définition d'une sainteté féminine." *Ons geestelijk erf* 66 (1992): 46–70.

————. "Expérience béguinale et récit hagiographique: À propos de la 'Vita Mariæ Oigniacensis' de Jacques de Vitry (vers 1215)." *Journal des savants* (1989): 61–103.

————. *La mémoire des ancêtres, le souci des morts: Morts, rites et société au moyen âge (diocèse de Liège, XIe–XIIIe siècles)*. Paris: Beauchesne, 1996.

————. "Praedicatio–Exhortatio: L'Église, la réforme, et les laïcs (XIe et XIIe siècles)." In *La Parole de prèdicateur, Ve–XVe siècle*, edited by R. M. Dessi and M. Lauwers, 187–232. Nice: Centre d'Études médiévales, 1997.

LaVere, Suzanne. "From Contemplation to Action: The Role of the Active Life in the Glossa ordinaria on the Song of Songs." *Speculum* 82, no. 1 (2007): 54–69.

Le Goff, Jacques. *Saint Louis*. Translated by Gareth E. Gollard. Notre Dame, IN: University of Notre Dame Press, 2009,

Le Grand, Léon. "Les béguines de Paris." *Mémoires de la société de l'histoire de Paris et de l'Île-de-France* 20 (1893): 295–357.

———. "Les Quinze-Vingts: Depuis leur fondation jusqu'à leur translation au Faubourg Saint-Antoine." *Mémoires de la Société de l'histoire de Paris et de l'Île-de-France* 13 (1886): 105–260.

Lerner, Robert E. "An 'Angel of Philadelphia' in the Reign of Philip the Fair: The Case of Guiard de Cressonessart." In *Order and Innovation in the Middle Ages: Essays in Honor of Joseph R. Strayer*, 343–364: Princeton, NJ: Princeton University Press, 1976.

———. "A Collection of Sermons Given in Paris c. 1267, Including a New Text by Saint Bonaventure on the Life of Saint Francis." *Speculum* 49 (1974): 466–498.

———. *The Heresy of the Free Spirit in the Later Middle Ages*. [1972.] Reprint, Notre Dame, IN: University of Notre Dame Press, 1991.

Little, Lester K. *Religious Poverty and the Profit Economy in Medieval Europe*. Ithaca, NY: Cornell University Press, 1978.

———. "Saint Louis' Involvement with the Friars." *Church History* 33, no. 2 (1964): 125–148.

Loats, Carol L. "Gender, Guilds, and Work Identity: Perspectives from Sixteenth-Century Paris." *French Historical Studies* 20, no. 1 (1997): 5–30.

Longére, Jean. "La femme dans la théologie pastorale." *Cahiers de Fanjeaux* 23 (1988): 127–152.

Mabille, Madeleine. "Les manuscrits d'Étienne d'Abbeville conservés à la Bibliothèque Nationale de Paris." *Bibliothèque de l'École des Chartes* 132 (1974): 245–266.

———. "Les manuscrits de Jean d'Essômes conservés à la Bibliothèque Nationale de Paris." *Bibliothèque de l'École des Chartes* 130 (1972): 231–234.

Makowski, Elizabeth. *"A Pernicious Sort of Woman": Quasi-Religious Women and Canon Lawyers in the Later Middle Ages*. Washington, DC: Catholic University of America Press, 2005.

McDonnell, Ernest W. *The Beguines and Beghards in Medieval Culture: With Special Emphasis on the Belgian Scene*. New Brunswick, NJ: Rutgers University Press, 1954.

McGinn, Bernard. *The Flowering of Mysticism: Men and Women in the New Mysticism, 1200–1350*. Vol. 3, *The Presence of God: A History of Western Christian Mysticism*. New York: Crossroad, 1998.

———. *Meister Eckhart and the Beguine Mystics: Hadewijch of Brabant, Mechthild of Magdeburg, and Marguerite Porete*. New York: Continuum, 1994.

McNamara, Jo Ann. "The Need to Give: Suffering and Female Sanctity in the Middle Ages." In *Images of Sainthood in Medieval Europe*, edited by Renate Blumenthal-Kosinski and Timea Szell, 199–221. Ithaca, NY: Cornell University Press, 1991.

———. "Rhetoric of Orthodoxy: Clerical Authority and Female Innovation in the Struggle with Heresy." In *Maps of Flesh and Light: The Experiences of Medieval Women Mystics*, edited by Ulrike Weithaus, 9–27. Syracuse, NY: Syracuse University Press, 1993.

McNamer, Sarah. *Affective Meditation and the Invention of Medieval Compassion*. Philadelphia: University of Pennsylvania Press, 2009.

Meersseman, G. G. "Les frères prêcheurs et le mouvement dévot au Flandre au XIIIe siè-cle." *Archivum Fratrum Praedicatorum* 18 (1948): 69–130.

Miller, Tanya Stabler. " 'Love Is Beguine': Labeling Lay Religiosity in Thirteenth-Century Paris," in *Labels and Libels: Naming Beguines in Northern Medieval Europe.* Edited by Letha Böhringer, Jennifer K. Deane, and Hildo van Engen. Turnhout: Brepols, 2014.

———. "Mirror of the Scholarly (Masculine) Soul: Thinking with Beguines in the Colleges of Medieval Paris." In *Negotiating Clerical Identities: Priests, Monks, and Masculinity in the Middle Ages.* Edited by Jennifer Thibodeaux, 238–264. New York: Palgrave Macmillan, 2010.

———. "What's in a Name? Clerical Representations of Parisian Beguines (1200–1328)." *Journal of Medieval History* 33, no. 1 (2007): 60–86.

Minnis, Alastair J. "*De impedimento sexus*: Women's Bodies and Medieval Impediments to Female Ordination," in *Medieval Theology and the Natural Body.* Edited by Peter Biller and Alastair J. Minnis. 103–139. York, U.K.: York University Press, 1997.

Mooney, Catherine M. "The Authorial Role of Brother A. in the Composition of Angela of Foligno's Revelations." In *Creative Women in Medieval and Early Modern Italy*, edited by E. Ann Matter and John Coakley, 34–63. Philadelphia: University of Pennsylvania Press, 1994.

———. *Gendered Voices: Medieval Saints and Their Interpreters.* Philadelphia: University of Pennsylvania Press, 1999.

Morenzoni, Franco. *Des écoles aux paroisses: Thomas de Chobham et la promotion de la prédication au début du XIIIe siècle.* Paris: Institut d' études augustiniennes, 1995.

Mosheim, Johann Lorenz. *De Beghardis et Beguinabus commentarius.* Edited by G. H. Martini. Leipzig: Libraria Weidmannia, 1790.

Muessig, Carolyn. "Prophecy and Song: Teaching and Preaching by Medieval Women," in *Women Preachers and Prophets Through Two Millennia of Christianity.* Edited by Beverly Kienzle and Pamela Walker, 146–159. Berkeley: University of California Press, 1998.

Mulchahey, Marian Michèle. *First the Bow Is Bent in Study: Dominican Education Before 1350.* Toronto: Pontifical Institute of Medieval Studies, 1998.

Mulder-Bakker, Anneke B. "Introduction." In *Seeing and Knowing: Women and Learning in Medieval Europe, 1200–1550*, 1–19. Turnhout: Brepols, 2004.

———. "The Metamorphosis of Woman: The Transmission of Knowledge and the Problems of Gender." In *Gendering the Middle Ages,* edited by Pauline Stafford and Anneke B. Mulder Bakker, 112–134, special issue of *Gender and History* (2001).

Müller, Ewald. *Das Konzil von Vienne 1311–1312.* Münster: Aschendorff, 1934.

Munro, John. "Silk." In *Dictionary of the Middle Ages*, edited by Joseph R. Strayer, 293–296. New York: Charles Scribner's Sons/Macmillan, 1988.

Newman, Barbara. "La mystique courtoise: Thirteenth-Century Beguines and the Art of Love." In *From Virile Woman to Womanchrist: Studies in Medieval Religion and Literature*, 137–167. Philadelphia: University of Pennsylvania Press, 1995.

———. *Medieval Crossover: Reading the Secular Against the Sacred* (Notre Dame, IN: University of Notre Dame Press, 2013).

———. "What Did It Mean to Say 'I Saw'? The Clash Between Theory and Practice in Medieval Visionary Culture." *Speculum* 80 (2005): 1–43.

O'Sullivan, Robin. "The School of Love: Marguerite Porete's Mirror of Simple Souls." *Journal of Medieval History* 32 (2006): 143–162.

O'Toole, Mark P. "Caring for the Blind in Medieval Paris: Life at the Quinze-Vingts, 1250–1430." Ph.D. dissertation, University of California, Santa Barbara, 2007.

Oliver, Judith. "Devotional Psalters and the Study of Beguine Spirituality." *Vox Benedictina* 9 no. 2 (1992): 199–225.

Olivier-Martin, François. *Histoire de la coutume de la prévôté et de la vicomté de Paris*. 2 vols. Paris: E. Leroux, 1922–1930.

Peters, Günter. "Die Bremer Beginen im Mittelalter: Entstehung und Struktur einer städtischen Frauengemeinschaft." *Niedersächsisches Jahrbuch für Landesgeschichte* 64 (1992): 131–181.

Peters, Ursula. *Religiöse Erfahrung als literarisches Faktum: Zur Vorgeschichte und Genese frauenmystischer Texte des 13. und 14. Jahrhunderts*. Tübingen: Niemeyer, 1988.

Petroff, Elizabeth. "Male Confessors and Female Penitents: Possibilities for Dialogue." In *Body and Soul: Essays on Medieval Women and Mysticism*, 139–160. New York: Oxford University Press, 1994.

Peuchmaurd, M. "Mission canonique et prédication: Le prêtre ministre de la parole dans la querelle entre mendiants et séculiers au XIIIe siècle." *Recherches et Théologie Ancienne et Médiévale* 30 (1963): 122–144, 251–276.

Philippen, L. J. M. *De begijnhoven, oorsprong, geschiedenis, inrichting*. Antwerp: Veritas, 1918.

Phillips, Dayton. *The Beguines in Medieval Strasbourg: A Study of the Social Aspect of Beguine Life*. Ann Arbor, MI: Edwards, 1941.

Pissart, Madeleine, "L'Administration du béguinage de Saint-Christophe à Liège." *Bulletin de la Société Royale "Le Vieux Liège"* 97 (1952): 113–130.

Poncelet, Edouard. *Chartes du prieuré d'Oignies de l'Ordre de Saint-Augustin*. Namur: Wesmael-Charlier, 1912.

Prévost, Danièle. *Le personnel de la chambre des comptes de Paris de 1320 à 1418*. Villeneuve-d'Ascq: Presses universitaires du septentrion, 2003.

Rapp, Francis. "Rapport introductif." In *Le clerc séculier au Moyen Âge: Actes du XXIIème Congrès de la Société des historiens médiévistes de l'enseignement supérieur public, Amiens, 1991*, 9–25. Paris: Publications de la Sorbonne, 1993.

Rashdall, Hastings. *Universities of Europe in the Middle Ages*, 3 vols. Edited by F. M. Powicke and A. B. Emden. Oxford: Clarendon Press, 1936.

Reichstein, Frank-Michael. *Das Beginenwesen in Deutschland: Studien und Katalog*. Berlin: Verlag Dr. Köster, 2001.

Richard, Jules-Marie. *Une petite nièce de Saint Louis: Mahaut, comtesse d'Artois et de Bourgogne*. Paris: H. Champion, 1887.

Roberts, Phyllis B. "Sermons and Preaching in/and the Medieval University." In *Medieval Education*, edited by Ronald B. Begley and Joseph W. Koterski, 83–98. New York: Fordham University Press, 2005.

Röckelein, Hedwig. "Hamburger Beginen im Spatmittelalter—'Autonome' oder 'fremd-bestimmte' Frauengemeinschaft?" *Das Mittelalter* 12 (1996): 73–88.

Roisin, Simone. "La méthode hagiographique de Thomas de Cantimpré." In *Miscellanea Historica in Honorem Alberti de Meyer,* 1: 546–557. Louvain: Bibliothèque de l'Université, 1946.

———. "L'efflorescence cistercienne et le courant féminin de piété au XIII siècle." *Revue d'histoire ecclésiastique* 39 (1943): 342–378.

Rouse, Richard H. "The Early Library of the Sorbonne." *Scriptorium* 21 (1967): 42–71, 227–245.

Rouse, Richard H., and Mary A. Rouse. *Preachers,* Florilegia, *and Sermons: Studies on the* Manipulus Florum *of Thomas of Ireland,* Studies and Texts, 47. Toronto: Pontifical Institute of Mediaeval Studies, 1979.

Roux, Simone. "Les femmes dans les métiers parisiens: XIIIe–XVe siècles." *CLIO* 3 (1996): 13–30.

———. *Paris in the Middle Ages.* Translated by Jo Ann McNamara. Philadelphia: University of Pennsylvania Press, 2009.

Ruh, Kurt. "Beginenmystik: Hadewijch, Mechthild von Magdeburg, Marguerite Porete." *Zeitschrift für Deutsches Altertum und Deutsche Literatur* 106 (1977): 265–277.

Schmitt, Jean-Claude. *Mort d'une hérésie: L'Église et les clercs face aux béguines et aux béghards du Rhin supérieur du XIVe au XVe siècle.* Paris: Mouton, 1978.

Schnerb, Bernard. *Armagnacs et Bourguigons, la maudite guerre.* Paris: Perrin, 1988.

Sells, Michael. *Mystical Languages of Unsaying.* Chicago: University of Chicago Press, 1994.

Simons, Walter. "Beguines, Liturgy and Music in the Middle Ages: An Exploration." In *Beghinae in cantu instructae: Musical Patrimony from Flemish Beguinages (Middle Ages–Late 18th Century,* edited by Pieter Mannaerts, 15–25. Turnhout: Brepols, 2009.

———."The Beguine Movement in the Southern Low Countries: A Reassessment." *Bulletin van het Belgisch Historisch Instituut te Rome/Bulletin de l'Institut Historique Belge de Rome* 59 (1989): 63–105.

———. *Cities of Ladies: Beguine Communities in the Medieval Low Countries, 1200–1565.* Philadelphia: University of Pennsylvania Press, 2001.

———. "Holy Women of the Low Countries: A Survey." In *Medieval Holy Women in the Christian Tradition: c. 1100–c. 1500,* edited by A. J. Minnis and Rosalynn Voaden, 625–662. Turnhout: Brepols, 2010.

———. "'Staining the Speech of Things Divine': The Uses of Literacy in Medieval Beguine Communities." In *The Voice of Silence: Women's Literacy in a Men's Church,* edited by Thérèse de Hemptinne and María Eugenia Góngora, 85–110. Turnhout: Brepols, 2004.

Smalley, Beryl. *The Study of the Bible in the Middle Ages.* 3rd edition. Oxford: Blackwell, 1983.

Smith, Margit. "The Medieval Girdle Book Project" (with Jim Bloxam). *International Journal of the Book* 3, no. 4 (2006): 15–24.

Stock, Brian. *The Implications of Literacy: Written Language and Models of Interpretation in the Eleventh and Twelfth Centuries.* Princeton, NJ: Princeton University Press, 1983.

Strayer, Joseph R. "France: The Holy Land, the Chosen People, and the Most Christian King." In *Medieval Statecraft and the Perspectives of History: Essays by Joseph R. Strayer*, edited by J. F. Benton and T. N. Bisson, 300–315. Princeton, NJ: Princeton University Press, 1971.

Sweetman, Robert. "Dominican Preaching in the Southern Low Countries, 1240–1260: *Materiae Praedicabiles* in the *Liber de natura rerum* and *Bonum universale de apibus* of Thomas of Cantimpré." Ph.D. dissertation, University of Toronto, 1988.

———."Thomas of Cantimpré, 'Mulieres Religiosae,' and Purgatorial Piety: Hagiographical 'Vitae' and the Beguine 'Voice.' " In *A Distinct Voice: Medieval Studies in Honor of Leonard E. Boyle, O.P*, edited by Jacqueline Brown and William P. Stoneman, 606–628. Notre Dame, IN: University of Notre Dame Press, 1997.

Szittya, Penn R. *The Antifraternal Tradition in Medieval Literature*. Princeton, NJ: Princeton University Press, 1986.

Tarrant, Jacqueline. "The Clementine Decrees on the Beguines: Conciliar and Papal Versions." *Archivum historiae pontificae* 12 (1974): 300–308.

Terroine, Anne. *Un bourgeois parisien du XIIIe siècle: Geoffroi de Saint-Laurent, 1245?–1290*, edited by Lucie Fossier. Paris: CNRS, 1992.

———. "Recherches sur la bourgeoisie parisienne au XIIIe siècle." Doctoral thesis, École des Chartes, 1940.

Thijssen, J. M. M. H., *Censure and Heresy at the University of Paris, 1200–1400*. Philadelphia: University of Pennsylvania Press, 1998.

Thompson, Guy L. *Paris and Its People Under English Rule: The Anglo-Burgundian Regime, 1420–1436*. Oxford: Clarendon Press, 1991.

Trexler, Richard. "Charity and the Defense of Urban Elites in the Italian Communes." In *The Rich, the Well Born, and the Powerful*, edited by Frederic Cople Jaher, 64–109. Urbana: University of Illinois Press, 1973.

Vauchez, André. "Prosélytisme et action antihérétique en milieu féminin au XIIIe siècle: La Vie de Marie d'Oignies (d. 1213) par James of Vitry." In *Propagande et contre-propagande religieuses*, edited by Jacques Marx, 95–110. Brussels: Editions de l'Universitaire, 1987.

Vidier, Alexandre. "Notes et documents sur le personnel, les biens et l'administration de la Sainte-Chapelle du XIIIe au XVe siècle." *Mémoires de la société de l'Histoire de Paris et de l'Île-de-France* 28 (1901): 213–383.

Vignat, Gaston. "Notes sur une des chapelles absidales de la basilique de Sainte-Croix d'Orléans." *Mémoires de la société archéologique de l'orléanais* 9 (1866): 100–144.

Waters, Clare M. *Angels and Earthly Creatures: Preaching, Performance, and Gender in the Later Middle Ages*. Philadelphia: University of Pennsylvania Press, 2004.

Wiesner, Merry. "Spinsters and Seamstresses: Women in Cloth and Clothing Production." In *Rewriting the Renaissance: The Discourses of Sexual Difference in Early Modern Europe*, edited by Maureen Quilligan, Margaret W. Ferguson, and Nancy J. Vickers, 191–205. Chicago: University of Chicago Press, 1986.

Wilts, Andreas. *Beginen im Bodenseeraum*. Sigmaringen: Thorbecke, 1994.

Ziegler, Joanna. "The *Curtis* Beguinages in the Southern Low Countries: Interpretation and Historiography." *Bulletin van het Belgisch Historisch Instituut te Rome/Bulletin de l'Institut Historique Belge de Rome* 57 (1987): 31–70.

———. "Reality as Imitation: The Dynamics of Imagery Among the Beguines." In *Maps of Flesh and Light: New Perspectives on the Religious Experience of Late Medieval Women*, edited by Ulrike Wiethaus, 112–126. Syracuse, NY: Syracuse University Press, 1993.

———. *Sculpture of Compassion: The Pietà and the Beguines in the Southern Low Countries, c. 1300–1600*. Brussels: Institut Historique Belge de Rome, 1992.

INDEX

Page references in italics refer to illustrations.

Abelard, on confession, 235n116
Ade of Senlis, 73; tax assessment of, 64, 72
Ad nostrum (decree), 4, 142–44
Agatha la Petite, property of, 202n141
Agnes (silk worker), 73
Agnes de La Tache, 66, 207n44; noble clients of, 79
Agnes de Senliz, 254n2
Agnes of Orchies, 27, 40, 187n101; tomb of, 109, *110*
Alexander IV, Pope, 21
Alice de Malaisie, 56
Alice of Saint-Joce, 64, 207n37, 254n7
Alice of Saint-Quentin, royal pension of, 245n30
almonry, royal, 149, 151, 164–65, 196n64; for laywomen, 195n59; under Louis IX, 181n12; under Philip IV, 147, 244n12
Alphonse of Poitiers, 44; bequest to beguines, 147, 244n16
Ameline (silk worker), 73, 213n101, 254n3
Amour verses (Old French), 121, 234n107
Andreas Capellanus, 230n57
Anne de Beaujeu, 170
Archer, Janice, 205nn18–19, 207nn39,45, 209n57
Arnoul le Bescochier, 120, 131–32
Arrode, Jeanne, 45
Auberde, Perrenelle, 55
aumônières, 69, 210n66

Babinsky, Ellen, 241n63
Baconthorpe, John, 128, 142
Baldwin, John W., 179n37
Basile (silk worker), 73, 213n101
Beatrice la Grande, 204n159; bequest to, 53, 77–78, 201n127

Beatrice of Nazareth, 106
beghards, 4, 141, 142; German, 177n22
beguinage, Parisian, 10; administration of, 30, 31, 40, 55–56, 151–54, 163, 193n28, 244n15; admission into, 45, 153; anniversary masses at, 106–7, 227n22; appeal of, 37; approximation of convent, 34; authority over, 28–30, 146, 203n157; Bonaventure's sermon at, 137; book culture of, 108–9; chapel of, 37, 135; chaplain of, 98, 152–53; Charles IV's statutes for, 145, 159–65; under Charles VII, 169; choir of, 106–7, 227nn19–21; communal life of, 41, 106–7; components of, 54; condemnation of, 107; decline of, 165–71; departures from, 59, 128, 204nn1–2; dining area of, 41, 194n41; documentation for, 27–28; Dominican responsibility for, 40, 55, 152, 163, 193n28; effect of civil wars on, 166–67; effect of Clementine Decrees on, 165; elite women in, 165–67; entrance fees of, 167; evictions from, 204n1; family support for, 54–55; in fifteenth century, 168–69, 252n141; Filles de l'Ave Maria at, 170, 252n132; finances of, 29; Flemish model of, 26; Flemish recruits in, 27; following Vienne Decrees, 158–65; Giles's defense of, 130–31; homes within, 41, 43, 57, 194n42; institutional identity of, 108; labor in, 47–48; lay support for, 35; life in, 37–41; living arrangements of, 54–55; location of, 27–28, *29*, 170–71, 188n110; Louis's foundation of, 1, 8, *9*, 14–17, 25–34, 145, 162, 181n15; Marguerite Porete and, 159; material support for, 31–33, 36, 43–44, 106–7, 153; mendicant involvement with, 31; Notre Dame's suit against, 167, 252n127; Parlement of Paris on, 170; pastoral care at, 83, 152–53, 189nn125–26, 252n140; patrons of, 28, 30,

ACKNOWLEDGMENTS

It is a pleasure to thank the many people who generously gave their time, advice, and encouragement throughout the process of researching and writing this book. My greatest debt is to Sharon Farmer, who gently pushed me to explore new approaches, sources, and interpretations, generously shared her research on the Parisian silk industry, and offered excellent advice over the years. I have benefited from her wisdom in more ways than I can possibly express.

Several institutions provided important financial and practical assistance as I conducted archival research in Paris. The History Department and the Medieval Studies Program at the University of California, Santa Barbara, generously supported several research trips to France. The French Department at UCSB provided me with the opportunity to spend a year in Paris, for which I am extremely grateful. Much of the research for this book took place at the Bibliothèque Nationale de France, the Archives Nationales, and the Archives de l'Assistance Publique. I thank the library staffs at all of these institutions for their help acquiring the materials I needed. In Paris, I spent many wonderful days at the Institut de Recherche et d'Histoire des Textes (IRHT), where I profited greatly from access to the unpublished research of Anne Terroine. I am particularly grateful to Caroline Bourlet at the IRHT for all of her help.

An Andrew W. Mellon fellowship at the Medieval Institute at the University of Notre Dame provided me with the time and resources to complete this book. The Medieval Institute was the ideal place to delve deeper into questions regarding the University of Paris, and it is very much due to the riches of the Astrik L. Gabriel Universities Collection that this book was transformed for the better. I thank the director, Olivia Remie Constable, for her kindness and support throughout my time at the institute. The associate director of the Medieval Institute, Roberta Baranowski, graciously helped me through several difficult moments. I also owe special thanks to Marina Smyth for her help locating microfilms and resources. Kent Emery Jr. and John Van Engen kindly offered their encouragement and advice.

I also thank my colleagues in the Department of History and Political Science at Purdue University, Calumet, for their support. I thank in particular my former department head, Richard Rupp, and Dean Dan Dunn for smoothing the way as I prepared to take academic leave. I also thank the department for generously providing financial support for the maps.

Parts of this project were presented at the California Medieval History Seminar at the Huntington Library and the Intellectual History Seminar at the Newberry Library in Chicago. I am grateful to the participants for their feedback. For helpful advice, criticism, and encouragement, I wish to thank especially Jennifer Kolpacoff Deane, who read almost every chapter, shared her own excellent research on German beguines, and helped refine my thinking on the nagging problem of labels. Sean Field somehow waded through more than one troublesome chapter, offering invaluable advice. I also owe a huge debt of gratitude to Nancy McLoughlin for her careful, insightful reading of several chapters. Parts of this book had their start in conversations with Nancy, whose own research on gender and intellectual authority has influenced my thinking. Katrin Sjursen also read several chapters and offered extremely helpful advice. I am so grateful for her friendship. I also thank Barbara Newman, Carol Lansing, Hilary Bernstein, Keiko Nowacka, Walter Simons, Jennifer Thibodeaux, and Shennan Hutton for their questions, comments, and criticisms at various stages in the writing of the book. Special thanks go to Dyan Elliott, William Chester Jordan, and Ruth Mazo Karras for reading the manuscript at an earlier stage and for participating in the public seminar discussion of the manuscript sponsored by the Medieval Institute at Notre Dame in 2011. I benefited enormously from their comments and criticisms. All three helped me to rethink the structure of the book, and I am deeply grateful for their support of this project. I also thank the anonymous readers from Penn Press for their comments and criticisms. My work would have been much poorer without their input.

It has been a pleasure to work with University of Pennsylvania Press. Many thanks go to Caroline Hayes, Rachel Taube, and everyone at the Press for their help in seeing this project to publication. I am particularly grateful to editor Jerry Singerman for his patience, counsel, and encouragement throughout the process.

My family and friends have given me so much love and support over the years. I owe an immense debt of gratitude to my mother, Priscilla Stabler, without whom this book would never have been completed. For her interest in my work and generous giving of her time (especially the many afternoons babysitting my children), I cannot thank her enough. My father, Jerry, always encouraged me to pursue my goals. I know he would have been proud of this book. My sister, Cherie, who manages to balance motherhood and scholarship with so much grace and humor, remains my role model and best friend. My wonderful parents-in-law, Floyd and Elizabeth Miller, cheered me on as I worked through the various stages of this project. I also thank my sister-in-law Liesl Orenic for her loving counsel and encouragement. I truly lucked out in the in-law department. I also thank the patient and talented John Fields for his friendship and excellent work on the maps.

My greatest thanks go to my children and husband, who have provided me with so much love and happiness. I thank Charlotte for understanding that "mommy needs to finish her book" and for all of her interesting suggestions for the title. Although Henry does not share his sister's understanding, his unconditional love and need for "UP" helps me keep things in perspective. My husband, Drew, has been with me from the very beginning of this project. From our first "dates" translating the letters of Abelard and Heloise to the present days of juggling teaching, research, and parenthood, he insisted that I should write this book even as I had my doubts. Over the years, he has offered pointed questions, half-joking (but ultimately useful) comments, and only an occasional "I told you so." For his unconditional love and support, even during the times when there was an unspoken fear that the book would never be finished, he has my eternal gratitude. It is to him that I dedicate this book.

An earlier version of chapter 6 appeared in the *Journal of Medieval History* 33 (2007): 60–86. A revised version is published here with permission.